Caste, Marriage and Inequality

Caste, Marriage and Inequality

Essays on North and South India

Pauline Kolenda

RAWAT PUBLICATIONS
Jaipur • New Delhi • Bangalore • Guwahati • Kolkata

ISBN 978-81-7033-799-7

Reprinted, 2021

Published by
Prem Rawat for **Rawat Publications**
Satyam Apts., Sector 3, Jawahar Nagar, Jaipur - 302 004 (India)
Phones: 0141 265 1748 / 265 7006 • E-mail: info@rawatbooks.com
Website: rawatbooks.com

New Delhi Office
4858/24, Ansari Road, Daryaganj, New Delhi 110 002
Phone: 011-23263290

Also at *Bangalore, Guwahati* and *Kolkata*

Typeset by Rawat Computers, Jaipur
Printed and bound in India

Dedicated to
the Chuhras of the western colony of Khalapur
and
to the other denizens of villages in
Uttar Pradesh, Rajasthan, Maharashtra, and old south Travancore
who taught me so very much

Contents

Preface

Never again in my life have I known all the members of a small community as I did the Chuhras, also called Bhangis, of the western colony in Khalapur, a large village in Saharanpur district, in western Uttar Pradesh. Usha Bhagat, my research assistant, and I visited them almost daily for sixteen months between October 1954 and June 1956. Four articles I wrote about their religion were reprinted in a first collection of my writings, *Caste, Cult and Hierarchy* (1981). In a second collection, *Regional Differences in Family Structure in India* (1987), was reprinted the paper "Widowhood among 'Untouchable' Chuhras" which relates very closely to the first paper in the present collection, "Living the Levirate". I continue to remember and re-live through my notes our fieldwork with the Chuhras in the second paper, " 'Untouchable' Chuhras through their Humor."

The first three parts of this new collection reflect three places where I did ethnographic fieldwork in India. The first part is made up of four papers concerning Khalapur. The first two draw on notes on the Chuhras from the 1950s, as I have said. The second two draw upon later fieldwork. I went back to Khalapur for about four months in 1984 to do a thirty-years-later study. Among other efforts, I tried to replicate a study I had done in 1955 on caste ideology reported in "Changing Caste Ideology in a North Indian Village," reprinted in *Caste, Cult and Hierarchy.* The replication appears in Part I under the title "Micro-Ideology and Micro-Utopia in Khalapur". I returned briefly to Khalapur in 1985, 1986, 1997 and 1998. The fourth paper in Part I is drawn from the study of a sample of 31 minimal patrilineages *(khandans)* in Khalapur that I began in 1984 and continued in my short stays in Khalapur in the 1980s and 1990s. In that paper, I break away from my usual preoccupation with Chuhras, the caste system, and family structure and take on a demographic topic, i.e., local forms of population control.

The second part, Kanyakumari, is also formed of four papers. In January 1967, I went for the first time to this southernmost tip of India in Tamilnadu.

My first visit to Dharmarajapuram, a Brahman *agraharam* near the Nadar and Vellala hamlets, was in the summer of 1969 for just an hour or so when I chatted with some elderly Brahmans retired there. When I brought 10 students from the University of Houston in the summer of 1971 to introduce them to India, it happened that one of the Tamil-speaking interpreters selected to help one of the students had been born in Dharmarajapuram. She became my research assistant and interpreter when I returned in 1974 to study the Brahmans. The first, second and third paper of Part II are about the Brahmans of Dharmarajapuram as I found them in 1974, 1978 and 1980. The fourth paper, "Foxes, Lions and Bears.." is derived from my fieldwork between 1967 and 1980 in five hamlets: one composed almost entirely of Nattatti Nadars and Saiva Vellalas, two composed only of Nattatti Nadars, a hamlet (or *agraharam*) of Brahmans, and a hamlet (or *ceri*) of Sambhava Parayas.

The third part in this collection pertains to Rajasthan. In the autumn of 1966, I spent four months studying two adjoining villages in Jaipur district of Rajasthan. A paper about that research was reprinted in the second collection of my papers, *Regional Differences in Family Structure in India* under the title "Sibling-Set Marriage, Collateral-Set Marriage, and Deflected Alliance among Annana Jats of Jaipur District, Rajasthan". In the late 1960s, I became interested in trying to research Indian family structure through data in the Census of India 1961. So, there is the paper published for the first time in *Regional Differences...* "Marked Regional Differences in Family Structure in India," co-authored with my student at the University of Houston, Lorraine Haddon. In Part III is another paper using the Census of India 1961 to explore family structure, "The Joint Family Household in Rural Rajasthan".

Perhaps it was inevitable that I would eventually try to compare the different places where I had done fieldwork. This I did in the two papers reprinted in Part IV. The first, "Woman as Tribute, Woman as Flower" compares women in Khalapur with women in the Nadar hamlets in Kanyakumari. The second, "Sibling Relations and Marriage Practices" makes comparisons between Khalapur, Rajasthan and Kanyakumari with respect to brother-sister relationships.

In Part V, I return to my longstanding interest in caste in India, in a paper presented at a conference marking the thirty-fifth year since independence. And in Part VI is a paper in which I ruminate about inequality in the United States of America as compared to inequality in India. The last paper of this collection has not been published before but is also concerned with inequality; in this case, the unfair treatment of Chuhras in a recent book about them.

Except for two papers, the last paper, "Demonizing Dalits", and one of the papers on the Brahmans of Dharmarajapuram, the papers were published elsewhere and they are reprinted in this volume by permission of the original publishers.

"Living the Levirate" was published in *Dimensions of Social Life: Essays in Honor of David G. Mandelbaum*, edited by Paul Hockings, by Mouton de Gruyter of Berlin, New York, and Amsterdam, in 1987.

"Untouchable Chuhras through their Humor" was published in *Divine Passions*, edited by Owen M. Lynch, by the University of California Press of Berkeley, California, in 1990.

"Micro-Ideology and Micro-Utopia in Khalapur" was published in *The Economic and Political Weekly* of Bombay, in the August 12, 1989 issue.

"Fewer Deaths, Fewer Births" was published in *Manushi* of Delhi in its March–April 1998 issue.

"Memories of a Brahman *Agraharam* in Travancore" appeared in *Religion and Public Policy*, edited by Keith E. Yandell and John J. Paul, published by Curzon of Richmond, Surrey, England in 2000.

El Colegio de Mexico of Mexico city published "Grandsons of the Shastrigals" in *South Asia*, papers from the Thirtieth International Congress of Human Sciences in Asia and North Africa, held in Mexico City in 1976, edited by Graciela de la Lama, Susana Gonzalez del Solar, and Benjamin Preciado Solis.

"Foxes, Lions and Bears" was published in volume 4 *Development and Ethnicity* of the multi-volume *Social Structure and Change*, honoring Professor M.N. Srinivas, edited by A.M. Shah, B.S. Baviskar and E.A. Ramaswamy, by Sage Publications of New Delhi in 1997.

"The Joint Family Household in Rural Rajasthan" was published in *Society from the Inside Out: Anthropological Perspectives on the South Asian Household*, edited by John N. Gray and David J. Mearns, by Sage Publications in New Delhi in 1989.

"Woman as Tribute, Woman as Flower" was published in the *American Ethnologist* (volume II) in 1984.

"Sibling Relations and Marriage Practices" was published in *Siblings in South Asia: Brothers and Sisters in Cultural Context*, edited by Charles W. Nuckolls, by Guilford Press of New York in 1993.

"Caste in India Since Independence" was published in *Social and Economic Development in India*, edited by Dilip Basu and Richard Sisson, by Sage Publications of New Delhi in 1986.

"How Should We Think About Inequality" was published in *Man in India* 1991 (volume 71, number 1) in 1991.

My review of Vijay Prashad's *Untouchable Freedom* that appears at the beginning of "Demonizing Dalits" was published in the *Journal of Social History* in 2002.

The second previously unpublished paper, "The Tamil Brahman Family as Affected by Out-Migration and Modern Occupations," I read as a participant in the Tenth International Congress in Anthropological and Ethnological Sciences in Delhi, in December 1978.

Let me finally acknowledge my dependence throughout my fieldwork on interpreter-assistants. Although I have studied both Hindi and Tamil, I never became proficient enough in either to be able to talk with villagers at the level of intelligence I wanted without the aid of an interpreter. I owe enormous thanks to Usha Bhagat (now Dave) who assisted me in Khalapur during 1954-1956 and to Indira Sapru who assisted me in Rajasthan in 1966 and 1967 and also in Khalapur in the 1980s and 1990s. Helping also in Khalapur in 1997 were Angela Gorewala and Shalini Parimwal. In Kanyakumari, I was aided in 1966-1967 by Saroja Chelliah, in the summer of 1969 by Prabha Joshua, in 1971 and thereafter on so many stints "in the field" by Prema Nathaniel. My assistant in interviewing Brahmans was S. Jayalakshmi of the Trivandrum *agraharam*. In early 1974, she and I traveled around India, visiting Madras, Bombay, Kanpur, Delhi and Ernakulam, visiting the sons of Dharmarajapuram who had gone out to find a decent living.

This list does not include individuals who helped me for short periods of time as interpreters, nor, of course, all those who helped me in other ways. My thanks to all.

Financing my research were many granting agencies. Especially important were the American Institute of Indian Studies, the National Science Foundation (USA), the Smithsonian Institution, and the Ford Foundation that funded Cornell University's village project in Khalapur back in the 1950s. My own University of Houston often helped with summer grants and limited-grants-in-aid as well as Faculty Development Leaves. My thanks to all of these.

Kensington, California **Pauline Kolenda**
February 20, 2003

Plates, Maps, Figures and Tables

PLATES

MAPS

FIGURES

TABLES

Part I

Khalapur

1

Living the Levirate

The Mating of an Untouchable Chuhra Widow

> "Mandelbaum (1957: 257) says that the 1891 census of India suggested that 60 percent of the population of Madras allowed and practiced widow remarriage" (Kolenda 1982: 198).

> "Where widows can remarry, the levirate is commonly preferred; a brother of the deceased husband becomes the next husband or at least he has the right of first refusal. Generally, a second marriage, whether for a man or a woman, is marked with a much simpler wedding than was the first and is not as prestigious an arrangement as the first might be" (Mandelbaum 1970: 78).

*

Haradi alternated between laughter and tears in our conversations with her. Her tears flowed when she spoke of her departed husband, Pratap. In the following passage, she praises his handsome appearance and explains the reason why she cannot marry either of his *chacha-tau* brothers (his father's brother's sons).

> He was a very good-looking man. You can't find the likes of him in the whole *basti* now. He was as tall as Kantu, well built and very fair and good. An honest man like him we can never find. He was in Lahore at the time of the riots [during the Partition of 1947], and he ran home from there saying, "My wife is alone." He left all his belongings in Lahore and even money and came back. Twice during his service in Lahore he came home to take me to Lahore, but all the people here in the *basti* told him not to take me, because then "the woman will breathe the city air."

> He was very fond of children. He would sleep with Kati and other children, fondle them, and he used to get annoyed when I drove them

out. He would say, "You are jealous because you do not have any children of your own." I said, "Yes, if God has not given us our own, why should we look upon other people's children? They create unnecessary dirt."

When I was expecting a baby, he said, "Now God will give us children too, and then you need not be jealous." When I had the stillborn baby, however, many people would not come [due to birth pollution]. They said, "She has a stillborn child," but he used to help me with everything... He used to cook all kinds of herbs for me and spend all the morning doing that... When I had serious dysentery, they all thought I was going to die. He ran in all directions calling doctors, and many people gathered. He kept beating his head against the wall. People told him, "If she dies, you will get another woman," but he said, "No, I cannot find another one like her." He came in despite other people's objecting, and he sat down beside the bed and took my hand. I, the wretched one, was saved however, and he died.

[Haradi's husband, Pratap, went into considerable debt in order to finance the wedding of his dead brother's son, Chiteru. This included a loan of one hundred rupees from Kalu, his *chacha-tau ka bhai* (his father's brother's son)].

Haradi explained: Kalu demanded his money many times, and every time my husband said, "We will give it to you." They were two – Kalu and his brother, Swami, while my husband was alone. His brother, Prithvi, was not here. One night in Phagun (February-March) they quarreled on the *chaupara* (men's sitting platform), and Kalu and Swami said, "You *Sasuras* (fathers-in-law) [referring to Pratap and Prithvi], you will both die, and we will keep your widows." My husband came straight home and placing his *pagri* (turban) at my feet, he said, "In this quarrel, one of us must die – either Kalu or I. And as I am alone, if I die, you must destroy yourself in any way. Do anything. Go away anywhere, but do not live with Kalu or Swami." Ram [the headman] was listening; he told my husband, "Don't be crazy. Brothers should not quarrel. Don't say such things to your wife." But Pratap asked me many times not to live with Kalu or Swami. He died two months later in the middle of Baisakh (April-May). When he died, we put a white cloth over him which he had bought for a *dhoti* (waistcloth) and shirt. Kalu all the time now, when he quarrels with me, taunts me saying, "We provided the shroud for your dead husband." And I reply, "Don't worry. I will put one on you when you die."

*

This is the story of Haradi, a widow, aged about 30, of the untouchable Sweeper (*Chuhra*) caste community in the village of Khalapur in northern India. A lithe graceful small woman with a moonface of oriental cast -- waxy yellow with somewhat slanted eyes -- she loved to sing and dance and tease her *devars* (husband's younger brothers), both real ones and those in relationship within the Chuhra colony. She was the delight of the *devars* but also of her other neighbors, both men and women. She was respectful to elderly women, going to help them bathe when they needed it, washing their backs, massaging their necks. She did her sweeping work for her Rajput and other higher caste *jajmans* well, going regularly and doing a thorough job.

But before Hardi's story, some background[1] is needed.

The Chuhra *basti* (colony) was on the west side of Khalapur. Usha and I used to cross the bridge at the east front of the village and walk along the north side road that edged the canal, passing Rajput houses of canal *patti*, and then the houses of watercarriers, and then Rajput houses of western *patti*. Sometimes, the Rajput or Watercarrier women would call us in, coming to the doorways of their windowless compounds to beckon, "*A jao. A jao* (Come in. Come in)." And, we would stop and visit them for a while. Four or five women of a joint family would cluster around us after we had been seated on a string cot and would examine our clothing. If I was wearing something from America, they would feel it and ask if I had made the machine-produced lace of a sleeve or the embroidery of a Guatemalan skirt. Then, after a few minutes we would leave, and they would go back to their spinning wheels or vegetable-cutting or grain-cleaning. All these activities were carried on in the open paved central space, bordered by single rows of separate rooms in which grain, food and implements were stored, or where clothing and jewelry were kept in metal trunks. Only in rainy weather did sleeping or cooking take place inside. Most of women's life went on in the courtyards beneath the clear blue skies and bright sun of the North Indian plains.

Plate 1

An 'untouchable' Sweeper woman at work in Khalapur. The most important part of a Sweeper's work was to gather up cow-dung, mix it with mud and straw, pat the mixture into loaves and leave them to dry in the sun. Cow-dung cakes are used as cooking fuel in north India. (Photo 1955, by J. Michael Mahar. See the first two papers in Part I)

Plate 2

An older 'untouchable' Sweeper woman at work in Khalapur, accompanied by her grandson. (Photo 1955, by J. Michael Mahar. See the first two papers in Part I)

But, on the whole, we were not especially noticed as we made our way to the Chuhras' colony. Some people accounted for our twice-daily trips as the egg-buying expeditions of non-vegetarians. They knew we ate eggs. When Bal Mal, a leading Bania shopkeeper and moneylender, would come to our project house to give me lectures on Hinduism, he would comment on the smell of eggs, and when on rarer occasions his wife came, she would even hold her nose because the odor of our breakfast presumably lingered on so strongly.

It would have been difficult for any of us to have got to know the untouchable Chuhras intimately if we had not been a *group* of researchers. Another anthropologist and his wife, as well as the psychologist and the linguist, together with their assistants, worked much of their time with the dominant landowning caste of Rajputs. An Indian graduate student in anthropology was studying the high priestly caste of Brahmans. The leaders of the village were being attended to. Thus, two of us ethnographers, along with our interpreter-assistants, could concentrate on untouchables. I worked with the Churha Sweepers. The other ethnographer worked with the Chamars, the field laborers, traditionally leather workers, and I worked with the Sweepers who made dung cakes (used for fuel in cooking hearths) in the higher castemen's cattle yards, and cleaned the latrines to be found in booths on the rooftops of high caste women's quarters.

Right after breakfast, Usha and I would leave the project house where we social researchers lived. It was just across the dirt road from the new high school, a few hundred feet up from the bridge crossing the canal to the village. Originally there was hope that we might live within the village itself, but the building of the new high school that had just been completed meant that all extra housing was taken by the teachers and students who had come in from the outside. So, the Cornell University project had built its own housing and compound; the anthropologist field director and his wife, John and Pat Hitchcock, and the other anthropologist in Khalapur, Toshio Yatsushiro and their Indian research assistants had spent much of the first year of the three-year project managing the building of the long nine-room barracks – eight double rooms for the researchers, plus a kitchen-dining room -- as well as separate quarters for the cooks. Those of us who came in the second year found that the housing and wall of the compound had been built, rapport had been established with the villagers by our predecessors, and our fieldwork could begin immediately.

Usha and I would often spend the morning in the Chuhra *basti*: Usha translating my questions into Hindi and the Chuhras' answers into English, I taking notes. We were usually concentrating on some particular cultural institution -- this month, the *jajmani* system, another month, kinship -- but we inevitably became involved in whatever human events were occurring in the lives of the Chuhras. We learned about the levirate in the course of listening to the daily gossip.

We would return to the project house for lunch. In the hot months, we, like everyone else, napped in the first part of the afternoon. If it was colder, I would type notes until three. Then Usha and I would have tea and a couple of vitamin pills (for strength) and work among the sweepers until six when it was supper time. In the evening I would again type notes. Only rarely did we go into the village at night. There was no electricity then, in the mid-1950s, and it was a mile or so to walk to the Chuhra *basti* in the dark. We did occasionally go, of course, to attend a special ceremony or to hear some crucial decision taken in the Chuhra men's council.

*

Beside the large women's quarters and men's sitting platform of the Rajputs of western *patti* was the waist-high brick shrine with a bulbous peak on top and a small indentation to accept food offerings and *diyas* (small clay oil lamps) dedicated to the village-god, Bhumiya. The Bhumiya is typically located in North Indian villages, as this one was, on an outer boundary. It stood on a slight hillock above the roadway looking out over a stagnant pond, perhaps a hundred feet across in both directions. Beyond the pond was the Chuhra colony of the western part of the village. There was another colony of sweepers in the southeastern part of the village with whom the western *basti* sweepers had enmity, because it was men of that colony who had helped to arrange the sale of Haradi, as will be told below.

As is customary all over India for untouchables, the Chuhras lived "outside" the clean castes' village (Dumont 1970: 134). Here they were separated by the pond; beyond them was only unoccupied sun-baked ground, a western *patti* Rajput's cattle yard, and then the fields. We would go around the pond to the rows of adobe women's houses forming two three-sided rectangles side by side, open toward the pond, built not on flat ground but on a gentle incline. The round solid brick well stood near the place where an outer wall of each of the two rectangles came together. The two rectangles, along with two men's platforms, constituted the main structures of the *basti*. The whole *basti* could not have covered much more than 1,000 square feet.

Whichever way we entered, we faced the two men's sitting platforms (*chaupara*). One belonged to Jhanki's *kunba* (patrilineal group), one to Ram's. To the south of Jhanki's were his women's quarters, behind a compound wall where his two sons' wives and children lived. Across from his sitting platform was a small compound belonging to an ex-daughter-in-law of Jhanki's *kunba* and her subsequent husband and their two married sons, their wives and children. The husbands, of course, slept on the men's sitting platform at night in the roofed, Moghul-arched men's dormitory at the back.

The ex-daughter-in-law, Sumi, was now a woman in her fifties. As a girl in her teens, she had gone through the first phase of wedding ceremonies (the *shadi*) with Jhanki's father's brother's eldest son. Before the second phase of wedding ceremonies (the *gauna*) her bridegroom died and she went through these rites with the groom's younger brother – a boy much younger than herself – following the Chuhras' rule of prescriptive levirate. It was then that she took up residence with her mother-in-law in her husband's parental household. As often seemed to happen when a mature woman married a childgroom, she eventually had an affair with an older man -- in fact with her husband's father's elder brother Shyam – a man with whom she should have had an avoidance relationship. She should have kept her face covered in his presence at all times and should not even have spoken to him; he was a kind of father-in-law to her, and thus should have been treated with the restraint a married woman should show all men outside her own patrilineage who were older than her husband. The lovers had no choice but to be found out and punished by the Chuhra men's council, or to run away. They ran away and worked in Hyderabad, a city in Sind where Shyam, the childgroom's father's brother, worked on a municipal sanitation crew, and Sumi worked as a servant in the homes of Europeans. The couple had two sons. After some years, Shyam died, and Sumi entered another secondary mating with a Chuhra from Khalapur -- a man of Ram's *kunba* who was also working in Hyderabad. This couple also had two sons. After many years of absence Sumi and Jammal and the four sons returned to the *basti*. Sumi's childgroom had died long before, and Jhanki was glad to have a family to swell the numbers of his smaller *kunba*, chronically at odds with Ram's *kunba*. Perhaps they had returned because the sons needed to be married, and it is easiest to arrange marriages when living within one's own caste community. So this family's *bagar* (women's quarters), a tiny single room, was built on a patch of wet soil right on the edge of the pond, across from Jhanki's *chaupara*.

Behind Ram's sitting platform along three walls forming a rectangle were the quarters of women whose husbands were descended from *bhanjas* (daughters' sons) or *salas* (wives' brothers) of Ram's patrilineage. Although, like most North Indian castes, the residence rule for the Chuhras was patrilocal -- a couple should live with the husband's patrilineal relatives after marriage – there was among the landless Chuhras a good deal of deviance from the rule. Frequently, a daughter who had been married out returned with her husband and children to live with her patrilineal kin; or a brother, dissatisfied in his father's village, joined his sister who had married into the *basti*. So, Ghasitu, now an elder in his seventies, had been the son of a daughter who had returned. Now, his two sons, men in their prime, were the beginnings of a new patrilineage. In the other way, Kantu's father had joined his sister Kreshani, who had married into the *basti*, so Kantu and the sons of his dead brother founded a new patrilineage. This same woman Kreshani's two married daughters had also returned with husbands and children. Each daughter had had a son, both now married, who would also start new patrilineages. There were six houses of *bhanjas* and one house of a *sala*'s son, while there were only six houses headed by men descendant from Ram's male ancestors in a strictly male line; these six were properly patrilineal and patrilocal. In addition, there was the house belonging to Gyarsi who had married Sumi and Shyam's son, Tikku, who had died. Now, Gyarsi remained in her first husband's home but had taken, in a kind of leviratic secondary mating, her mother-in-law's brother's son, her dead husband's mother's brother's son. The advantage of this uxorilocal mating, the widow living in the house she had shared with her dead husband, was that the *ghar jamai* (uxorilocal son-in-law) could not easily sell her, protected as she was by her dead husband's *basti*-men.

In the seventeen houses of Chuhras there were never more than 100 people during the twenty months that Usha and I knew them. There was a certain amount of flux in their population as daughters came to stay with their parents, and daughters-in-law went to visit their parental villages. Some of the men worked in sanitation crews in cities of the region; all of the adult men had done so at one time or another. So men came and went. One or two families moved in and one or two families moved out during the time we were there.

The men could absent themselves from the village, because the *jajmani* work was carried on very largely by the women. A pair, mother-in-law and daughter-in-law, or mother and daughter, or two brothers' wives, would serve a dozen or so *jajmans*, higher caste clients – cleaning their latrines and cattle yards where they patted the animal dung into cakes, which when dried, served as fuel for cooking.

Culture as Constituted

The general Hindu idea which the Chuhras of the western colony also accepted was that although a man could marry more than once, a woman could marry only once; she should have in her lifetime only one husband (Dumont 1964: 82). Among the higher Hindu castes of India – for example, the Rajputs, Banias and Brahmans of Khalapur – a widow remains celibate staying in her dead husband's house and raising her children or being cared for by her adult sons. Among lower castes widow remating is widely practised (Singh 1947: 169; Crooke 1907: 209; Mandelbaum 1957: 257; Dube 1955: 122: Mayer 1960: 234–235; Carstairs 1957: 136; Dumont 1957: 180; Beals 1962 31; Lewis 1958: 190–191; Vatuk 1980: 289). The Hindi term used in Khalapur was *karawa* – the widow comes in *karawa* and "sits with" *(baith dena)* her new mate. Anthropologists (O'Malley 1932: 92; Blunt 1969: 72; Dumont 1970: 111) refer to the custom as a secondary marriage or an inferior form of marriage; from the native view, it is not a marriage but a permanent liaison. I hesitate to use the term which some British observers used for widow remating among Hindu peasants, "concubinage", because the children of the secondary marriage had full status as offspring of their father.

In Khalapur, among some clean castes like the watercarriers and potters, and among some unclean or untouchable castes like the Chamar agricultural laborers or the Chuhra sweepers, there was a rule of levirate (a widow should mate with her husband's brother). The levirate is not as widespread as widow remating, but it is widespread among middle and lower castes in northern India (Singh 1947: 169); it is less prevalent in southern India (Karve 1965: 224; Chattopadhyay 1922: 41). The commencement of the leviratic liaison is only briefly ceremonialized and feasted (Singh 1947: 167; Crooke 1907: 93; Stevenson 1930: 67; O'Malley 1932: 93; Kolenda 1982: 202) in comparison to the lengthy set of double ceremonies for the wedding of a virgin. The workings of the levirate are not well known. In Khalapur I came to know only the way the levirate worked among the Chuhras of the western colony (see Kolenda 1982 for a theoretical treatment and p. 201 of that article for a brief description of the levirate as I found it in the Jaipur district of Rajasthan, among Jats.).

The proscriptive rule, always followed among the Chuhras of Khalapur, was that a widow must marry her dead husband's unmarried brother. Since siblings of the same sex marry in order of age, an unmarried brother of a married man usually is younger, but it is possible that an elder brother is a widower or is for some other reason unmarried. The widow was supposed to be assigned to a new mate at the thirteenth day ceremony after her dead husband's cremation. Her father or brother usually attended the ceremony and agreed that she should go in secondary mating to the husband's unmarried brother.

Culture as Lived-in

The assignment of a widow to her dead husband's brother at the end of the death period often resulted in the situation in which Sumi had found herself, mated to a childgroom. Often, the women so assigned did not wait until the boy had grown up to become sexually active again; such women often took lovers and, like Sumi, ran away with them. Whether the couple was ever accepted back into the colony or not after running away depended on whether the lover was also a Chuhra; if he were a Muslim or a Chamar or a man of some other caste, they would never be accepted; but if he was a Chuhra, the likelihood for re-acceptance after some years of absence, as in Sumi's case, was good. If the lovers were caught in an illicit affair, the Chuhra man might be required to pay the woman's dead husband's family for the widow; otherwise they would separate her from the lover and sell her. A man of another caste or religion could not legitimize the mating by paying the woman's dead husband's family for her.

The proscriptive levirate rule was inadequate, not just because childgrooms were immature and unready to mate with the widow of an elder brother, but because it was a rule that did not succeed in allotting many widows. It was not unusual for the husband's younger brother to be married already; in that instance the custom was that the widow, as well as the man and his wife, must all accede to the polygynous arrangement that would result if the widow joined the household. The general community assessment was that co-wives fight all the time. Neither Chuhra widows nor married brothers' wives agreed to the polygynous solution without hesitation, so this solution was rarely chosen although, as we shall see, Haradi did prefer it.

Then, there was the common possibility of a dead husband having no brothers. To allow for these two kinds of failure of the leviratic rule, that the dead man's brothers were all married or that there was no brother, it was customary for the Chuhra elders to suggest that the widow accept a substitute for the husband's full brother and take as a mate the dead husband's cousin -- usually, his father's brother's son; more rarely, a mother's brother's son or even more rarely, a father's sister's son; or even a more distant cousin of the dead husband might be proposed. Hindi kinship terminology uses the same term *bhai* for all male cousins; they are all called "brother". However, the distinction between a man's full brother, and a "cousin-brother" is carefully noted, and the distance makes a difference.

If a woman mates with her dead husband's full brother, he cannot sell her. There is the idea that she came as a virgin to the whole household of the first husband, that she came in a sense as a virgin to the husband's brothers as well as to the husband. This entails the rule that the husband's full brother cannot sell the leviratic mate. The rule seems to hinge on the ideal of the lineal-fraternal joint family; the woman comes in marriage to that joint household. However, cousin-brothers are not considered to be part of the husband's household, and the introduction of a factor of lateral genealogical distance from the original husband entails the secondary husband's right to sell the woman. The Hindu pollution concept, so important in understanding caste ranking and untouchability (Kolenda 1978: 62--85; Stevenson 1954; Davis 1983; Marriott and Inden 1973), extends to the purity of women (Yalman 1963). A woman is impure for any sexual partner subsequent to the partner to whom she was taken as a virgin. The Chuhra modification of this Hindu ideal seems to be that she is pure for all the men of the patrifraternal contingent of her husband's joint family (his brothers and father) but she is not pure for a man outside that family. Once she is taken by a second mate, she is impure and presumably "spoiled" and thus saleable. This is not stated explicitly by the Chuhras but it is a Hindu way to account for this right of the cousin-brother of the dead husband to sell the secondary wife (see also Kolenda 1982: 206.) If a cousin-brother accepting the widow takes her to live in another village, he must pay her first husband's male family member for her; if on the other hand he resides in the same village, he does not pay for her, but may sell her. A woman who has been bought can be resold.

Women are usually sold to widowers, because widowers generally have a hard time convincing the guardians of young virgins to arrange marriages with them. Widowers may be left with children to raise and may have no choice for a mate except to buy a widow. The sale of a widow by her dead husband's cousin-brother or by anyone else is usually by deception. I never heard of a widow consenting to being sold. If she is sold by deception, it is done secretly and she may lose her entire complement of relatives, both those of her natal village and those in her first husband's village, for none of these is likely to be informed about her whereabouts, at least for some time, and there is not likely to be anyone in the buyer's village whom she knows (although fortunately for Haradi, there was in the village into which she was sold a man related to a man of her dead husband's village). It is this alienation from all her relatives, the deception and secrecy, the lack of ceremonialization or of any public affirmation that sharply distinguish the sale of a woman from marriage by brideprice, a custom also prevalent in India, especially among lower castes. A woman who is sold is stigmatized; there is the implication that she has engaged in an illicit affair; often women who are sold are already pregnant through such an affair. A wife who has come to a family in a first marriage or a virtuous widow should not be sold. Among the 27 adult Chuhra women of the western colony who had married into the *basti*, 15 were still married to their first husband, six were in leviratic marriages, two were elderly widows and three were women who had been sold to men of the *basti;* one other widow had taken a lover who had paid her dead husband's family men for her. It was not an unusual destiny for a widow or (even though it was against the rule) for a wife to be sold although, as we shall see with Haradi, a widow may try hard to avoid being sold.

While North Indian kinship culture seems to place a heavy emphasis upon the sibling relationship as one of solidarity, needless to say, the real relationships in which people live do not always follow these ideals of loyalty and love. Hostility between brothers is common, but even more common is hostility between cousin-brothers, who are the sons of full brothers. Such patrilateral parallel cousins belong to households founded by men who once shared a household and then separated, men who belonged to the same parental and later the same joint family. When brothers divide a joint household, they seldom do it without bad feelings. Thus, the cousin-brothers inherit their fathers' hostility; there have probably been bad feelings between their households for much of their lives. By implication, the widow may have good reason to fear that if she agrees to "sit with" her dead husband's cousin-brother, he may be motivated to sell her.

The marriages of virgins are arranged in India. The widow who has not been automatically assigned to sit with her dead husband's unmarried brother has choice, or at least veto power over her subsequent mate. Her agreement must be taken concerning her mating with either her husband's married brother or with her husband's cousin-brother. She may also choose to remain a celibate widow. However, if she chooses to be a celibate widow and she is still in her childbearing period of life, she is likely to be under pressure from the elders of her caste/community to accept a man who can be construed to be a brother of the dead husband.

Haradi's Story

The story of Haradi (see Figure 1.1) is pieced together from twenty-two conversations which Usha and I had over a year and a half with Haradi herself as well as thirteen other members of the Chuhra community. Of these, Kali, Mahendi, Bhuli, Kishandai (Chuhris) and Kantu (a Chuhra) are cited in the passages below.

Figure 1.1
Haradi and Some Kin

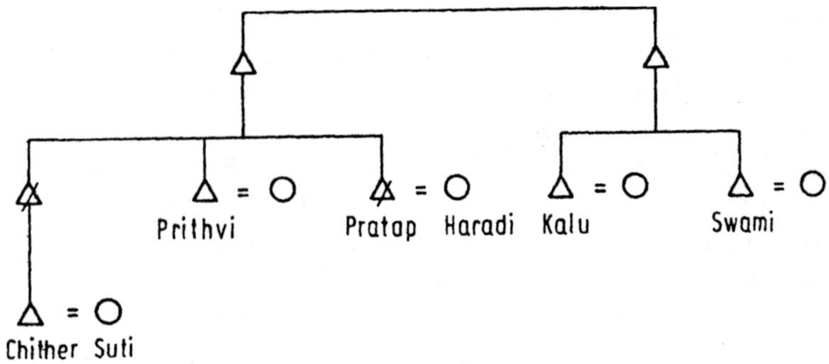

Outline of Haradi's Career as a Widow

1946 — Widowed, at about the age of 23.

1946–48 — Remained in village where she worked with Prithvi's wife, wife of her dead husband's brother, absent in Delhi. When Prithvi failed to return, both women went to their parental villages.

1948–49 — In her home village, her brother and his wife made Haradi feel unwelcome so she returned to her dead husband's village.

1950 — Elders suggested that Haradi should "sit with" Mahinder, her dead husband's father's father's brother's daughter's son. After a short time, Haradi turned him out of her house.

1952 — Haradi was sold by her dead husband's brother's son Chiter, who was under pressure to pay off debts from the expenses of his own wedding. Haradi was rescued by the elders and *devars* of the western Chuhra *basti* of Khalapur.

1953 — At Mangal's wedding, elders suggested that Haradi should "sit with" Kalu, her dead husband's father's brother's son. Both Kalu's wife and Haradi refused that arrangement.

1954–56 — Haradi was under pressure from Kalu to "sit with" either himself or his brother, Swami.

195? — Haradi "sat with" Prithvi, her dead husband's full brother.

196? — Haradi died.

Haradi, born in Manohar village, had a father who married three times and took widows to wife *(karawa)* twice. Haradi told us:

> My mother came last [thus in a *karawa* widow remating]. I had only one full brother, Radhu. Only one of my father's first four wives had a child, a girl married in Kishan village.... I don't remember much about my mother. She died when I was about 6 years old. People tell me she looked like me. She died at about my age [30]. At first, we both [Haradi and Radhu] went to live with our *bhuwa* (father's sister) in Surenderpur village. *My bhuwa* nursed my brother. Then one of our previous mothers who had run away earlier came hack, and we

> returned to Manohar village. She lived with us there. My father was as old as Jammal [perhaps late sixties] and looked like him also. We liked everything about him. He kept us very well and loved us very much. He had lots of money, but when he died my *tau*'s (father's elder brother's) son took all the money, as my brother was very young and I was married here. My father kept asking for me when he was dying, but I could not go. I went later. When I reached there, everything in our house had been removed by my *tau*'s son who had pretended to take my brother into his house.

Haradi was very popular with the Sweepers of the *basti* because she loved to joke and tease, to dance and sing, often making up songs presented extemporaneously. The North Indian culture prescribes avoidance between a woman and men older than her husband who are not of her own patrilineage, but it also prescribes a joking relationship with men younger than her husband in his patrilineage and by extension in his residential community. Haradi loved to indulge in joking with her *devars*. Thus, I recorded in my notes:

> Haradi was teasing old Dharmi (a really ancient widow, perhaps in her seventies), telling us how Dharmi's wedding had been arranged. Haradi laughed, "I told my *sasura* (father-in-law) to go and look for a bride for my *dadasara* (husband's father's father). Then I plastered the house [in preparation for a wedding] and had a man stand beating the drum, so everyone would know that my *dadasara* had brought a new wife."

Here, the joke is in the age reversal, a granddaughter-in-law having arranged her grandmother-in-law's wedding. Similarly, in the next joke, she plays on the absurdity of a woman in her thirties being mated with a boy of twelve and having to keep her face covered from men in their late teens and twenties, because they were men older than her adolescent husband:

> "If I become Suku's (a boy of twelve) wife, I'll have to keep *ghungat* (face covered with end of sari or head covering) from you (to Moti, a male of early twenties) and from Nathu (a boy of 17)."

The reader may refer to the beginning of the paper for Haradi's perceptions of her dead husband and for the reason why she could not marry either of her husband's *chacha-tau* brothers (father's brother's sons), Kalu and Swami.

Haradi's husband, Pratap, had had two brothers. One, the father of Chither, was dead but the other, Prithvi, who had a reputation for being a gambler, was still alive in 1956, working in Delhi. Pratap and Prithvi had quarreled over the division of the house and utensils when their joint family divided into two nuclear families. Kali told us that Prithvi lived in the city not because he liked the city but because of the quarrel with his elder brother. "He said when he left, "I'll never come back." Pratap turned Prithvi and his wife out."

When Haradi was first widowed in about 1946, she lived and worked with Prithvi's wife, but this woman returned to her home village in about 1948 because Prithvi had been away in Delhi so long without returning. Neither Prithvi nor his wife were ever seen in the Chuhra colony during our time there in 1954–56.

We asked Bhuli why Haradi had not gone back to live in her natal village. Bhuli said that Haradi was very independent. She had indeed gone to live in her home village for three or four months after her husband's death, but her brother said she should get mated. "After all," he said, "ours is a working caste *(kaum)*, and you should have a man." Her brother's wife complained about Haradi being dependent upon them for food and support, and Haradi, being sensitive, did not like that, so she returned to live in her mother-in-law's house, from which no one could eject her. "It's hers as long as she lives," Bhuli said. Bhuli praised Haradi's chastity, pointing out that if Haradi had ever had an affair she would have become pregnant, but that had not happened.

Later on, the Chuhra elders had proposed that Haradi should "sit with" a man who was her dead husband's father's father's daughter's son and thus a father's cousin sister's son to her husband. My notes read:

> Mahendi, an elderly lady, then urged Haradi to sing us a song, "Oh, my Mahinder, don't go to the gram fields." Haradi said, she couldn't sing it because there were men present. We told Moti and the others to go, but Moti said that Haradi wasn't at all modest or shy about singing with them (*devars*) present. Mahendi explained that many years ago, after Haradi was widowed, the elders – Ram, Ghasitu, and her brother, Radhu -- decided that Haradi should be made to sit with

Phatu's brother. Mahinder (her husband's father's father's brother's daughter's son, a distant cousin brother). Haradi complained about him – that he smelled – and she would sing this song to him, "Oh, my Mahinder, don't go to the gram fields." Haradi would not sing the song, but she offered to show us how he walked. She got up and jerked one shoulder and then the other, imitating Mahinder's walk. Haradi then went away.

Mahendi told us that the elders had had Haradi "sit with" Mahinder. Laughingly she said that when Mahinder was in the house, Haradi would be out. When Haradi was in, Mahinder was out. She only stayed with him a few days. "He was so greedy for something he didn't get," laughed Mahendi "that he would go and collect the dung all alone and not ask Haradi to work at all". She would cook his food, but when he came and said, "Come in the house and give me food," she would say, "Take it. It's there." "I don't want to live with him," she would tell other people. Upon coming into her house, he had taken his share of grain from his brother. She kicked Mahinder and his grain out of her house. So then Mahinder left the village. No one knows where he is now.

Bhuli told us on another occasion, "But Mahinder was just like a wandering dog. He'd come once a month. He didn't want to keep her [Haradi], and 'she didn't want to stay there, so they broke up.' Kalu and Swami have always been afraid she'd take another man." Kali also told us that Mahinder had been arrested for "loitering at night". Kali didn't know where he was now. She said, "Many times letters come, sometimes from Saharanpur, sometimes from Jalabad or Roorki [cities of the region]. He used to live here; for a while, he came every ten or fifteen days, but he hasn't come for a year. Maybe he has been arrested." She said that he had no family; both his wife and two daughters had died. "He was a man older than Phatu (thus past 40). He didn't steal. He was whimsical. He'd go pick someone's dung one day; then he'd do some service somewhere else the next day."

Although Haradi had managed up to 1956 not to settle down with any of her husband's *chacha-tau* (father's brothers' sons) or *maman-phuphi ke bhais* (mother's brothers' or father's sisters' sons) she was once sold – by her husband's dead brother's son, Chiter.

One of the sweeper men, Sukhar, told us the story:

Pratap-ki-bahu (Pratap's wife -- Haradi) was taken by Chiter by deceit and sold by him in Nangal village. A year and a half ago, Chiter had two sons. The elder one was sick. Chiter said to his wife, "Let us go to Devton, and see a medical man there." He told his *chachi* (father's younger brother's wife), Haradi, to come along. Suti, his wife, and the two children all went too. After they had been to the doctor, Chiter suggested that they take a *tonga* (horse-drawn cart) home. Chiter had already received the money for Haradi, so he had had a great deal of money. *"Chachi,"* he said, "let us go in a *tonga."* "No," she said, "it is too expensive. Let us go on foot. Besides there is no *pakka* (paved) road to Khalapur." Chiter suggested they take a *tonga* to Gyarsipur village, then walk from Gyarsipur to Khalapur. He pushed Haradi into a *tonga*, and the *tonga* shot off toward Nangal village. Haradi didn't realize where they were going because she was all the time talking. Two miles this side of Nangal village, the wheels of the *tonga* broke, so they started walking. They entered Nangal village. Haradi said, "Is this Gyarsipur village?" Chiter said it was. He had taken her where he had sold her.

The people of Marchwa (the southeast quarter of Khalapur Chuhras) -- three men, Paltu, Saresh, and Balwant -- were also involved in this sale of Haradi. Chiter had taken five hundred rupees. They had each taken one hundred. These men had already arrived in Nangal village. No one from our *basti* knew about the transaction at all. The people of Nangal village were expecting them. They had a good feed. The women went into the house and the men stayed out, and they ate with good will. Now Suti, Chiter's wife, was in the house. To go home, Chiter wanted to get Suti out, but without Haradi. He sent in a messenger saying that Chiter's father was there and that Suti should come out. Haradi need not come out because *samdhi* and *samdhin* (daughter-in-law's father and son-in-law's mother) should not see each other. Haradi said, "I'll come too, for I must go home." Suti said, "No, I'll be back." So she came out with her two children.

Later when it was getting late, Haradi said, "Where is my *bahu* (daughter-in-law)?" She tried to get out but they stopped her. The man who had bought Haradi had a grown-up daughter with two small children. She caught hold of Haradi and said, "Where are you running away to? You have come to be my *mausi* (mother's sister) [thus equating the man's second wife with his first as sisters]." Haradi realized what had happened. She started crying, shouting, and abusing people. The man who had bought her, Kaliram, came in and some others caught hold of her. She ran and ran. She ran to the top of the roof, and along the way her *orna* (head covering) had been snatched off, and she stood on the roof saying, "May you people of Gyarsipur village die! May your sons and grandsons die, and everyone else die too." She threw stones and cowdung at them. The people laughed and laughed. The people of the village gathered around. They said, "You have brought her here by deceit. She doesn't even know where she is. You should send her back if she does net want to live here. Don't shout and cry!" The sweepers there who had brought her caught her and put her in a guarded room. She lay on the *charpai* (string cot). Then she put her *charpai* on end and with the help of a couple of baskets and her *orna* (head covering), she climbed over the wall and came out of Nangal village. She walked until she came to another village, Surwan. She didn't go into this village, but there was a stream there. She thought, "If I try to cross this stream, I'll die." So she sat there. By this time, the people of Nangal village were out searching for her. They came along where she was in Surwan saying, "We don't know where our *bahu* went." She said to them out loud, "I'm sitting right here. My brain is not right. I have gone mad." So the people of Nangal took her back.

Manpal's *sala* (wife's brother) is from Nangal village. He came visiting in Khalapur. He told Manpal, "I have tried to make a home for Kaliram, but such a wife we have bought for him! She refuses to eat or drink. She cries and weeps all the time. She is mad, too." Manpal asked where he had bought her. He said, from Khalapur. They knew that Haradi was missing, but Chiter had said that he had married her off and that she was happy and had been married by her own will. They realized that this couldn't be true if she was weeping and crying. So on the next day after the *sala* had come, several men of the *basti* -- Swami, Chaman, Phatu, and Kalu's wife (Kalu himself was working in the city of Roorki) went to Nangal village.

When they got to Nangal village the people there wouldn't let them see Haradi. They didn't even let *Kalu-ki-bahu* (Kalu's wife) see her, because they were afraid that she would talk her into coming away.

The Nangal people said, "We won't let you take her away. In case you decide about the money, we'll give her back." By this, they meant that the Khalapur people should return the money Chiter had gotten for her. The Khalapur people said, "In case you don't give back our *bahu*, if she is in any way harmed we will take revenge on you, your children, and your grandchildren." Saying this, they came back to Khalapur.

The next day they went with a letter from the village *sarpanch* and *pradhan* (elected officials, both Rajputs, members of the dominant caste). They had a big form with the signatures of *sarpanch, pradhan*, and influential men of the village on it. They told the sweepers, "Seeing these signatures, they should send her back. If they don't, the whole village will accompany you there next time."

They went to Nangal village and stayed there for the night. The whole village of Nangal was alert that night in case they should try to take the bride and run away with her.

Another part of the Khalapur Sweepers had gone to find Chiter. On the day after selling Haradi, he had gone away – to his in-laws (his wife's natal village). He did not know that the Sweepers had decided to demand her back. Nangal, Chaman and Mangal went to find Chiter. (Nine men: Kantu, Ghasita, Manpal, Itwari, Moti, Gana, Phatu, Sohu, Kishan had gone to Nangal village.) Chiter had already spent quite a bit of the money, but they got from him what was left and took some other money from him. Chaman, Ram and Kalu each contributed 50 rupees. And they got 100 rupees from the people of Marchwa (the other Chuhra quarter of Khalapur) by having a *panchayat* at which it was decided that they should contribute too. Thus they got enough money together to buy Haradi back. They got the money from the Marchwa quarter people by threatening them. The Chuhra (Sweeper) *panchayat* of both *bastis*, the elders of Marchwa themselves agreeing, threatened the men from Marchwa who had been in on the plot. They threatened them with punishment and said they would sue them for the money.

The Nangal *sarpanch* also handed down some punishments. When those men were taken to Nangal, both the men from Marchwa and Chiter were tied up by their hands from the roof from which they hung for an hour. Then they had to sit with their ears between their knees for an hour, and they had to apologize thoroughly for acting so wickedly. Each man was fined ten rupees by the Nangal *sarpanch* too. Both Chiter and his wife had to pay ten rupees. They saved Suti, Chiter's wife, from being hung by her hands and so on, because it would have been an insult to have a *bahu* punished in that way. They got her out of these punishments by saying that she did not know what was happening, that she had no knowledge of what Chiter was doing. She actually started saying, "My son was ill, and I went to show him to a doctor. I was called away by deceit."

The Nangal *panchayat* was a full *panchayat* of that village. Many people from Khalapur and from "all four sides" attended. Some relatives such as Baliram's daughter's people from Karcha near Nangal attended. Chiter and the Marchwa men were present. It was the regular *panchayat* that decided the punishment.

Haradi had not come home yet. The Khalapur men had got Chiter to go to Nangal by telling him, "What's done is done. Come, let us go and bring her back." This was after they had gathered the rupees for Haradi. They had told the Marchwa men to come in the same way.

It was the Khalapur Sweepers who had gone to the *sarpanch* in Nangal village and told him, "Today it is our *bahu*. Tomorrow it will be someone else's. These men should be fined and punished as much as possible." They felt that if these men had trapped our *basti*, they should be punished. There was no question of punishing Kaliram, the man who had bought Haradi because he had not troubled her in any way. He had behaved very decently to her. He had paid for her honestly.

All of the Khalapur delegation had talked to the Nangal *sarpanch*. Ram and Ghasitu, elders, had done most of the talking but they had all chimed in.

Later the men were punished by a Sweeper *panchayat* (caste-men's council) held in Khalapur. The men from Marchwa, and Chiter were fined five rupees each. This was after the Nangal punishments. This money was taken and kept by the *panchayat* for an emergency. There was also a case filed in the *gawn panchayat* (village elected *panchayat)*, but the Marchwa people probably bribed the *sarpanch, so* that he

> asked that the case be taken to our own *biraderi panchayat* (caste chapter *panchayat*). Both *panchayats* should have punished these men. The *sarpanch* in Nangal told us that they should be punished in Khalapur. All he could punish them for was breaking the laws of Nangal. The law of Nangal that had been broken was selling a woman without her consent. The case with the *sarpanch* at Nangal was initiated by the Chuhras of Nangal. They wanted to have made the first report in case anything went wrong. They had told him, "We have bought a woman, and she doesn't fit in very well. We think she has been sold to us by deceit." They wanted to report first, so that if there was a report against them they wouldn't be held part of the plot.

Had the letter with the signatures of the important men had any influence upon the Chuhras of Nangal? "The Nangal people were not trying to be unreasonable. They said, "Give us back our money. We'll give you back your *bahu* (daughter-in-law)."

How had the people in the Sweeper basti treated Chiter after this?

> Haradi was angry with Chiter for a long time. For six months no one in the *basti* spoke to Chiter. They wouldn't let him smoke their *hukkas*. Finally he apologized thoroughly and said to all the people of the *basti*, "I did a great misdeed." He said this to *chacha* (Ghasitu) and to Ram and to all the men met together. He put his shoe on his head and clasped his hands. All the men were there. Chiter said, "You are my babas (father's fathers). Excuse me. In the future, I won't do such a thing again." Chiter had decided to make this apology himself.

Chiter indeed had so little community support that he left the *basti* soon after our arrival and his wife Suti returned home with her child. She told us, "My child is well only at my mother's. He is never well here. We have no one of our own here; no elder here looks after us. The whole *basti* dislikes us, so I am going home." The community's image of Chiter was of a lazy fellow who had run away and was loafing somewhere, a man who never took the advice of the elders, and did not wish to obey them or show his respect for them.

In the spring of 1956, Swami's wife died, leaving three small children, and Swami's brother Kalu now pressured Haradi to marry his brother. She still continued however to have the support of the community in her refusal to sit with a *chacha-tau bhai* of her husband's. Bhuli told us:

> On Chaudas day recently, Haradi was getting ready to go the *mela* (fair). Kalu went and asked her whose permission she had taken to go. Haradi doesn't have any real *jeths* (husband's elder brothers), *devars* (husband's younger brothers) or husband so whose permission should she take? She was just going herself. Kalu went and pulled her out of her house and beat her, pushed her and gave her a slap and said, "You go and have affairs with everyone. Why don't you sit with him (Swami) instead of going around to other people?"
>
> After all, Haradi is young. She likes to dress up and wear nice clothes. She talks pleasantly to people, and sometimes she laughs and jokes with younger men who are *devars* in relation. For all this, he accused her of being flirtatious. Haradi has a *bhatiji* (brother's daughter) married into Marchwa quarter. Sometimes she goes there, so he accused her of having affairs with people there. Haradi told me, "See, I should have died the death of a worm, and worms should eat me up. Everything bad should happen to me if I have done anything bad." Kalu abused her calling her "*sali*" (wife's sister) and "*sasu*" (mother-in-law). Haradi told me, "If they trouble me too much, I might have to go away somewhere."
>
> Swami had been nice and said, "No, no, let her alone. We don't want her. Let my children live. I don't want her."
>
> (We asked if the *bare admi* (big men) of the *basti* couldn't force Haradi to sit with Swami.) No, no, everyone's sympathy is with her when she doesn't wish to go there. The whole village -- the *pradhan* (headman of the village) and the *jemindars* (landholders of the village), everyone is with her. They told her if she was troubled at all, she should come to them and they would take care of her. Her brothers also told her, "If they trouble you, and it is not your wish, tell us, and we will come and rape their daughters."

Haradi continued to be under pressure while we were there to sit with Kalu, so that he might take on the debts which her husband Pratap had owed. Haradi explained to us that as a widow she is not obligated to pay these, but whatever man she decides to re-marry would have to shoulder these debts. Since the debts were taken to marry off Chiter, Chiter's motivation in selling his *chachi* had been to clear some of those debts. Thus, the bridegroom in whose behalf the debts had been taken might also be expected to pay them off. Indeed, at one time, before the sale of Haradi, when Chiter was very ill, the *bhagat* treating Chiter found that it was the ghost *(bhut)* of Pratap that was stuck to Chiter, and the *bhut* pronounced through Mangal the shaman *(bhagat)* that he was making Chiter sick because he had not repaid these debts and had been bothering his wife, Haradi. Kali told us that Mangal had not been able to control the *bhut* of Pratap very well, because "he was a real *chacha* (father's younger brother) of Chiter's and even the gods *(devtas)* cannot have much control over spirits playing on members of their own family."

Pratap had demanded that a cow be given in his name, and that cow was still in the *basti* in 1956; it could never be sold, Kali told us. Kali also pointed out to us that Pratap's *bhut* observed Haradi closely and made her sick whenever she wanted to leave the *basti* for a visit elsewhere. Kali warned, "Now you'll see. She wants to go to her *bhanja's* (sister's son's) wedding (in another village), and she will surely come home sick."

Last year at Holi some of the visitors thought that Haradi had thrown color on them (it was actually another woman). Kalu, hearing them say, "Haradi is our *sali*. That is why she threw color on us," came in with a *lathi* (a weighted bamboo pole used as a weapon) and told Haradi, "You do not get remarried or sit with us, but go out after other people who visit. I will cut off your genitals." She said, "First bring your wife and cut off hers and then bring your daughter and cut hers, and then cut mine!" "After that, he abused me no more."

Another Sweeper, Bhuli, told us that Kalu's wife's parents said when Haradi became a widow, "It is not Haradi who has been widowed, but it is our daughter. Her husband has eyes only for Haradi, and our daughter will be neglected." Bhuli affirmed that Haradi did not want to marry either Kalu or Swami and she told her people (her brother) not to give a rupee to either of them (the gesture of agreement to her "sitting with" one of them).

Kishandai, another Sweeper, however, assumed that there had been a sexual relationship between Haradi and Kalu, and said that if Haradi had a baby by Kalu, it would be perfectly legitimate and accepted as the child of a leviratic second husband. Kalu's wife would of course be jealous. Kishandai sighed, "What can a woman do? No woman likes another one in her house. They have twenty-four hour disputes."

Since Haradi likes to laugh and joke, she sometimes does so with men of the village or *basti* who are *devars* in relationship to her, Bhuli told us. Kalu even went to her home village and told her people that their daughter was going "bad". They sent back word that she should "sit with" Kalu, or they would never come to see her again. Haradi said, "Let those copulators never come. I don't care."

While there has been some friction between Swami's wife and Haradi, because the former feared that Haradi might "lure" her husband, Haradi and Kalu's wife seem to get along well. Kalu's wife does have to bear a certain amount of teasing. Thus, when Kalu once went to fetch Haradi from her home village, a number of women teased his wife saying that Kalu had gone to "get a new wife".

Kati explained Haradi's acceptance of the basic rule of the levirate, that a widow should marry her husband's full brother. She said, "If a woman's husband dies, and if any of her *devars* (husband's younger brothers) or *jeths* (husband's older brothers) are single, then she can live with one of them. Mostly, that is only if one is single. Sometimes it happens that two wives live together, but then there is much quarreling. For example, if two live together and one is given clothes and jewelry by the husband and the other isn't, there is a quarrel. Now with Haradi and Kalu's wife, when Haradi's husband died, both Swami and Kalu wanted her, but she wouldn't sit with either because she said, 'I don't want to sit in a full house, one where there are women and children. Why should I go there? I will spend my days here. If Prithvi my *jeth* comes, I will stay with him.' "

We asked about Prithvi. "His wife lives at her mother's house. She hasn't come back here for the past five or six years. If he came, Haradi could stay with him. She still says, 'If you find him, I'll stay with him.' When Haradi's husband died and Prithvi ran away, those two (Prithvi's wife and Haradi) lived and worked together. Then Prithvi's wife went away."

Haradi is a childless widow who refused either to take one of three leviratic mates or to be sold.

When we returned to Khalapur for a brief visit in 1967, we learned that Haradi had finally remarried her husband's full brother, Prithvi, the man who had been lost in Delhi. He evidently had reappeared meanwhile. In 1974, when we again visited, we learned that she had died.

To summarize Haradi's career as a widow -- she successfully resisted pressures from her brother, the Sweeper *basti panchayat*, and from the man in question himself, to remarry her married husband's *chacha-tau ka bhai* (father's brother's son). She managed this, first, by claiming a promise made to her husband that she would not marry either of his two *chacha-tau ke bhais;* secondly, by citing the regularity with which co-wives quarrel, and thus that she and Kalu's wife would quarrel; and thirdly, by maintaining a reputation for chastity, based on the very real fact that she had not become pregnant. Furthermore, she was regular in her sweeping work done for higher-caste households in the village, so these clients thought well of her. She had also won the support of the elder Chuhras by showing unusually great respect to them, and she was pleasant and entertaining to the other Chuhra women and to her *devars* (husband's classificatory [*basti*] younger brothers). When her husband's dead brother's son tried to sell her without her permission, she not only won the sympathy of the people to whom she had been sold but also had the immediate aid of the elders and of the other adult men of her first husband's *basti*.

Haradi had indeed briefly tried "sitting with" a distant cousin of her dead husband's, but she broke off that relationship with the sympathy and support of the community, because he was a wandering fellow who was not a solid member of the Chuhra community. She eventually did conform to the prescriptive levirate rule that a widow should marry her husband's full brother. We do not know, however, whether Prithvi, the husband's full brother, was married or not at the time she mated with him; her willingness to enter that polygynous situation was indicated right after her first husband's death when she lived with Prithvi's wife until this woman, deserted by her husband, returned to her natal village.

How are we to understand Haradi's story? I do not think we should see Haradi as manipulating the cultural rules in pursuit of her own self-interest as Marett, Malinowski, Bailey, Barth and Turner have written (Kuper 1975: 30, 38), nor is she to be understood as a person in a situation in which norms are in flux or in conflict as Leach and Gluckman (Kuper 1975: 191) have written. Haradi conformed to the social norms of the Chuhra community. She had fun within the prescribed joking relationship with husband's younger brothers, and she fulfilled the more onerous norms of "sitting with" a husband's real brother, doing her *jajmani* work, and doing respectful chores for older women. The norms themselves however are not totally patriarchal in this patrilineal-patrilocal culture. They do allow the widow choice of a mate if there is no dead husband's unmarried full brother. And Haradi used the right of choice steadfastly, especially with respect to the cousin-brothers whom her husband hated, and she disputed her lot of being sold, quite within her rights as a virtuous widow. Perhaps what Haradi represents is a woman who took full advantage of the rights built into her small social system, but did the duties required of her by the other norms impinging upon her. By so doing, she won the support of most of the members of her small community and with that their protection. By some scorings, she may be seen as both a brave and good woman.

Note

1. I carried on fieldwork among the Chuhras of Khalapur (Saharanpur district, Uttar Pradesh) between October 1954 and May 1956 as a post-doctoral fellow of the Cornell University India Project. Usha Bhagat (now Mrs. Mahendra Dave of Tarzana, California) was my research assistant during the years in Khalapur.

References

Beals, Alan R. (1962), *Gopalpur*, New York: Holt, Rinehart and Winston.

Blunt, Edmund Arthur Henry (1967), *The Caste System of Northern India with Special Reference to the United Provinces of Agra and Oudh*, London: Humphrey Milford, Oxford University Press; Delhi: S. Chand; orig. 1931.

Carstairs, G. Morris (1957), *The Twice-Born: A Study of a Community of High-Caste Hindu*, London: Hogarth Press.

Chattopadhyay, K.P. (1922), "Levirate and Kinship in India", *Man* 22: 36--41.

Crooke, William (1907), *Natives of Northern India*, London: Archibald Constable.

Davis, Marvin (1982), *Rank and Rivalry: The Politics of Inequality in Rural West Bengal*, Cambridge: Cambridge University Press.

Dube, Shyama Charan (1955), *Indian Village*, London: Routledge and Kegan Paul.

Dumont, Louis (1957), *Une Sous-Caste de l'Inde du Sud, les Pramalai Kallar*, Paris: Mouton.

— (1964), "Marriage in India: The Present State of the Question", Part 2 *Contributions to Indian Sociology* 7: 77–102.

— (1970), *Homo Hierarchicus: The Caste System and its Implications*, Chicago: University of Chicago Press.

Karve, Iravati (1965), *Kinship Organization in India*, Bombay: Asia Publishing House.

Kolenda, Pauline (1964), "Toward a Model of the Hindu *Jajmani* System", *Human Organization* 22, no. 1: 11–31.

— (1978), *Caste in Contemporary India*, Menlo Park, Cal.: Benjamin/ Cummings.

— (1982), "Widowhood among 'Untouchable' Chuhras", *Concept of Person: Kinship, Caste, and Marriage in India*, edited by Akos Ostor, Lina M. Fruzetti and Steven Barnett, Cambridge, Mass.: Harvard University Press, pp. 172–220.

Kuper, Adam J. (1975), *Anthropologists and Anthropology: The British School 1922--1972*, Harmondsworth: Penguin Books.

Lewis, Oscar (1958), *North Indian Village*, Urbana-Champaign: University of Illinois Press.

Mandelbaum, David Goodman (1957), "The Family in India", *Introduction to the Civilization of India: Changing Dimensions of Indian Society and Culture*, Chicago University of Chicago, Syllabus Division; orig. in *Southwestern Journal of Anthropology* 4: 123–139, pp. 247–262.

— (1970), *Society in India*, Berkeley and Los Angeles: University of California Press.

Marriott, McKim, and Ronald B. Inden (1973), "Caste Systems", *Encyclopaedia Britannica*, Chicago: Encyclopaedia Britannica Inc., 3: 982–991.

Mayer, Adrian Curtius (1960), *Caste and Kinship in Central India*, Berkeley: University of California Press.

O'Malley, Lewis Sydney Steward (1932), *Indian Caste Customs*, Cambridge: Cambridge University Press.

Singh, Mohinder (1947), *The Depressed Classes: Their Economic and Social Condition*, Bombay: Hind Kitab.

Stevenson, Henry Noel Cochrane (1954), "Status Evaluation in the Hindu Caste System", *Journal of the Royal Anthropological Institute* 4: 45--65.

Stevenson, Margaret Sinclair (1930), *Without the Pale: Life Story of an Outcaste*, London: Oxford University Press.

Vatuk, Sylvia Jane Dutra (1980), "The Aging Woman in India: Self-Perceptions and Changing Roles", *Women in Contemporary India and South Asia*, edited by Alfred deSouza, Delhi: Manohar Books, pp. 142--163.

Yalman, Nur (1963), "On the Purity of Women in the Castes of Ceylon and Malabar", *Journal of the Royal Anthropological Institute* 3, pt. 1: 25--58.

2

'Untouchable' Chuhras Through their Humor

"Equalizing" Marital Kin Through Teasing, Pretence, and Farce

What is at issue, briefly, is the over-all "discursive fact," the way in which sex is "put into discourse."

—Michel Foucault, *The History of Sexuality*, Volume I

Remember, people joke about only what is most serious.

—Alan Dundes, *Cracking Jokes*

The various genres of humor are for the purpose of entertainment. They relate to emotions because, although they require a cognitive prerequisite (one must "get" the joke), if appreciated, they bring pleasure to their audience.

There is a belief in the United States that the English cannot quite "get" American jokes; there is even a series of jokes about that (Dundes 1987: 150--58). That many ethnographers may sympathize with the English predicament is indicated by the scarcity of ethnographic treatments of humor. People construct jokes, farce, and satire out of cultural materials, and as a minimum, the ethnographer must, just as with a cockfight (Geertz 1973) or a ritual (Bateson 1936), know the other culture rather well to grasp its humor.

Although jokes primarily entertain, they can also be seen as commentaries that people are making, consciously or unconsciously, on aspects of their own society and culture. Dundes above warned us that jokes are about serious matters, and Mary Douglas (1975: 104) has suggested that jokes are usually against the social structure: "they attack classification and hierarchy."

Jokes often seem to express a strain of defiance toward the official social structure and proper cultural values. Part of what makes some jokes funny is the casualness with which the sternest mores are broken in the often upside-down world fantasized in the joke. Perhaps it is the countercultural values expressed in the various genres of humor that contribute to making them difficult for an outsider to grasp. One must not only know much of the other culture but also appreciate its practitioners' discomfort and dissatisfaction with many of its parts, some of which they may imaginatively and even rebelliously play with in genres of humor.

To their audiences, jokes may be "truer" than propriety; they can have a kind of wisdom as they tear away the masks of propriety revealing that both high and low are all-too-human (or all-too-animal). If anthropologists look more closely, they may see that one set of masks has been replaced in joking or farce by another and that the disguises of propriety shape the disguises of humor.

Habermas (1988:310) has suggested that when people laugh at the humor of wit they temporarily regress to an infantile prelinguistic stage of life. But I would say that it is not back to a prelinguistic stage but back to the early years of childhood, when they had to learn the most basic social and cultural rules, that jokes – that themselves permit the ready breaking of these rules – carry them. Certainly, joking and farce are forms of play during which raconteur or actors and the audience may behave like kids. Perhaps that aspect of humor is universal, but the content of jokes is very much culturally constructed.

In this chapter, I am concerned with some aspects of humor among Hindu peasants of North India, specifically with culturally prescribed uses of humor, derision, and insult in the relations between equals, between men who are "brothers," and between married women of the same generation, on the one hand, and between unequal affinal relatives, the wife's kin and the husband's kin, on the other. These latter are what anthropologists have called ritual joking relationships.

Although ritual joking relationships are found widely throughout the world, including India, the *content* of the institutionalized joking between affines (people related as brothers-in-law or sisters-in-law or brother-in-law/sister-in-law or co-parents-in-law) is seldom recorded. Apte makes the point forcefully that the ethnographic record is lacking in descriptions of actual joking behavior. He defines a joking relationship

> as a patterned playful behavior that occurs between two individuals who recognize special kinship or other types of social bonds between them; it displays reciprocal or nonreciprocal verbal or action-based humor including joking, teasing, banter, ridicule, insult, horseplay, and other similar manifestations. usually in the presence of an audience (Apte 1985:30–31).

Later he writes:

> A major weakness in the existing studies of the joking relationship from the viewpoint of the student of humor is that much emphasis has been put on the relational aspects of the joking relationship and not enough on the phenomenon of joking itself. Relatively few ethnographic accounts describe in detail what actually happens by way of joking, irrespective of how the term is understood by the investigator. Detailed information about the verbal, gestural, and action-based manifestations of joking is often lacking (Apte 1985:34).

In this essay, I shall describe "what actually happens" in culturally prescribed joking relationships, as I found them among North Indian untouchable Sweepers, called Chuhras or Bhangis, in village Khalapur, western Uttar Pradesh, in the mid-1950s.[1] It is important to see that these joking relationships balance avoidance-respect relationships in the North Indian Hindu cultural context, a characteristic of joking relations noted by Radcliffe-Brown (1952a, 1952b) for some peoples in Africa, Asia, Oceania, and North America. In North India, avoidance and respect relationships between affines of different generations or between those with large differences in age in the same generation, follow an elaborate etiquette that has been described in considerable detail by scholars treating women, *purdah* (seclusion and veiling of women), and family life in northern India (Beech 1982; Bennett 1983; Das 1976; Hershman 1981; Jacobson 1970, 1977, 1982; Jeffery 1979; Luschinsky 1962; Madan 1965, 1975; Mehta 1982; Minturn and Hitchcock 1966; Papanek 1982; Papanek and Minault 1982; Sharma 1978; van der Veen 1972; Vatuk 1982; Vreede-de Stuers 1968). The following passage will give only a flavor of the Chuhras' extensive description of deference etiquette between affines.

Among the Chuhris (feminine for Chuhras; the latter term is both generic and masculine), especially when discussing the relationships between an in-married woman and her affinal kin, the word repeatedly spoken is *kayda,* a rule of etiquette manifesting an attitude of deference. There is *sasu ka kayda,* the etiquette for the mother-in-law, and *jeth ka kayda,* the etiquette for the husband's elder brother, *nanand ka kayda,* for the husband's sister, and so on. The combination is a code for hierarchical relationships between junior affines and senior affines, maritally related kin of different ages. The various *kayde* (plural) involve respectfulness, graciousness, concern for the others, and even hospitality.

But I will let the Chuhris speak for themselves about *kayde;* in quoting from my field notes I use NQ and a number. Bhati told us about the *sasu* (the mother-in-law) and in the course of her discussion, spoke of *kayda* (etiquette of deference):

> NQ 1 One should behave toward a *sasu* as toward one's own mother. (How should one show this?) Press her feet when she comes from outside, fill the *hukka* [water-pipe for smoking tobacco], rub her back in the morning, be affectionate toward her. (How should a *sasu* treat her *bahu* [daughter-in-law]?) She should be very affectionate, bring things for her – food, cosmetics, and toilet articles, keep her well-dressed. (Should the *bahu* obey the *sasu?* If she doesn't obey her, it's very bad....
>
> If the *sasu* and *bahu* are young, they might talk pleasantly to each other. I and my mother-in-law used to eat together. I kept one important kind of *kayda* [etiquette]. Unless she ate, I wouldn't eat. I wouldn't eat unless food was given me by my mother-in-law. There was great affection between us. Unless she is sleeping, a *bahu* serves her mother-in-law. The mother-in-law tells her to do everything. When the *bahu* has learned, she does it herself....
>
> For those who do keep *kayda,* affection is great....
>
> My mother-in-law had four or five *bahus. I* had five *devranis* [husband's younger brothers' wives] and *jethanis* [husband's older brothers' wives]. She used to beat them if they didn't do their work, but I was never beaten. If she told me to do ten jobs, I would say, "I have so much to do. Please wait," and we both would laugh. She was very affectionate. If I ever came here [to parental village], my mother-in-law would come along, crying, for half a *kos* [one mile]

> after me. She missed me so, she'd say, "Oh, *bahu,* come back soon." The other *bahus* would sass back and be disobedient. If she said, "Ey, *bahu,* do this right away," the others would say, "I can't do it."

> [A *kayda*-practicing *bahu*] covers her face if her husband comes in, and if the *sasu* sits on a cot the *bahu* sits on a *pirha* [*stool*], so she is lower than her mother-in-law. She keeps a *ghumghat* [*covers* her face with the end of her sari] from the *taisera* [husband's father's elder brother's wife] and *pittisera* [husband's father's younger brother's wife], too.

The Chuhris indicated the specific acts by which a subordinate displayed respect, reverence, or deference to a superordinate. In return, the superordinate should show affection.[2] Suffice to say, in-marrying women should be silent and cover their heads and often their faces when in the presence of father-in-law, elder brother-in-law, and husband's other kin older than the husband, both male and female.

Similarly, in-marrying men are respectful toward a wife's older kin, just as they are respectful toward their own older kin. Male respect etiquette is not as dramatic as female. A man does not smoke, joke, or talk about sexual matters in the presence or hearing of older men.

Between people of the same generation, close in age, joking may be allowed and even prescribed among North Indian peasants. Balancing or opposed to deference between seniors and juniors is derision (*ganda majak banana*, to make a dirty joke), insult (*gali dena*, to give an insult), and joking (*hamsi-makhaul karna*, to make a laugh-joke), expressed in asymmetrical relations between affinal kin of the same generation and close in age. A recognition that heavy purdah regulations are balanced by the gaiety and fun involved in this all-too-often risqué discourse may modify an impression that a culture so addicted to hierarchy as is North Indian, expressed in caste ranking and age-and-generation ranking, is unrelievedly obsequious.

My essay is divided into three parts: first, North Indian hypergamy; second, Chuhra marriage customs; third, joking relationships, which are subdivided into four parts: everyday joking, teasing the bridegroom, brothers-in-law, and co-parents-in-law.

The North Indian Hypergamous Milieu

Hypergamy was first conceptualized as a label for certain marriage patterns in the Punjab by a Mr. Coldstream, according to British census ethnographer Ibbetson (1881: 356), cited in Dumont (1964: 87--88), and it means a preference for the bride to marry "up". Although seemingly only a few castes have grades of families (Dumont 1970: 109–129), between which hypergamous marriages take place, the bride at marriage moving from a family of lower grade into a family of higher grade, in many more castes, the bride, her natal family members, and the members of her *khandan* (minimal patrilineage), *basti* (colony), or village caste-chapter are considered inferior to the groom, his natal family, *khandan*, *basti*, or caste-chapter; the differential ranking is instituted with the establishment of the marital alliance at the time of the arrangement of the marriage. In fact, some ethnographers report that marriages usually are established between families of about equal wealth and community standing. A number of scholars (Dumont 1964, 1966, 1975; Vatuk 1969, 1975; van der Veen 1972; Pocock 1972; Khare 1975; Madan 1975; Das 1976; Hershman 1981; Bennett 1983) have recognized that a central feature of the North Indian marriage system is the inequality between the groom's kin (the wifetakers) and the bride's kin (the wifegivers); indeed, Dumont has spoken of Hindu North India as a "hypergamous milieu" (Dumont 1966: 94, 110), referring to the bridetaker-bridegiver ranking. The original inspiration for such analysis is Lévi-Strauss (1969: 240, 245, 261).

The inequality between the bride and groom's sides is expressed in unilateral "perpetual gift giving" (Vatuk 1975: 174) and various ritual gestures showing reverence and respect to the bridegroom (Dumont 1966: 94) and his kinsmen. Dumont (1966, 1975), Vatuk (1969, 1975), Khare (1975), Madan (1975), Fruzzetti and Ostor (1976), and Inden and Nicholas (1977) have debated the issue of whether the inequality between the bridegivers and bridetakers is also expressed in North Indian kinship terminology -- an issue addressed to some extent later in this chapter.

Although all the scholars listed have studied almost entirely Brahmans or higher castes, in one of the earliest village descriptions of the asymmetrical system -- for Kishan Garhi, Aligarh district, Uttar Pradesh (Marriott 1955: 101) -- it appears to be shared by all twenty-four castes.[3] For the "Cornell" village, Khalapur, Minturn and Hitchcock (1966: 58) found that among the Rajputs, the high dominant landed caste, "the status of a wife's family is always subordinate to the status of the groom's." The Rajputs, Hitchcock found (1956: 56--60), practice a kind of "directional hypergamy," resting on strict rules of arranged marriage, village exogamy (a marriage partner must reside in another village), and patrilocal residence; brides come from Rajput villages to the south and east, and daughters are given in marriage to the north and west. As far as I am aware, all twenty-five Hindu castes of Khalapur have marriage systems in which bridetakers are superior to bridegivers.[4] In this essay, I am primarily concerned with culturally expected humor concerning sexuality and marriage alliances in North India, as illustrated by the untouchable Chuhras of Khalapur.

Marrying Among the Chuhras of Khalapur

Khalapur, in western Uttar Pradesh, just to the east of Haryana and Punjab, is ninety miles north of Delhi, capital of Muslim empires for more than eight hundred years. So, although the population is over 90 percent Hindu, some Muslim-inspired customs endure. There were more than thirty different caste-communities among the five thousand people of Khalapur in 1955. The population was about 9700 in 1984 when I returned there to do fieldwork.[5] It is a Rajput village; the Rajputs are the dominant landowning group, making up two-fifths of the population, with around twenty-four hundred people in 1955. The second largest caste, the untouchable Chamars, numbers about six hundred; they drag away other people's dead cattle to tan the hides, their traditional caste work, and labor in the Rajputs' wheat and sugarcane fields. The Chuhras are the fourth largest caste (after the Brahman priests), divided into two colonies (*bastis*). "Our" community, the Chuhras of the western *basti*, numbers about one hundred. Their work is cleaning cattle yards and ladies' latrines in the high-caste women's quarters. Most people in Khalapur would agree, even if the Chuhras would not, that the Chuhras are the bottom of the local caste ranking system. Between the high-caste Brahmans, Rajputs, and merchants, and the unclean Chamars and Chuhras are clean serving and artisan castes – goldsmiths, barbers, washermen, potters, weavers, shepherds, carpenters, and blacksmiths, among others. The 10 percent of the population who are Muslim include Muslim Rajputs, oilpressers, and tailors. Caste-communities live in their own neighborhoods, especially untouchables like the Chuhras who live in an isolated, detached colony (*basti*) on the outskirts of the village.

There are two wedding ceremonies in North Indian marriages. In Khalapur, the first, the *sadi,* takes place when the bride is between the ages of ten and sixteen, and the groom is twelve to eighteen years old; the *cala* takes place one to five years later. The purpose of marriage is the reproduction of offspring, especially males, to continue the patrilineage. The first wedding ceremonies (*sadi*) bind together the two families, minimal lineages, and caste-colonies of the bride and groom. After each set of rituals at the bride's home and village, she goes with the groom and his all-male wedding party to his village where she stays with the women of his joint family in the women's quarters. After the *sadi,* she may not see her bridegroom at all. Only after the second set of ceremonies (*cala*) is the couple's marital relationship consummated.

Because women are hardly allowed to travel except between their natal and marital villages, male elders arrange marriages. The bride's elderly males propose marriage to the groom's. Mates must be found outside the child's own village (village exogamy) but within her or his *jati* (endogamous set of caste-chapters in a set of nearby villages). Unlike South Indians and some Indian Muslims, North Indian Hindus prohibit marriage with cousins or second cousins through a prohibition on marriage in three or four *gotras* or patri-sibs. A child cannot marry anyone belonging to his or her own, the mother's, the father's mother's, and the mother's mother's *gotra.*

Because marriages are arranged between unrelated lineages, in Khalapur, and in much of northern India, mother-in-law and daughter-in-law are always unrelated strangers, as are the two fathers-in-law (father of the groom and father of the bride, both *samdhi* or the two brothers-in-law (the bride's brother [*sala*] and her husband [*jija, bahanoi,* i.e., sister's husband]). Because women cannot travel about, the two mothers-in-law or sisters-in-law (bride's sister and groom's sister) are unlikely ever to meet.

The bride's family usually tries to find a bridegroom whose family's resources are better than their own. The bride's family, however, bear most expenses of the wedding entertainment, as well as the expenses of the bride's *trousseau*, gifts for the new affinal relatives, and gifts of money and clothing for the bridegroom. Gift giving is heavily one-sided; the bride's side gives the gifts, and the groom's side receives. Furthermore, a married woman's brother should bring her gifts three times a year at the festivals of Tij (in August), Diwali (in October or November) and Holi (in March).[6] Whenever a daughter visits her parental home, she must take back with her gifts for her affinal kin, as well as clothing for herself.

Exchange marriage between two lineages is prohibited. The two parties to a wedding are permanently bridegivers and bridetakers to each other; the former gives gifts to the latter throughout the life of the marriage binding them together, and beyond, because a child's mother's brother (*mama*) must bring gifts for the child's marriage, even if the linking woman, the child's mother, is dead.

Basic to North Indian kinship is the strong positive relationship between brother and sister (Dumont 1966: 99–100; Vatuk 1969: 101; Pocock 1972: 100–103). Both Das (1976: 21–22) and Hershman (1981: 133) emphasize the importance in the Punjab of the brother's caring for and protecting his sister; he may even protect her *against* her husband. Minturn and Hitchcock (1968: 36) write about the dominant caste Rajputs of Khalapur: "The relationship between a brother and his sister or female cousins also seems warmer and less restrained than the marital one and is considered sacred" (see also Dorschner 1983: 128–129).

Chuhras frequently state their own belief in the strength and priority of this relationship over others.

> NQ 2 One Chuhri married into another village who feels much affection for her younger brother said, "As far as affection goes, it is greater for one's brother, because you can always get another husband if he dies. One's affection is always greatest for a brother. You can't get a new brother."

Gyarsi, a female informant in her thirties, also believed in the priority in a woman's affections for her brother.

> NQ 3 A woman loves her brother above her son, and her son above her husband.

Because a woman marries into another village, into a household of strangers, potential support from her father and brothers in her natal village can be crucial for her welfare. The assumed bond of strong affection and obligation between brother and sister has much to do with the initially hostile relationship assumed to exist between a woman's bridegroom and her brother, which I discuss below.

High-caste Hindus, like the Brahmans and Rajputs of Khalapur, prohibit the remarriage of widows, but the Chuhras, and other untouchables, as well as the middle castes, allow widow remarriage, often practicing the levirate (Kolenda 1982). Marriages across generations are prohibited; thus, a widow could not take her dead husband's father's brother as her second husband.

Strongly influenced by Muslim culture, Khalapur has the institutions of seclusion and veiling of women, purdah, and villagers largely accept the Islamic ideology concerning sexuality. According to this ideology, people have very strong sexual impulses that must be controlled to prevent social anarchy, and sexual interest distracts the devout believer from concentrating upon Allah and spiritual goals (Sabbah 1984: 63–78; Jeffery 1979: 17–22). This Muslim ideology is similar to the belief in mystical Hinduism that sexual interest distracts the holy man from his spiritual goal (Carstairs 1957: 98–99). Thus, in both religious traditions, there is a denigration of sexuality. Among the Chuhras and other North Indians, a young virgin is referred to and addressed as a *devi*, a goddess; auspicious, she is given offerings in some religious ceremonies, just as Brahmans and cows are; however, a married woman is a *suhagin*, a woman who is auspicious because her husband is alive, but she herself is not considered divine in any way. Degrading a *devi* by making her partake of sexual activity makes her brother who gives her into marriage curse-worthy.[7] The reason for both the hierarchical relationship and the lowness of the bride's brother relates to religious traditions that devalue sexuality. Because the Muslims in Pakistan scorn the *sala* (a wife's brother), one may suspect this northern custom is both Muslim and Hindu.

There is a segregation not only of castes but also of the sexes in Khalapur. A set of patrilineally related women, the wives of brothers, fathers, and sons lives in its own quarters; compounds of rooms are built about inner open courtyards. Men of a minimal patrilineage sleep in their club house (*caupal*), a room at the back of a platform built above the narrow village path. Men sit or sleep on cots on the platform. Women are forbidden to set foot on the men's *caupal*.

In other words, husband and wife do not share a sleeping room: a woman sleeps with her daughters and small sons in a room in the women's quarters; her husband sleeps with other men and boys of his joint family and minimal patrilineage at the club house or cattleshed. Sleeping arrangements seem to deny that sexual relations occur, consistent with the negative sexual ideology briefly described.

The subjects of my essay are untouchable Chuhras who work as servants of higher caste people. How many of the rules of purdah apply to the Chuhris, the Chuhra women? Adult Chuhris leave their homes daily to go out to work in homes and cattle yards of others. They always go in pairs, never alone, however, and they are always veiled as they move through the village, even when they are carrying baskets of waste on their heads to compost heaps. They are not fair game for strange men, and any illicit sexual relationship is strongly disapproved of. Except for the outings required by their work, Chuhri women remain at home; they do not work in the fields. Like higher caste women, they do not travel out of the village unescorted by a man. Women have their own quarters; men have their *caupals*.

Everyday Joking and Derision

The rule among the Chuhras against talking about sex before elders is matched by a rule against unmarried girls' listening to their brothers' wives' and the *basti*-brothers' wives' talk about sex. Both rules, however, are balanced by permission for married people of the same sex, close in age, to talk about sex quite freely, usually in a jocular vein. Married women often talk about another's sex life. Here are two examples from my field notes on the Chuhras:

> NQ 4 Surti, a girl of fifteen, had just returned from her *cala*. A *basti bhavaj* [brother's wife] told a group of other married women, "Here, let me tell you something about this girl. She says that when she went to her in-laws and her husband came to visit her at night, she said, 'Wait, let me spread my *orhna* [long head-covering] on the cot, so that the cot will not get spoiled.' At this, her husband said, 'No, take some old cloth or old *orhna*. Don't spoil the new one.'" The women listening to the story looked incredulous, put their fingers on their mouths, laughed, and shook their heads in disapproval. Another

> *bhavaj* said, "What an unwise thing to say! Her husband might have thought she was well up in such things, must have had practice before. He must have been a simple man. Otherwise, he might easily have become suspicious and caused trouble. Girls should try to show more innocence and not make such suggestions."
>
> The first *bhavaj* said further that Surti had told her that she had pushed her husband away twice when he advanced toward her, before she let him touch her. At this, the women again laughed disapprovingly.

In the above passage, Surti's seemingly knowledgeable behavior, the *bhavajs* seemed to think, might have raised doubts in her new husband's mind about her total innocence.

The second example is usual daily fare.

> NQ 5 A group of women were sitting together. One said something about having sore eyes. Tarkhi said in a low tone that her genitals also were sore, and Anandi remarked, "How can that happen? That person who can make them sore [her husband] is far away, not here!"[8]

How are we to understand such a joke? As Bhati mentioned above in NQ 1, there is considerable rivalry between daughters-in-law for a mother-in-law's approval, and there is likely to be tension, even quarreling, between women over shares of work. Gossiping and joking together is at least an amiable pause in the day's occupations. Relations between the women are not hierarchically structured at such times, although rivalries and put-downs may manifest themselves in these exchanges between equals. Her brothers' wives in NQ 4 are certainly criticizing and putting down Surti, and a married daughter of the *basti,* Anandi, in NQ 5 may be questioning her sister-in-law's (Tarkhi's) virtue.

Mutual put-downs in a sexual discourse may become a kind of contest between equals among the Chuhras as in NQ 6. Conversations like NQ 6 take place on the men's sitting platform of the *caupal* where men spend their leisure hours. In the following passage, Kharu, a young man in his twenties, matches wits with Sadhu, a man in his late thirties; Sadhu and Kharu are third cousins.

NQ 6 Kharu told us that the night before last, he had been sitting on the *caupal* and he said to Sadhu's ten-year-old son, "Your mother will soon be here [Sadhu's wife had been in her natal village for some weeks], and your father will have a good time!"

Sadhu started abusing Kharu. Referring to Kharu's wife, Ramkali, Sadhu said, "She's your *tai* [father's elder brother's wife]; she's your *caci* [father's younger brother's wife]." [Thus, Kharu's "mothers," so suggesting that Kharu was having an incestuous cross-generational sexual relationship with his leviratic wife, Ramkali. The latter is probably fifteen years older than Kharu.] Then Kharu kidded Sadhu about still sleeping in his house rather than on the *caupal.* Sadhu said he slept in the house because his wife was alone there. "There is no one to keep her company." Kharu twitted, "You have grown old. You have no more children. You should lend your wife out for six months or a year. Then see if she doesn't have children." [Here Kharu is teasing about a human female as though she were a cow. People in Khalapur often give a cow out "half-and-half" to someone who will feed and care for the animal; then as calves are born, the lender and the borrower alternate in ownership of them.]

Kharu said that one day he told Sadhu to give his wife out "half-and-half" to M's father, a "fat, dark Chamar" [an untouchable who the Chuhras like to pretend is of lower caste rank than themselves].

Sadhu retorted, "All right, I'll give her away. In case she doesn't have a child, though, you'll have to give the one-eyed bad one [he is referring here to Kharu's wife] to me!"

Note the various metaphors used in this discourse of mutual abasement which Kharu considered to have been hilarious. First, Kharu breaks the rule of the silence between father and son on matters of sex by calling to Sadhu's son's attention the sexual relation between his parents. Then Sadhu accuses Kharu of incest by making Kharu's leviratic wife into a "mother". Kharu then accuses Sadhu of first liking sex too much (staying with his wife in her house) and then of impotence (indicated by her having no more children). He also "makes" Sadhu's wife into a cow who should be loaned out and impregnated. The offspring of such a mating would then be split between genitor and *pater* half and half. On some occasions, Kharu has suggested that the genitor in this half-and-half arrangement should be an untouchable Chamar. The men run the gamut of sexually outrageous behavior -- excessive sexual appetite, incest, prostituting one's wife, prostituting her to a low-caste man and then accepting (presumably as legitimate children) the offspring (or half the offspring), and finally agreeing to give one's wife out to a "brother" for adultery.[9] They use various idioms of hierarchy, those of caste, humans *versus* animals, wife *versus* prostitute/concubine, primary wife *versus* secondary wife, demeaning the other by putting him on the down side of each.

This joking discourse between Kharu and Sadhu appears to be based upon a number of cultural suppositions. First, women's purpose is primarily to bear children and, while still of childbearing age, to continue to bear children; men's duty is to make them pregnant. Sadhu is already the father of four, but he does not protest that he and his wife already have enough children. If his eldest son, at this time a youth of fifteen, had already been married, Sadhu could have used, as his excuse for seeming impotence, the cultural proscription on parents' having sexual relations after their eldest child is married. North Indian villagers believe it wrong for both mother and daughter to be producing babies at the same time, but Sadhu could not yet use that excuse.

In their sallies, both men take advantage of their intimate knowledge of each other's sexual vulnerabilities. Sadhu may well be feeling his age and feeling less virile than formerly. It was well known that Kharu, who had inherited his older brother's widow in the Chuhras' prescribed levirate, was less than enchanted by his wife, well into her forties while he was still in his early twenties. She was already the mother of four children, the eldest aged nineteen, and she was hardly a beautiful woman; her face was marred especially by a heavy cataract over one eye. Kharu, on one occasion, asked us for some medicine to stimulate some sexual desire in him for this wife. She sometimes taunted him that when she died, she would haunt him, causing trouble (severe illness) to him and the new wife she expected he would immediately take after her death. Sadhu knew all this and used it to advantage in replying to Kharu's jibes.

Kharu does not hesitate to explain Sadhu's wife's infertility as due to Sadhu's failure, not to hers. She would surely bear a child if she were given out to a Chamar who would impregnate her successfully. So a lowly Chamar has power that Sadhu lacks. This taps, no doubt, into the chronic anxiety men in a caste system have about men of lower caste (or higher caste) taking their women.

Note that this joking is reciprocal; both men insult and tease each other, and both men, in effect, make the other into a pimp. Kharu suggests that Sadhu arrange a profitable relationship for himself by giving his wife to a Chamar, and Sadhu suggests that Kharu give his wife to *him*. Such casual suggestion of prostituting one's wife or forcing her to commit adultery, of course, reverses the seclusion of women that the purdah system in Khalapur provides and its protection of women so that they remain always chaste and faithful to their husbands. The anxieties about women's chastity and fidelity, that the purdah system seems to bespeak, are indeed spoken of indirectly in such joking between brothers as equals.

Lila Abu-Lughod (1986) has spoken of different discourses going on about and among women in purdah elsewhere. Among the Chuhras and other North Indians, hierarchical behavior with strict deference and respect forbids mention of the topic of sex between relatives and non-relatives of different generations; this is the more public, unmarked discourse. But in private, among equals, another discourse speaks frankly of prohibited sexual activities.

Other anthropologists (Burkhart 1974; Parry 1974; David 1974, 1977; Carter 1975) have also written about non-unequal relations in South Asian caste or egalitarian contexts in India, both economic and religious.[10] I may add these joking relations between brothers close in age and sisters-in-law close in age to that list of egalitarian relationships in South Asia.

The discourse between "brothers" who are good friends, as Kharu and Sadhu are, is in a "language of intimacy" rather than a "language of social distance" (Douglas 1975: 106). In NQ 6, that language is one in which wives and sexual difficulties are talked about openly and laughingly; neither man takes offence. All the evils that purdah is erected to prevent are taken for granted as truths – incest, adultery, pimping – in the joking mode. Although the discourse of deference and respect supports the social structure, the discourse of joking between both female and male equals turns it upside down.

The Bridegroom and the Bride's "Sisters"

A young Chuhra bridegroom described himself to us as shy (*saram lagna*) as he anticipated his visit after his *cala* to his wife's parents and relatives, as much strangers to him as his relatives were strangers to his new wife. Why should the bridegroom feel shy? He would not have to stay at the bride's village and home very long. He would take her and leave her there. But probably he remembered his previous experiences among her relatives, when at both the *sadi* and the *cala* his bride's sisters and brothers' wives, as well as her brothers, teased him.

Sukhar, a man in his thirties, reminisced about his wedding day. Among the Chuhras, it is the custom to take the new bridegroom around to the various farmers who retain the Chuhras to work for them. In the village where Sukhar was married, the dominant caste was probably Tyagi, but it also had some untouchable Chamars as well, and the women of these castes pinched and needled the young Chuhra bridegroom. He said,

> NQ 7 "When I went to get married, all the Tyagi girls and Chamaris came. They pinched me and put needles in me, and they gave me the same treatment when I went for my *cala.*"

> Were you taken around, or was this in the *basti?* He explained that "*salam mangna*" [greeting with a *salam* and begging] is done. The groom takes a *thali* [metal tray] and asks for things from the farmers [the landed families who employ the sweepers]. Wherever the groom goes, the girls laugh, joke, and are naughty. Sukhar said, "One Tyagi girl gave me a small bottle of oil and a comb. She said, 'Ey, let's see you comb your hair in the *Angrezi* [English] style.' Another gave me a piece of soap. She said, 'Ey, *jija* [sister's husband], go and bathe with this'."

The fiction that the village is all one family is sustained in this example. All the girls of the village, though of higher caste-rank than the Chuhras, are, nevertheless, the bride's fictive sisters, and the in-married young wives are her fictive brothers' wives. And both sisters and brothers' wives of the bride can have a fling at teasing the new bridegroom. They give him hair oil, comb, and soap to help the bridegroom improve his appearance, presumably helping him to prepare for his meeting with the bride's womenfolk and, eventually, the bride.

Their mothers are, of course, fictive mothers-in-law to the groom, and, as upper generation women to the groom, women to whom he must show avoidance respect and who show respect for him, they do not enter into the fun.

The day after the main wedding ceremonial at the time of the *sadi*, the groom is brought into the women's quarters to be fed. While he tries to eat, the bride's sisters (full sisters, female cousins, and *basti*-sisters, i.e., his *salis*) and her *bhabhis* and *bhavajs* (brothers' wives, cousin-brothers' wives, and *basti*-brothers' wives, i.e., his *salhajs*) tease him, saying he is the lover of his own mother (*ma ke yar*) and the son of a lewd woman (*lucci ka*), suggesting that he commits incest with his mother and that his mother was or is a prostitute. They have not seen him before because women other than the bride do not attend the main wedding ceremony, but they assess his appearance saying that he looks like a runt and probably lacks sexual prowess. During these tauntings, the bridegroom must maintain his dignity as best he can. Above all, he must not break down by either becoming angry or weeping. It is a brave bridegroom who can make clever retorts. Most sit stiffly with head down, trying to concentrate on the food and be deaf to these strange harpies.

In the joking over the meal in the women's quarters, the women are rejecting the bridegroom as an acceptable mate for their bride: he is the son of a prostitute; he commits incest with his mother; he is impotent. He has to put up with whatever they deal out to him and to the members of his male party until they and he finally get the bride.

On the night before the *barat* (all-male marriage party) departs with the bride at either the *sadi* or the *cala*, the *bahanoi*, his brother, and members of his *barat* who are his age are serenaded by the *salis* (wife's sisters) and the *salhajs* (wife's brothers' wives) with *sithani*, obscene songs which question the groom's virility, the virtue of his mother, and so on.[11] Remembrance of such ordeals is enough to make any young bridegroom shy in anticipation of more encounters with his affinal kin.

There is a female solidarity among the women of the bride's village, especially among the unmarried girls and brothers' wives of her own generation, a common voice of protest at the coming of this stranger to take away one of their own. Their resentment and hostility cannot become actual resistance, so teasing the interloper is indulged in with delight.

The cross-sex relations between affines of the same generation allow an older *bahanoi* [sister's husband] to tease his younger *sali*s [wife's sisters] and for them to tease him. In this culturally prescribed teasing, both the *bahanoi* and *sali* speak of the desirability of her going home with him along with her sister. The *sali*s may often, probably usually, initiate such joking conversations. The couple may be seen to be playing out a kind of mock marriage, parallel to the real marriage between the *bahanoi* and the *sali*s' sister. The joking may also anticipate a sororate marriage later on. The Chuhras and other middle- and low-caste people of this region do not go in for sororal polygyny, but a sororate marriage does occasionally occur.[12]

Relationships between Brothers-in-Law: Respectful, Abusive or Joking?

In *Social Structure*, his multicultural study of kinship practices, Murdock (1949: 279) states:

> Although the author unfortunately did not gather data on social behavior between male relatives, he has a distinct impression from general reading that the relations between brothers-in-law are commonly characterized by respect or reserve, especially by a marked tendency to avoid mentioning matters of sexual import. This is not unnatural in view of the fact that, with respect to the same woman one of the two men enjoys unrestrained sexual freedom whereas the other must observe one of the strictest of incest taboos. Any allusion to sex by the former is likely to arouse unconscious anxieties in the latter, whereas an allusion by the latter might imply to the former a lack of respect for the woman who unites them or even suggest the possibility of of an unpardonable incestuous connection with her.

Much of the writing on the North Indian relationship between wife's brother and her husband, brothers-in-law, has suggested that it is a relationship of distance or respect. The inequality between the brothers-in-law is expressed in respect rituals; Hershman writes (1981: 197) about villagers in Jullundur district, Punjab: "Just as a younger brother touches the feet of an elder sister, so he also touches the feet of an elder sister's husband."

At several places Hershman speaks of the great honor and respect the bridegroom and his brother receive at the bride's natal home (1981: 194, 196, 199, 203, 206); he also speaks of avoidance between brothers-in-law (1981: 203). Hershman never talks, however, about a joking relationship between *sala* and *bahanoi,* although he mentions the fact that *sala is* a curse word when used as an appellation in address. Similarly, Nicholas (1965: 33) says that "in Bengali the most common term of abuse is *sala.*" He notes, however, that "the relation between a man and his wife's brother is formally distant and frequently hostile."

The consciousness or awareness of sexuality and the need for respect between affines is expressed by prohibiting use of the descriptively correct kinship terms in either reference or address between them. The Hindi terms for husband (*pati*) and wife (*pativrata, patni*) are never used; a woman might refer to her husband as "that one" or "someone"; a man similarly refers to his wife. Sometimes a man refers to his wife as the "lady of the house" (*gharvali*) or by his child's name -- for example, Bharat's mother (*Bharat ki ma*) -- or the woman refers to her husband as the "master" (*malik*) or Bharat's father (*Bharat ka caca*).[13] In reference, a woman is so-and-so's wife -- Bharat's wife is *Bharat ki bahu.* If a woman finds herself in a position of being asked to give someone's name that is the same as her husband's, she becomes flustered, and other women laugh embarrassedly. If a woman by chance lets her husband's name slip out, other women think it is breathtakingly shocking and very funny, embarrassing indeed. These prohibitions on the use of either names or kinship terms by husband and wife for each other is not so much a matter of deference as of sexual embarrassment. One hints at the sexual relationship between husband and wife by saying "that one," but one never openly admits to the relationship by using a name or even more explicitly using the kin term.

Other affinal kin terms are never used in address. A man never addresses his wife's mother; he can address his wife's father, but he would never address him as *sasur* (father-in-law); a woman never addresses her husband's father; she can address her husband's mother, but she would never address her husband's mother as *sasu* (mother-in-law). She would call her *ma* or *mataji* (mother).

The affinal kin terms used for the wife's immediate relatives, her parents, and siblings, all seem suffused with the connotation of embarrassing sexual relationship connecting the two families of bride and groom. Some affinal terms do not share this stigma, such as *bahanoi* (sister's husband), and *nandoi* (husband's sister's husband). These are males who actually have sexual relations with one's sister or one's husband's sister, but they are not considered demeaned or despicable because of this; the men who have *given* their daughters or sisters into this plight are demeaned. The term daughter-in-law, *bahu,* the woman who is used sexually, is similarly not demeaned, and the Chuhras say that one should neither joke about *bahus* nor ever treat them disrespectfully. The women being given and presumably being used sexually are not looked down upon, nor are the men who so use them; only the men who have given them as sexual partners for other men's pleasure are demeaned.

Curse words in Hindi are *sala* (wife's brother) and *sasur* (wife's father); their connotation approaches that of pimp in English. The *sala* and *sasur* are men who have given their sister or daughter in marriage; they have given her to be used by other men sexually, and the connotation is that they are low, curse-worthy because of this.

Hershman (1981: 191, 197) writes:

> A brother gives his sister in marriage to another man and in so doing not only makes a gift of that which he most jealously guarded but also exposes himself to the possibility of personal dishonour. In Punjabi culture the most taunting abuse is for one man to inquire of another: *tun mera sala lagda* which literally means "are you my wife's brother?" but which carried with it the emotive power of "are you the man who gave me his sister to violate?" To give a woman in marriage is to place oneself in a position of inferiority to the taker....
>
> ...The relationship which is most inegalitarian in nature is that between brothers-in-law. The word for sister's husband, *sala*, is never used as a form of address and some men even avoid using it as a term of reference by employing a circumlocution such as saying, "my child's mother's brother." *Sala* may be used as a term of abuse, and a choice use of insult is to call a man *sale ka kutta* "the dog of a wife's brother." The reverse of this is the term for sister, which is generally *bhanoia* and an honorific. Brahmans employ the highly honorific Hindi word *jija* in address and reference to an elder sister's husband, while other castes use the *bhaia* which is also a term carrying a great

deal of respect and may be employed for any senior male such as the father's father.

(Notice that the above paragraph from Hershman is actually muddled. *Sala* is first translated as sister's husband instead of wife's brother, and later in the same paragraph *bhanoia* is translated as sister rather than sister's husband.)

Although Nicholas and Hershman suggest that the relationship between brothers-in-law is abusive in their absence (i.e., behind their backs) but distant in their presence, others do recognize the existence of an institutionalized joking relationship between brothers-in-law. Dumont (1966: 102) states that there is a joking relationship, but he does not describe it, saying only that "outside its proper denotation, the word *sala* is a term of abuse." Madan (1975: 226) also does not suggest that joking exists between the brothers-in-law among the Pandits of Kashmir; rather they are allies; he does, however, say that brothers-in-law in Uttar Pradesh use the term *sala* in banter rather than hostility; again, he does not label it a joking relationship. Naik's (1947) description of joking relationships shows considerable diversity in the content of the relationship, as he found it in the literature on Indian tribals, among whom the sister's husband sometimes bullies the wife's younger brother and sometimes the wife's brother bullies the sister's husband. Apte (1985: 42) also recognizes and treats the joking relationship between brothers-in-law in India:

> In societies with patrilineal kinship and strong male dominance, an asymmetrical joking relationship may exist between a person and his wife's brothers. Wife givers are generally inferior to wife takers in such societies, so that a man can make fun of his wife's brother with impunity, knowing full well that his brother-in-law cannot and will not respond in kind. Among the Hindus in North India, a wife's brother is always regarded as someone to be made the butt of joking.

This description does not fit the joking relationship between a man and his wife's brother among the Chuhras. In the instances of the relationship that I collected in the mid-1950s, the *sala* makes a butt of his *bahanoi*.[14]

My own review of the ethnographic literature for North India and tribal India, some of which I cited above, confirms Apte's observation that the ethnographic descriptions necessary for comparison have not been published, so the variations in the joking relationship between a man and his wife's brother for North India cannot be analyzed. Now I will consider the joking between brothers-in-law as I found it among the Chuhras.

> NQ 8 Kharu explained to us that there are clean jokes (*hamsi-makhaul*), ridicule in fun; or *hamsi-majak,* funny jokes. This is the type Kharu might have with Gyarsi [*devar* (husband's younger brother) – *bhavaj* (older brother's wife) joking].
>
> We asked if the type of joking one did with a *samdhi* [one's son or daughter's father-in-law] or a *sala* [wife's brother] was *hamsi-majak.* Kharu said it was all the same thing. But one can abuse his *sala* through his sister and abuse his *samdhi* through his wife. You can't joke with a brother in this way. Abuses of that sort are *ganda majak* [dirty jokes] or *gali* [abuse]. One can't beat and throw a brother around as one can a *samdhi.*

Among the Chuhras, the ritual of insult (a joking relationship) between the *sala* and *bahanoi* involves a reversal in roles. The *sala* pretends that he has married the *bahanoi*'s sister rather than the reverse, and he greets the *bahanoi* by hugging him and kissing or biting him on the cheek. The *bahanoi* must put up with this, remaining passive saying little in response.

> NQ 9 (We asked Kharu what kind of behavior was shown in joking relationships.) He said that there was much laughing, joking, and kidding, and they might start quarreling and slapping each other with their hands. "For example," he said, "if I and my sister's husband [*bahanoi*] are sitting, and someone asks, 'What are you to each other?' I would say that he was my *sala* [wife's brother], the opposite from what is the truth. Then he might start abusing my sisters. We might even come to blows. When my sister Kraceni's husband comes, I will say that I am married in this fellow's house. Then we might come to blows. I might spit in his face or make him impure by kissing him. Then we would have a big fight. At the time of Anandi's wedding, I bit Kraceni's husband so hard that the mark on his face could be seen for days. He had two guests with him. They had a plan. They called me over asking me to fill the *hukka* for them. When I went they caught hold of me and took big bites, and we slapped each other, and I ran away.

Note the variety of ways of insulting the *bahanoi* that Kharu used: first, making him impure by spitting in his face, biting, and kissing him;[15] second, physically attacking him; third, mocking foreplay to sexual relations with him as the sex object; and in so doing, fourth, treating him as though he were a female. All this suggests the sexual nature of the relationship between the two parties.

Kraceni's husband and his friends get back at Kharu. Passivity on their part is no longer as necessary as it was during Kraceni's wedding when the groom and his party did not yet have the bride. Once they do have her, after the wedding, they do not have to take a *sala*'s attack stoically. Kharu, of course, reported all this as great fun.

Another example of reversal in roles occurs between Bhartu, a *basti-sala* (bride's brother by membership in the same Chuhra colony) to Chandni's (Kharu's brother's daughter's) bridegroom, Paltu.

> NQ 10 Bhartu sat in front of his *bahanoi,* Paltu, and the latter's brother, Pannu. Bhartu lit a cigarette and then gave it to Pannu to smoke. He knocked off the burning tip and almost burned his clothes with it. Bhartu said, "Why have you broken my cigarette? Now either give me my cigarette back or one of your sisters. Look, I am spreading my *pala* [bottom of shirt] before him and asking him to give me one of his sisters. And see, I'm saying the same thing to Paltu."
>
> Pannu said, "Let me make a suggestion. You have given us a girl already. Give us each another one, and then we'll try to think of making some arrangement for you, too."

Here Bhartu proposes an exchange marriage, an impossibility to the Chuhras and to most North Indian Hindus.[16] The groom's brother, not the groom himself, has the courage to reply; in his reply he suggests polygyny, not so abhorrent because it is sometimes practiced but rather unusual.

The reversal in roles I interpret as a culturally prescribed "reaction formation" on the part of the *sala,* who by joking denies his own shameful role in having given his sister for sexual use. The reversal, given the *sala* is the joker and the *bahanoi* the jokee, saves the *sala* from teasing about the *bahanoi's* sexual relationship with the *sala's* own sister. He also does not reverse the relationship so that he is married to the *bahanoi's* wife, who, of course, is his own sister; he does not joke about an incestuous relationship. He reverses it in the way least likely to anger the *bahanoi* or entrap himself.

This Chuhra move modifies Murdock's speculation, quoted above, that brothers-in-law do not joke because the idea of brother-sister incest might be invoked. They joke through role reversal and suggesting an exchange marriage. As I have shown in the joking both between Kharu and Sadhu (NQ 6) and between the *salis* and the bridegroom, the Chuhras do not quake at the notion of accusing a jokee (victim of the joke) of incest (between son and mother). Nevertheless, the Chuhras' ingenious pretence of a role reversal in joking between brothers-in-law makes possible sexual joking without bringing in incest, rather than their being limited to a respect or reserve relationship that Murdock and others might have led us to expect. The reversal in relationship between *sala* and *bahanoi* (and, as I shall show below, *samdhi* and *samdhi,* the two fathers-in-law) is motivated by the bridegivers' resistance to accepting their subordinate status; Minturn and Hitchcock (1966: 58) state that the practice of female infanticide by Rajputs of Khalapur in the past was partly due to the "heavy financial burden which dowry represented" and partly due to

> the reluctance of the male members of the bride's family to assume a subordinate status in relation to the members of the groom's family....
>
> ...Furthermore, since a girl must marry into a family of higher status than her own, her male relatives are always subservient to the men of her husband's family. Many of the men do not take kindly to this inferior position.

Sensitivity to the abuse one was subject to as a *sala* was carried to the extreme by at least one Muslim nobleman, the Nawab of Bahawalpur state (on the border between the Punjab, Sind and Baluchistan, now in Pakistan). Tandon (1961: 174--175) wrote about this treatment for the sisters of the Nawab of Bahawalpur in the 1920s:

> The sisters of a Nawab, according to custom, were not permitted to marry. In the north the word for wife's brother, *sala*, has somehow become a term of abuse. The Nawabs therefore considered it an

> unbearable insult to become a *sala* to someone; they would rather not marry their sisters. But it was a risk to keep them in the palaces for fear of some scandal arising, and they were therefore banished to an old inaccessible fort in the desert. There, under a heavy guard, they lived their long lonely lives like prisoners, lost to the world and looking back to their childhood, the only short spell of happiness they had ever tasted. Relations rarely came to see them, and thus condemned they could only have received scant attention from the fort authorities.

That being a *sala* is experienced as a scourge and a disgrace at least by some North Indians and Pakistanis is suggested by this extreme custom.

Co-Parents-in-Law

The joking between the bride's and groom's male elders, father, father's brothers, and so on, both of whom are *samdhi* to each other, similarly involves a reversal. The elderly male of the bride's family accosts, hugs, and kisses the elderly male of the groom's family and teases him, again a role reversal and a kind of defense against admitting one's own role in giving a daughter into a sexual relationship.

> NQ 11 Kharu had told us that last night Soma had whipped the *samdhi*, Hari. At the *caupal*, we asked about this. Soma got up and took one of the boys' *cadars* [small blanket], wound it and doubled it over to make a kind of whip. Ram said that last night when the girls were singing, and the men were preparing a bundle to put on the *samdhi*'s head, and the "girls" [Kharu and Soma] were preparing the whip, the *samdhi* had come to Ram's bed and said, "Oh, please save me." "And," said Ram, "I said, 'All right, I'll save you.' Then when they came to hit him, I sat in front and protected him." Soma contradicted him, saying that the *samdhi* had been hit twice. The *samdhi* denied that he had been hit. Ram said he had been pushed around a great deal in the process of trying to save Hari. We asked who had hit him. Ram said it was Pal *ki bahu* Chamari. It seemed Kharu and Soma had dressed up like girls and were Pal *ki bahus*.

Multiple insults are heaped on Hari, the *samdhi*. He is made into a menial carrying rocks on his head, while he is whipped by Chamar women. We did not know Pal, but we may suspect that Pal's wife or wives were not the most appealing women as prospective sexual partners.

> NQ 11 (continued) The *samdhi,* Hari, said, "When you come to our place, our 'women' will also come and give you the same treatment." Soma said, "Oh, if your women come, then we'll hug them."

Here the men are debating the virtue of Hari's women. He is saying that they will also command and force their *samdhi*s to carry rocks on their head. But, the latter are saying that no, these women will be amenable to being hugged by their *samdhis*. In other words, they will not resist the sexual overtures of these strange men, never mind beat them and drive them about.

> NQ 11 (continued) The men said the *samdhi* jumped from cot to cot last night when they tried to put a bundle of rocks on his head. Also they made him worship the well – clasp his hands and bow to it while Mukanda beat the drum. Ram said that this was the custom, to tell the *samdhi* that it was customary to worship the well in their *basti.*

Here, the *samdhi* is insulted by making him behave like a woman; only women worship the well. It is as though the giving of a bride makes her male relatives (here Kharu, her father's younger brother, her leviratic "father"; and Soma, a *basti*-father's younger brother) also female, and humor may involve the attempt to make the male relatives of the groom play at being female, too.

> NQ 11 (continued) The *samdhi* was alone. He was the only barati who could be joked with. The brothers, *bahanoi* [sister's husband], and so on are *samletas* [affines of a junior generation] to Kharu and Soma, so they could not joke with them.
>
> It seems that the *samdhi*s can initiate joking with the opposite *samdhi*s in their own [the formers'] village. When Kharu and Soma go to the *samdhi*'s village, they will be kidded, too. Shyam and Soma sat up very straight to show how staunchly they would take it all. The *samdhi* said, "We'll beat you, beat you." Kharu said, "Memsahib, tell them that they can't beat your boy." Pauline said, "We'll protect you." Kharu explained that Pauline was Chandni's *dadi* [father's

> mother]. Pauline asked if *dadis* were beaten, too.[17] When they go to the *samdhi*'s, the men said they would take Mian (old Govardhan) with them. Mian said, "If you beat us, we'll put our *samdhan* in the car and bring her away."

Here joking between *samdhi* (son's "father-in-law") and *samdhan* (daughter's mother-in-law) is brought in. A *samdhan* is either one's married daughter's mother-in-law or one's married son's mother-in-law. Similarly, a *samdhi* is either one's married daughter's father-in-law or one's married son's father-in-law. Both pairs of same sex terms are reciprocal: *samdhan-samdhan* and *samdhi-samdhi.* The joking in NQ 11 is between *samdhi* (Kharu, Hari's brother's son's father-in-law) and *samdhi* (Hari, Kharu's step-daughter, Chandni's father-in-law's brother). Joking involving the *samdhan* will be discussed below, after NQ 11.

> NQ 11 (continued) Kharu asked Pauline if she saw any resemblance between Hari, the *samdhi,* and his son, Laki. Kharu joked that the reason there was so little resemblance was because Laki's mother had gone to live with a Grainparcher, and then Laki was born. Then she came back to live with Hari.
>
> Naga said, "Look at the *samdhi;* he looks like a bear. Look at Kharu; he's a lion." Somehow, Laki was referred to. Kharu said, "Oh, don't say anything to poor Laki. He's only got one father." There was some discussion among the men of the *caupal* as to whether a person could have more than one father. Someone said, "Ask his father how many fathers Laki has." Someone else said, "But even Laki's father wouldn't know that. Ask Laki's mother where all she's been. She'll tell you how many fathers he has." Hari said, "Such a thing couldn't happen." Jumlal, an elder in his seventies, said, "Why, do you keep locks on them?" The *samdhi* retorted, "Do you keep locks on yours?" Jumlal replied, "No, we go with them."

Here the *samdhi* is insulted by the accusation that his wife was adulterous; even worse, her adultery was with a man of another caste (Grainparcher), and the *samdhi* had so little pride that he accepted the illegitimate child of the adultery as his own. Although the Chuhras value virginity and expect it in brides (see NQ 4 above), they seldom talk about honor, *izzat.* But much of this joking discourse is concerned with *izzat.* Because a man's honor is especially closely tied to the virtue of his unmarried sisters and daughters and to his wife's chastity and fidelity, these seemingly endless jokes about seduction and abduction of the women of the opposing party attack the opponents' honor. In the above passage, the suggestion that Laki might have more than one father is such an attack. Laki's mother was supposedly so promiscuous that she was having several affairs at once; thus, Laki could have been sired by any one of several men. When Hari has a chance to assert the resistance and virtue of his women, he passes up the chance, either purposely or not, allowing the bride's elder to assert the virtue of the bride's side's women who are always chaperoned by their men: "We go with them."

> NQ 11 (continued) Kharu said that theirs was a good *samdhi,* because he did not get angry at all, but agreed with whatever they said. Mostly the *samdhi* sat quietly, with a half-smile on his face. The men on the *caupal* said they would talk and kid until midnight, but the *samdhi* would not sleep at all tonight. He didn't sleep at all last night, we were told, "out of fear." Kharu said that such kidding went on all through the time the *calavalas* were here.

> NQ 12 Some of the men had put eggs under the *samdhi.* Then when the eggs broke, they said, "Oh, see, our guest has laid an egg."

The *samdhi* here is an animal – in this case, a chicken who can lay eggs. In this insult, the *samdhi* is not only an animal but also a female animal. The essentially sexual reproductive nature of the relationship between the two wedding parties is perhaps suggested by the fertility symbol – the egg.

Both the *bahanoi* and the *samdhi* (daughter's father-in-law) are victims of rites of degradation at the hands of the *sala* and opposite *samdhi* (one's son's father-in-law). In multiple ways, each is "put down," by being likened to an animal, by being hugged, tackled, chased, shoved and beaten, and by being touched by supposed untouchable Chamar women and treated as though he were a woman.

The relationship between *samdhi* and *samdhan* is more imaginary than real, but the content is one of flirtation.

> NQ 13 At the time of Chandni's *cala,* we asked if the *samdhan* didn't joke with the *samdhi.* Chatu, a guest *samdhi* [bride's father-in-law in

> relationship], said that last night when no one was looking, he had decided to go to visit his *samdhan* [son's mother-in-law]. Kharu said, "We saw him slipping away, but we didn't stop him because we knew our women were brave. We thought, 'Let him taste a bit from our women, too. ' Just when he walked in, the *samdhan* caught hold of him and started beating him. And he said, 'Please let me go.' Then we went and got him free."
>
> At this, one of the Chuhra men, a *samdhi* [groom's father-in-law] pulled Chatu back and shook his fist at Chatu as though he were threatening to beat him.

Here again, the virtue of the local bride's women is attested to. Chatu, a guest *samdhi*, probably was trying here to insult the hosts by indicating that he had gone to have sex with the bride's mother, but again Kharu asserts that the women accosted the invader and beat him. Evidently, one of the groom's men was displeased that Chatu's salvo had boomeranged.

Another example of a fantasy flirtation between *samdhan* and *samdhi* comes from Kanti's life history.

> NQ 14 At the time Kanti was to have her *sadi* and go to her bridegroom's village, Kanti's mother's *jija* [sister's husband] teased her, saying, "Why don't you go with Kanti? Go with your *samdhi*. Go as his wife!"

Here Kanti's mother's sister's husband suggests that his wife's sister, Kanti's mother, go along with Kanti when Kanti marries, in order to have "a good time" with Kanti's father-in-law, Kanti's mother's *samdhi*. In this example, a sister's husband teases his wife's sister, a culturally prescribed joking relationship, and in his joke he refers to a largely imaginary joking relationship between *samdhan* and *samdhi*.

Not all flirtations are just imaginary, however. Sometimes *samdhans*, faces covered with headclothes, go up to the edge of the *caupal* and say, "We'll throw color on our *samdhis*." But their own men threaten the women. Sometimes, however, the women succeed in throwing colored powder on the *samdhis*. Colored powder is thrown during the spring festival, Holi, and seems to be a symbol of fertility (see note 11 for accounts of *samdhans* singing to *samdhis*).

The joking relationship between a *samdhi* and his *samdhan* is a cross-sex joking relationship that, contrary to what Brant's (1948: 160–162) hypothesis might have led us to expect, is not one between potential spouses.[18]

Because *samdhan* (groom's mother-in-law) never meets *samdhan* (bride's mother-in-law), the joking takes place by means of messages with hidden sexual insults sent by way of their husbands or son or daughter to each other. One will send a message telling the other to take hold of a thorn bush (penis?). It is said that if they were to meet, both *samdhans* would have faces covered but would joke through their headclothes.

Devar (Husband's Younger Brother) and *Bhavaj* (Elder Brother's Wife)

It might seem that the new bride suffers nothing but shyness and embarrassment in her new role in the household of her mother-in-law. Many scholars of the North Indian family and kinship point to the relief that the young newly in-married daughter-in-law may enjoy in the culturally prescribed *hamsi-makhaul ka rista* (joking relationship) between herself and her husband's younger brother. It is also commonly pointed out that this is a relationship between a couple who might eventually marry, especially if a caste, such as the Chuhras, practice the levirate. Because the right to joke with the husband's younger brother (*devar*) extends to the male cousins of the husband and to *gamv-basti devars* (village-colony husband's younger brothers), a woman like Gyarsi who delights in this sexy flirtatious joking may have many partners with whom to joke.

Although the ethnographic literature on northern India is bereft of examples of joking between *devar* (husband's younger brother) and *bhavaj* (elder brother's wife), mention of its existence is frequent.[19] Space precludes explorations of that relationship here.

In all three types of cross-sex joking – that between *bahanoi* (sister's husband) and *sali* (wife's sister), *samdhi* (bride's father-in-law) and *samdhan* (groom's mother-in-law), *bhavaj* (older brother's wife) and *devar* (husband's younger brother) – there is a pretence that the two should have or are already having a sexual relationship or that the two are already married. Women usually initiate the horseplay and wise-cracking in which some women revel.

A man can joke only with his wife's younger sisters, not her older sisters; a married woman can joke only with her husband's younger brothers, not his older brothers. A husband's older brother cannot joke with his younger brother's wife; this is an avoidance relationship, and a woman should be veiled and should not speak to her *jeth* (her husband's elder brother), who is like a small father-in-law.

Among the lower castes of Khalapur and much of northern India in which levirate and sororate are practiced, a *bhavaj* may indeed be married in a secondary marriage to her *devar* after her husband's death; thus, a *sali* could, indeed, become wife to her dead sister's husband.

Conclusion

As Radcliffe-Brown (1952a) perceived, the two parties, that of the bride and that of the groom, are two separate groups, now attached through their marriage. Clear in the joking relationships between affinal relatives close in age is that sexuality is spoken about or expressed in gestures. Some cross-sex joking, like that between *bhavaj* and *devar* and *jija* and *sali,* seems to anticipate a future sexual relationship. Some cross-sex joking like that between *samdhan* and *samdhi* is a flirtation that, if not entirely fantasized, suggests a replay of the relationship between their children, with each other. That relationship, as well as the singing of *sithanis* to the groom and his "brothers," and the same sex joking between *samdhi* and *samdhi* and between *sala* and *bahanoi,* is fraught with sexual content and innuendo and seems to direct the wedding parties' attention to the sexual nature of their relationship. The joking reiterates the fact: "We two groups are joined by a marriage."

All the mock sexual relations – those between *sali* and *bahanoi, samdhan* and *samdhi, samdhi* and *samdhi, sala* and *bahanoi* – act out in anticipation the sexual relationship between bride and groom. Sideplay statements during the wedding feast serve as a counterpoint to the religious ceremonies that also go on during the *sadi,* the profane opposes the sacred. Both profane and sacred rites unite bride and groom: the one carnally (at least in anticipation), the other spiritually, religiously, and legally (wrought by the *mantras* themselves).

Radcliffe-Brown (1952a) also suggested that the joking relationship mixes both hostility and affection. His observation holds for the *sala-bahanoi* and *samdhi-samdhi* relationships among the Chuhras. The two parties are initially strangers. Because elders usually arrange marriages, it is likely that the *sala*'s father or grandfather actually went to the *bahanoi*'s village to give the rupee and engage the *bahanoi* as a bridegroom for the daughter/granddaughter, so it may well be that at the time of the *sadi* neither young man has met the other before. The negotiation between the two wedding parties (the groom's are to be guests at the bride's, the bride's are to be the hosts) is often fraught with misunderstanding, even anger. The hosts try tactfully to hint that the groom's party should not be too large, for the hosts must feed them all for three or four days; the groom's party is touchy and can use their ultimate sanction of breaking off the engagement because the hosts are so penurious. So the feeling between *sala* and *bahanoi* upon first meeting and between *samdhi* and *samdhi* at the time of the wedding ceremonies is likely to be one of mild hostility.

Of course, the fundamental fact to be understood in this joking is the *sala*'s and *samdhi*'s (groom's father-in-law's) resentment in having to give sister/daughter away in marriage to the *bahanoi/jamai* (sister's husband/daughter's husband). The reversal in relationship between *sala* and *bahanoi* and between *samdhi* and *samdhi,* possible when the groom's party is on the bride's home ground, is one way to quash the bride's father and brother's feelings of guilt and resentment. They thus resist the situation in which they find themselves.

The joking relationship in which the *sala* plays that he is the *bahanoi* seesaws him from the low subordinate position to the high superordinate one in this limited hypergamous system. He plays this game while the wifetakers are still dependent; they have not yet received the bride. The joking takes place at the *sadi* and the *cala* before the bride has been transferred to the groom and the other men of his party who have come to take her back to the groom's father's village and before the sexual relations between the groom and bride have commenced. The groom and his brothers must bear up with joking both from his new wife's sisters and from his wife's brothers, not only to win their respect, but also presumably so that they will not falter in their transfer of the bride. His father and his brothers must do the same. The reversal in the relationships is the key trope in this play, and this can be seen as a kind of ritual of rebellion

(Gluckman 1963), a statement that the *sala* or *samdhi* (groom's father-in-law) wishes that the relationship were the reverse of what it is.

Such an analysis, however, does not account for the *content* of the humorous insults that the bride's men dole out to the groom's men, much to the enjoyment of the others in the bride's party. As detailed above, these dirty jokes (*ganda majak*) and insults (*gali*) repeatedly attack the honor (*izzat*) of the guests in a situation in which the guests are helpless. The effect of this use of the discourse of forbidden sexuality -- accusations of incest, exchange marriage, adultery, bastardry, and cuckoldry – is that the hierarchical relations between the bridetakers and the bridegivers are leveled. They also use the discourse of caste and pollution and override the usual vast gulf between humanity and animality, between male and female. The Chuhra jokers frequently demean a man by "making" him into either an animal or a woman.

Seen against a background of caste and arranged marriage the primary purpose of which is to ensure that bride and groom are of the same caste and from good families (ones in which incest and adultery presumably would not take place), such joking says that the groom's party is not worthy of taking the bride because the groom and his father and their brothers have broken the most basic rules of caste and family purity (Yalman 1963; Kolenda 1985: 62--85). The logic of such joking would seem to be: because you are of bad family and impure caste, you cannot take our daughter/sister. Through such insult, the groom's party is discredited and proven unworthy of being given the bride, who is presumably from a good family and a pure caste.

I began this chapter with a quotation from Foucault suggesting that the research scholar must see how sexuality is used in discourse. Between bride's people and groom's people during wedding ceremonial visits in the bride's people's village, the joking and farce express rebellion on the part of the subordinated, and they attempt to discredit the bridetakers to deprive them of their superior status. The content of the joking, thus, is not accidental but closely related to the intergroup situation. Such analysis suggests that there is considerable value in ethnographers' reporting the contents of joking and not just covering it with a single adjective like obscene, which is a common practice.

Mary Douglas has suggested that jokes are antistructural; this is true in the reversal of roles between the *sala* and the *bahanoi.* Douglas also claims that joking may well foster *communitas,* "unhierarchised, undifferentiated social relations" between the parties (Douglas 1975: 104). During the *sadi* and *cala,* not only does the bride's party resist the new relationship, but it also resists giving the bride. However, they do come to accept the relationship, and the bride is eventually given over.

Given the rules of patrilineage and village exogamy as well as caste endogamy and the asymmetrical ranking of bridetakers and bridegivers, plus the North Indian ideology of sexuality, one can see that the North Indian wedding is fraught with tension between the bride's and the groom's wedding parties. This tension could be dealt with in various ways, including avoidance, aloofness, and great formality in their interactions. Indeed, these interpersonal strategies are culturally coded, creating avoidance relationships between daughter-in-law and men older than her husband in her husband's party; the groom is silent before his mothers-in-law and fathers-in-law, those women and men in the bride's party of the parental generation.

The ambivalence in the encounter of the strange men brought together by a wedding presumably could teeter in one direction rather than another. Those anthropologists who characterize the relationship between *sala* and *bahanoi* as hostile or distant suggest that in some North Indian localities and groups the ambivalence has tipped that way. Among the Chuhras, the groom, knowing that he will be teased, feels shy; he anticipates the humiliation that the *sala* is likely to deal out to him. However, in the Chuhra scheme of things, *sala* and *bahanoi* should become good friends. It is said that they should love each other far more than the *bahanoi* loves his wife, who is, of course, the *sala*'s sister. Humor relaxes tension, and this strategy is used between members of the two parties of the same generation. The relaxation of tension through farce and humor makes possible more friendly relations between the two opposed parties. This seems to be what the Chuhras expect; out of the joking in which the *sala* attacks the *bahanoi* a relationship of affection will develop.[20]

Obviously, the bride, as well as her brothers and parents, benefit if there is a friendly relationship between her father and her husband's father and father's brothers and a friendly relationship between her husband and her brother and their age-mates. That this, in fact, takes place is indicated at the end of the story about Chandni's wedding.

As the bullock-cart departs, taking Chandni, Kharu's step-daughter, away at her *cala,* her younger brothers walk with the young men of her husband's *barat* (all-male wedding party), their arms around each other; her father and her husband's father bid each other fond farewell; her husband's brother says that the relationship is now forever in reply to her brother's regret that his *bahanoi* must leave. Out of the tomfoolery comes *prema* or *pyara*, affection and love. Out of the barrage of abuse, insult, and jokes emerges and triumphs intimacy (Douglas 1975: 98).

In conclusion, I make three points about the insult-joking relationships at the Chuhra wedding. First, the mock flirtations and pretend sexual relations between certain assigned pairs of affines reiterate the purpose of the contact between the two groups – to establish a sexual relationship between a male member of one group and a female of the other. Second, much of the farce and joking is a pretense of diminishing the superior status of the groom and the bridetakers by discrediting their claims to purity either from regular endogamous relations or obedience to incest tabus; all this "in-play," jolly rituals of rebellion that can last for only a few hours or days, occurs before the jokers must succumb to the real superiority of the wifetakers and give them the bride. Third, the ritualized joking is a transformative process, the middle phase in a rite *of passage* (Gennep 1960: 10–13) as the brothers-in-law pass from the statuses of strangers to those of friends.

The joking, both between equal brothers and equal sisters-in-law and between unequal affinal relatives, makes a travesty of the purdah system and the concept of *izzat*, the local versions of shame and honor. In fact, Mary Douglas (1975: 96) suggests:

> The joke merely affords opportunity for realising that an accepted pattern has no necessity. Its excitement lies in the suggestion that any particular ordering of experience may be arbitrary and subjective. It is frivolous in that it produces no real alternative, only an exhilarating sense of freedom from form in general.

Notes

Earlier versions of this essay were presented at the Asian Studies Colloquium of Michigan State University on April 8, 1987, and at a panel on Joking in India at the meetings of the Association for Asian Studies in San Francisco on March 26, 1988. I owe thanks to the audiences including Judith Pugh, Rita Gallin, and Bernard Gallin, and to discussants of the latter panel, Mahadev Apte and Alan Dundes, who raised provocative questions and made telling points. I also thank Owen Lynch, editor of this volume, who offered me much sound advice and suggested leads that I might follow, and to Paul Toomey, a contributor to this volume, for stimulating comments.

1. My research assistant, Usha Bhagat (now Mrs. Mahendra Dave), and I were members of a Cornell University interdisciplinary research group studying Khalapur from 1953 to 1956, and financed by the Ford Foundation. I owe special thanks to Usha Bhagat Dave, our Chuhra friends, Director Morris Opler, Field Directors John Hitchcock and the late Edward LeClair, and the Ford Foundation. With financial support from the Smithsonian Institution, I returned to do fieldwork in Khalapur from January to June 1984.

   The native Hindi terms for the two divisions within the category of servant and artisan castes is *suddh* and *asuddh,* clean and unclean. The unclean castes tan leather, make shoes, sweep streets, and clean latrines, work Hindus consider unclean. The term *untouchable* was first used by the Maharaja of Baroda before the Depressed Classes Mission of Bombay in 1909 (Galanter 1972: 298) and became much more widely used than unclean. Discrimination against citizens considered unclean or untouchable is against Indian law and its Constitution (see Kolenda 1985, chap. 4). Old customary practices and beliefs persist, however.
2. The psychoanalyst, Alan Roland (1982), has characterized the Hindu family as thoroughly hierarchical, one in which deference and obedience from children is rewarded by affection from elders. Here in NQI Bhati has presented the same analysis: *Kayda*-keeping (deferential and solicitious) daughters-in-law win their mothers'-in-law affection, she asserts, presumably on the basis of her own experience.
3. Although Marriott's may well be the earliest account of the North Indian superiority of the bridetaker's side over the bridegiver's as a form of hypergamy (as distinct from hypergamy between grades of families), anthropologists' recent focus upon the phenomenon stems

from Dumont's (1957, 1961, 1966, 1970) concern with marriage alliance; his inspiration came from Lévi-Strauss (1969: 269) who found that "generalized exchange" (unilateral asymmetrical giving of brides) "extends over a vast area of Southern Asia."

If North India is a hypergamous milieu, there is, of course, a problem in the definition of the boundaries and territory of North India. Hierarchical relations between bridetakers and bridegivers have been found in studies done in the Indian states of Kashmir (Madan 1975), Uttar Pradesh (Marriott 1955; Dumont 1966; Khare 1975; Vatuk 1975), Delhi (Vatuk 1975), and the Punjab (Hershman 1981), and in the country bordering northern India, Nepal (Bennett 1983). But there are exceptions in the north. Fruzzetti and Ostör (1976: 109) state "that hypergamy as status difference between wife-giving and wife-taking groups on-the-ground is a distortion of the Bengali evidence." Sirkanda villagers (Berreman 1963), in the foothills in northern Dehra Dun District, Uttar Pradesh, also fail to follow this North Indian system of inequality as do the mostly brideprice-giving middle and lower Hindu castes of Rajasthan (Kolenda 1989). It is, thus, doubtful whether some parts of Bengal, the sub-Himalayas or Rajasthan, can be included in a North Indian hypergamous region.

4. Dumont (1966: 108--110) addressed the question of the kinship systems of lower castes in localities in Gorakhpur District in eastern Uttar Pradesh; he concluded that, in contrast to high castes like the Sarjupari Brahmans, they lack coherent kinship systems. I did not find this to be the case (Kolenda 1982). All Hindu castes in Khalapur seem to have essentially the same system. The main difference between the Rajput and Brahman kinship systems and those of the merchants and the middle and lower Hindu castes in Khalapur is the practice of widow remarriage, prohibited by the former two and prescribed by the latter three social categories.

   The Rajputs are one large caste-complex in northern and central India famous for its ranked clans (sets of families). For a discussion of such ranking by the Rajputs of village Khalapur, see Hitchcock (1956: 51--54).
5. Throughout this essay, I use the present tense for Chuhra and Khalapur doings and conditions as they were in 1954–56. There have been major changes in Khalapur in the intervening thirty years, but the general conditions as I describe them here have not changed.
6. Describing or mentioning similar celebrations of the brother-sister relationship are Minturn and Hitchcock (1966: 36), Dumont (1966: 98), Pocock (1972: 97), and Bennett (1983: 247--252).

7. That even marital sexual activity demeans a woman is asserted by Salman Rushdie in *Shame*, his novel about Pakistani Muslim Punjabis. "It was believed that the mere fact of being married did not absolve a woman of the shame and dishonour that results from the knowledge that she sleeps regularly with a man" (Rushdie 83: 76).
8. Das (1976: 6) speaks of a Punjabi sister-in-law (brother's wife) bantering with her sister-in-law (husband's sister) about sexual matters. Bennett (1983: 177), writing about eastern Nepali village women, says:

   > There is a great deal of vigorous sexual joking carried on among the women – sometimes even within earshot of the men. Unmarried girls were told that first intercourse would burn the vagina just as chili-peppers burn the tongue. The suggestive nature of keys being fitted into locks or of the shapes of bananas and cucumbers (and which of their neighbors was thought to relish these foods the most) was a source of endless joking among the women.

   Jeffery (1979: 75) also implies that in conversations between Muslim women friends in Nizamuddin, Delhi, intimate sexual topics are discussed.
9. That Rajput men when among equals also discuss sex is reported by Dorschner (1983: 119).
10. See my discussion of these studies and egalitarian relations within the caste system (Kolenda 1977: 181–182, 1981: 313–314).
11. Owen Lynch brought to my attention Briggs's (1920: 75, 86) mentions of Chamar women related to the bride singing obscene songs to the men of the groom's party during weddings. Jacobson (1982: 96) also mentions obscene songs sung to the bridegroom at weddings, to which *samdhis* (bride's fathers-in-law – that is, the father-in-law and men in his generation including his brothers, cousins, and so on) are expected to take no offence; she writes:

    > In these songs (*gari git*), the women name the *samdhis* and accuse them and their womenfolk of engaging in immoral and indecent acts. At some of these gatherings, the bride's womenfolk throw colored water on the visiting affines, tie cowbells around their necks, rub their face with wet flour, and even dress them ridiculously in women's blouses and forehead spangles. Throughout these raucous performances, the women keep their faces properly veiled. The *samdhis* are expected to take no offense at these songs and insults.

    Hershman (1981: 164–165, 187, 196–197, 206) makes much of joking between bridegroom and his *salis* and bride's women: "The songs sung cruelly satirise the paucity, poverty and ill looks of the members of the marriage party" (165).

12. In her treatment of cross-sex affinal joking relationships between brother's wife's brother and sister's husband's sister, husband's younger brother-older brother's wife, and sister's husband-wife's sister, Vatuk (1969: 107–109) sees the applicability of Brant's (1948: 160–162) generalization that cross-sex joking relationships occur between persons who are potentially marriageable, but she points out that there is no likelihood of such marriages among the high-caste populations she studied (Vatuk 1969: 109).

    Widow remarriage is common among the Chuhras and other middle and lower castes in Khalapur; a woman might marry her husband's younger brother or her sister's widower-husband. These men are definitely considered as possible mates in secondary marriages for a widow (see Kolenda 1982), and joking relations do occur between these potential mates.
13. *Caca is* a father's younger brother. A child never calls the father *bap* or *pita*, correct terms, while his or her father is of child-bearing age; instead, the child avoids suggesting procreative activities of the parent by calling him *caca*, a person who may well not yet be married.
14. After his description of the relationship between Hindu brothers-in-law, Apte cites a proverb about making a maternal uncle the butt of a joke "among the Marathi speakers on the west coast of India." Because Apte himself is aware of the paucity of descriptions of the relationship between wife's brother and sister's husband, he would probably be quite willing to admit that his own description of the relationship is probably not accurate for all Hindus of North India.
15. Hindus believe any bodily *exuviae* or product is polluting, including saliva; hence, they find biting, kissing, or licking someone polluting.
16. In discussing a joking relationship between a brother's wife and a husband's sister, Vatuk says (1969: 109) that "one aspect of the humour is the suggestion that an exchange of women has or will take place." Among many North Indians, exchange marriage is unthinkable (Karve 1965: 125; Dumont 1966: 104–107; Kolenda 1978: 266, 1987: 202–203).
17. Kharu's making of the author, Pauline in these notes, into a father's mother (*dadi*) was probably a way of showing respect, but perhaps it was also a way of recognizing that she moved about the village freely the way only a *dadi*, an elderly woman among them, would do.

18. Apte (1985: 43) states, "The existing ethnographic literature also indicates that institutionalized joking rarely occurs between females of the same generation." He then mentions only three instances he found in the literature. This institutionalized joking between *samdhan* and *samdhan*, the two mothers-in-law of a married couple, among the Chuhras would make a fourth instance.

    Relatively few recent ethnographers mention the relationship between parents-in-law. Bennett (1983: 160) says that the relationship between the two sets of parents-in-law is particularly "strained." She goes on to say that "all affinal relations are marked by distance-respect behavior. " Jacobson (1982: 95) says that a Bhopal Hindu woman veils her face in the presence of her *samdhi* but that, if two *samdhans* meet, they both should be veiled although able to speak to each other.

    Hershman also makes no mention of joking between *samdhi-samdhan* but speaks of respect between them (Hershman 1981: 203). Vatuk (1969: 107--109) does not discuss joking relationships between male affinal relatives, such as that between *samdhis*. In fact, Vatuk (1975: 183) characterizes the latter relationship as an avoidance relationship, as are relationships between co-parents-in-law involving the opposing mothers-in-law and the opposing mother-in-law and father-in-law. Such respect relationships are the opposite of the joking relationships between the co-parents-in-law among the Chuhras.

19. Jacobson (1982: 92) speaks of the elder brother's wife teasing her husband's younger brother "about his love for his wife." Hershman (1981: 175) says that "when she first enters her husband's household [she] jokingly demands payment in order not to veil her face from him [the husband's younger brother]," and a joking relationship between them thus begins (1981: 195). Others speak of the relationship as one in which the woman does not have to veil her face (Mehta 1982: 142) or like the relationships the daughter-in-law is used to in her natal home (Bennett 1983: 213).

    The most thorough treatment of the *devar-bhavaj* relationship is by Hivale (1943) who describes it among two tribal groups, the Gonds and the Pardhans of east Mandla, Madhya Pradesh. There are many aspects to the relationship, partly depending upon the difference in age between the *devar* and *bhavaj*. The joking he transcribes (Hivale 1943: 162--164) in which *devar* suggests that the *bhavaj*'s brother has come in order to have sex with *her* (thus brother-sister incest); then the *bhavaj* replies that her *nanand* (husband's sister) is nearby to accommodate her brother's sexual impulse (thus an exchange marriage or sexual liaison). This indicates that joking about incest is not tabu, contrary to what Murdock and others might have supposed, nor is joking about exchange marriage. Another good treatment concerning mostly tribals is by Naik (1947).

20. That relations between male affinal kin are commonly friendly is also suggested by Minturn and Hitchcock (1966: 33):

> Easy, friendly relations are also common between a man and his wife's father and brothers. The husband usually accompanies his wife when she goes to visit her parents and returns to pick her up. On both occasions he often stays for a day or more, and most men look forward to these visits. Although the husband is treated with some deference by his wife's people, for they are culturally defined as somewhat lower than he in status – a fact which may account for some of his pleasure – the general tone of the relationship is comradely and without strain.

Jacobson (1982: 100) notes for her Bhopal Hindus:

> But the ridicule and insults, offered as they are within the limits of the prescribed joking relationship, virtually never cause ill-will and instead contribute to ostensibly friendly relations between the two affinally-linked groups.

Hershman (1981: 196) also suggests that friendly relations develop between affinal male kinsmen. Lévi-Strauss (1969: 302–303) was the first to suggest that groups involved in a one-directional cycle of bride-giving were likely to develop hierarchical relations that they might or might not equalize through affection.

References

Abu-Lughod, Lila (1986), *Veiled Sentiments*. Berkeley: University of California Press.

Apte, Mahadev L. (1985), Joking Relationships. In *Humor and Laughter: An Anthropological Approach*, pp. 29--66, Ithaca: Cornell University Press.

Bateson, Gregory (1936), *Naven*, London: Oxford University Press.

Beech, Mary Higdon (1982), The Domestic Realm in the Lives of Hindu Women in Calcutta. In *Separate Worlds: Studies of Purdah in South Asia*,

Hanna Papanek and Gail Minault, eds. pp. 110–138, Columbia, Mo.: South Asia Books.

Bennett, Lynn (1983), *Dangerous Wives and Sacred Sisters: Social and Symbolic Roles of Highcaste Women in Nepal*, New York: Columbia University Press.

Berreman, Gerald D. (1963), *Hindus of the Himalayas*, Berkeley: University of California Press.

Brant, Charles (1948), On Joking Relationships. *American Anthropologist* 50: 160–162.

Briggs, George W. (1920), *The Chamars*, Calcutta: Association Press.

Burkhart, Geoffrey (1974), Equal in the Eyes of God: A South Indian Devotional Group in Its Hierarchical Setting, *Contributions to Asian Studies* 5: 1–14.

Carstairs, G. Morris (1957), *The Twice-Born*, London: Hogarth Press.

Carter, Anthony T. (1975), Caste "Boundaries" and the Principle of Amity: A Maratha Caste Purana. *Contributions to Indian Sociology*, n.s. 9: 123–139.

Das, Veena (1976), Masks and Faces: An Essay on Punjabi Kinship, *Contributions to Indian Sociology*, n.s. 10:1–30.

David, Kenneth (1974), And Never the Twain Shall Meet? Mediating the Structural Approaches to Caste Ranking. In *Structural Approaches to South Indian Studies*. Harry Buck and Glenn Yocum, eds. pp. 43–80. Chambersburg, Pa.: Wilson Books.

— (1977), Hierarchy and Equivalence in Jaffna, North Sri Lanka: Normative Codes as Mediator. In *The New Wind: Changing Identities in South Asia*, Kenneth David, ed. pp. 179–226, The Hague: Mouton.

Dorschner, Jon Peter (1983), *Alcohol Consumption in a Village in North India*, Ann Arbor: UMI Research Press.

Douglas, Mary (1975), Jokes. In *Implicit Meanings: Essays in Anthropology*, pp. 90–114, London: Routledge and Kegan Paul.

Dumont, Louis (1957), Hierarchy and Marriage Alliance in South Indian Kinship. Occasional Papers of the Royal Anthropological Institute of Great Britain and Ireland, No. 12, London: Royal Anthropological Institute of Great Britain and Ireland.

— (1961), Marriage in India: The Present State of the Question, *Contributions to Indian Sociology* 5: 75–95.

— (1964), Marriage in India: The Present State of the Question, Postscript to Part One and Part Two, *Contributions to Indian Sociology* 7: 99–102.

— (1966), Marriage in India: The Present State of the Question, Part Three: North India in Relation to South India, *Contributions to Indian Sociology* 9: 90–114.

— (1970), *Homo Hierarchicus: An Essay on the Caste System*, Chicago: University of Chicago Press.

— (1975), Terminology and Prestations Revisited, *Contributions to Indian Sociology*, n.s. 9: 197–215.

Dundes, Alan (1987), *Cracking Jokes: Studies of Sick Humor Cycles and Stereotypes*. Berkeley: Ten Speed Press.

Foucault, Michel (1980), *The History of Sexuality, Volume 1: An Introduction*, Robert Hurley, trans. New York: Vintage Books.

Fruzzetti, Lina, and Akos Ostor, (1976), Is There a Structure to North Indian Kinship Terminology? *Contributions to Indian Sociology*, n.s. 10:63–96.

Galanter, Marc (1972), The Abolition of Disability: Untouchability and the Law. In *The Untouchables in Contemporary India*, J.M. Mahar, ed. pp. 227–314, Tucson: University of Arizona Press.

Geertz, Clifford (1973), Deep Play: Notes on the Balinese Cockfight. In *The Interpretation of Cultures*. pp. 412–452, New York: Basic Books.

Gennep, Arnold van (1960), *Rites of Passage*, Chicago: University of Chicago Press.

Gluckman, Max (1963), Rituals of Rebellion in South-East Africa. In *Order and Rebellion in Tribal Africa*. pp. 110–136, New York: Free Press of Glencoe.

Habermas, Jurgen (1988) [1970], On Hermeneutics' Claim to Universality. In *The Hermeneutics Reader*, Kurt Mueller-Vollmer, ed. pp. 294–319, New York: Continuum.

Hershman, Paul (1981), *Punjabi Kinship and Marriage*, Delhi: Hindustan Publishing House.

Hitchcock, John T. (1956), The Rajputs of Khalapur: A Study of Kinship, Social Stratification, and Politics, Ph.D. dissertation, Sociology and Anthropology Department, Cornell University.

Hivale, Shamrao (1943), The Dewar-Bhauji Relationship, *Man in India* 23: 157–167.

Ibbetson, Sir Denzil (1881), Report on the Census of the Panjab. Lahore: Government Press.

Inden, Ronald B., and Ralph W. Nicholas (1977), *Kinship in Bengali Culture*, Chicago: University of Chicago Press.

Jacobson, Doranne (1970), Hidden Faces: Hindu and Muslim Purdah in a Central Indian Village. Ph.D. dissertation, Anthropology Department, Columbia University.

---- (1977), Flexibility in Central Indian Kinship and Residence, In *The New Wind: Changing Identities in South Asia*, Kenneth David, ed. pp. 263--283. The Hague: Mouton.

---- (1982), Purdah and the Hindu Family in Central India. In *Separate Worlds: Studies of Purdah in South Asia*, Hanna Papanek and Gail Minault, eds. pp. 81–109, Columbia, Mo.: South Asia Books.

Jeffery, Patricia (1979), *Frogs in a Well: Indian Women in Purdah*, London: Zed Press.

Karve, Irawati (1965), *Kinship Organization in India*. 2nd ed. Bombay: Asia Publishing House.

Khare, R.S. (1975), "Embedded" Affinity and Consanguineal "Ethos": Two Properties of the Northern Kinship System. *Contributions to Indian Sociology*, n.s. 9:245--261.

Kolenda, Pauline (1977), The Hierarchical Renouncer and the Dutiful Person: Insights from the Meeting of Themal and Structural Analyses of Indian Culture. Papers in Anthropology (University of Oklahoma) 18(2): 167–200.

---- (1978), Sibling-set Marriage, Collateral-set Marriage, and Deflected Alliance Among Annana Jats of Jaipur District, Rajasthan. In *American Studies in the Anthropology of India*. Sylvia Vatuk, ed. pp. 242--277. Delhi: Manohar.

--- (1981), *Caste, Cult, and Hierarchy*, Delhi: Manohar.

---- (1982), Widowhood Among "Untouchable" Chuhras. In *Concepts of Person: Kinship, Caste, and Marriage in India*. Akos Ostor, Lina Fruzzetti, and Steve Barnett, eds. pp. 172--220, Cambridge: Harvard University Press.

---- (1985), *Caste in Contemporary India: Prospect Heights*, Ill: Waveland Press.

---- (1987), *Regional Differences in Family Structure*. Jaipur: Rawat Publications.

---- (1989), The "Joint-Family" Household in Rural Rajasthan, In *Society from the Inside Out*, John N. Gray and David J. Mearns, eds. pp. 55--106. New Delhi: Sage.

Lévi-Straus, Claude (1969), *The Elementary Structures of Kinship*. James Harle Bell, John Richard von Sturmer, and Rodney Needham, trans. London: Eyre and Spottiswoode.

Luschinsky, Mildred Stroop (1962), The Life of Women in a Village of North India. Ph.D. dissertation, Sociology and Anthropology Department, Cornell University.

Madan, T.N. (1965), *Family and Kinship: A Study of Pandits of Rural Kashmir*, New York: Asia Publishing House.

--- (1975), Structural Implications of Marriage in North India: Wife-givers and Wife-takers among the Pandits of Kashmir, *Contributions to Indian Sociology*, n.s. 9:217--243.

Marriott, McKim (1955), Social Structure and Change in a U.P. Village. In *India's Villages*, M.N. Srinivas, ed. pp. 96--109. Calcutta: West Bengal Government Press.

Mehta, Rama (1982), Purdah Among the Oswals of Mewar. In *Separate Worlds: Studies of Purdah in South Asia*. Hanna Papanek and Gail Minault, eds. pp. 139--163, Columbia, Mo.: South Asia Books.

Minturn, Leigh, and John T. Hitchcock (1966), *The Rajputs of Khalapur, India*. New York: John Wiley.

Murdock, George Peter (1949), *Social Structure*. New York: Macmillan.

Naik, T.B. (1947), Joking Relationships. *Man in India* 27: 250--266.

Nicholas, Ralph W. (1965), Factions: A Comparative Analysis. In *Political Systems and the Distribution of Power*. Michael Banton, ed. pp. 21--92, London: Tavistock.

Papanek, Hanna (1982), Purdah: Separate Worlds and Symbolic Shelters. In *Separate Worlds: Studies of Purdah in South Asia*. Hanna Papanek and Gail Minault, eds. pp. 3--53, Columbia, Mo.: South Asia Books.

Papanek, Hanna, and Gail Minault, eds. (1982), *Separate Worlds: Studies of Purdah in South Asia*. Columbia, Mo.: South Asia Books

Parry, Jonathan (1974), Egalitarian Values in a Hierarchical Society. *South Asian Review* 7:95121.

Pocock, David F. (1972), *Kanbi and Patidar*, Oxford: Clarendon Press.

Radcliffe-Brown, A.R. (1952a) On Joking Relationships. In *Structure and Function in Primitive Society*, pp. 90--104. Glencoe, Ill: Free Press.

---- (1952b), A Further Note on Joking Relationships, In *Structure and Function in Primitive Society*, pp. 105--116, Glencoe, Ill: Free Press.

Roland, Alan (1982), Toward a Psychoanalytical Psychology of Hierarchical Relationships in Hindu India, *Ethos* 10(3):232--253.

Rushdie, Salman (1983), *Shame*, New York: Knopf.

Sabbah, Fatna A. (1984), *Woman in the Muslim Unconscious*, New York: Pergamon Press.

Sharma, Ursula (1978), Women and Their Affines: The Veil as a Symbol of Separation. *Man*, n.s. 13:218--244.

Tandon, Prakash (1961), *Punjabi Century*, New York: Harcourt, Brace and World.

Vatuk, Sylvia J. (1969), A Structural Analysis of the Hindi Kinship Terminology, *Contributions to Indian Sociology*, n.s. 3: 94--115.

---- (1975), Gifts and Affines in North India, *Contributions to Indian Sociology*, n.s. 9: 155–196.

---- (1982), Purdah Revisited: A Comparison of Hindu and Muslim Interpretations of the Cultural Meaning of Purdah in South Asia. In *Separate Worlds: Studies of Purdah in South Asia*, Hanna Papanek and Gail Minault, eds. pp. 54--78. Columbia, Mo.: South Asia Books.

Veen, Klaas W. van der (1972), *I Give Thee My Daughter*. Assen: van Gorcum.

Vreede-de Stuers, Cora (1968), Parda: A Study of Muslim Women's Life in Northern India. Assen: Van Gorcum.

Yalman, Nur (1963), On the Purity of Women in the Castes of Ceylon and Malabar. *Journal of the Royal Anthropological Institute* 3 (I): 25--58.

3

Micro-Ideology and Micro-Utopia in Khalapur

Changes in the Discourse on Caste over Thirty Years

> ...it is not men in general who think, or even isolated individuals who do the thinking, but men in certain groups who have developed a particular style of thought in an endless series of responses to certain typical situations characterising their common position (Mannheim 1936: 3).

> In this village, people are in favour of the caste system. They think it is a good way of ordering society. It was a teaching of their forefathers to think in this way. The feeling is still strong among the villagers, although the government is very much against caste and preaches against it (a Rajput elder of Khalapur, 1955).

The topic of ideology has been treated and defined in many ways over the past century. Marx and Engels gave the term a definite political content; ideologies were world-views of social classes that explained and justified the superiority of the social class that made up its main adherents, and justified the necessity for other social classes to accept *that* social class' definition of things. An ideology masked the self-interest of its main adherents from the audience, those the adherents were interested in taking advantage of, but whom they also hoped would accept their hopefully-not-too-feeble excuses.

But ideology has been defined in other ways. Louis Dumont (1970, 1978), the French social-cultural anthropologist, defines ideology as the principal values of a society, and his units of study are entire nations or even large portions of continents, so Dumont can write about the hierarchical person of the East, meaning primarily India, and the individualistic person of the West, meaning primarily France. In such a definition of ideology, I am reminded of Ruth

Benedict (1934) who characterized a culture as pervaded by a dominant drive that shapes all its institutions – the Zuni and other Pueblo Indians were Apollonian, the Kwakiutl were megalomaniacal paranoids, the Plains Indians were Dionysian – except that while Benedict saw styles, rather like styles in art, Dumont sees core ideas, kernel-assumptions. Dumont rejects a multi-ideological approach (Dumont 1970: 263–64); a society has a single global ideology, he asserts, and that is what he is interested in. In the singleness of the style or idea, Benedict and Dumont are alike.

Both Marx and Engels (1948) and Althusser (1970) have emphasized the consistency between the human relationships in the production of commodities and the teachings or ideologies promulgated in other institutions, especially, for Althusser, churches and schools. Theirs is a kind of functional analysis that also looks for ulterior motive.

Max Weber, unlike Althusser or Dumont, raised the issue of the relationship between ideology and social and economic change. He was concerned with unplanned change as opposed to Marx and Engels (1948) who might be said to have been concerned with planned social and economic change purposefully brought about by the use of rather drastic measures. In relating the Protestant ethic to the development of capitalism, Weber not only suggested that ideology must be consistent with the economy, the relations of production, but that changes in ideology precede changes in the economy (Gerth and Mills 1946: 321). Recently, a historian of capitalism, Chandra Mukerji (1983) has challenged Weber's interpretation, agreeing that there were changes in ideology before the flowering of capitalism, but that they were not ascetic in content as in the ascetic Puritanism backed by Weber, but rather luxury-loving in a new consumption-orientation diffusing from "the *nouveaux riches,* the courts, and the aristocracy" (Appadurai 1986: 37). In this interpretation of the ideological changes preceding capitalism, Mukerji and other historians are following the lead of Werner Sombart (1967), rather than Weber.

Most interesting to me is the treatment of ideology by Karl Mannheim (1936), because he seems more than other theorists to address the empirical situation as I have found it. There is seldom one ideology among the members of a community. While Mannheim did not emphasize the multiplicity of ideologies, he did see that there might be a contention between ideologies. He called the established ideology, ideology, and the new challenging ideology, one advocating change, utopia, and he saw this contention as one between social classes. In Khalapur I do not find contention so much between higher and lower castes as between old ideology and new, the new being set by the Congress party leadership in the central government in the 1950s and 1980s and by the Indian urban educated middle class in the 1980s. These new ideologies challenge rural people, especially the village intellectuals, responsible educated and articulate male leaders.

Michel Foucault (1970, 1980) has suggested that discourse within a society or a sector of a society changes over time. One of the topics for discourse in India has been the caste system. It has been a topic for discussion throughout the nineteenth and twentieth centuries. In this paper, I can only treat the recent past, but I do raise the question: Has the discourse about caste changed in the last generation? And if so, how?

The major ideologue concerned with caste in the first part of the twentieth century was Mohandas K. Gandhi. He made the issue of untouchability integral to the cause of independence from the British. The major change he advocated was the end of mistreatment of untouchables by higher castes. Bhimrao Ambedkar, the author of the Indian Constitution, himself born an untouchable Mahar, saw to it that untouchability was outlawed in the Constitution of India (Joshi 1954), established in 1950. This document contains passages such as the following, "untouchability is abolished and its practice in any form is forbidden" (Article 17), "all citizens shall have the right to practise any profession or to carry on any occupation, trade or business" [Article 19 (g)], and "no citizen shall be denied admission into any educational institution maintained by the state or receiving aid out of the state funds on grounds of religion, race, caste, language, or any of them" [Article 29 (2)].

In the mid-1950s, I spent sixteen months doing ethnographic fieldwork in a village of 5,000 people in western Uttar Pradesh, as one of a social sciences group from Cornell University.[1] I was particularly interested in the caste system and in untouchables. In 1958, my paper 'Change in Caste Ideology in a North Indian Village' was published. In that paper, I summarized the views of four older men of the village, who were respected members of four different castes, two of high caste and two of low. One was of the largest landed patrilineage of the village Rajputs, another was a wealthy shopkeeper and moneylender, the third was the headman of one of the two untouchable sweeper colonies, and the fourth was an elder of the untouchable Chamars, once leather workers, now mostly agricultural labourers.

While I had interviewed at length and in considerable depth, all four of the men, as well as others whose opinions were not included in the published article, I also had an interview guide of questions (Appendix I) that I had each of them answer. When I returned to Khalapur in 1984 to do a thirty-year-later study, I interviewed two of the four men again; the other two had died; and I interviewed seven other men of different castes using the same interview guide. The nine men whose caste ideologies I shall explore are from the Rajput, Baniya, Chamar, sweeper, watercarrier, and goldsmith castes. Most of these men I also interviewed more broadly. What I wish to do in this paper is say something about how caste ideology seems to have changed over thirty years in the village of Khalapur. In a longer work, I hope to treat changes in several other aspects of the caste system in Khalapur.

First, however, let me say something about Khalapur. It is located in western Uttar Pradesh, about 100 miles north of Delhi, in a prosperous sugarcane-growing region. In 1954, the population was about 5,000 people; in 1984, it was about 9,700. The dominant caste was and is Pundir Rajput; about 40 percent of the population belongs to one or another of the minor or minimal patrilineages of the maximal patrilineage of Pundir Rajputs. Virtually, all male Rajputs trace their descent from the founding brothers who conquered the Jats who held Khalapur about 300 years age (Hitchcock 1956: 131). They own, even after *zamindari* abolition, 90 percent of the land and control all land. The rest of the population live in Khalapur at the invitation and sufferance of the Rajputs. No other caste begins to be as large as the Pundir Rajputs, but there are a few hundred in each of the larger castes, the Brahmans, untouchable Chamars, untouchable sweepers, and the Baniya shopkeepers. The other twenty-five castes have smaller numbers of people; they include goldsmiths, barbers, carpenters and blacksmiths, washermen, oil-pressers, and so on. About 10 percent of the population are Muslim; 90 percent are Hindu.

In the 1950s, Khalapur was slated for change. Three important change factors had been introduced: first, it was one of the pilot villages for the new Community Development Programme that the

Government of India began in 1952; second, partly as part of this latter programme and partly because a local man had become the deputy planning minister for the state of Uttar Pradesh, sugarcane as a crop of the region received many catalysts in the form of agricultural programmes, irrigation facilities, price supports to the farmer, cooperative credit facilities; and thirdly, a high school was established in Khalapur in 1949. The changes programmed have indeed taken place. The amount of sugarcane grown in Khalapur has increased manifold, and the money flowing to the large landlords from cane receipts ran by the 1980s into many crores. The enrolment in the high school had increased over the years from less than a hundred boys in 1949 to over 1,200 boys and over 300 girls in 1984.[2]

Many facilities have come to the village. The number of shops has tripled, but given the doubling of population that is about what we should expect. However, a bank was established, a branch of the State Bank of India by the latter part of the 1960s; later came a small hospital. New to the village are three or four teashops. None existed in 1954. Also new is the bus service and the paved roads. A bus comes each way once a day, but horse-drawn platforms, called *boogis*, go to the nearby town, five miles away, all morning, and they return all afternoon. We counted over twenty of them in 1984. The number of primary schools has increased from two to seven, and the enrolment in primary school has increased from 200 boys to 923 boys, and from 40 girls to 543 girls.[3]

The intellectual level of the village is at its highest among the masters who teach at the high school, and to some extent it is also set by teachers who teach in the primary schools, as well as the government medical doctor at the hospital, not a villager. There is still no one in the village who speaks English with facility, although two or three of the primary schools claim to be "English-medium". The high school consisting of grades seven through twelve is not English-medium, but Hindi-medium.

Many men have worked outside the village for years at a time, especially Rajputs and some Chamars who have been in the military or in the police of the region. Untouchable sweepers have worked on the municipal garbage crews of various cities. Others have worked in factories or shops in cities, as well. There are two nearby towns, one four or five miles away, the other eight miles away, and many modern amenities are available in these towns, including radio and TV shops, tractor and lorry repair shops, cinemas, barbers who do fashionable cuts, tailors who can stitch a three-piece suit, shops selling synthetic *saris* and terylene for sports shirts, and so on. There are no repair shops in the village, although in 1984 there were about 80 tractors in the village and 40 television sets. One of the most noticeable changes in Khalapur as between the 1950s and 1980s is the absence nowadays of very many bullocks. Because tractors do the heavy ploughing, bullocks are not needed, and the male water buffalo has become the main draught animal, drawing extremely full carts of cane from the fields to the sugar mill in the nearby town.

In the mid-1950s I interviewed three Rajput elders, a Baniya shopkeeper, two untouchable Chamars and an untouchable sweeper using the Caste Sanctions Interview Guide, reprinted in Appendix I. Trying to understand the caste system from the point of view of the Khalapur villagers and using these village intellectuals as my sample for village ideology, I found that the Khalapur villagers spoke of the local caste system in terms of six binary pairs: the *raya* (or *jemindar)–raya* relationship, the *khasgar--lagdar* relationship, the *jijman* (or *jemindar*, or *kirsan)–lagdar* (*or kamin*), the *kirsan--hali*, the *uncha-nicha* system and the *bara-chhota* system (see Kolenda 1978).

Let me briefly suggest what was meant by each of these. The *rai* (pronounced 'rye') is a chieftain or king and the *raya* (pronounced 'rye-ya') is subject. The elder Baniya (shopkeeper) explained:

> For example if I have one or two bighas of land and I build on it a few houses, the people living there are *raya*. The *rai* takes *begari* (forced labor) from *rayas*. When the Chamars (untouchable leather and field workers) sat in *raya* on the land of *jemindars* (landholders), they had to do all sorts of work, and they had little money and education.

It was agreed by all, both the Rajput *rais* and the non-Rajput *rayas*, that Khalapur was 'a Rajput village' and that Khalapur belonged to the Rajputs. The other caste communities had all been invited by the Rajputs, and even though some might have been there for ten generations, they still could be evicted at any time. One of ploys in enticing a community of washermen or weavers to live in the village had been the offer of housesites -- land upon which they could build their houses. It was well known to whom the land belonged, which

Rajput minimal lineage, and the *rai* had the right to ask the *raya* to work for him; he also had the right to the cowdung and other waste that might be composted as the *raya* accumulated it: he also retained the right to take back the land at any time. One of the rights which the *rayas* attained with the passing of the U.P. Zamindari Abolition Act in 1952 was the ownership of their housesites; the *rai* could no longer evict the *raya*.

The *khasgar* is a 'master'; the *lagdar* is a servant, one who fetches and carries (from the Hindi verb *lagna).* One of the Rajput elders used these terms in the following statement:

> With growing cane, the khasgars profited They grew more cane and got more money. Lower castes benefited, because khasgars were rich, and thus, they employed more labour. If the khasgars in a country are happy, everyone else will be happy. Even the shopkeepers in a city are dependent on the khasgars...The khasgars produce the grain and sell it, and the rest of the world buys it.

The core of a local village caste system is the exchange of services that goes on between specialists of different castes. The second largest caste in Khalapur was and is the Chamars, once leather workers and now mostly agricultural labourers *(mazdurs).* Some of these, as well as men from other castes, used to be *halis,* ploughmen, who did the ploughing of a khasgar's fields as well as other land cultivation. His wife, a *haldan,* did the grinding of grain and other heavy household chores for the khasgar's wife.

Seven of the Khalapur castes were engaged in the *jijman-kamin* (patron-worker), more commonly referred to as *kirsan-lagdar* (farmer-servant), relationships. These were the washermen, the barber and his wife, the sweepers and their husbands, the potter, the carpenter, and watercarrier. The seventh, the Brahman, was never referred to as a lagdar but rather as a *purohit,* a household priest; he came to perform *pujas* (religious offering to gods) within the women's quarters on almost two dozen Hindu holidays; his wife sometimes helped in the jijman's kitchen, and groups of Brahman women usually sang at weddings and birth ceremonies of the jijmans. Payments to these lagdars varied, but all received three *dharis* (about 30 pounds) of grain every six months. Since each lagdar served several jijmans, they earned almost enough grain for their families in this way. The Brahmans had their own land; the watercarriers had bits of land. All the others were landless. The sweepers got daily mid-day meals from their kirsans, yearly sets of clothing, food at the time of all festivities (religious holidays and lifecycle rites such as marriages and birth ceremonies). All lagdars had the right to get fodder for their animals and tender leaves of vegetables to make cooked greens from the khasgar's crops, and to graze their animals on the khasgar's fallow fields. When we asked one Rajput elder if a potter wouldn't be better off selling his pots for cash, the Rajput elder listed for us all the sanctions which could be brought to bear to make it clear to the potter that he should supply his khasgar with pots and not attempt to find other outlets for his product. These included not allowing him or his family to defecate in the khasgar's fields, or to graze their donkeys there, or to let their donkeys drink in the canal passing through the khasgar's fields.

The *uncha-nicha* or the high-low system of castes refers to a system of dirt and pollution and involved rules for untouchables and lower castes both for keeping their distance, not touching higher castes, and not expecting the higher castes to accept food or water from them. Chamars are *niche,* low, because they are dirty. In the *bara-chhota* (big-little) system, the terms have to do with authority and the monopoly on physical force. The *bari* castes command the *chhoti* castes, and it is their duty to use physical force to ensure obedience if necessary. To a considerable extent physical force was threatened or used to ensure that the *chhoti* castes remained *nichi,* that is low and dirty (see Kolenda 1978 for more details).

The Rajputs in Khalapur very much fancied themselves to be just what their name means, "sons of kings". They believed that their *dharma,* their religious duty, established at the first sacrifice of the superman *(purusha)* was to rule and to protect their subjects, as well, of course, as to conquer. It was the duty of the other castes to follow their dharma, whether that of the Brahman priest and religious scholar, or that of a potter or weaver. Society would remain in harmony with nature if every caste fulfilled its dharma. The passage in the classic *Bhagavad Gita* which among other Sanskrit religious works teaches about dharma is "better to do one's own dharma badly than the dharma of another well". One of the Rajput elders whom I interviewed both in 1955 and in 1984 told me this story from the *Mahabbharata,* the great Hindu epic.

> Dronacharya was the guru of the Pandavas and the Kauravas. He used to teach them how to shoot the bow and arrow. One day a Bhil (a tribal) boy came there. Drona taught only boys belonging to the high *khaps* (castes), not boys belonging to a lower castes (or presumably to tribal people either). The Bhil said, "Teach me, too". Drona said that he taught only Rajput boys, so he couldn't teach the Bhil. That boy went away. He made a figure of clay and called it Drona. Every morning, he would bow before it, and he would start practising with his bow and arrow. One day, there were some Pandavas and Kauravas who came there. They aimed their arrows, and he did, too. And the Bhil boy defeated them. When Drona heard this he was very upset that his princes should be defeated. He went to the Bhil. He said, "Whose *chela* (pupil) are you?" He said, "Drona's". Then Drona said, "I never taught you". Then, the Bhil boy explained that he had made a clay figure and worshipped it and had practised every morning. Drona said, "All right. I am your guru, but you haven't given me *guru dakshina* (gift for one's teacher)." The Bhil boy said he would give him whatever he asked. Drona said, "Give me your right thumb". Of course, without that thumb, he would be unable to shoot a bow and arrow. So that boy gave his thumb. The meaning of the story is: a person who uses arms should only be a Rajput.[4]

In the 1950s I saw the old caste ideology of Khalapur as the combination of a belief in *jati dharma* (caste duty) and Rajput dominance, while the constitutional rights I saw as the Congress government's form of 'utopia', an ideology proposing fundamental changes in the social structure; and I asked how four of the elders, one Rajput, one Baniya shopkeeper and moneylender, an untouchable Chamar elder, and an untouchable sweeper elder reconciled in their own thinking the contradiction.

The caste ideology of an ordinary person is not a coherent, consistent set of ideas, but is composed of thoughts from here and there heard over the years in the discourse on caste, as well as of observations of events going on around him, or those in which he was himself involved. The content for men of the same age and village is similar although like plaid cloth the pattern made by the various strands of ideas differ for each according to his experiences and his own caste's interests or sufferings. Clifford Geertz has suggested that there are two kinds of theories of ideology, viz., interest theories and strain theories (Geertz 1973: 201). Among men of different castes, we may expect that the caste ideologies of high caste men are more likely to be interest theories while those of low caste men are more likely to be strain theories.

The four men I interviewed were arranged on a continuum with 'ideology' at one end and 'utopia' at the other. The Rajput elder, Hukam Singh, falls at the ideology end as the most conservative, and Jivan Mal, the Baniya, falls at the other end as the most utopian. The two untouchable elders fall in between, Randhir, the sweeper closer to Hukam, and Mithan, the Chamar closer to Jivan Mal. Let me turn to the ideologies of each of these men in turn.

Hukam is a scion of the wealthiest Rajput minor patrilineage in the village. His views on caste in the 1950s were the most orthodox of the four men. He said:

> It is written in the *Vedas* (ancient Sanskrit religious hymnals) that there should be particular lives for each caste. There is one for Brahmans and one for Shudras (servant castes). If you believe in your books and act according to what your ancestors tell you, that is good. If you don't, your *karma* has fallen... One's *karma* is to perform the occupation of one's caste. The occupation of the Rajputs is to help the poor and to protect them and not to take other people's women. If their *karma* falls, they do many bad things. If a Chamar does good things now, he will be born in a higher *dharma*. Those Rajputs who do bad now will be reborn as Chamars and sweepers.

Hukam uses argument of the *Bhagavad Gita*: one should do the duty of one's caste. Bad events will occur otherwise.

At the other extreme from Hukam, at the 'utopia' end of the continuum, is Jivan Mal. Jivan Mal, the Baniya, had been active in Congress party politics in the 1930s. Of the four men, he was the most educated, having eight years of schooling, while Hukam had perhaps four as had Randhir, the sweeper. Mithan Chamar had had no schooling. Jivan Mal knew the Congress programme against caste well. He said:

> The Congress gathered Chamars, Muslims, and all together as one in order to bid farewell to the British. No single creed alone could have

done it... That was the basis of the whole thing, equality. Mahatma Gandhi was a Vaishya and Nehru was a *pandit* (a Brahman). They might have thought, "We will keep apart from the untouchables", but they did not... God is with those who do not discriminate. There should not be caste...

Jivan Mal was a Gandhian. Like Gandhi, he tried to live his life according to the four *ashramas*,[5] and when we knew him, he was in the third ashrama; he was a *vanaprashta,* one who had retired from ordinary life to devote himself to religion. He explained that he and his wife were "like brother and sister"; he had given up sexual activity. Consistent with his religiosity and his Gandhianism was his strict vegetarian diet, but inconsistent with his Gandhianism was his inability to consort with untouchables, to be near them or to take food or drink from them or with them. It is not surprising that Hukam Singh Rajput, the conservative also disapproved of such Congress social intercourse with untouchables. Hukam said:

> Now, we have started eating everywhere. At first, we ate nowhere except at the Baniyas' and the Brahmans'. Even there, we ate only fried *(pakka)* food. Ever since the Congress came, even the big leaders eat at the Chamars' and the sweepers'. What can others do?... I am a modern man. I take both boiled *(kachcha)* and fried *(pakka)* food at the Tagas' and the Jats' (high agricultural castes) and at the Baniyas'. We now even eat at the goldsmiths'... Even if we object, what are we to do?

So Hukam indicated that he had relaxed his personal prohibitions on eating with some other higher castes, but he could not bring himself to approve of eating and drinking with untouchables and low-caste people. Aware that the old ways were being challenged, he remains unconvinced, saying:

> The caste system is necessary. As long as the old people are alive, caste will not disappear. But, the lineages will become badly mixed and the Rajput will keep a Chamar woman, and the Chamar will keep a Rajput woman.

At the other end of the ideology -- utopia continuum -- Jivan Mal though unable to bring himself to consort with untouchables, nevertheless condemned the caste system.

> [The caste system] is a way of destroying the world. Since the time that caste came to India, India has been under foreign rulers... If the Rajputs are ruling, they keep untouchability restrictions with the sweepers and the Chamars. So, in time of trouble, they will not help the Rajputs. Now we have fallen from our *karma* by non-unity, especially through untouchability.

Jivan Mal's ideology, though strongly Gandhian and anti-caste, nevertheless, included a strand of nostalgia for the old days when the caste system operated ideally, as it should. In those days, he said:

> The Brahmans had hold of the whole world. They were the protectors of the country. India was considered the centre of learning. Wherever an Indian walked, people would pick up the dust and place it on their foreheads. It was a land of gods...

Hukam's ideology was consistent. Again aware of the challenge of change with respect to education and middle-class jobs for untouchables, he again rejected it saying:

> [In the past] they were not prevented from being educated simply because they lacked natural ability, but because the leaders would not have liked it. Now, the government says all should become one. We are afraid of that.
>
> Now we can't get anyone to work for us. If they are all clerks and gentlemen, who will plough our fields? Even now it is hard to get laborers. It used to be you could get a man for five rupees to work for you. Now they ask thirty or forty... (We asked if one could pay less.) How could we do that? The government helps them. If we try to make them take less, they will sue in the courts.

Hukam expected the worst in the future; just as the *Gita* and other religious sources have taught, the mixture of castes would lead to destruction of the world which would necessitate the coming of a savior to put things right. He predicted:

> When the Congress rule ends, there will be a rule of devils (*rakshas*). The untouchables and the lower castes will rule, and they will trouble the Rajputs and Brahmans. They will then be kept low. Then (god) will come... During the rule of devils, there will be no caste,

> and there will be no dharma and karma. Then *Kalkiavatara* (god in man's form) will be born. Then he will start castes all over again.

The untouchable elder closest to Jivan Mal in his views was Randhir, the sweeper. He also approved of the Congress' goal of equality, but in 1955 he had begun to doubt its attainment. He said:

> These Congress people said that we are all equal. So why don't they give us equal treatment? For seven years they have been in power, and they have done nothing. Untouchability still goes on... these Congress people are not good in their hearts.

He was especially doubtful that caste discrimination would end in the village. He remarked:

> It is written in books now that they must let everyone take water at the pump, but they do not. We have to live in the village, so we don't want to make reports against people and turn them against us.

His helplessness in the village where the dominant Rajputs continued to hold sway in the traditional way is voiced in this passage:

> We consider the Rajputs to be our kings. Nobody can do anything against the kings, unless they unite against them... People don't unite because they are weak. We are poor and dependent upon the Rajputs for animals, food, and everything.

Unlike the untouchable Randhir sweeper, untouchable Mithan Chamar did not approve wholeheartedly of the Congress and Gandhian attempt to do away with the rules of untouchability. He was already anguished concerning the frequent exploitation of Chamar women by Rajput and higher caste men; now, if there were restraint from the feelings of disgust for untouchables, the untouchable women would be troubled even more. He, like the other three men, idealized the past when the local caste system worked well. He said:

> The Rajputs and low-caste people should be like parents and children. It used to be that if anyone else troubled us, the Rajputs would protect us. Now they themselves oppress us.

That the higher castes in Khalapur have tried equality and rejected it, is indicated in Mithan's account of the first meeting of the new democratically-elected village council. He was an untouchable member of the council. He said:

> When India got its independence, there was an order from the higher authorities. This is when the elections were being held and then people started living more in unity because of that order, for about six weeks. They even started letting us take water from their wells in the fields, and during council meetings all fifty-two members used to sit on clothes spread on the ground. Then about three months after independence, Rajputs started sitting on cots and made the lower castes all sit on clothes on the ground. Still later, even the clothes were not spread and the old state of affairs was resumed, with Rajputs and higher castes on the cots and lower castes on the bare ground.

So, Mithan, like Randhir, held little hope that the strictures of untouchability would be relaxed in Khalapur.

My analysis of the four elders' ideologies in the mid-1950s had six conclusions:

First, enthusiasm for equality had dissipated.

Second, the concept of progress was strikingly lacking. All four men looked back to golden days of the past either when Rajputs were rulers (for Hukam) or when Brahmans ruled (for Jivan Mal) or when Rajputs were parental toward their servants (for Randhir, the sweeper and Mithan Chamar).

Third, three of the elders, Hukam Rajput and the two untouchables, felt victimized and helpless.

Fourth, all set conditions for the future success of the government. Jivan, the merchant and Randhir, the sweeper required intercaste equality. Hukam required power for Rajputs. He and the Chamar predicted an era of evil manifested in intercaste sexual relations and intercaste marriages that would end in the destruction of society and the coming of a saviour to set things right again.

Fifth, no one except Hukam any longer expected people to follow the dharma of caste occupation.

Sixth, none could envision a social order free from restrictions on intercaste social intercourse.

Clearly, the issues of the 1950s were educational and occupational access for low-caste and untouchable people, and practices of untouchability like using wells, sitting as equals or sitting hierarchically, giving and taking of food and water, sharing waterpipes together, and so on. My feeling in the 1950s was that villagers in Khalapur could not conceive of a society that was not caste-organized. Equal treatment was a foreign urban Congress party issue. Occasional politicians came and advocated and even demonstrated equality, but rural Rajputs could ignore it and untouchables had to suffer non-enforcement of their rights if they wanted to continue living in the village.

In 1984, two of the four elders were still alive, Hukam Rajput and Mithan Chamar, and among other conversations I had with each, I re-interviewed them with the same Caste Sanctions Interview Guide. In the 1950s the impact of education upon Khalapur was slight, but over the past thirty years, all of the men whom I interviewed, including four older men and five younger ones, had sons or grandsons who were high school or even college-educated, or were highly educated themselves. To replace Jivan Mal, I interviewed Durga Lal, a Baniya, a man in his late fifties or early sixties. When I asked him about the origin of the caste system, he said, "Ever since the world has been populated, there have been jatis". When I asked, "Was there a creator?" he said, "A *sciencewala* can tell you."

Durga Lal, who had eight years of education, has six daughters and four sons. Four of the daughters studied to eighth class, one to twelfth, and the youngest was in tenth in 1984. Durga has one son who finished twelfth and works in his shop. The other three sons work outside the village. One has a B.Sc. degree; one is an engineer; and one is a postgraduate science teacher, perhaps the *sciencewala* Durga had in mind. Durga, in fact, has lots of *sciencewale* in his family.

The impact of education has changed the discourse in the village from phantasies about the past to expectations of the future. *Parivartan*, change, is the word on the tongues of the young high school- and college-goers, of the teachers and office workers.

Four of those I interviewed in 1984 were aged late-fifties to eighties. One of these was Durga Lal, the merchant, who had eight years of education, unusual for a man in his late fifties or early sixties, but who had, nevertheless, lost confidence in the worth of his own opinions saying, "I don't have much education." The eldest of the four older men interviewed was Raghunath, a goldsmith, I remembered well from thirty years ago. Raghunath is one of the few I spoke to who still talks about the etiquette of untouchability. When we asked, "Is *jat-pat* (caste system) a good or bad way of ordering society?" he said, "How can I tell? It is from before *(pahale se).* Actually, it is good *(achcchaa hai).* The lower castes that visit me cannot sit on my cot, but sit on the ground -- the sweeper, barber, washerman, weaver, oilpresser and tailor."

Hukam Singh Rajput, the conservative interviewed in 1955, now in his seventies, has changed his views drastically since thirty years ago, saying that "caste is rotten; it is not right", but his statement seemed perfunctory, especially as he immediately went on, saying, "The difficulty is that you have to have different *hukkas* (waterpipes)", and he reminisced about the old days when he had no place to stay or to eat when he had to spend the night in a nearby Chamar village.

One of the three teachers whom we interviewed, a Rajput schoolmaster, in contrast, said that the caste system was a bad way to order society. He then commented: "In some families now *achhut*s (the unclean, that is, untouchables) can prepare food and serve it, prepare *hukka*s for *chaudhuri*s (the important men). They can sit on our cots."

But, the issues in the discourse on caste have changed. No longer are the issues of access for facilities, intercaste etiquette and untouchables' rights to jobs and education. These changes have been absorbed. When we asked Durga Lal, "Do you know of some castes advancing? What do you think of a Chamar teacher or a Nai (barber caste) doctor?" he said, "I can't tell, but you know everything is being done for these (the untouchables) to bring them up." We asked, "From the village?" Durga Lal did not reply, but his son who works in the shop said, "From the government." There are now untouchable teachers and *babu*s (clerks) living in the village. People now live with the ideal of egalitarian etiquette, even though they feel uneasy with it and probably do not practice it. But, the issues now are new issues in a new discourse on caste. These are intercaste marriage, a questioning of caste as a social system, and the expectation of social change.

When I began to ask Hukam Singh Rajput the list of questions on the Caste Sanctions Interview Guide, he launched immediately into the issue of intercaste marriage. As a man now in his seventies or eighties, he still accepts the idea that castes are different species. Within intercaste marriage, he said: "The offspring will be changed. Like a donkey mates with a horse, a mule is born, not a donkey."

Raghunath, the goldsmith said that intercaste marriage simply "isn't done. One must marry in one's own caste."

Mithan Chamar, also now in his seventies, said, however, that he wouldn't object to a Rajput woman marrying a Chamar man, "but", he exclaimed, "the Rajputs would object!"

Among the younger men, those in their thirties to fifties, however, attitudes are different from those of the elders except for the untouchable Mithan Chamar who agrees with the younger men, all of whom pronounce *jat-pat* a *kharab* (rotten) or *bahut bura* (very bad) way of ordering society. The young men are a Rajput high school teacher, a Baniya school teacher, and an untouchable sweeper primary school teacher. One is a watercarrier by caste who failed tenth class as a boy; he works as a *chaprasi*, a peon, in the high school. He is seeing to it that his son is educated, having had a study room built on the roof of their small compound for the boy's sole use. And, the fifth is one of the first educated men among the untouchable Chamars, a man we knew as a youth in the 1950s who got his education under very difficult circumstances in the late 1930s and 1940s; he and the three other untouchable boys in the school had to sit separately from the others, and were prohibited from drinking at the school pump; his father suffered periodic beatings by high castemen, and was made to do unpaid labour, because he kept his son in school.

Here are these younger men's comments on intercaste marriage:

(1) The Rajput high school teacher said: "Some people say you should not marry in other castes. If it happens by chance, they become angry. With an educated person, an educated bride and groom if they do so, I think, in society, it is not thought so bad. Our KS [the late principal of the high school, an outsider, a government-appointee, but a Chauhan Rajput and principal for a quarter of a century] – his elder son married a girl of Kayastha caste. When KS and his elder brother came to know, they were happy; they did not object."

(2) The Baniya school teacher said: "I don't think it wrong, but *samaj* (society) does not accept it. Because of social pressure, even if one wants to marry a son or daughter out of caste, one cannot. Men of one's caste brotherhood apply such pressure on any of their caste people who try to marry into another caste; those who do so have to give up their own caste. In this village, there were such marriages long ago. One such family was

thrown out of our caste for a long time. All recognized them as people among whom an intercaste marriage had taken place. AS [a neighbor] his grandfather [father's father] married a sweeper woman. He defied his caste brotherhood. He just brought her and kept her. He had had *pheras* [been properly married] with a Rajput woman. He kept both women at once. They lived separately. At first, he kept the sweeper outside and then in the cattleshed. She was never in the women's quarters of his family.

"Then four years ago, a Rajput boy here married a girl whose caste is not known. We presume she is a Chamar. He is a supervisor in a factory in G [a city in the district]. He is not allowed to come into the village nor does anyone go there. Two months after marriage he came with his wife. They let him stay the night only, then sent him away next morning."

(3) Ramlal, the watercarrier caste school-peon said: "I would like people of different castes to marry, but that is my own individual idea. I wouldn't mind my son marrying into some other caste, but I have relatives who would object."

(4) Tirlok, the untouchable sweeper school teacher, said: "That is the best thing. I am not averse to that. I would like that so that all *jats* (castes) are broken up. Under Sanjay[6] they started a movement – if a lower caste marries a higher caste, the couple would be given presents by the government."

Thus, these men represent a range of opinion, but intercaste marriage is still something outside, something that might be done by educated people in the city, advocated by the government in the city, but not yet something that might be acceptable in Khalapur. But this was very much the status of egalitarian intercaste etiquette and equal rights to jobs and education for untouchables in the 1950s.

I was very much surprised at the unanimity among the seven younger men against caste as a system; among the older men Mithan, the Chamar joins them saying, "It is harmful *(nuksan, phaida nahin).* Each caste keeps away from the other. [We: would it be better if they did not keep separate?] Yes, there would be more love *(prema)* if they were not so separate."

As mentioned above, even Hukam Singh reluctantly says the system is *kharab* and *thik nahin* ("rotten" and "not right"). Nowadays, only very elderly folks like Raghunath in his eighties can still say the system is good, and men in their sixties like Durga Lal may just hold their tongues.

In the 1950s I felt Khalapur villagers could not conceive of any different social system. To quote the remarks of the younger men:

(1) The Rajput high school teacher said caste was a bad way to order society, and he went on as mentioned above about untouchables even serving food and the *hukka* to high-caste people. He added: "Untouchable sweepers and Chamars are well-educated. I had a sweeper class fellow who is in the central district administration military office (as a lawyer). He goes to the *pradhan*'s (village headman) and *chaudhuri*'s (important man) houses. He takes tea with us (Rajputs)."

(2) The Baniya school teacher pronounced the caste system *kharab*. He said: "According to my views, it is wrong. Every human being was created by a creator (*usi*). It is a *nuksan* (a loss or harm) to a human being to think of another as lower than himself, because of his work."

(3) The watercarrier caste school clerk also said the system was *kharab*, going on to say: "We are all human beings. A man should be treated like a man. There is difference only according to work."

(4) The Chamar educated "first" also said the system was *kharab*, saying: "Among human beings, God made all of the same blood, so why this difference between one and another."

(5) The untouchable sweeper primary school teacher was the most impassioned in his response to our question, "Is the caste system a good way or a bad way of organizing society?" He said it was "very bad. Our country cannot progress because of this. Indira Gandhi is fighting against it. I am as educated as a Brahman and Rajput. I read religious books. I have education and give education. Yet only under government pressure will a Brahman eat with us. In his heart, he thinks, 'He's an untouchable sweeper!' Indira Gandhi is against it, wants rid of it, so the country can go forward."

The species kind of thinking done by Hukam is rhetoric of a past discourse on caste. Ideas about equal etiquette and equal rights are becoming ideology in Khalapur. The discourse concerning intercaste marriages the questioning of caste as an entire system, the expectation of change, are parts of a new utopian ideology.

Appendix I
CASTE SANCTIONS QUESTIONNAIRE

1. What is the origin of the caste system? How did it start ?
2. What is the basis of the caste system? How was it that people doing different work were divided into castes? How was it when there were four *varnas* originally, there are now thirty-six castes? How did *chhutchat* (untouchability) come about?
3. Is *jat-pat* (casteism) a good way or a bad way of ordering society?
4. Do you agree or disagree that one's virtue depends on fulfilling one's own caste's duties, and not on doing the duties of another caste?
5. What do you think of people who do not do their caste's work, but some other kind of work? Such as a Chamar school teacher, or a Dhobi (washerman) doing farming, or a Nai (barber) doctor?
6. Is it is wrong to do work which is not your own caste's work? If you don't want to do your own caste's work, is that wrong? What advice would you give to a member of your caste who wanted to do some other work?
7. What is the origin of untouchables? How did they get started? Why is it bad for people of different castes to marry? Who were the ancestors of the untouchables?
8. Do Rajputs and Brahmans have high positions, because of their good *karma* in past lives? How did their high position come about?
9. Do you agree or disagree:
   (a) "The highest duty of the Shudra is to serve a Brahman".
   (b) "Killing a Brahman is the worst crime on earth."
   (c) "A Brahman be he ignorant or learned is a great divinity."
10. What is *karma?* What is *dharma?* How are *karma* and *dharma* related to caste?
11. Why are some castes lower than others? Are some castes lower because they allow widow-remarriage?
12. What would you do if your Nai (barber) or Bhangi (untouchable sweeper) refused to work for you?
13. Is it necessary for one's *ijjat* (honour) to have a Bhangi? a Brahman? a Nai? a Dhobi? a Badhai (carpenter)? a Kumhar

(potter)? Would you give up your Bhangi if you no longer needed him?

14. Is your own position in the caste system due to past deeds in past lives?
15. What do you think of various castes trying to improve their position?
    Do you know of any caste groups trying to improve themselves by taking up the wearing of the sacred thread? by giving up widow remarriage? in other ways? giving up meat?

Notes

[This paper was originally read in a seminar at the University of Texas at Austin, September 24, 1984.]

1. My research in Khalapur between October 1954 and June 1956 was supported by a Post-doctoral Fellowship from the Cornell University India Programme; writing of a number of articles on Khalapur including 'Changing Caste Ideology...' was supported by grants from the American Philosophical Society (in 1957–58) and the American Association of University Women (in 1958–59). The research in Khalapur from January to June 1984 was supported by a grant from the Smithsonian Institution. I am grateful to all of these organizations.
2. The figures on high school enrolment were copied from the school records by Shyamsher Singh, a high school teacher.
3. The figures on primary school enrolments for 1955 are taken from Minturn and Hitchcock 1966: 91. The figures for 1984 were collected by a research assistant, Deepika Anand.
4. Hukam Singh made reference to the same story in 1984, but then he only said that Dronacharya had taught Arjun, the Pandava warrior-hero of the *Mahabharata*, one of Dronacharya's pupils referred to in the 1955 story. In 1984, he did not mention the Bhil boy or his thumb.
5. The *ashramas* are the four stages of life which Hindu religious law books prescribe for upper caste men. For one-quarter of his life, he should engage himself in religious study with a guru. For one-quarter of his life he should be a married householder, raising children. For one-quarter of his life, he and his wife should retire to the forest and pursue religious ends; this is the *vanaprashta ashrama*. For the last quarter of his life, he should be a renouncer, beg for his living, and seek union with the absolute (Basham 1954: 158–59).
6. Sanjay Gandhi, who died in 1980, was the younger son of Prime Minister Indira Gandhi. During the 1970s, he was head of the Congress party's youth organization, and he worked for many social and economic reforms, including abolition of caste abuses. Here, Tirlok refers to the newspaper reports of government-approved weddings between people of different castes.

References

Althusser, Louis (1970), 'Ideology and Ideological State Apparatuses (Notes Towards an Investigation)' in *Lenin and Philosophy and Other Essays* translated by Ben Brewster, New York and London: Monthly Review Press.

Appadurai, Arjun (1986), *The Social Life of Things: Commodities in Cultural Perspective,* Cambridge: Cambridge University Press.

Basham, A.L. (1954), *The Wonder That Was India,* New York: Grove Press.

Benedict, Ruth (1946) (originally 1934), *Patterns of Culture,* New York: Penguin Books.

Dumont, Louis (1970) (originally published in French in 1966), *Homo Hierarchicus* translated by Mark Sainsbury, Chicago: University of Chicago Press.

— (1978), *From Mandeville to Marx,* Chicago: University of Chicago Press.

Foucault, Michel (1970), *The Order of Things,* New York: Vintage Books.

— (1980), *The History of Sexuality,* Volume 1: *An Introduction,* New York: Vintage Books.

Geertz, Clifford (1973) (originally published in 1964), 'Ideology as a Cultural System' in *The Interpretation of Cultures,* New York: Basic Books, pp. 193–233.

Gerth, Hans and C. Wright Mills, editors and translators (1946), 'The Protestant Sects and the Spirit of Capitalism' in *From Max Weber: Essays in Sociology,* New York: Oxford University Press.

Hitchcock, John T. (1956), *The Rajputs of Khalapur: A Study of Kinship, Social Stratification and Politics,* PhD Dissertation, Cornell University Press.

Joshi, G.N. (1954), *The Constitution of India,* London: Macmillan.

Kolenda, Pauline (1958), 'Changing Caste Ideology in a North Indian Village', *Journal of Social Issues, 14:* 51–65.

— (1978), 'Hindu Caste in a Regal Tradition: The Native View', in *Cultural Context: Essays in Honor of Edward Norbeck,* Christine M.S. Drake (editor) Rice University Studies 66 (1): 125–36.

Mannheim, Karl (1936), *Ideology and Utopia,* New York: Harcourt, Brace and Company.

Marx, Karl and Frederick Engels (1948) (originally 1848), *The Communist Manifesto*, New York: International Publishers.

Minturn, Leigh and John T. Hitchcock (1966), *The Rajputs of Khalapur*, New York: John Wiley and Sons.

Mukerji, Chandra (1983), *From Graven Images: Patterns of Modern Materialism*, New York: Columbia University Press.

Sombart, Werner (1967), *Luxury and Capitalism*, Ann Arbor: University of Michigan Press.

Weber, Max (1930), *The Protestant Ethic and the Spirit of Capitalism*, translated by Talcott Parsons, London: George Allen and Unwin.

4

Fewer Deaths, Fewer Births

Decline of Child Mortality in a UP Village

In her classic anthropological work, *Birth in Four Cultures: A Cross-cultural Investigation of Childbirth in Yucatan, Holland, Sweden and the United States* (Montreal, Canada: Eden Press Women's Publications, 1978), Brigitte Jordan convinced readers that the Dutch obstetric system was the best of the four. There, at least in the 1970s, most births took place in the comfort of home, with a midwife who had attended the woman pre-natally and was well-trained to spot any emergency requiring medical intervention. With such a system, Holland had extremely low rates of infant mortality, close to the lowest in the world, low rates of caesarian section, epis iotomies, use of labor-inducing injections (pitocin) and women dying in childbed. The overwhelming majority of Dutch births required no medical intervention. Following Jordan's lead, Robbie Davis-Floyd (see her *Birth as an American Rite of Passage*, Berkeley: University of California Press, 1992) and others have critiqued the medicalization of birthing, showing that hospital births as they have been carried out in the U.S.A., involving widely used technological measures, and pharmacological and surgical interventions, are more for the convenience of the medical personnel than they are for the benefit of the birthing mother; much of the technology and medical intervention is unnecessary, these critics say; some of it is, indeed, harmful. There has been a considerable movement in the United States to return childbirthing to trained midwives, relaxed scheduling, and the home.

Jordan has tried to face up to the problems of birthing in the Third World countries, concluding:

> Because of the efficacy of technological biomedicine in dealing with pathological cases, some accommodation between cosmopolitan

obstetrics and the traditional ethno-obstetric systems should be sought. 'Cosmopolitan Obstetrics: Insights on the Training of Traditional Midwives' (*Social Science and Medicine* 28(9): 937–945, 1989).

In Khalapur village in Saharanpur district, in western Uttar Pradesh, in 1997, almost all births took place at home attended by a midwife -- a Harijan midwife. I regret that in a short paper l can only outline the Khalapur birthing situation, and must leave out a great deal of contextual data.

In 1984, in a thirty years later study of Khalapur, with a population at that time of about 9,700, I took a 5 percent sample of all the patrilineal segments (*khandans*); that, I was able to do, because another social-cultural anthropologist, J. Michael Mahar, aided by a schoolmaster and some educated young men of the village, had just completed a census of Khalapur, taken in terms of khandans. The advantage of using khandans as the sampling unit was that in the initial interview with members of each, l could do a genealogy, going back to the apical head of the khandan (the oldest living male whose male descendants form the core of the khandan) and include all women, both living and dead, both wives and married daughters, as well as their husbands and children.

In 1984, I collected various information about the people in the 32 khandans that had fallen into the 5 percent sample. In winter 1985, I went back to collect reproductive histories for all of the married women, both married daughters and wives. While there are some fascinating differences between wives and married daughters – Khalapur, like much of northern India, practises village exogamy, so all daughters of all castes, both Hindu and Muslim, go to live with their husbands elsewhere -- I cannot here go into those differences, nor can I go deeply into differences between castes, or between Hindus and Muslims.

The reproductive histories included caste and khandan membership, age and education of both wife and husband, husband's name and occupation, age of the woman at the time of her first wedding ceremony (*shadi*), her age at the second wedding ceremony (*chala*) -- that used to take place as much as two or three years after the first ceremony, her age at her first birth, the names and ages of all her children -- both living and dead, causes of death of children, where she had each child – whether in her mother-in-law's house or at her parents' house in another village, who the midwife (*dai*) was, whether there had been any medical personnel involved, whether there were any injections, length and ease or difficulty of labor, use of birth control, illnesses of children, medical treatment of children, and so on. In April-May 1997, I returned to Khalapur to take the reproductive histories of women married since 1984 and to re-interview other women, especially to record details about births since 1984.

Table 4.1

Crude Birth Rate, Crude Death Rate, and Population Growth of Village Khalapur, 1983 and 1996 (Based on a 5 percent sample of the 1984 population collected by khandan units)

Village Resident Population		
	1983	*1996*
cbr	33.54	22.86
cdr	12.58	3.81
pg*	2.096	1.905
Village Population *(Including Outpopulation)*		
	1983	*1996*
cbr	37.03	19.46
cdr	11.11	2.99
pg*	2.592	1.647

cbr = crude birth rate; cdr = crude death rate; pg = population growth
**Population growth per annum*

1983 population: 477(487 in 1984–10 children born in 1984)
1996 population: 525(529 in 1997–4 children born in 1997)
1983 population: 477(living in village+63 living outside)=540
1996 population: 525(living in village+143 living outside)=668

Comparison of the figures in Table 4.1 indicates the change in crude birth rate, crude death rate and population growth in 1983 and 1996. (Crude birth rate is the number of births in a year per 1,000 population; crude death rate is the number of deaths in a year per 1,000 population. Here, the "population" is 477 persons in the 5 percent sample in 1983 and 525 persons in the same sample in 1996.) The figures are presented in two ways: first, those based on people resident in the village, and second, those based on the village residents, plus those who, by rules of patrilineality and patrilocality, should be living in the village, but were living outside. (The 1983 population including those living outside numbered 540; in 1996, it numbered 668.) Either way, population growth in Khalapur was over 2 percent a year in 1983, but it had come down to around 1.9 percent by 1996 for the village population, and to 1.6 percent, if villagers living outside are included. Both birth rate and death rate have gone down sharply, although overall decline in population growth is slight – from 2.1 percent to 1.9 percent – for the population living in the village.

The total number of living people in my 5 percent sample resident in Khalapur rose from 487 in 1984 to 529 in 1997, almost 9

Plate 3

With improved incomes from cash-crops, Khalapur Rajputs dress their children in warm sweaters and head coverings (Photo: Pauline Kolenda)

percent (8.62 percent) over 13 years, suggesting that the Khalapur population was now around 10,600 in 1997. If the villagers who would normally, by rules of patrilineality and patrilocality, be living in the village, but who are living outside are added to the village populations, then the change is from 550 to 672 persons, an increase of 22 percent.

But, let us look at the 170 Khalapur wives in the 32 khandans of my 1997 sample. This includes 136 wives, 12 widows and 20 dead wives, 1 wife whose husband deserted her, and 1 divorced (Muslim) wife. Almost half of them (80 or 47 percent) belong to the dominant landed caste of Rajputs. Other high castes, Brahmans and Banias, make up 15 percent; middle castes (carpenters, shepherds, watercarriers, *jogis,* weavers, potters, goldsmiths) make up 18 percent; Harijans, 11 percent, and Muslims, 9 percent. In the calculations for this paper, I omit two women for whom I lack adequate accounts. So, the number of wives considered is 168.

The oldest woman in the sample, a dead wife, was born in 1907; she was a Rajput woman who bore 8 children, of whom three died. When we interviewed her in 1985, she said that her first child, a son, died of dysentery, at age 1; another son, her fourth child, died of TB, at age 20; and a third son, her last-born, died of diarrhoea, at age 10. She had two sons and three daughters living. Married at age 15, she did not have her first child until she was 19; she bore her eighth and last child at age 45. The youngest wife in the sample, also a Rajput, was born in 1978; married at 18, she had her first child, a son, at 19, born in early 1997.

Neither the oldest woman in the sample nor the youngest had had any schooling. It is only the most recent cohort, the youngest women in the sample, the 27 wives born in the 1970s, women in the early part of their reproductive careers, who have less than half of their number (32 percent) in the totally unschooled category. Of those born in the 1960s, bearing children in the 1980s and 1990s, more than half (51 percent) had had no schooling. For the sample as a whole, 70 percent had never gone to school.

Virtually all Khalapur women's births take place home; over 85 percent in the women's quarters of the mother-in-law's house; about 6 percent in the mother's house – in another village, of course. Only 4 percent of deliveries, 13 in all, in the 305 deliveries in a sub-sample of 73 women for whom we got information on place of birth, took place in hospitals; in addition, one delivery took place in a nursing home in a nearby town, and one wife having a miscarriage went to the hospital to try to prevent the miscarriage, but lost the premature baby. In the sub-sample of 73 wives, 8 women had hospital births. Most births at the hospital are motivated by unusual conditions – forceps delivery, twins, swelling of the pregnant woman's body (possibly eclampsia), the death of a previous baby. Two of the 8 women subsequently had home deliveries after having had a baby at the hospital.

Table 4.2

Education of Khalapur Wives (Including Widows, Remarried and Dead Wives) by Decade of Birth

Birth Decade:	*1900--39*	*1940s*	*1950s*	*1960s*	*1970s*	*Total*
Education						
0	(45) 92%	(15) 75%	(21) 84%	(22) 54%	(9) 35%	(112) 70%
1–4	0	0		(4) 10%	(1) 4%	(5) 3%
5	(3) 6%	(5) 25%	(2) 8%	(8) 19%	(3) 11%	(21) 13%
6–9	(1) 2%	0		(3) 7%	(9) 35%	(13) 8%
10 or more	0	0	(2) 8%	(4) 10%	(4) 15%	(10) 6%
Total	(50) 100%	(20) 100%	(26) 100%	(45) 100%	(27) 100%	(168) 100%
Don't Know	(1)		(1)	(4)	(1)	(7)

In 1997, some of the women we interviewed mentioned the current occurrence of hospital births. One Bania (merchant caste) mother whose daughter had just had a hospital birth noted the comparative expenses. She said, "It is very expensive to have a baby at the hospital. At home, it costs Rs.250–300, but at the hospital Rs.6,000." An older Rajput (b.1939) commented, "We are very simple people. The *(dai)* massages and we wait for the delivery." Another Rajput widow (b.1949) said, "We don't have to go to hospital. One will have pain wherever one is. One might as well be comfortable at home."

Khalapur women feel quite competent to handle birthing -- with the aid of a Harijan midwife, of course, to absorb the pollution entailed. Already in 1984, at the time of my restudy, Harijan midwives had received some training and knew how to avoid tetanus infections by using a new razor blade or scissors rather than a rusty sickle, sometimes used in the past. Even earlier, in the mid-1950s, when I first worked in Khalapur, the government's newly introduced Community Development Project (CDP) employed a trained midwife. Since I worked closely with the Harijan sweepers, I find in my 1950s notes references to the CDP midwife working collaboratively with Harijan midwives then. The CDP midwife

Plate 4

Rajput mother with her child (Photo: Pauline Kolenda)

supervised while the Harijan midwife actually received the baby and did the cleaning up. While my notes do not mention the CDP midwife's instructions for cutting the umbilical cord, it is likely she did prescribe a sanitary instrument. In 1997, at least upper-caste people were aware of the dangers of tetanus. So, a Rajput farmer who had cut his foot on a tiller was not only well-bandaged, but was also injected against tetanus, administered by one of the local private doctors. The most recent death of a new baby from tetanus among the ten reported by the women in our sample was in 1981.

Brigitte Jordan has suggested that one measure of the adequacy of an ethno-obstetric system is whether many mothers or babies die during birthing. Of the 170 wives in my sample, only one died during childbirth – about 0.5 percent. This woman died in late 1984 at the age of 15 or 16. She was a Muslim Nilgar. Her mother-in-law told us that she was very sick during her pregnancy, swollen and with dysentery. She delivered the child in her eighth month. Both mother and child died. The midwife was a widely-used Harijan sweeper. The dead woman's husband's Muslim khandan is extremely poor, the men working as agricultural laborers. Their traditional caste work of dyeing cloth was abandoned long ago. This family feels they cannot afford to go to a doctor. Perhaps if the woman had received some treatment for her dysentery and swelling, she might not have had her baby prematurely. Then again, she was unusually young, only 15 or 16. Among the wives over age 45 (born in 1952 or earlier) past the child-bearing age, the average age of first birth was almost 19 (18.88), and the average age for bearing the last child, almost 34 (33.72).

The reason for early average cessation of having children is in part due to a custom known to me in the mid-1950s and still followed – that a woman who is a grandmother should not bear any more children. A strong positive valuation upon celibacy probably contributes to abstinence from sexual relations among Hindu grandparents. In subsequent writing, I plan to take up the issue of use of birth control to terminate child-bearing and to space births by the Khalapur women in our sample.

So mothers very seldom die in these home deliveries. What about children? Out of the 799 births that these 168 Khalapur wives have had – 4.76 per woman -- 211 children died, or 1.26 per woman on average. Of course, some women have lost many children, some have lost few. At the extreme was one woman who had lost 8 of the 10 children she bore, the first 7 dying. The numbers and proportions of mothers in the entire sample by the numbers of children lost to death appear in Table 4.3.

Table 4.3

Number of Children Lost to Death by Numbers of Mothers

Children who died	*Mothers who lost so many*	*% of mothers*
0	80	49%
1	31	19%
2	19	12%
3	15	9.25%
4	3	2%
5	7	4.25%
6	3	2%
8	4	2.5%
Total	162	100%

N = 168. 2 women were barren, 4 were young married women who had not yet had children. So 168 – 6 = 162.

Almost half of all the wives in the 1997 sample had lost no children to death, 19 percent had lost only one, but over 31 percent had lost 2 or more.

At another extreme, there were only two wives who can be considered to be confirmed as barren, an elderly (b.1934) Harijan widow (widowed in 1984) of the Jatiya shoemaker caste, and a younger (b.1968) Rajput wife, married in 1988. The latter adopted the newborn daughter of her brother-in-law's sister-in-law, when its mother died during a Caesarian-section operation. Among the other 4 women in the 1997 sample who had no children, two were pregnant at the time of our April-May 1997 interviews, one a *Kumhaar* (potter) wife, born in 1969 and married in 1992, the other a Rajput wife born in 1973 and married in 1993. The other 2 women were both recently married.

That only two married women out of 168, slightly over one percent, should be barren is a low rate, and, of course, we cannot be sure whether their childlessness was due to deficiencies in the women or in their husbands. Even if one of the 2 recently married women turns out to be unable to conceive, 3 barren women out of 168 is not even 2 percent. Stanley and Ruth Freed (see *Fertility, Sterilization, and*

Population Growth in Shanti Nagar, India: A Longitudinal Ethnographic Approach, New York: American Museum of Natural History, 1985) in their 1978 study of a largely Jat village in Delhi also found about 2 percent of the ever-married women to be barren. They point out that this proportion agrees with the proportion found by Wyon and Gordon in their 1960s study of Khanna villages in Ludhiana district, Punjab.

Mothers stated causes, and ages of death for 137 of the 207 children who died; of the 82 women who had lost children,73 gave causes of death. There are various observations to be made about the mothers' reports. First, there were only two reports that deaths had been due to shadow-spirits *(opri).* This represents a considerable change from the 1950s when an elaborate indigenous theory of

Plate 5

In the 1950s, most people believed diseases and epidemics were caused by goddesses. A Jogi waits by the Kali shrine to receive offerings. (Photo: Patricia Hitchcock)

diseases held sway, complete with disease goddesses (Shitala, Ujali, Kali, etc.), malignant ghosts, sorcery, evil eye, and curses – fascinating to a graduate student who had just taken a course in Anthropology of Religion; but I prefer the current theories of disease in Khalapur. The villagers now name diseases or ailments – pneumonia, measles, tetanus, TB, diarrhoea, dysentery, jaundice, rickets, boils – familiar with the idea that there is an "English medicine" to cure each, an expectation already well-established in 1984. Some of the mothers' diagnoses were vague – "sick" or "fever".

Plate 6

A thing of the past: In the 1950s, Khalapur villagers put pots of water on their roofs, in hopes that Mata, the smallpox goddess would cool herself by bathing in the pot of water, and then move on. (Photo: Patricia Hitchcock)

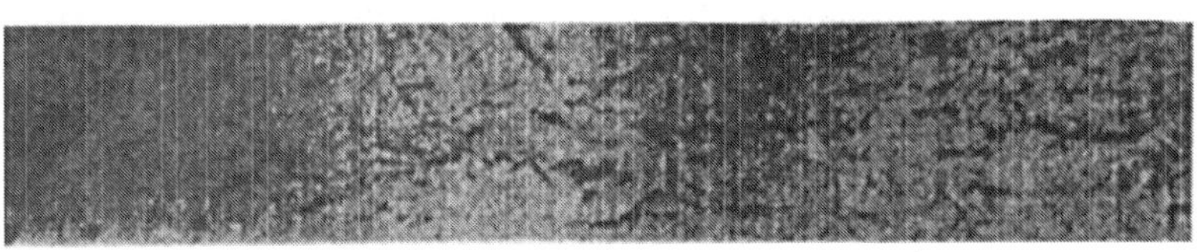

An elderly Rajput widow (b. 1932) told us in spring 1997 that she is now a disciple of Radha Saomi Byas. The women of her khandan still give offerings to Shitala and Ujali [pox goddesses, called *Mata*], but the widow believes only in Byas. Concerning the *Mata*, she said, "I fold my hands and tell her not to come. I only show my children to doctors. God is the keeper. I don't believe in going to *bhagats* [those who cure by communicating with spirits]."

Even in 1984, in our eliciting of accounts about treatment of children's illnesses, only one elderly Harijan woman (b. 1917) spoke of consultations with a *jogi* who did *jhars* (ritual sweeping with a broom to rid a sick person of bad spirits) and a *siana* (wise man) who used *pan* leaf emulsions for cures. Belief in "English medicine" and medical doctors is well-established even in the minds of elderly women.

The second feature of the mothers' reports about their children's deaths had to do with the time of death. The distribution of times of death appear in Table 4.4.

Table 4.4

Time of Children's Deaths from Wives in 5% Sample of Khalapur Khandans

At birth	30 cases	22%
After birth, but in first month	26 cases	19%
After first month, but up to 1 year	21 cases	15%
Between ages 1 and 5	48 cases	35%
Between ages 6 and 10	4 cases	3%
Over 10 years of age	8 cases	6%
Total	137 cases	100%

What were the causes of deaths at birth ? Eleven were still-born, seven were premature, and nine died at birth or immediately after. One baby had an intestinal obstruction; another had no anus; and one was a breech birth.

Among those who died in the first month, there were ten reports of tetanus, one measles, eight "fever", one pneumonia, three could not suckle, two "sick", and one ghost (*opri*).

So, a first point on babies who died at birth – less than half of the children's deaths are reported to have been connected with birth (56 out of 137 reports), if we count all the deaths at birth or within the first month.

A second point is that deaths of children have gone down dramatically. Table 4.5 shows the wives divided by decades of their births, noting the decades during which they gave birth to their children, the average number of children born, the average number who died, and the average number who survived. What this table, developed from the reproductive histories of the 168 Khalapur wives, shows is that the number of children dying for the average wife has gone down sharply from the situation before Independence when the average mother lost more children to death than she had surviving. After Independence, in the 1950s and 1960s, the death rate was halved. It went down a further 33 percent in the 1960s and 1970s, went down by more than half again in the 1980s, down to no children lost to death so far for wives born in the 1970s who are now in their reproductive phase.

Table 4.5

Khalapur Wives from a 5% Sample of Khandans Subdivided by Decade of Birth and Decade of Child-bearing: Children Borne, Lost to Death

Born:	*Pre-1920*	*1920s*	*1930s*	*1940s*	*1950s*	*1960s*	*1970s*
Bearing in	1920–40s	40–50s	50–60s	60–70s	70–80s	80–90s	90s-
No. of women	13	15	22	20	26	45	27
Avg. no. born	6.92	6.33	6.82	6.60	5.50	3.29	1.52
Avg. no. died	3.75	3.27	1.64	1.20	1.38	0.47	0
Avg. no. survived	3.17	3.06	5.18	4.4	4.12	2.82	1.52
Percent mo loss*	85%	80%	73%	60%	65%	31%	0%

*This is the percentage of mothers who lost one or more children to death.

By the 1980s, it would appear that villagers had recognized that children's chances of survival had greatly improved. Women born in the 1960s, most of whom had completed their families by 1997 had borne about 3 children on an average. half the number their mothers-in-law and grandmothers-in-law had borne.

Another way to look at the change in the numbers of children dying is to compare the percentages of women in each age cohort who lost one or more children to death. In the oldest group born before 1920, 85 percent of the mothers lost one or more children. Among the mothers born in the 1960s, bearing their children in the 1980s and 1990s, only 31 percent lost one or more children. In the youngest cohort, born in the 1970s, no Khalapur wife has yet lost a child to death.

A third way to look at the change in child mortality is to divide the children by the decades of their births and to calculate the proportion of children who survived to the age of 10. In Table 4.5 all children who died were included, whatever the age of their deaths. In Table 4.6, the fates of the children of 150 women in the 5 percent sample is given according to their survival to the age of 10. 90 percent of the 205 children's deaths occurred before the age of 10. Indeed, among the 99 females who died, 86 percent died by the age of 3; among the 106 males who died, 81 percent died before the age of 3. Out of the 99 deaths of females, only 4 occurred over the age of 20; among 106 deaths of males, 7 occurred over the age of 20.

Table 4.6

Proportions of Children who Survived to the Age of Ten According to the Decade of Birth among the 746 Children Born to 150 Women in the 5% Sample from Khalapur Village

Children Born	*% Females to 10*	*% Males to 10*	*All to 10*
1920s	-(0)	40%(5)	40%(5)
1930s	38%(13)	54%(26)	49%(39)
1940s	57%	44%(45)	50%(80)
1950s	61%	64%(42)	62%(103)
1960s	83%(58)	74%(65)	78%(123)
1970s	88%(89)	87%(70)	87%(159)
1980s*	74%(65)	86%(80)	81%(145)
1990s*	87%(46)	98%(46)	92%(92)

* Of course, children born since 1987 have not had enough time to survive 10 years, but they are included here for completeness.

The decline in child mortality in Khalapur is again shown dramatically by a perusal of the proportions in Table 4.6. Note the rise in the proportions surviving to age 10 of those born in the 1950s as compared to those born in the 1940s, an increase from 50 percent survival to 62 percent survival. There is another 16 percent increase between the 1950s children and the 1960s children, from 62 percent to 78 percent, and a further 9 percent increase between the 1960s children and the 1970s children, from 78 percent to 87 percent. Almost all the children born in the 1990s, none of whom have had ten years in which to survive, were alive in 1997; their proportion of survivors is over 85 percent. Notice also that over the decades, the survival rate of male children is not consistently higher than that of female children.

This enormously impressive decline in child mortality has come about with hardly any hospitalization for birthing. I should add that although there are a dozen private doctors in the village, as well as one government doctor, none of these doctors includes obstetrics as part of his practice, although 3 have been reported by some women in our sample to have given labor-inducing injections. All dozen doctors are male. The strict *parda* in Khalapur has meant that parents have been slow to permit daughters to attend school. This continues to prohibit them from going to a male doctor. The few women, who have gone to a hospital in a birth emergency, have been treated in hospitals in nearby towns by female doctors or midwives.

We may explain the changes in child mortality with the availability of treatment for childhood ailments. So after Independence came the Community Development Project with a Village Level Worker who reported that he had performed 1,388 vaccinations in 1954 (see S.C. Dube *India's Changing Villages*, Routledge Kegan Paul 1958: 69); of the 10 children's deaths that mothers reported to have been due to smallpox, the most recent was in 1972; there were three each in the 1930s, 1940s and 1950s. The CDP also encouraged cleaning of wells, paving of muddy village paths, and the adoption of high-yielding seeds. The sugarcane cash-crop revolution that took off after Independence in western UP meant that landed households in Khalapur installed hand-pumps in their women's quarters' courtyards in the 1950s and 1960s, putting out of work the women of the watercarrier caste who had lugged pots of water from the village wells to women in *parda*, but probably drinking water was much cleaner thereby, since buffaloes, cows and bullocks are rarely tied near the pumps in the women's courtyards as they are commonly tied near village wells. Cleaner water should have lowered rates of dysentery and diarrhoea. The sugarcane earnings and higher wheat harvests also meant better food, resulting in reduction in rickets and hunger, one might expect, and, especially important with respect to pneumonia and colds, warm clothing in the winter and for some footwear all year round.

While in the mid-1950s, there was only one doctor, a Unani, in Khalapur, in the late 1970s and early 1980s, village sons set up offices to be village doctors. Not one of them had an MBBS degree; even the government doctor in 1997 lacked an MBBS degree. The latter and most of the private doctors have a Bachelor in Ayurvedic Medical Science (BAMS). Two Muslim doctors have Bachelor in Unani Medical Science (BUMS) degrees. Whatever their training all prescribe almost entirely "English medicine" – vitamins, pills, ointments, injections (antibiotics, glucose), eye washes, clean bandages.

Both the old and the new government Primary Health Care Centre buildings remain empty. The new one, erected in 1996, is supposed to have a ward for 6 or 8 beds, an operating theatre and sterile wash-up room, but it was unfurnished in May 1997 except for the desks of the doctor and the pharmacist. It would remain unfurnished until the arrival of an MBBS female doctor, we were told.

Plate 7

In mid-1954, the Village Health Worker of the Community Development Project inoculated over a thousand children in Khalapur (Photo: Patricia Hitchcock)

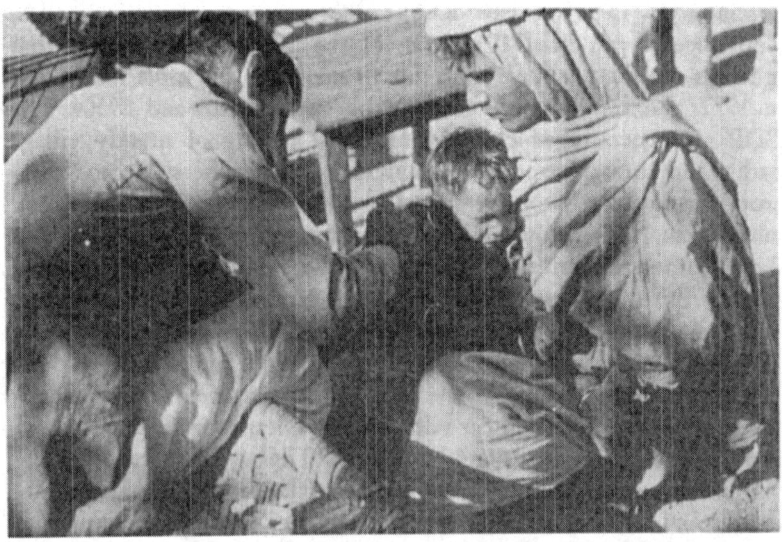

The government health workers who staff the Primary Health Care Centre (PHC) keep, at best, very short daily hours, since except for the sweeper, they all live outside the village, mostly in the nearby town. The villagers do not complain since they shun almost all of them as strangers anyway. The most effective of the staff is a upper-caste woman who lives in a town thirty miles away, with a tenth class education (Intermediate), trained as a Basic Health Worker and an Auxiliary Nurse-Midwife (ANM), who has been stationed in Khalapur since 1984. In spring 1997, she ran a wednesday inoculation clinic where small numbers of children received inoculations.

In the households of only four of the thirty-two *khandans* in the sample was it mentioned that members had been contacted by women workers from the Primary Health Centre -- three Rajput and one watercarrier household. Three of these are located near the edge of the

Plate 8

The old Primary Health Center, dedicated in 1962, unused in 1997. (Photo: Pauline Kolenda)

village closest to the PHC. One young Rajput mother (b. 1967) from the fourth khandan, whose aunt had had a PHC nurse attend her birthing, commented, "When labor is at night, the center is not open, and many births are at night."

In fairness, I should say that the shortage in attention from the health centre staff is not just because the doctor and health workers live outside Khalapur and are often late or absent, but because the doctor, at least, must serve other villages on alternate days of the week, and Khalapur is supposed to be served by a second doctor – the MBBS woman doctor who has not yet arrived. Another reason is that Khalapur is a very large village.

However, Khalapur is also a very prosperous village. Nineteen of the 32 khandans in my sample have land. In the 19 khandans were 385 persons, 73 percent of the 487 in the 1997 sample. And the landed, at least, avail of doctors and medical facilities in nearby towns. Some report even going as far as Meerut, Delhi, and Simla for special medical care. Better-off families already had their children immunized against various childhood diseases in 1984. The worst-off are the declining numbers of Muslims of Khalapur, most of whom are too poor to afford medical care. However, I did see some Muslims getting their children inoculated and visiting the free government doctor while we were in Khalapur in spring 1997.

All this far-less-than-ideal health care has worked, insofar as children's deaths have just about ceased. So there seems no need to hospitalize childbirth in Khalapur. The worst aspect, the tetanus from rusty sickles, seems to have been taken care of as Harijan midwives have learned to use new razor blades or scissors to cut the umbilical cord. Childhood diseases seem to have declined through vaccinations, inoculations, better nutrition, warmer clothing and shoes, cleaner drinking water, and "English medicine" dispensed by Ayurvedic or Unani doctors.

There continues to be in Khalapur almost no prenatal, natal or post-natal care. Almost all births are in a room in the women's quarters where a birthing mother sits on a pair of parallel bricks and pulls on the cot posts, or lies on a cot with a sister-in-law pushing on her swollen womb from behind and the Harijan midwife at her foot, ready to massage the would-be mother and catch or pull out the baby, and then clean it, the mother, and the birth room that have become 'polluted'. All three – mother, midwife and baby – are in the company of the new mother's mother-in-law and sisters-in-law and maybe some neighbours.

The major finding of this longitudinal study is that child mortality has declined to almost zero in Khalapur over the past 50 years, while births have declined substantially but still take place in much the same way -- at home with the help of a Harijan midwife and without the involvement of MDs or other modern medical practitioners. Several changes in standards of living and health environment, as well as in the child bearing beliefs and practices of these mothers are likely to be the reasons for the lower child mortality rate.

Acknowledgments

Thanks are owed to Mrs. Indira Sapru who accompanied me on most of the khandan interviews in the 1980s. In April-May, 1997, Angela Gorewala assisted me most of the time, with Shalini Parimwal assisting me at other times. Other 1980s researchers included Deepika Anand and Savitri Suri.

I offer thanks to both researchers and funding agencies, which supported my work as well as to J. Michael Mahar who allowed me to select a sample from the census he had directed, and to the gracious Rajput family whom I deem best to keep anonymous here, who hosted me and my team during 1984, 1985 and 1986, and again in 1997.

Part II

Kanyakumari

5

Memories of a Brahman *Agraharam* in Travancore

It was Martanda Varma, the conqueror, founder and king of Travancore, who, in 1753, had eighteen families of Tamil Brahmans come from the Thanjavur-Chidambaram area of the Tamil country, to receive from him the gift of 200 acres of tax-free inalienable land, two watering tanks, and a community of lower-caste slaves to do the cultivation for them. The two hundred acres the Maharaja purchased from the Kanyakumari temple which was not yet within the territory of Travancore (it was ceded to Martanda Varma's successor in 1766) (Velu Pillai 1940 II: 364--374). A village or area of land granted to Brahmans is called in Sanskrit an *agrahara*, or in Tamil, an *agraharam*.

This paper is about the descendants of the grantee Brahman families and other Brahmans who lived on the Brahman street called Dharmarajapuram in the revenue village of Kanyakumari in southern Tamilnadu (formerly southern Travancore) in the 1970s and early 1980s.

In his paper, "Recent Writings on the Social and Cultural Aspects of Modern South Indian History," in a volume edited by Robert E. Frykenberg and myself some years ago, G.A. Oddie says:

> A second problem is what happened to the Brahmans as a result of the rise of the non-Brahman movement? How did they attempt to counteract anti-Brahman agitation and adapt to a new and difficult situation? Apart from a few references in Irschick and in one or two other works very little has been written on the subject (Oddie 1985: 177).

Here I treat the reactions of ordinary, mostly elderly retired south Indian Tamil Smarta ("Iyer"[1]) Brahmans, whose sons work in scattered cities over India (Kolenda 1982) – in Madras, Bombay,

---

Revised version of a paper presented at the Nineteenth Conference on South Asia at the University of Wisconsin-Madison in a symposium: "Religion in South Indian History: An Interdisciplinary Perspective: In Honor of Robert E. Frykenberg", November 3, 1990.

Plate 9

Some of the houses on the south side of the Brahman street in Dharmarajapuram. (Photo: August 1978, by Pauline Kolenda)

Plate 10

Some of the houses on the north side of the Brahman street in Dharmarajapuram. (Photo: August 1978, by Pauline Kolenda)

Calcutta, Delhi, Kanpur, whom I got to know as an ethnographer in summer 1971, spring 1974, and summers 1978 and 1980.[2] As people in their fifties to eighties, some remembered as far back as the end of the nineteenth century, and thus experienced in their lives the sharp decline in the status of South Indian Brahmans throughout the twentieth century. These agraharam dwellers are not the people who were in the eye of the storm, but were at a distance watching. Yet their lives were strongly influenced by the anti-Brahman meteorology.

I
Introduction

Is there any other living group in any part of the world whose occupation has retained the precise content of its work, ritual and religious practices, its identity, its high status, as have the Vedic Brahmans of India? Such is the unbroken continuity of the Vedic Brahman's role that the pages of Basham's history of *ancient* India is informative about the Dharmarajapuram Brahmans of *today*, Brahmans still devoted to learning the *Rg*, *Sama* and *Yajur Vedas*, composed three thousand years ago, still performing the *sandhyas*,

> the morning, noon, and evening devotions which included reciting the Gayatri,[3] restraint of the breath, sipping and sprinkling water, and pouring libations of water to the sun .... (Basham 1954: 163);

and the myriad life cycle rituals, the *samskaras*, including the all-important ritual thread ceremony for adolescent boys, the *upanayana*, and the *shraddhas*, the commemorative ritual feeding of ancestors; and the Five Great Sacrifices thrice a day. These Tamil Brahmans still

Figure 5.1
Towns and Settlements Near Land's End Mentioned by the Brahmans of Dharmarajapuram

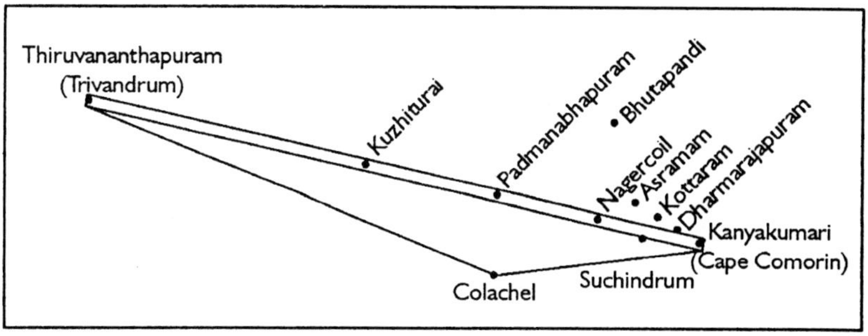

maintain the eight primeval *gotras*, the exogamous sub-divisions among Brahmans going back to the sages (*rishis*) (Basham 1954: 159, 161, 155, 170, 154).

In the Hindu state of Travancore (1729–1949), the Brahmans were privileged in much the way the Hindu law books, the *Dharmashastras*, said they should be. They lived under the patronage of the king, on grants of tax-free land, farmed for them by peasants -- in Dharmarajapuram, by untouchable agrestic slaves. As far back as Mauryan emperors in the fourth century B.C., "religion was protected by liberal grants to learned Brahmans..." (Basham 1954: 89).

The Brahmans have been held by the Hindu law books, assumed to have been written by Brahmans, to have the highest rank in the Hindu caste system. Other lower ranking castes/communities showed their respect for Brahmans by keeping their distance from them, not touching them, or passing on the contagion of their pollution through food or water, serving them, and leaving to them the care of the great temples and the gods, and above all, transmitting Vedic learning from one generation of Brahmans to the next.

The status and the welfare of the Dharmrajapuram Brahmans depended heavily upon the support of the Maharaja of Travancore, a Hindu king. There is a considerable literature on the relationship between the Brahman and the Hindu king. Louis Dumont claimed that the disjunction between the role of priest and the role of king was established in ancient Hindu doctrine and has persisted throughout Indian history. In *Homo Hierarchicus* (Dumont 1970a) and in his essay, "The Conception of Kingship in Ancient India" (Dumont 1970b), Dumont explained this basic principle of the caste system. He wrote:

> It is a matter of an absolute distinction between priesthood and royalty. Comparatively speaking, the king has lost his religious prerogatives: he does not sacrifice, he has sacrifices performed. In theory, power is ultimately subordinate to priesthood, whereas in fact priesthood submits to power. Status and power, and consequently spiritual authority and temporal authority, are absolutely distinguished (Dumont 1970a: 71–72).

The clear-cut distinction in the roles of king and Brahman means that the Brahman performs sacrifices and never rules; the king as Kashtriya rules, but never performs sacrifices. The latter is dependent upon the former for the necessary rituals by which the king receives supernatural reinforcement and support, or, at least, by which he buys off supernaturally evoked or induced obstacles or harassment. While the ruler is dependent upon the Brahman and is inferior to him, because of this lesser purity and incapacity to communicate with the divine power, still the Brahman cannot, within the duty of Brahman, rule in the secular sphere.

Thus, in Hindu tradition, there is an interdependence between the king and the Brahman, between the politico-economic and the religious powers. This tradition falls midway along a continuum of interdependence of the politico-economic and the religious. At one end of such a continuum would be societies like ancient Egypt in which the king was also the high priest, thus embodying both secular and religious powers. At the other end of the continuum would be societies, like those of the modern west, in which the political is almost completely secularized and almost absolutely separate from the religious. With the disjunction of the Hindu tradition, the politico-economic is only "relatively autonomous" (Dumont 1970b: 87), for in the dominant Hindu tradition, the politico-economic is dependent upon, and must defer to the religious.

The willingness of Brahmans to be religious mentors for rulers *of any stripe* may also be understood in terms of the anciently established ideology of the Hindus, according to Dumont, an ideology that did not support political unification of the Indian territory into a stable state or even into a series of stable states. So Dumont explains wryly:

> Not the slightest value or intellectual interest is attached for example to the stability of dynasties: there is nothing in the texts on this point. If someone stronger imposes his rule by doubtful methods, one can imagine that if he lavishly endows the Brahmans and 'toes the line' he will not lack henchmen (Dumont 1970a: 196).

Throughout Indian history, rulers, whether they were Muslim, Hindu, Buddhist or Christian, have depended upon Brahmans to be close advisers and aides, to be ministers, bureaucrats and officials. Such functions would seem to stem partly from the ancient role of the Brahman *purohita* or household priest of the king, advising the king about his proper duty, as well as sacrificing to the divine on his behalf. It can be seen then to have been a very traditional move for Brahmans in various parts of India to have striven to join the service of the British government; they had so striven for other rulers before.[4]

There are probably few places in India where the way of life of the ancient Vedic Brahmans was lived with such integrity as in the

Hindu state of Travancore, and lived so up to contemporary times. Originally Brahmans learned in the Vedas and Shastras[5], some of the Dharmarajapuram Brahmans became officials in the Maharaja's government. The learned Brahmans of the agraharam did, as well, take on the sins of the Maharaja by accepting his gift of land and food, sins which they expunged from themselves through devoted chanting to the gods and Vedic learning.

Samuel Mateer, a London Missionary Society minister, who wrote a fine book on Travancore, published in 1871, described the Brahmans in Travancore as follows:

> The Brahmans in Travancore have secured for themselves a singularly high and unfair superiority over all other classes – very different from their present position in British India. Though comparatively so few in number (little more than three percent of the whole population), they are the only class that are free from all social and religious disabilities, and enjoy perfect liberty of action. The whole framework of Hinduism has been adapted to the comfort and exaltation of the Brahman. His word is law; his smile confers happiness and salvation; his power with heaven is unlimited; the very dust of his feet is purifying in its nature and efficacy.... He is professedly the pure and exalted priest, separate from all that is "common or unclean" (Mateer 1871: 31–32).

> Hinduism is the established religion of the state, and is sustained and supported by all its power, wealth, and social influence. The theory is that all other classes are created for the service of the Brahmans, and that the highest possible virtue consists in obedience and homage being rendered to them. Their influence and authority are supposed to extend over all the acts and relationships of life, and everything enjoyed or possessed by others comes, they affirm, from the favour of the Brahmans, and belongs properly to them... This state is still therefore one of the great strongholds of Hinduism and caste in the south of India, and is distinguished as "the Land of Piety and Charity" for its liberal support of the Brahmanical religion and priesthood (Mateer 1871: 158–159).

In the 1860s, almost one-third of the revenues of the state went to support Hindu temples, feeding houses for Brahmans, and religious ceremonies, Mateer tells us (Mateer 1871: 72, 159).

Dharmarajapuram is not the only agraharam or Brahman street in old south Travancore. There is an agraharam two miles to the south, around the great temple to Kanyakumari, the virgin goddess, once to-be-bride of Shiva, and another six miles away around the great Dravidian temple, Suchindrum, and another near Suchindrum, called Asramam. The municipality of Nagercoil, twelve miles to the north of Dharmarajapuram, absorbed into its boundaries, as it expanded, the agraharams at Meenakshipuram, Vadiveeswaram, Krishnankoil, Parvatipuram and Ozhuginasery. The Brahmans of Dharmarajapuram have close marriage ties with all those agraharams. And in those agraharams also the old orthodox way of life has been followed, as closely as possible, given the condition of modern times. This network of intermarrying Brahmans are Tamil-speakers. Thus, the Tamil Brahmans of Dharmarajapuram originally came from Chidambaram, another great temple center, three hundred miles to the northeast in Tamilnadu.

The Vedic Brahman way of life, traceable back for two or three millennia, has been on a lingering deathbed throughout this century. The district of Kanyakumari, once part of the kingdom of Travancore, is now part of the modern Indian state of Tamilnadu, home of the most vigorous anti-Brahman political movement known in contemporary Indian history. Brahmans make up only a tiny percentage of the population of Tamilnadu – about 3 percent – and the vast majority of non-Brahmans and low-caste people in a modern democratic state have grasped political power and rejected the high status of Brahmans of old times. As Tamil Brahmans in Travancore for two hundred years, the Dharmarajapuram Brahmans were a component of the two or three percent Brahmans of that state (Jeffrey 1976: 330).

This paper tries to treat the issue of Brahman reactions to the anti-Brahmanism of the non-Brahman movement by listening, if very briefly, within the confines of a short presentation, to the voices of Tamil Brahmans who lived in an agraharam in southern Kanyakumari district of Tamilnadu. Kanyakumari district, as part of the old princely state of Travancore, after Indian independence, was part of the new state Travancore-Cochin between 1949 and 1956. As part of states' reorganization, Kanyakumari district broke off from the rest of Travancore and joined the new state of Tamilnadu, beginning in 1956. The rest of Travancore was merged with old Cochin and Malabar to form the state of Kerala (Schwartzberg 1978: 77–78, and End Cover Insert). Thus, the Brahmans of Dharmarajapuram are the descendants of grantees from the Maharaja of Travancore, but are now living in the state of Tamilnadu.

In talks with more than a score of agraharam natives and residents, they told me of their lives there, of the history of their agraharam, and interpreted their Brahmanhood for me. I emphasize the "for me", because I have come to see that their stories leave out certain crucial elements, revealed when I compare theirs with the stories told by historians of South India like Robin Jeffrey and others. Their stories might have been fuller or different in many ways if told to someone else.

An issue that must has been of long concern to the Dharmarajapuram Brahmans and to their forebears was the activities of Christian missionaries and of their converts over the past century and a half in southern Travancore. In northern Travancore, there were communities of Syrian Christians whose history goes back to the early centuries after Christ, and there were Roman Catholics in various parts of Travancore, including the fishermen in nearby Cape Comorin. While there had been Roman Catholic missionaries since the coming of the Portuguese to southwestern India in the late fifteenth century, the Protestant missionaries did not come until the early nineteenth century, and the first Protestant missionary in Travancore came to a village within a few miles of Dharmarajapuram; the town of Nagercoil, twelve miles to the north, became one of the major Christian centers of south India. The Protestant missionaries were especially successful with the local *avarnas* or low castes, namely, the Shanars, more recently called Nadars, whose caste occupation was climbing palmyra palm trees to tap tubers for their sweet sap, made into palm sugar or toddy, and the Parayas, untouchables, locally known as Sambhavars, usually agrestic servants of higher castes.

Indeed, the eighteen families of slaves whom the Maharaja had given the eighteen families of Brahmans in 1753 were Sambhavars. These families were freed from slavery in the latter part of the nineteenth century, and in the 1970s none of their descendants worked any longer for the Brahmans, but their past was well known, and the Brahmans must have found it galling that their former slaves had converted to Christianity in considerable numbers.

About one-third of the population of both Kanyakumari district and Agasteeswaram taluk, where Dharmarajapuram is located, is Christian, as compared to almost two-thirds Hindu; there are a few percent Muslims. Within a quarter of mile of Dharmarajapuram live many lower-caste Christians.

But the topic of Christianity rarely came up in my conversations with the Brahmans. They never asked me my religious affiliation, but probably categorized me as a Christian. They were not so reticent about the British, with whom they might also have associated me, although all the men were at least high school educated and knew the difference between Britain and America; their comments about the British were mixed: some positive, some negative.

Most of the talk quoted in this paper took place in 1974. The Head Trustee of Dharmarajapuram, Subramaniam, spoke to me in English. Others spoke Tamil and what they have said is translated. In all instances, the words spoken are theirs. The characters are *not* composites of a number of persons. Only their names have been changed, and, of course, the words are only a small excerpt of what each said to me and my female research assistant, also a Tamil Brahman, born in the agraharam, but brought up in Trivandrum. Before hearing from them, some background to the situation of Brahmans in the former princely state of Travancore might be helpful.

II

Background: The Princely State of Travancore

Unlike much of the rest of the South Asian peninsula, the southwestern Kerala strip that composed Travancore was very little influenced by Islamic culture or by Muslim rulers. The most serious threat was that of Tippu Sultan and his father, Hyder Ali, rulers of parts of Mysore to the north of Malabar. The Travancore army, aided by an unseasonable monsoon, and a British diversionary threat of attack upon Mysore, repelled the invading Tippu in 1790, after he had taken Malabar and Cochin to the north of Travancore (Velu Pillai 1940 II: 216–221). Thus, a traditional Hindu kingdom endured there until 1949 when the Maharaja of Travancore ceded the state to new independent India.

Despite a century of modernization through the intervention of British residents and *dewans* (prime ministers), and later through educated South Indian dewans and officials, the most rigid caste restrictions in Hindu India persisted there up to the 1930s (Hutton

1951: 79–85), as did the exalted position for Brahmans, devoted worship of the gods, and remarkably substantial support for Brahmans and temples from the Maharajas.

The princely state of Travancore was established by a process of unification – partly through conquest, partly by treaty – carried out by Martanda Varma, the king of Venad, a small principality, located about eighteen miles northwest of Dharmarajapuram. He was aided by British and French arms, and a firm alliance with the British East India Company; he won at the expense of factions of princes within Venad, and of neighboring rival princes, and of the Dutch who were defeated decisively at the port of Colachal, twenty-two miles west of Dharmarajapuram.

During its history, from 1729 up to 1949, Travancore was reputed to be a Dharmaraj, a country ruled (*raj*) according to ancient Hindu religious law, *dharma*. The founder, Martanda Varma, who reigned from 1729 to 1758, dedicated his kingdom to Padmanabha, a manifestation of the god Vishnu, to whom the great Dravidian temple in Trivandrum is dedicated. The king thus became the god's servant or *das*; a title of the Maharaja of Travancore was Padmanabhadas (Velu Pillai 1940 II: 347 ff; Pillai 1941: 15). Martanda Varma also greatly increased the elaborateness and number of ceremonies to be held at the great temples of his kingdom -- at the Padmanabhaswami temple in Trivandrum, the Suchindrum temple, the Kanyakumari temple at Cape Comorin and many others.

In order to free himself from the kinship networks, factions and intrigues of the native Malayalam-speaking landed Nayars and Nambudiri Brahmans, Martanda Varma brought in Tamil Brahmans to administer his new territories, including his prime minister or *dewan*, Rama Aiyar (Menon 1878: 110–111, cited by Jeffrey 1976: 3; Low 1978: 379). Under the supervision of his dewan, Rama Aiyar, Martanda Varma had several *uttupuras* (feeding houses) and *valiyampalams* (rest houses) constructed for the convenience of Brahmans. The *uttupuras*, attached to Travancore temples, gave Brahmans free meals daily throughout the year. In 1851, there were 41 such feeding houses for Brahmans in various parts of Travancore (Jeffrey 1976: 7, 274, citing the *Travancore Calendar* of 1851). A title of the Maharaja of Travancore was "Annadatha", giver of food. While such charity to Brahmans was a long established institution in the kingdoms of Kerala, Martanda Varma considerably extended the largesse of his constituent territories (Velu Pillai II: 337–338).

Although Martanda Varma succeeded in his unification through the aid of the British merchants' soldiers, the rulers of Travancore did not accept British paramountcy until 1795, and the British resident stationed in Trivandrum did not take a strong hand in Travancorean affairs until there was a rebellion against the prime minister which British troops managed to put down in 1805 (Woodcock 1967: 189).

Major John Munro, the Resident representing the British Indian government from 1810 to 1819 at the Maharaja of Travancore's court, and dewan of Travancore from 1811 to 1814, began a series of reforms, including the state's taking over control of hundreds of temples of the kingdom. He brought with him a number of administrators who were by caste Desastha Brahmans, Marathi-speakers from Tanjore, in the Madras Presidency. Between 1817 and 1877 the dewans of Travancore were Desastha Brahmans or Tamil or Telugu Brahmans (Jeffrey 1976: 6,8).

Throughout the nineteenth century, however, most Travancore government employees were Nayars. Nayars were Hindus of middle caste rank, cultivators and soldiers, famed for their matrilineages and matrilineal descent, natives of Travancore for centuries, who composed between 15 and 30 percent of the population of Travancore during the nineteenth century (Jeffrey 1976: 330). In 1847, there were 8,000 or 9,000 government servants, all of whom were either Nayars or non-Malayali (almost entirely Desastha or Tamil) Brahmans (Jeffrey 1976: 34); lower castes, like the Iravas and Shanars, were excluded from government service, as were Christians and Muslims (Jeffrey 1976: 9, 197). Although the non-Malayali Brahmans were very small in number in Travancore, composing between one and two percent of the Travancore population during the nineteenth century (Jeffrey 1976: 330), they were disproportionately wealthy. Only the Malayali Brahmans, the Nambudiris, were more wealthy; the Nambudiris never became government servants. But, the Dasastha and Tamil Brahmans were wealthier proportionate to their sizes than were the Nayars (Jeffrey 1976: 29). And, the non-Malayalis, Dasashta and Tamil Brahmans, were represented in the government in disproportionate numbers. There were 2,900 of them out of a total of 8,000 or 9,000 government servants in 1847, and many of them had high positions, including the dewanship (Jeffrey 1976: 8, 28).

One of the arguments for the need for Brahmans in the government was the requirement that only Brahmans could supervise the Hindu temples and the Brahman rest and feeding houses under the government's surveillance (Jeffrey 1976: 197–198). The non-Malayali Brahmans were reputed to have great influence with the Maharajas during the nineteenth and twentieth centuries (Jeffrey 1976: 26).

The Nayars, as Hindus, respected the Brahmans as holders of higher religious and ritual status , even giving their women as sexual partners to Brahmans as a meritorious gesture (Jeffrey 1976: 13, 184). Some of their western-educated members, however, began to doubt the value of their matrilineal system and their traditional Hindu values in the latter nineteenth century. By the 1880s, there was a noticeable number of unemployed western-educated Nayar men, and some Nayar educated leaders mounted an anti-Brahman campaign, criticizing the Brahman (Dasastha) dewan, the Maharaja, and the Maharaja's favorite counselor, also a Brahman (Tamil), and complaining that the non-Malayali Brahman element in the government was maintained "while the number of educated, unemployed Nayars was increasing" (Jeffrey 1976: 159–163, quote from 163). Advantages enjoyed by the Brahmans, besides their high positions in the Travancore government, were their immunity to taxation and their right to feed at the "choultries" (Brahman feeding houses) at public expense, complained the members of the Nayar-led society, the Malayali Sabha, in a 1891 Memorial to the Maharaja (Jeffrey 1976: 169).

The new dewan who came in shortly thereafter, a Tamil Brahman named Shungarasoobyer, tried to right the situation for Nayars, by promoting Nayars already in the government and hiring more new Nayar recruits (Jeffrey 1976: 178). As a very religious Brahman, he came to be seen as the enemy of the Christians seeking jobs in the government, however, rather than the enemy of the Nayars (Jeffrey 1976: 179–180, 190–199, 204).

This late nineteenth century anti-Brahmanism in Travancore probably affected the Brahmans of Dharmarajapuram. As many of their comments attest, they were especially sensitive to the condemnation of them as privileged persons regularly fed free at temples. They saw their later loss of this privilege as seriously affecting their welfare.

Another nineteenth century movement that undermined Brahman status was Christian missionizing. At the beginning of the nineteenth century, the British East India Company relented in its firm exclusion of missionaries from India, and by 1806, there were English Protestant missionaries in Travancore. The Governor-General of Madras did not hesitate to interfere in Travancore affairs when necessary, and that sometimes was at the behest of Travancore missionaries, as in the breast-cloth controversy of 1859, well-described by Robert Hadgrave's *The Nadars of Tamilnadu* (Hardgrave 1969: 65--69). The Nadars are a major caste population of low rank in southern Travancore and southern Madras Presidency (now Tamilnadu), many of whom converted to Christianity.

The Maharajas of Travancore emerge through the historical accounts as supporters of missionary educational endeavors. So Maharaja Swathi Tirunal invited J. Roberts, headmaster of a school in Nagercoil, to establish an English school in the capital at Trivandrum in 1836, called the Rajah's Free School (Nagam Aiya 1906: II: 247--248). But, the Maharajas were also highly religious Hindus; none of them converted to Christianity, and they were able to sustain an intensely orthodox Hindu regime, and to have ensured the high position of Brahmans right up through the mid-twentieth century.

The Christian missionary activities affected Brahmans in two ways. First, it was largely through missionaries in Travancore that western-style education was introduced -- a form of education that soon became more prestigious and useful than Sanskritic Hindu education. Secondly, lower-caste people were given access to education, upsetting the caste regime that excluded lower castes from Sanskritic Hindu education, reserving it only for the higher castes, particularly the Brahmans.

III

Dharmarajapuram and Some of its Denizens

Along the Cape-to-Nagercoil road between Nagercoil and Cape Comorin are to be seen bastians of fortifications erected by de Lennoy, the Flemish engineer who worked for Martanda Varma in the 1720s and 1930s. One such opaque rectangular brick solid stands near the bus-stop where one gets off the bus to go in to Dharmarajapuram. These brick oblongs in a line separated Martanda

Varma's kingdom, on the west of the narrow expanse of land, perhaps four miles wide, from that of the Nawab of Arcot and the immediate lands of the Kanyakumari temple on the east.

Crossing the road to get to that cart-track leading in, one sees a pilgrims' rest house, an arcaded white-washed room, still usable but built long ago. Rice from land held by the Dharmarajapuram Trust is designated to be used to feed nine Brahman pilgrims each day, as they rest here on their journey between the Suchindrum temple to the north six miles and the Kanyakumari temple to the south two miles. To do this feeding is the duty of one of the temple *pujaris* in the employ of the Dharmarajapuram Trust, but I was not aware, when I worked in Dharmarajapuram in the 1970s and 1980s that this feeding was done anymore. The rest house is a remnant of the days when Travancore was a *dharmaraj* and the Dharmarajapuram Brahmans could afford to give charity to pilgrims, indeed of days when pilgrims walked from great temple to great temple rather than tootling from one to another by bus.[6]

On the other side of the lane leading into the agraharam is a small Pillayar temple. This is one of the two Dharmarajapuram temples taken over by the government, and is administered by the Tamilnadu State Devaswam Board[7] which employs a pujari to care for the temple and its deities.

If we walk in from the Cape road a hundred yards or so, we see a huge, beautiful tank, more like a lake. Besides 200 acres, the 18 Brahman families received two tanks in the original *danam* from which to water their fields. The larger one, near the entrance of the village, still is used in cultivation, but the other became silted up and eventually became a paddy field that is owned communally by the village and is looked after by the agraharam trustees. The produce from that land is used to employ two *purohitas* or household priests to serve the families of the agraharam, as well as a temple priest for the Shiva and Shasta temples. The two "government temples", the Pillayar and Krishna temples, are cared for by a pujari employed by the State Devaswam Board. The trust land also pays the costs of *pujas* in the temples and for other religious celebrations. There are, in addition, various lands willed to the trust by former residents, to pay for the employment of a Vedic teacher and the costs of various religious rites.

Beyond the tank, we can see some of the paddy fields belonging to the agraharam. The original 200 acres were divided among the heirs of the original ancestral families at the turn of the century. Much of the land has been sold by individual owners, but some of it is still owned by Brahmans of the agraharam, some of whom are direct descendants of the original 18 families, some of whom are descendants of relatives by marriage with the danam families, some of whom are descendants of ancestors who moved in after the danam, but a century or more ago, some of whom have bought Dharmarajapuram land more recently.

Off in the distance beyond the tank, lost among a stand of palm trees is the *cheri*, the settlement of Sambhavar Parayas, whose ancestors were the Brahmans' slaves. They were "freed" in the 1880s, and none of them now work for the Brahmans. Those in the Brahmans' employ in the 1970s and 1980s were mostly Nadars from nearby hamlets.

We now turn away from the tank to the entrance to the agraharam. Near it is a white stuccoed gracefully arcaded brick stand, a resting place for the goddess Kanyakumari when she comes to hunt in October. She comes from Cape Comorin "riding a silver horse" -- actually carried on poles -- and after her "hunt", she rides through the Brahman street, blessing one and all.

The gateway to the Brahman street was barricaded up to the mid-1930s; people of other castes or religions were prohibited from walking on the Brahman street. The stone supports for the gateway are still there, but there is no gate.

Just inside is a huge (perhaps five feet tall) *lingam* marking the place where a great grandfather of one of the presently resident danam descendants died while in *samadhi*, in religious trance. His body, still sitting in trance, is said to be beneath the *lingam*. In the minds of some of the village residents, this represents the supremacy of the *jnana marg*, the mystical path to union with the divine.

To the left, before we are actually onto the street, is the brick high-walled village bathing *ghat*; one has to go inside a doorway in the wall to see the water tank itself. Especially the temple pujaris must bath here before beginning their daily work in the inner sanctums of the temples, but others also bathe here before entering temples.

To the east of the tank is the small Shiva temple, and next to it is a two-story building, the *Bajan Mandam*, where a group of young men gather from time to time to sing devotional hymns.

And still before we are onto the street of Brahmans proper, we pass, on the right, large houses quite recently built, and after three such houses comes the impressive trust building where the paddy from the common fields are stored, the accounts books are kept, and the head trustee does his administrative and office work. There are large rooms in the building serving as *kalyanam mandabam* -- a place for weddings.

Then comes the long, long street itself. Across from the trust building and heading the street is the Krishna temple. The portal of the small, red-and-white-striped temple looks out on the houses in two long rows facing each other across a broad street, about 30 houses to a side. Like the brownstones of London or Brooklyn, or rows of slave quarters in the American south, there is no space between the sides of the long, narrow houses. Like railroad cars, the rooms in a house stretch back one behind the other, from a verandah (porch) where lower-caste people and strangers may be greeted, to inner ones like the family sitting room, then puja room, then kitchen, then cattle shed, and finally a long garden and yard.

In the evening when the *arti* takes place at the Krishna temple, Brahmans can just step out of their houses and face toward the temple and be blessed by the priest waving the tray containing burning camphor and coals and a tiny oil lamp, a means of connecting god and humans. So, the street forms the antechamber to the inner sanctum that is the temple.

Subramaniam, the head trustee, was in his eighties when he spoke to me in 1974. A thin graceful elder, dignified and eloquent, he sometimes wore bushshirt and trousers, appropriate to his former work as a construction manager in the town of Nagercoil, sometimes simple *dhoti* and sacred thread, appropriate to a religious learned Brahman. He is the manager of the trust lands, keeping accounts, arranging for sale of rice, rental of land, and use of the produce for religious purposes. A danam descendant, his home is in the nearby town of Nagercoil, but he spends much time in Dharmarajapuram managing the trust.

Subramaniam: My father was Shankaranarayan. His father was Bagavate Ishwara Shrotigal. His father was Subramaniam. His father was Abatatorna. That is as far back as I can trace – that is probably back to the time of the danam.

The story goes that the Travancore highness was at the forefront of battle, fighting for large areas of land against the Muslim conquests of Tippu Sultan and Mukhdum[8] and he killed many. He felt, "I am a sinner. It is my duty as a king to conquer. But warfare is not necessary, the loss of lives." He felt he was a sinner. He was advised by astrologers to expiate his sins by extending relief to Vedic scholars.

The danam was given so the Brahmans would give *tapasya*[9] for the welfare of the community, so the Maharaja can expiate his sins. He invited Brahmans and made them a gift of a certain area, and provided facilities for their stay. The Maharaja feels mental consolation by having gifted sufficient wealth and set up certain Brahman families in different parts of the state. They are supposed to think of him, pray for him, remain loyal to him, and do the duties expected of them as Brahmans.

My father was an Ishwara *sevai*[10], paid from the Maharaja's private income. He and some others went every morning at 6 to the Kanyakumari temple to pray for the Maharaja. Just as at the Trivandrum temple, there were 22 Brahmans to pray for the Maharaja, at the Kanyakumari temple, there were six – four lived here in Dharmarajapuram. I myself did such praying, taking my father's place, when my father could not go. For this praying, each Brahman got rice, oil, and two rupees from the Kanyakumari temple. The praying involved prostration before the goddess, saying portions of the *indrajit* while thinking of the Maharaja.

PK: This is Krishna, a retired teacher, who devotes himself to religious study. He, too, is thin and dignified, but his face is more smiling and kindly than the authority face of Subramaniam. Unlike Subramaniam, he always wears dhoti, sacred thread, and ashes across his forehead and shoulders, for he seldom leaves the agraharam.

Krishna: I was born in the agraharam at the Kanyakumari temple in Cape Comorin in 1905. Two or three families of Iyers are *arcakkars*[11] in the Kanyakumari temple there. There are also some Iyer peons and two Potti families who do puja. The rest of the Brahmans there are landlords.

This danam was given by Martanda Varma by purchasing Kanyakumari temple land and then giving it to Brahman families *gratis*.

Plate 11

A Dharmarajapuram Brahman and his wife. The husband, aged 80 in 1974, was a teacher for thirty years in various places in Travancore. For much of that time, he was the headmaster of a teachers' training college. When interviewed in July, 1978, he spoke in English. He said that he had been born in the *agraharam* in the village of Kanyakumari, but because his mother died shortly after his birth, he had been brought up by his mother's brother in Trivandrum. At age 12, he married his mother's brother's daughter who was aged 8 or 9. He took both a B.A. degree and B.T.(Teacher), probably in Trivandrum.. In the photo, he wears a sacred thread and the stripes of devotion to Shiva, bestowed on his forehead by the temple-priest. He said that he had spent the thirty years since his retirement studying religion, reading books both in English and in Tamil. He learned to read Tamil after his retirement. He commented, "It takes many rebirths before one is an enlightened one *(gnani)* and has no desires." (Photo: Spring 1974, by Pauline Kolenda)

Plate 12

A Brahman, aged 76 in 1974, a retired schoolteacher who had lived in Dharmarajapuram, his father's mother's village, for more than 50 years. After seven years of schooling in a nearby village (where his father worked for the Travancore government as a temple-priest), he started teaching at the age of 17 in various elementary schools of the area, teaching in both Malayalam and Tamil. He married at age 21 to the first of his four successive wives, aged 12. She died in 1919 of smallpox, five months after the wedding. After his retirement from teaching in 1974, he worked as the postmaster for Dharmarajapuram for 15 years. (Photo: Spring 1974, by Pauline Kolenda)

Plate 13

Photograph of the Vedic chant group on their outing to Marutimalay, 1942

My father did not work. He had half an acre of paddy land in Dharmarajapuram. He got two free meals a day at the Kanyakumari temple – at the *namaskaras* in the morning and at the *uut* in the evening. His father-in-law was rich, having 15 acres, and his sisters' husbands were also rich.

As a teacher, I taught Malayalam, maths, history, everything except drawing and music. I came to Dharmarajapuram when I retired from teaching in 1960.

PK: What was the villagers' view of the Maharaja?

Subramaniam: The Maharaja is considered to be a Pradiksha Devam – a god whom one can see. People still feel that way about Chitra Tirunal. He goes daily to the Padmanabha temple in Trivandrum to pray. He still thinks of himself as a servant of Sri Padmanabha. He is just a servant – his *das*.

PK: Premavati, an ochre-sari'd widow in her seventies, who also devotes her entire time to religious activities, told us that she had seen first Maharaja Mulam Tirunal and then Maharaja Chitra Tirunal. The Maharaja used to come to Cape Comorin for two weeks, and she would see him. What was he like?

Premavati: The king is like a god. It is not for us to ask what he is like. Now these ministers and all are ordinary people, but the king was a god.

PK: Brahmans served in the Travancore administration as taluk officers, police inspectors, excise inspectors, teachers, administrators of temples and clerks of court. According to Robin Jeffrey, the Travancore government employed 25,000 people in the 1930s (Jeffrey 1978: 143). "The government service was the preserve of caste-Hindus" (Jeffrey 1978: 144). While Brahman males were the most literate of any of the major caste communities (Jeffrey 1978: 142), and the Brahmans of Dharmarajapuram were among the four-fifths of male Brahmans who were literate, according to the 1931 and 1941 censuses of Travancore, there were relatively few Brahmans who were literate in English; in 1931, there were only 8,226 Brahmans literate in English out of all Brahman communities in Travancore as compared to 37,296 Christians and 18,606 Nayars.

This is Sita and her husband. Her husband is a danam descendant. She also is a danam descendant through her mother.

Sita, wife of Ananda: I was married at the age of ten in 1919. I was born here in 1909. This is my mother's parental village, but my parents were living here when I was a small child, while my father, an official in the Maharaja's government, was working at the taluk[12] office nearby. He worked in several places in Travancore, from Trivandrum to Cape Comorin. My father's father was from Suchindrum. I went to school in Suchindrum and in Kuzhiturai[13], studying up to the 6th class.

My husband was 25 at the time of marriage.[14] The wedding took place at Bhutapandi[15] because my father was employed there then. My father knew English, because he had studied in Trivandrum up to matriculation.[16] My father's brother was also a taluk officer in Trivandrum.

I brought a small dowry of between 300 and 500 rupees. My *mama* spent this on clothing for the groom's sisters and others in the family to be present at the wedding. Now dowries cost 5,000 or 6,000 rupees and one can pay 500 for one sari. My husband's elder sister who was already married tied the *tali.*

After the wedding, I stayed with my parents for five years. Then I came to Dharmarajapuram in 1924 to live with my *mama* and *mami* and *patti* and my husband's tambi and two *tangachis.*[17] Upon marriage, I lived in this house.[18]

My brother was police inspector in Nagercoil. My husband's first younger sister was married in Trivandrum; her husband was an excise inspector. His other younger sister was married in Asramam; her husband was a teacher. His younger brother was also a teacher in a school in Kottaram.[19]

My husband worked for the Devaswam Board, and he lived in so many places, from Trivandrum to Cape Comorin. The Devaswam Board transferred him every year. At the time of our daughter's weddings, we were living in Nagercoil, and my son was studying at Sita Lakshmi Bai High School.

My son is a clerk in a second class magistrate's court in Tuticorin. He is a Tamilnadu state government servant. He is transferred every three years.

PK: In the view of many of the villagers, Brahmans are above all the repositories of the Vedas. A good Brahman should know the Vedas. A number of men used to meet in the 1930s to chant Vedas, beginning at three or four in the morning. Sons of these men have a photograph in their homes of the Vedic chant group of Dharmarajapuram taken on their outing to Marutimalay, a nearby mountain peak, in 1942, I was told (Plate 13). The son of the *vattiyar* or Vedic teacher who instructed them was a danam descendant who died in 1978 leaving no sons to carry on the tradition.

But a good Brahman also celebrates a series of life cycle rites called *samskaras*, as well as a series of calendrical rites. He prays to a series of gods in *sandhya vandanams* three times a day.

This is Rama, a purohita, wearing dhoti and sacred thread with his long hair knotted in a bun at the nape of his neck.

Rama, purohita: I am a Telugu priest who has been here for years, coming from Malapavur, near Tenkasi.[20] My ancestors came there from Velanadu, Andhra, 500 years ago. We speak Telugu in our houses. Tenkasi is a dry area. The climate does not suit people, and people there commonly go out for jobs. I had heard that in *this* village the purohita was paid monthly by the Dharmarajapuram Trust.

Here, I am in charge of the religious functions of the village, done by the villagers in their own homes. I serve all families here for birth, *upanayanam*, *simamtan*, *vivaham*, *jatakarna*, *namakarana*, *annaprashna*, *chowla*, birthday , 60th, 81st, death and *shraddhams.*[21] The latter should be done monthly during the first year, then annually.

Ladies' *vratas* include: Vinayaka Chaturthi, Karttigai Somavara puja, Navratri Devi puja, Shankarandi Suryanarayana puja, Shivratri, Amasomavama puja, Vaikashi puja , Krishna Jayanti, Ramanaumi, Rishipanchami, Saptarishi puja, as well as others.[22]

PK: There are many important life cycle rites. One of the most important is veneration of ancestors in shraddhams.

Subramaniam: We venerate our forefathers in the shraddhams. These rites help us to remember them , follow them and their ways. We think of our forefathers as gods themselves. We feed Brahmans at the shraddhams. We don't feed many -- just two, one on the mother's side and one on the father's side. It is not an ordinary feast. Only close relatives, those who claim a right of partnership in the *dyadhi*[23], hereditary rights in the property, participate. Only they can take food left after feeding the two Brahmans. One Brahman represents the father and his forefathers, and one represents the mother's side. We feed them, considering them as representatives of the dead ancestors on both sides. It is akin to idol worship.

The Brahmans selected as competent to be fed or to accept such feeding must possess ample religious faith. They must be ones doing penances, to cast away the sins committed. Such Brahmans must chant the Gayatri mantra at sunrise and do *sandhya vantanam* morning, noon and at sunset. The sin attached to the food goes to them, but we get mental consolation. They eat. This is conduct of the rituals as set down in the Vedas.[24]

PK : The gate to the Brahman street has long been open. The tenants of the Brahmans deliver paddy to their front doors now. Non-Brahman, even Christian, children go through the street on their way to school. Separation and aloofness from non-Brahmans and untouchables persists among the elderly Brahmans.

Subramaniam : After finishing at Scott Christian College,[25] I worked for ten years or so as a clerk in the judiciary. I was employed by many lawyers who thought well of me. I met many prominent lawyers that way. Then I went into the construction business with a Pillai, a Vellala,[26] a man who used to work for my father when my father was supervising the repair of the tanks here.

When I was going to school, that Pillai used to help me in various ways. As a clerk in the judiciary, I was earning 25 rupees a month, and I had heavy responsibilities – this was between 1100 and 1110 (1924--1934) before my daughter was born. I had to look after my parents who lived to a ripe old age. I had my sister's sons to help and some cousins also.

As for being a partner of that Pillai, I am unorthodox in that way. I mix with those of other caste. I don't eat with them or intermarry with them,[27] but they are people. I like people.

You can't reach the top of the ladder all of a sudden -- you must start at the bottom and climb up. The barber is to shave. The warrior is to fight. The Brahman is to do *tapas*, prayer for the welfare of all. Life must be in the service of mankind, for the welfare of humanity, not for oneself.[28]

PK : The Travancore Tamil Brahmans are a subordinated elite, a toppled elite. How do they react to this rejection of Brahmans? There were various milestones in that subordination in the view of the Dharmarajapuram Brahmans. A first was dewan Munro's taking over of the temple lands early in the nineteenth century.

Krishna, teacher: I read that under Maharani Lakshmi Bai, the dewan was Munro, and the temples then had plenty of lands. Munro had each temple manager come to Trivandrum, and had them calculate exactly what the needs of each temple were. Then he had all lands taken by the government and it gave each temple sums of money. He had them reduce their needs to the barest minimum.

PK: A second milestone in the history of their decline in the Brahman view was the Justice Party and the activities of E.V. Ramaswami Naicker.

Here is Mahesh Sharma, the purohita, a short, portly, round-faced man in his fifties, usually wearing bushshirt and dhoti. He works outside the village as a household priest and also supervises the cultivation of lands owned by Brahmans no longer residing in the village.

Mahesh Sharma, purohita : I am a Sama Veda purohita who served this village for over twenty years. I also looked after the Vinayakar and Shasta temples.

I was born in 1921. I attended a Vedapathshala between 1930 and 1942. I started at the age of nine and studied at Madurai, Chidambaram and Trivandrum.[29] I moved with my guru, Mahalinga Shrowdigal, as he moved from place to place.

Brahmans have had a hard time since independence. The British respected us. The first anti-Brahman party was the Justice Party founded by E.V. Ramaswami Naicker who died recently.

PK : Mahesh's twenty-year-old son, described some terrible things the D.K. Party, a successor to the Justice Party, had done, such as garlanding nude Rama and Laxman with strings of shoes.[30] He said the main slogan of the D.K. Party was: "Those who believe in God are fools."

Mahesh : The Justice Party complained that Brahmans were just lazy fellows being fed for free. All government jobs were held by Brahmans. Brahmans alone learned English. The non-Brahmans were uneducated.

PK : Mahesh Sharma is not quite correct in attributing to E.V. Ramaswami Naicker the founding of the Justice Party,[31] although Naicker was associated with it from 1925 on. Naicker was long a member of a pro-Congress Party group called the Madras Presidency Association, also proposing non-Brahman representation in the Madras Council (Irschick 1969: 61, 68). Mahesh is correct, however, in seeing the Justice Party as an important force in toppling the Tamil Brahmans from their government and religious positions under the British in the Madras Presidency.

Eugene Irschick's excellent history of the Justice Party in the Madras Presidency (Irschick 1969) shows that it was founded in 1916 by some educated non-Brahmans living in the city of Madras. The leadership included T.N. Nair,[32] a medical doctor and specialist on diabetes, and P. Tyagaraja Chetti, editor of a weekly, the *non-Brahmin*, who dedicated the party to gaining seats for non-Brahmans in the Legislative Council of the Madras Presidency and then gaining positions for non-Brahmans in the government bureaucracy.

By the late nineteenth century, the presidency government, headed by British officials, was staffed very largely by Indian educated men of Brahman caste. South Indian Brahmans had been especially quick to send some of their sons to learn English and to attend English-medium schools with English-style curriculum which included geography, sciences, mathematics, and English language and literature. Rather few non-Brahmans followed suit. There was a growing concern among the British officials by 1900 that their government was being run by these Brahmans. Irschick writes:

> After the 1850s the Telugu and particularly the Tamil Brahmans, who together comprised only 3.2 percent of the total population, enhanced their position in the social system by gradually filling the great majority of administration and educational positions then open to Indians. (Irschick 1969: 5) In public administration there was a marked preponderance of Tamil Brahmans, with Vellalaṣ and Telugu Brahmans occupying second place, followed by Nairs and Balija Naidus. In positions concerned with law, instruction, and letters, the pattern was similar (Irschick 1969: 13).

> As the possessors of learning, they were more and more indispensable in the government bureaucracy. But their very usefulness and skill aroused mistrust, because they were increasingly in command of large areas of the British administration and therefore in a position to suit their own, rather than British, ends (Irschick 1969: 19).

By 1916, the Indian Independence Movement led by the Congress Party was under way, especially strong in the areas around Bombay and Calcutta. Some educated non-Brahmans of Madras feared that with independence for India, rule in Madras would be transferred from the British to the Brahmans (Irschick 1969: 74). The Justice Party supported the continuance of British rule in return for the reservation of a proportion of the seats in the Madras Legislative Council for non-Brahmans.

The Justice Party waged election campaigns in 1919 and 1920 to prove that it could win even more seats than those reserved for non-Brahmans; it proved that non-Brahmans could be politically effective. Its elected representatives did succeed in getting the Council to pass legislation to hire government staff in better proportion to the caste components of the population (Irschick 1969: 236–244). So, according to M.N. Srinivas, the government order number 1129, dated December 15, 1928, issued by Public Service Department, provided that out of twelve posts "five had to go to non-Brahmin Hindus, two to Brahmins, two to Muslims, two to Anglo-Indians or Christians, and one to the Depressed Classes (Harijans)" (quoted in Srinivas 1966: 109).

The Justice Party representatives on the Madras Council also achieved passage of the Hindu Religious Endowments Act in 1925 that put the administration of the funds of Hindu temples and monasteries (*maths*) under the Government of Madras (Irschick 1969: 253).

E.V. Ramaswami Naicker, a non-Brahman and a Kannada Balija Naidu from Erode[33] (Irschick 1969: 332) had been one of the first members in 1917 of the Madras Presidency Congress Committee which was against British rule and in support of the policies of the national Congress Party (Irschick 1969: 332). He also was involved in the demonstrations at the Vaikom temple, the next milestone in Brahman decline, related below; for his speeches at Vaikom, Naicker was imprisoned in Travancore (Irschick 1969: 269). After the leadership and organization of the Justice Party declined, many of its members joined the Congress Party. Naicker himself broke from the Congress Party in 1925, worked in the Justice Party (Irschick 1969: 332) and founded the Self-Respect movement.

Naicker was the most flamboyant and popular of the non-Brahman politicians in the anti-Brahman movement, speaking in colloquial Tamil and addressing the untouchables most particularly. Like some others, he took up the message emerging from the scholarship of the nineteenth century missionaries like Robert Caldwell that there had been a high Tamil culture and civilization before the coming to South India of Aryan Brahmans, bearing Sanskrit religious learning and a rigid caste system, which allotted the Tamil indigenous people to the lower rank, and that there was a rich and old literature in the Tamil language (Irschick 1969: 277–281, 342).

One of the themes in Naicker's campaign of de-legitimization of the Brahmans was a new Dravidian interpretation of the great Hindu epic, the *Ramayana*, in which the king of Sri Lanka who had captured Queen Sita was the hero, and King Rama was an ineffective defeated wimp (Irschick 1969: 283–284, 294). The Hindu law books, the *Dharmashastras*, especially that by Manu, was denounced as an ancient but long-credited charter of the caste system and the subordination of Tamil non-Brahmans. At a number of meetings at which Naicker was present, copies of the *Laws of Manu* were burned, as a symbolic repudiation of the caste system (Irschick 1969: 339). Irschick explains:

> And it was the Brahman as the leader of the social and religious life of Tamilnadu who was the target of Self-Respect attacks: the Brahman was to blame for the present state of the Tamil country, with its highly stratified social system and its vast social distance between Brahman and untouchable since it was the Brahmans who had supposedly introduced all that was impure and foreign into the once pure or Dravidian culture. Self-respecters upheld a total disbelief in the religious validity of Brahmans....(Irschick 1969: 339)

Naicker and the Self-Respect Party moved into the Dravida Kazhagam, a party, founded in 1944, that was anti-Brahman in its ideology, and non-Brahman in its leadership and membership. Its successor, the Dravida Munetra Kazhagam (DMK), founded in 1949, became a Tamil regional party, that advocated a separate Dravida Nad, a separate Tamil state, as its goal; it became the dominant party in Tamilnadu from the elections of 1967.

Throughout this anti-Brahmanism in Madras in the first half of the twentieth century, Dharmarajapuram was, of course, in Travancore, but since 1956 it has been in Tamilnadu, the state in which the DMK and other regional parties with a long history of anti-Brahmanism have held the chief ministership and most of the high offices both at the capital in Madras and in smaller centers for the past quarter of a century. Like other Brahmans, those in Dharmarajpuram have felt excluded from jobs and higher education in Tamilnadu, due to anti-Brahman laws and policies.

A third milestone was the Temple Entry Proclamation of 1936 and the ending of feeding of Brahmans at the temples, both connected in the Dharmarajapuram Brahmans' minds with the dewan, Sir C.P. Ramaswami Aiyar, who also introduced a basic tax on all land.

C.P. Ramaswami Aiyar, a lawyer and a renowned public servant, was a Tamil Brahman from the Madras Presidency, so he belonged to the same caste-complex as the Tamil Brahmans of Dharmarajapuram.

The movement for entry of *avarna* caste--communities[34], sometimes called untouchables and backward castes, into the Hindu temples of Travancore, from which they had been traditionally excluded, had begun in 1917 when the editor of the newspaper *Deshabhimani*, T.K. Madhavan (1885--1930), himself an educated member of the low-caste Iravas, called in an editorial for such access. Robin Jeffrey says:

> The temple-entry question simmered throughout the first nine months of 1921, as the non-cooperation movement boiled in British India. Madhavan and his supporters took temple-entry propaganda into the villages of central and northern Travancore, and their meetings, which often attracted audiences of two to three thousand, provoked counter-demonstrations from orthodox Hindus. The state's armed police was alerted to prevent riots (Jeffrey 1978: 150).

The movement received the blessing of Mahatma Gandhi when he came to Travancore later in 1921.

The avarnas in Travancore had not only been excluded from Hindu temples, but also from roads and streets near the temples, and the first mass protests concerned not *entrance* to the Vaikam Shiva temple in northern Travancore, but the right to use the roads and streets near the temple. Non-violent protestors were in the area for twenty months. News media focused the attention of the nation upon them, and they received Gandhi's personal advice on non-violent methods of protest, as well as his aid in the attempt to negotiate. The culmination in 1926 was the government's building of special streets and roads near the Vaikom temple for the avarnas' use (Jeffrey 1978: 150--153). In the palace of the Regent Maharani, Tamil Brahmans (some of whom were related by marriage to the Brahmans of Dharmarajapuram) opposed temple entry and influenced the regent's policy to continue to support prohibitions against temple entry for the "polluted" avarnas (Jeffrey 1978: 157–158). It was not until her son came to the throne in 1931 that a new policy became possible.

Plate 14

The green rice fields, orchards and mountains of Kanyakumari district in southernmost Tamilnadu. (Photo Spring 1967, by Konstantin Kolenda)

In 1932, a Temple Entry Enquiry Committee was appointed; as a result of its report, most roads, wells and tanks were opened to all castes in 1934 (Jeffrey 1978: 161).

Then the Irava newspaper editor, C.V. Kunjuraman (1871–1949), and other publicists began a campaign calling for the Iravas and other avarnas to convert to another religion, most probably Christianity. The non-Brahman threat to the established order had been accentuated.

When in 1936 C.P. Ramaswani Aiyar became the dewan of Travancore, temple entry for all communities was opened almost immediately.

Trivandrum is 53 miles to the northwest of Dharmarajapuram, and Vaikom is even further away, 200 miles. There are very few, if any, Iravas in southern Kanyakumari, then southernmost Travancore, but by 1936, sons of Dharmarajapuram had served in the Travancore government in various capacities – as school teachers, as officials – and some had been stationed in Trivandrum, so that the people of Dharmarajapuram must have been aware of the temple entry movement through personal contact. All the males of the community were literate and would have read newspaper accounts, as well. Furthermore, one of the *jathas* (marching demonstrators) at the Vaikom protests was a similar protest and demonstration demanding temple entry at the Suchindrum temple, only six miles away from Dharmarajapuram, in 1926 (Jeffrey 1978: 167). This, the Dharmarajapuram Brahmans must have been all too aware of.

The basic land tax that most of the Brahmans of Dharmarajapuram mentioned was evidently designed by the dewan, C.P. Ramaswami Aiyar. He felt a " Christian threat to the character of a Hindu state" (Jeffrey 1976: 158), and to retain a caste-Hindu majority in the state's legislation, he wanted only landholders paying a certain tax to be able to vote. Since most of the Christians were low-caste converts, fewer of them were sizeable landowners paying land taxes, and hence few were able to vote. The dewan evidently also wanted to unite the Hindu population, both high-caste and low-caste, solidly behind the government and saw the abolition of prohibition on temple entry as a gesture in that direction.

Subramanian: We named the marriage hall in honor of C.P. Ramaswami Aiyar. He came to this village several times and listened to our petitions. We were against the temple entry. He did not agree with us always, but he listened. He said, "Well you can carry on your own worship in your home. Leave off the temple."[35]

Two of our temples were taken over by the government -- the Pillayar temple and the Krishna temple. Untouchables came to our temples only once or twice. We did not purify the temple afterwards, because we obey the law.

Mahesh: C.P. Ramaswami Aiyar, the dewan of Travancore, during the Regency of Parvathi Bai, when Chitra Tirunal was a minor, had stopped the feeding of Brahmans and endorsed the temple entry, because he feared that all the non-Brahmans would become Christians. Also he did not want to encourage lazy Brahmans who just ate from the state.

Gandhi had started the temple entry movement in North India, although success was first proclaimed in Travancore.

The real problem was untouchability. Brahmans would not let other castes into their villages because rituals might be going on which they were not to see. They made people stand at a distance of a mile or two. The four *varnas* are laid down in the Shastras. Keeping others at a distance is in the Shastras. Thus, Brahmans were to blame themselves because of the rules of untouchability.

The untouchable Sambhavars here used to be very respectful, not wearing shoes or a headcloth before Brahmans, wrapping the headcloth around their waists and holding their shoes in their hands. It was Sambhavars who had served Brahmans. They used to address the Brahmans as 'Nayinar' and 'Nachchiyar', and still some very old ones do. The younger ones used 'Amma' and 'Ayya'.[36]

Krishna, teacher: My father originally came from Parakat near Suchindram. He sold his land there and bought land here thinking it was tax free as danam land. But C.P. Ramaswamy Aiyar, the dewan of Travancore, introduced the basic tax on all land, so danam land was taxed like other land -- 1 pie per 1 cent of land.

PK: A fourth milestone in the Brahmans' own history is states integration. Travancore had never been directly under British rule, even though there had been a British Resident at the Maharaja's Palace in Trivandrum since 1800. When India became independent in 1947, the new federal government set about the task of persuading the 532 princely states that made up about one-third of the South Asia peninsula to merge either with Pakistan or with India. In the process, Travancore was joined with princely state of Cochin, to form, for eight years, the state of Travancore-Cochin. Later, this was merged with Malabar to from the state of Kerala. There was a campaign, however, led by the educated Christian Nadars of the nearby town of Nagercoil, to make southern Travancore part of the state of Madras, where Tamil was spoken, rather than, part of Kerala, where Malayalam was spoken. The justification for this annexation was that the culture and language of southern Travancore was Tamil. Southern Travancore, transferred to Madras state, was called Kanyakumari district.[37] As a result, the temples and religious schools of south Travancore came under the Madras state administration. The committee supervising temples was called the Devaswam Board.

Mahesh: The Vedapathshala[38] that I attended was entirely financed by the Maharaja. After states integration, the head of the Devaswam Board said that the pathshala must be opened to people of all castes. The gurus refused to teach non-Brahmans and the pathshala was closed. The head of the Devaswam Board was Mannath Padmanabhan of the Nair Service Society.[39] Padmanabhan said that the pathshala spent Rs. 50,000 of the state's funds, funds paid by all people, and their money could not be used to support an institution meant only for Brahmans. There were 100 students at the pathshala studying the various Vedas when I attended. Now, at Conjeeveram, the Shankaracharya has hardly 7 or 9.

PK: Part of the reaction to anti-Brahmanism is a mourning for a lost way of life, or a way of life that is just barely surviving.

Mahesh: I found that despite the extremely hard time one has learning a Veda that one makes no money at it. Purohitas make little money, because people are not celebrating their *samskaras* in a grand style anymore. This is because they do not believe in them any more. And that is due to westernization. If it had not been for the British, Hinduism would still be strong in India, and the Brahmans would be respected, but now everyone wants to imitate the west. Previously, the Brahmans were not dependent on offerings from householders, because they were supported by the king, but with states integration, the king could no longer support the Brahmans.

So I learned Hindi, so I could be a Hindi pandit. I taught for over twenty years at St Anthony's High School in Cape Comorin. Then, the DMK government did away with Hindi, so now I teach geography, history and mathematics in the first, second and third form at St. Anthony's. They cannot sack me at St. Anthony's since I have taught there for so long.

In the evening now, I am studying the Rg Veda. I would like to be able to do purohita work for followers of the Rg Veda as well as the Sama Veda.

PK: There are other social types in the agraharam. Some are cultivators. There are several widows, some of whom wear ochre-colored saris and self-consciously live the lives of renunciates. But, the future belongs to the young. All the sons of the longtime residents and the ancestral danam families finish high school, take training in stenography and typing and leave for the cities of India – Madras, Calcutta, Delhi, Kanpur, Bombay, Ernakulam – and the daughters marry such young men once they are settled in the distant place (Kolenda 1982). Often these weddings are held in the village *kalyanam mandabam* (wedding hall).

And, the children of these far-flung married children in large numbers come back to the village to live with their retired grandparents and to be educated through the Tamil language in Tamil-medium schools.

So, we leave a Brahman street, still surviving, because of the recency of its destruction as a residence of learned Brahmans and temple priests, through its trust which provides "all Vedic facilities", and because of its beauty.

Let me finish with a few quotations from the *Laws of Manu*:

> For that (money which is given) to Brahmans is declared to be an imperishable treasure for kings (Manu VII, 82).
>
> Neither thieves nor foes can take it, nor can it be lost; hence an imperishable store must be deposited by kings with Brahmans (Manu VII, 83).
>
> The offering made through the mouth of a Brahman, which is neither spilt, nor falls (on the ground) nor ever perishes is far more excellent than *agnihotras* (Manu VII, 84).
>
> A gift to one who is not a Brahman (yields) the ordinary (reward); a gift to one who calls himself a Brahman, a double (reward); a gift to a well-read Brahmana, a hundred-thousand fold (reward); (a gift) to one who knows the *Veda* and the *Angas* (*Vedaparaga*, a reward) without end (Manu VII, 85).

Notes

1. Iyer or aiyar is often used as the surname of the Smarta Tamil Brahmans. They are distinct from the Tamil Brahmans with the surname of Iyengar, who are worshippers of Vishnu.
2. The American Institute of Indian Studies generously financed most of my research. That done in 1971 was supported by the Group Projects Abroad Program of the Department of Health, Education and Welfare.
3. The Gayatri mantra is a prayer to the sun.
4. There has been considerable discussion of kingship since Dumont's writings cited here, but the role of the Brahman with respect to the Hindu king has been sustained. See Heesterman 1978: 4–5.
5. *Shastras* are religious teachings.

6. Bus service came to this area around 1925.
7. The Devaswam Board is an agency of the state, either Travancore before 1956, or Tamilnadu, since 1956, that supervised hundred of important Hindu temples.
8. Subramaniam's history is off by 37 years. Dharmarajapuram was established in 1753. Tippu Sultan attacked Travancore in 1789--90. Mukhdum Sahib was the commander of the forces of Hyder Ali who moved into the Palghat area of Malabar, now part of northern Kerala (Woodcock 1967: 175). The state of Travancore was actually established before the son of Hyder Ali, Tippu Sultan, and his forces threatened Travancore. According to Woodcock (1967: 182):

   > Cornwallis had already recognized that the conquest of Travancore would be intolerable to British interests, and had reversed the neutralist policy, instructing the Company's officers at Tellicherry to regard themselves as at war with Tippu.... As soon as he realized the magnitude of the alliance ranged against him, Tippu abandoned his campaign in Travancore and hurried back to Mysore to prepare his defences.

   According to the historian of Travancore, A.P. Ibrahim Kunju, (1976: 6):

   > By the time of the Mysorean invasions, Travancore had consolidated her positions and the threat of foreign conquest had made even bitter opponents of Travancore in the conquered territories join her ranks to resist the invasion. Here again it was a powerful and united kingdom that was able to put up an effective opposition to the Mysorean invasion. Had the principalities of southern Kerala remained scattered and quarreling they would have fallen easily like the principalities of northern Kerala before the invading armies of Mysore.

9. *Tapas* or *tapasya* is a kind of heat, a kind of magical power derived from asceticism (Basham 1954: 247, 249).
10. *Sevi* in Tamil means to worship. *Sevai* is a worshipper.
11. *Arcakkars* are temple priests.
12. A *taluk* is a sub-division of a district.
13. Kuzhitural is a village about 30 miles to the northwest of Dharmarajapuram, in Kanyakumari district, quite near the border of Kerala.
14. The orthodoxy of the Brahman descendants of the danam is possibly reflected in the almost perfect conformance in the marriage ages of Sita and her husband to the *Laws of Manu* (Chapter 9, verse 94), "A man, aged thirty years, shall marry a maiden of twelve who pleases

him, or a man of twenty-four a girl eight years of age...." She was ten, her husband twenty-five. See Buhler 1886: 344.

15. Bhutapandi is about 15 miles to the northwest of Dharmarajapuram.
16. Sita's father knew English, but Sita did not. In the 1970s, it was still not common to educate Brahman daughters in English. I only met one Brahman woman associated with Dharmarajapuram who spoke English – the wife of a college professor who was an Iyer, originally from Trichur, Kerala. The college professor lived in Dharmarajapuram while he taught at a nearby college.
17. A *mama* is a mother's brother or father-in-law. A *mami* is a mother's brother's wife or a mother-in-law. A *patti* is a grandmother or here a husband's father's mother. A *tambi* is a younger brother; a *tangachi* a younger sister.
18. Located in Dharmarajapuram.
19. Asramam is another agraharam, about eight miles to the northwest. Kottaram is a small market town about a mile away from Dharmarajapuram.
20. Located in Tamilnadu, about 100 miles straight north of Cape Comorin.
21. Rama purohita is listing here some of the major Hindu samskaras, life cycle rites performed in the home, prescribed in the *Vedas*, *Grhyasutras*, *Dharmasutras*, and other ancient Hindu ritual manuals. Tamil speakers tamilise the titles of these rites, especially by adding a suffix to the Sanskrit title. Simantam refers to the *Simantonnayana* or *Simanta* or hair parting, a ceremony for a pregnant woman to bless her and her unborn child. According to Pandey (1949: 109), the Hindu law books held that her husband should part her hair with various auspicious grasses, sticks, fruits and so on. As celebrated in Dharmarajapuram, the pregnant woman is adorned with new glass bangles in a ceremony run by the older women.

    The *jatakarna* is a set of birth ceremonies. The *namakarana* is a name-giving ceremony. *Anna-prashana* is first feeding of the baby with solid food. The *chowla* of *chuda* is a ceremony for first cutting of the hair. The *upanayana* is the ritual bestowing the sacred thread upon male adolescents of the high castes initiating them into their roles as religious scholars and into their positions at the apex of the caste system. *Vivaham* or *vivaha* is marriage ceremonies. *Shraddhas* are memorial rites honoring dead ancestors.
22. A *vrata* is a fast. Typically, women cook delicacies and special foods during the day while they fast, then break their fasts after the sun sets

and enjoy the feast food. Rama Purohit's list includes calendrical religious celebrations honoring the gods Shiva (Shivratri), Vinayaka (Vinayaka Chaturthi), Surya (Shankaranda Suryanarayana), Krishna (Krishna Jayanti), Rama (Ramanaumi), and Durga (Navratri Devi puja); and special meritorious offerings to Brahmans (Saptarishi puja, Rishipanchami). Presumably, Rama performs *puja* or other rituals in the worshippers' homes at the time of these religious celebrations.

23. *Dhyadi* are the male members of a minimal patrilineage, descendants of a common great grandfather, tracing their descent back through male links.
24. What Subramaniam is saying is that the Brahmans take on the sins of the *shraddha*-celebrators' ancestors through actually eating the food offered to the ancestors; thus, they facilitate the celebrators' ancestors' passages through the after-world. To rid themselves of the sin so acquired, the Brahmans must chant the *Gayatri mantra* many times – some say 1,000 times – and do rituals like the *sandhya vantanams.* Many of the more modern of the Dharmapuram Brahmans refuse to accept *shraddha* food, because they do not think their religiosity is sufficient to be able to expunge such sin from themselves.
25. Scott Christian College is located in the nearby (12 miles away) town of Nagercoil. The work activities Subramaniam is talking about he also did in Nagercoil.
26. A Vellala is a member of the highest Shudra landowning cultivating caste in Tamilnadu, whose rank is slightly below that of Brahman.
27. If a Brahman eats with or marries a Vellala, he would be polluted, according to orthodox Hindu conception.
28. Subramaniam here outlines a theory of rebirth. Through successive lives, a soul might move up the caste hierarchy.
29. Madurai and Chidambaram are cities in Tamilnadu. Trivandrum is the capital city of Kerala.
30. Rama was the king in the Indian epic, the *Ramayana.* Laxman was his brother. Rama has been deified and considered by many Hindus to be an incarnation of the god Vishnu.
31. Mahesh is also not quite correct in saying that the British respected the Brahmans. Irschick (1969: 102–122) lists a series of influential writings that fed a British "Brahmanophobia". The Justice Party received help from the Madras government partly because of the British distrust of Brahmans and their view that "the Brahmans possessed far too much social and religious control over the non-Brahman caste Hindus and the untouchables" (Irschick 1969: 353).

32. Dr. Nair was a Nayar. Nayars are the major non-Brahman caste in the state of Kerala, and in old Travancore. I talk below about their anti-Brahman movement in the 1880s and 1890s.
33. A Kannada Balija Naidu of Erode. Erode is a town in north-central Tamilnadu. Naidu is a title of respect (Thurston V: 138). Balijas are a trading caste who have sometimes claimed to be Kshatriyas, second in rank to Brahmans (Thurston I: 134--135).
34. *Avarna* means lacking *varna*. The four *varnas* of the Rg Veda are the Brahman priests, the Kshatriya warriors, the Vaisya cultivators and the Shudra servants. The class of untouchables are the avarnas. The five class system is commonly known by Hindus throughout India, and they apply it to their local complement of castes.
35. Jeffrey says that one of the reasons for the delay in the temple entry proclamation was "an exaggerated fear of a violent reaction from orthodox caste-Hindus if the temples were opened" (Jeffrey 1978: 161). Possibly Dewan C.P. Ramaswami Aiyar made it a practice to try to console resistant Tamil Brahman. He had the enormous advantage of being a member of their caste community.

    His suggestion that the Brahmans could leave off going to the temple is the response that a Nambudiri Brahman is reported to have made to Mahatma Gandhi in a debate in 1925 when Gandhi was advocating opening orthodox Hindu temples in Travancore to avarnas. See Desai 1937:20.
36. *Nayinar* and *ayya* mean 'master' or 'lord', *nachchiyar* and *amma* here mean 'lady'.

    Jeffrey's conclusion about the temple entry movement was the following:

    > The government had, unintentionally, done much to create the temple-entry demand. Its land reforms in the 1860s had established a secure and independent body of small proprietors, some of whom were low-caste men. Its encouragement of cash crops and the coir industry had similarly given a certain independence to men and women who had not enjoyed it before. Its heavy expenditure on education -- far greater than anything British government attempted -- made it possible for the newly independent to put their children to school. To modernize to such an extent, yet still try to preserve the old social disabilities, was an impossibility (Jeffrey 1978: 164).
37. Robin Jeffrey summarizes the process of integration of Travancore into India as follows:

Sir C.P. Ramaswami Aiyar announced in June 1947 that Travancore would become an independent state after the British left India. Opposition to the independence plan united most groups in the state. In July Ramaswami Aiyar was attacked and wounded on the face in Trivandrum. Soon after, Travancore signed the act of accession, and he resigned the dewanship.

Responsible government in 1948 made real power available to Travancore leaders and intensified their struggles with each other and with the economic conditions of the state. In the period from 1948 to 1956 Travancoreans had seven governments and an interval of President's rule from New Delhi. In 1949 Travancore and Cochin were integrated into a single state of Travancore-Cochin. In 1956 Malabar district was added and Kerala state formed; the Tamil-speaking taluks of south Travancore were ceded to Madras (Jeffrey 1976: 262). The Maharaja of Travancore, Chitra Tirunal became Raj Pramukh, or governor, when the state of Travancore-Cochin was formed in 1949. He now lives in Trivandrum and takes no part in public life (Jeffrey 1976: 329).

38. School where *gurus* taught the Vedas.
39. "Mannath Padmanabha Pillai, the general secretary of the Nair Service Society, which had little following in south Travancore, dramatized the divergent outlooks of the new, competitive caste-Hindu middle class and the old, orthodox caste-Hindus of Trivandrum in a speech shortly before T.K. Madhavan's death in 1930. Padmanabha Pillai offered to help in organizing Irava volunteer corps to enter temples by force. He claimed that the Malayali Brahmins of north Travancore were prepared to support temple entry, but the Maharani Regent was misled by Tamil Brahmans, in the palace in Trivandrum" (Jeffrey 1978: 158).

References

Basham, A.L. (1954), *The Wonder That Was India*, New York: Grove Press.

Buhler, G. (1886), *The Laws of Manu*, Oxford: Clarendon.

Desai, Madev (1937), *The Epic of Travancore,* Ahmedabad: Navajivan Karyalaya.

Dumont, Louis (1970a), *Homo Hierarchicus,* Chicago: University of Chicago Press.

— (1970b), 'The Conception of Kingship in Ancient India.' *In Religion/Politics and History in India: Collected Papers in Indian Sociology,* Paris: Mouton Publishers, pp. 62–88.

Hardgrave, Robert R., Jr. (1969), *The Nadars of Tamilnadu,* Berkeley: University of California Press.

Heesterman, J.C. (1978), 'The Conundrum of the King's Authority.' *In* John Richards, editor, *Kingship and Authority in South Asia.* Madison, Wisconsin: South Asian Studies, University of Wisconsin-Madison, Publication Series, Publication Number 3, pp. 1–27.

Hutton, J.H. (1951), *Caste in India: Its Nature, Function and Origin.* Second Edition, London: Oxford University Press.

Irschick, Eugene F. (1969), *Politics and Social Conflict in South India: The Non-Brahman Movement and Tamil Separatism 1916--1929,* Berkeley: University of California Press.

Jeffrey, Robin (1976), *The Decline of Nayar Dominance: Society and Politics in Travancore, 1847--1908,* New York: Holmes and Meier.

— (1978), Travancore: Status, Class the the Growth of Radical Politics, 1860–1940: The Temple-Entry Movement. *In* Robin Jeffrey, editor, *People, Princes and Paramount Power: Society and Politics in the Indian Princely States.* Delhi: Oxford University Press, 1978, pp. 136–169.

Kolenda, Pauline (1982), 'Gransons of the Shastrigals: Migration and Identity Transformation among Dharmika Brahmans of Travancore.' *In* Graciela de la Lama, Susana Gonzalez Del Solar, and Benjamin Preciado Solis, editors, *South Asia 2,* papers from the Thirtieth International Congress of Human Sciences in Asia and North Africa, Mexico City, 1976, Mexico City: El Colegio de Mexico, pp. 29–61.

Kunju, A.P. Ibrahim (1976), *Rise of Travancore: Study of the Life and Times of Martanda Varma,* Trivandrum: Kerala Historical Society.

Low, D.A. (1978), '*Laissez-faire* and Traditional Rulership in Princely India.' *In* Robin Jeffrey, editor, *People, Princes and Paramount Power: Society and Politics in the Indian Princely States,* Delhi: Oxford University Press, pp. 372–387.

Mateer, Samuel (1871), *The Land of Charity,* London: John Snow.

Menon, P. Shungoony (1878), *A History of Travancore,* Madras: Higginbotham.

Nagam Aiya, V. (1906), *The Travancore State Manual*, Trivandrum: Travancore Government.

Oddie, G.A. (1985), 'Recent Writings on the Social and Cultural Aspects of Modern South Indian History.' *In* Robert Eric Frykenberg and Pauline Kolenda, editors, *Studies of South India: An Anthology of Recent Research and Scholarship*, Madras: American Institute of Indian Studies and New Era Publications, pp. 171–194.

Pandy, Raj Bali (1949), *Hindu Samskaras: A Socio-religious Study of the Hindu Sacraments*, Bhadaini, Banaras: Vikrama Publications.

Schwartzberg, Joseph E., ed. (1978), *Historical Atlas of South Asia*, Chicago: University of Chicago Press.

Srinivas, M.N. (1966), *Social Change in Modern India*, Berkeley: University of California Press.

Thurston, Edger (1909), *Castes and Tribes of Southern India*, Madras: Government Press.

Velu Pillai, S. (1940), *Travancore State Manual*, Trivandrum: Government of Travancore.

Woodcock, George (1967), *Kerala: A Portrait of the Malabar Coast*, London: Faber and Faber.

6

The Tamil Brahman Family as Affected by Out-Migration and Modern Occupations

Anthropologists who have described the South Indian Brahman family have tended to emphasize its "patrilineality". Its structure was to be understood in terms of inheritance of land from father to sons. Hence, typically, there was a strong authority relationship between father and sons, and often tension between inheriting brothers. Daughters did not inherit land, but received security through placement in a "good" marriage. Family wealth might be expended for a daughter's dowry and other costs of her wedding and for the maintenance of subsequent affinal relations. A patrilineal joint family, one composed of parents and a married son, his wife, and children, might occur, but a fraternal joint family, one composed of married brothers, their wives and children, was rare (Gough '1956; Harper 1958). Even within the home, patrilineality was the tone. Thus, Gough describes the Tanjore Brahman family:

> In fact, in everyday life in the home, a young mother is prevented by household tasks and by partial seclusion in the kitchen from regularly tending her children after the age of one or two. They are then monopolized by the father who has greater leisure than the mother and who is at home for a large part of the day. In an extended family household, the child is also cared for by the father's parents and sometimes by the father's widowed aunt or sister, all of whom tend to support the father's rather than the mother's claims in the child (Gough 1956: 835).

In this paper, I am concerned with family structure among Iyers, Tamil Brahmans, whose native place is an *agraharam* (a Brahman street) in southernmost Tamilnadu, very close to land's end at Cape Comorin, in Kanyakumari district. This part of Tamilnadu was previously part of the princely state of Travancore. Many of the older residents of the agraharam served the Maharaja of Travancore in various capacities. Indeed, such service continues to a small extent. Thus, one of the village priests (*pujaris*), a graduate of the *pathshala* (religious academy) in Trivandrum, was one of the *arcakkar*s (chanters) at the ex-Maharaja's sixtieth birthday celebrations in 1974. The original eighteen families of the village were donees, receiving a grant of about 200 acres of land from an early Maharaja in 1753. The giving was a meritorious act on his part, helping to wash away the stains of his warrior sins. Most of the residents of the village are either descendants of the original *danam* (gift) families, or else they are descendants of Iyers who married into the village or bought land in the village at least two or three generations back.

The present social structure of the agraharam must be understood in terms of the dynamics of out-migrations and the adoption of modern occupations. Since many of the residents of the agraharam are old people, it is easy to conclude – prematurely, as I hope to show – that the village will soon disappear and join the number of deserted agraharams which dot more northern Tamilnadu (Béteille 1965: 170; Mencher 1970: 207). The focus of my paper, however, is upon the family structures resulting from the needs of taking up modern occupations and the out-migration required to do so.

To give you a feel for the data, let us look at the series of families through which one of the successful members of the agraharam has passed. Now a man of 64, a medical doctor, his mother was a direct patrilineal descendant of a receiver of the danom. His father's father's mother had also been a patrilineal descendant of a danom family. Both sets of his grandparents lived in the agraharam, combining religious specialization with supervision of cultivation. His father, brought up in the house next door to his mother's, was the son of a priest serving in one of the Maharaja's Shiva temples.

Subramoniam was the eldest of six children. He was born in 1914 in the house of his mother's parent, just next door to his paternal home. After his mother's confinement and delivery in her parental home, she and the infant returned to a household composed of Subramoniam's parents, his father's mother, and his father's younger unmarried sister. His father was the eldest of four sons and was the cultivator in the family. His father's three younger brothers were living with their mother's brother in the nearby town of Nagercoil and going to an English high school there. One later became a teacher, another an agent for a landholder in another village, and the third a distiller in a distillery in Nagercoil. His mother's four brothers similarly resided with their mother in Nagercoil, attending school there. The related bilateral families as they were at Subramoniam's birth looked like this:

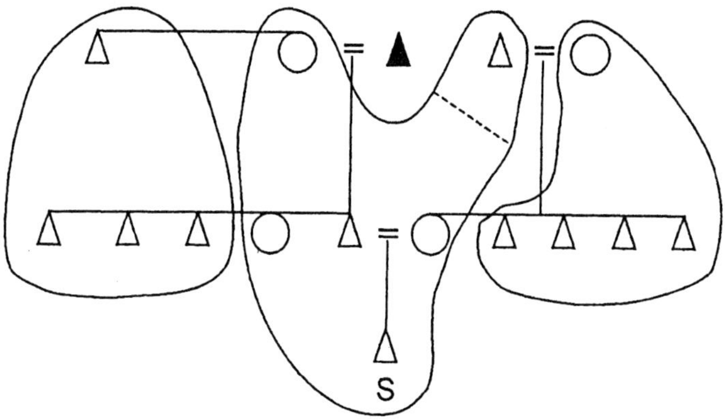

Subramoniam's mother's parents were living separately, his mother's mother in Nagercoil looking after her sons, his mother's father living alone, but eating from his daughter's kitchen. Upon finishing school, one of Subramoniam's mother's brothers became a health inspector in northern Tamilnadu. One of his younger brothers went with him there, to continue his schooling.

Subramoniam had a brother born in 1917, another born in 1920, another in 1923, a sister born in 1925, and a last brother born in 1927. At the age of seven, having completed two or three years of schooling in the village, Subramoniam went to live in Nagercoil with his mother's mother and with one of his mother's brothers who was studying in the local college at the time. During his studies, this mother's brother married. Gradually, Subramoniam's younger brothers joined this household, as did two other boys from the agraharam who were Subramoniam's mother's mother's brother's sons. Subramoniam lived with his mother's mother and his mother's brother in Nagercoil for eight years while he completed the six forms of middle and upper school and the two years for intermediate at the local college. Meanwhile, his mother's brother finished his intermediate, and he and his wife had a baby daughter.

On weekends Subramoniam and his brothers walked home on Friday evenings, more than fourteen miles, and walked back again early Monday mornings, carrying with them rice, coconuts and bananas for their Nagercoil larder. In 1928, the household looked like this:

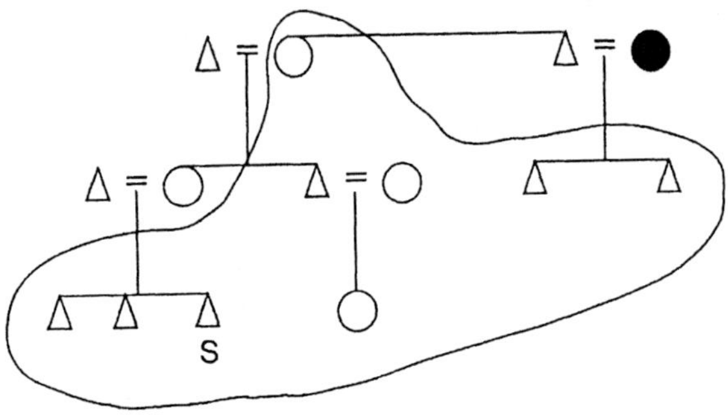

While studying in intermediate in the college in Nagercoil, Subramoniam was married. He was age 14; his wife was age 9. His wife continued to live with her parents who lived in northern Travancore. Subramoniam's father-in-law insisted that Subramoniam should take up medical studies, even though Subramoniam's own father thought that medicine was "dirty and menial work". Subramoniam left Nagercoil after completing intermediate to enter medical school in Madras. There, he lived in a hostel. He was then 15 years old. His wife, who remained with her parents, matured. Subramoniam would visit her at her parents' home during holidays. Their first daughter was born during his second year in medical school. Notification reached Subramoniam in Madras by means of a telegram.

Subramoniam finished medical school in 1934, and he proceeded to hold various positions in the medical service of the Travancore government. Meanwhile, his wife and daughter continued to live with his wife's parents and her unmarried younger brothers and sisters. (She was the eldest, with four younger brothers and four younger sisters.) It was not until 1939 when Subramoniam was 25 and his wife 19 that they were able to live together in their own home. They had been married eleven years. His daughter, now aged eight, continued to live with her mother's parents.

Subramoniam and his wife had a second daughter in 1943. In 1945, his first daughter, aged 13, was given in marriage to her first mother's brother. This was against the wishes of Subramoniam, who wanted her to study further ("She had come first in the SSLC."). But, her grandfather insisted. Thus, even after marriage, the daughter continued living in her mother's father's household, married to her mother's brother whom, presumably, she had known throughout her life. Subramoniam, her father, had seen her perhaps half a dozen times a year -- during her school holidays.

Around the time of his eldest daughter's wedding, Subramoniam received a posting in Cape Comorin near enough to his native agraharam that he could take up residence there again with his parents.

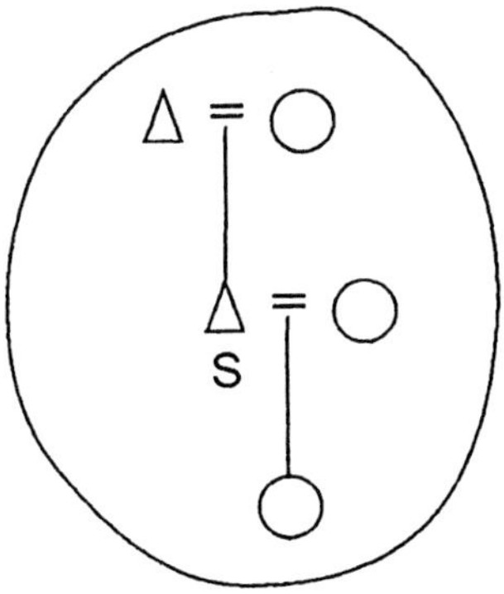

So at the age of 31, he moved back to live in his native village. He had not lived there since he was seven years old, nor had he lived with his parents since age seven.

In 1958, he accepted a position in Tinnevelly district. From there, in 1967, he gave his second daughter in marriage. She was twenty-four years old. He retired to the agraharam in 1969 at the age of 55, to live with his wife and aged mother. His mother died in 1976, and now he lives alone with his wife.

The case history of Subramoniam illustrates a number of the common features of the family life of Iyers in southern Tamilnadu. These include:

(1) Long residence with maternal relatives -- most commonly with the mother's parents, but frequently with the widowed

mother's mother, the mother's brother, or the mother's sister, even a mother's mother's sister. There are a few cases of residence with father's parents or with father's sister, but these were instances in which the child's mother was dead or mentally deranged. The link person, the mother, was essentially absent.

It has been not only common, but the standard pattern, for the sons and daughters (the few who have gone beyond the elementary grades) of the agraharam to have their education while in the care of a maternal relative. This maternal relative may already live near good schools, or he or she purposefully may take up residence in a place with good schools, just for the sake of the daughter's or sister's children. This pattern was adaptive for children residing in the village. They had to go and live in town. It is also adaptive to a father's modern occupation which involves frequent transfer. Other circumstances may have brought about "being raised by mother's mother". Thus, two brothers who resided in the agraharam even after elementary school, going to a high school in the next village, claim to have been raised by their mother's mother. Their mother became a widow and went to join her widowed mother. Although their mother was in the household, they see themselves as having been brought up by the grandmother.

(2) Residence with maternal kin is not always a matter of the needs of education. The maternal kin are not always wealthy or childless. Children residing with maternal kin may well have been able to get a good Tamil education in their parents' place. Thus, Subramoniam's mother's brother has had his daughter's son living with him since the boy was two or three years old. The boy just entered the university. His mother and father live permanently in Calcutta where the boy could have attended a good Tamil-medium school. It is a matter of affection, the grandfather explained.

(3) The old people residing in the agraharam are not all cultivators whose children have left them, as a first impression might suggest. Many of them are themselves people who worked "out", "in service", who at a relatively young age of 55 have retired to their ancestral village, or to their wife's ancestral village. Their own children may well have been raised by the

wife's relatives. They, in turn, may be raising their daughter's children, because the son-in-law is "in service".

(4) Patterns of emotional closeness follow residence patterns in many instances, rather than genealogical closeness. Thus, the two brothers above who felt more affection for their mother's mother than for their own mother are an example.

Marriages develop out of cousins or uncle and niece residing in the same household. Subramoniam's daughter married her mother's brother, a young man of her own household. In another instance, one of the few college-educated daughters of the agraharam lived with her mother's sister while in school. She lived with this mother's sister's daughter in the hostel while in college. The two girls lived together later while both worked in Madras. The mother's sister's daughter was the matchmaker in arranging the marriage between her brother and her cousin – again a young man the latter had known while living with her mother's sister. When we last talked to this young woman, she had just borne her first child. She was about to leave her husband in Calcutta to return to her "in-laws" in Madras. There her mother-in-law would look after the baby while the girl worked as a telephone operator. The mother-in-law was the girl's mother's sister, and the baby's mother's mother's sister. So, a new generation is raised by matrilateral kin.

In an instance from Subramoniam's family – his brother who had lived with his mother's brother for several years while in school in Nagercoil married this mother's brother's daughter, a little girl in the household where he resided while going to school.

Residence with such maternal kin may persist after marriage Such was the case with Subramoniam's daughter. In another case of a seemingly nuclear family, that of an agraharam son living in Madras, it turned out that the flat next door was occupied by the wife's mother's brother and her mother's mother. The wife had, in fact, been raised by her mother's mother, and she had had a close "sisterly" relationship with her mother's brother which now continued after her marriage. It had been her mother's brother who had rented the two flats next to each other when the couple returned to Madras from Calcutta where the husband had been stationed in his company.

Now that they were transferred to Tamilnadu, an old matrilateral residence pattern could be resumed.

Mother's brother's sons or mother's sister's sons are frequently mentioned as people whom agraharam sons now living in large cities helped upon their migration. Such cousins often resided for years with their cousins as they adapted to Calcutta or to some other strange locale.

Conclusion

It has been said that in northern India when villagers migrate to the city or town, they leave their wives and children behind in the village, to be looked after by their joint family members. It has also been said that in South India when a villager went out to work, he took his family, wife and children, with him. What these data suggest is that a frequently-transferred man working out does have his wife with him, but his older children are very likely with his wife's parents who have retired and/or are cultivators back in Tamilnadu. There are a number of value commitments involved in these patterns, of course.

First, there is no assumption that children must be raised by the mother. By the age of three or four, they may be taken by maternal kin to be raised.

Secondly, there is a strong commitment to continuity in education to be found in attending schools in one place. Success in education emerges out of a very competitive process. Stability in residence is probably a competitive advantage to a student. One concludes that success in education with the potential of entry to modern occupations with middle-class salaries is more important than maintaining the nuclear family unit intact (if that value was important ever in the past).

Thirdly, although it is not expected that mothers must be the child-rearers, there does seem to be an assumption that children should be raised by the mother's parents, brother, or sister.

Fourthly, there is a strong commitment to the home culture, home area, even home village. One retires to the agraharam – often to associate with men and women with whom one went to school or played with in childhood.

The idea that with modern occupations requiring much geographical mobility, the appropriate family form is the nuclear family is belied by these data. The nuclear family must be supplemented with families which include sister's or daughter's children, the offspring of the ever-transferred man "in service".

References

Béteille, Andre (1965), *Caste, Class, and Power*, Berkley: University of California Press.

Gough, E. Kathleen (1956), Brahman Kinship in a Tamil Village, *American Anthropologist* 58: 826--853.

Harper, Edward (1958), Economic Structure of a South Indian Village, Ph.D. Dissertation for Cornell University.

Mencher, Joan P. (1970), A Tamil Village: Changing Socioeconomic Structure in Madras State. *In* Ishwaran, ed., *Change and Continuity in India's Villages*, Columbia University Press.

Sivertsen, Dagfin (1963), *When Caste Barriers Fall*, London: George Allen and Unwin.

7

Grandsons of the Shastrigals

Migration and Identity Transformation among Dharmika Brahmans of Travancore*

> ...many of the mechanisms of adjustment which once made for psychosocial evolution, tribal integration, and national or class coherence are at loose ends in a world of universally expanding identities (Erikson 1968: 72).

In his book, *When a Great Tradition Modernizes,* Milton Singer dealt with the reinterpretation of Tamil Brahman Hinduism by Smartha Brahmans in the city of Madras. His focus was upon the religio-cultural traditions. He spoke of the decline in religious education, and hence a change in the religious capacities and needs of the urban western-educated Madras Brahmans. In this paper, I shift the focus from religion to the western-educated Smartha Brahman himself, asking the question: What new conception of *self* does the western-educated migrant Smartha Brahman from Tamilnadu formulate in a new urban setting, for his own psychological use and support?

This paper is part of larger study of a Tamil Brahman (Iyer) *agraharam* (village) in Kanyakumari district of southern Tamilnadu. The *agraharam* of study was occupied by learned Brahmans supported by a gift of land, house-sites, and agrestic laborers, granted by the Maharaja of Travancore in 1753 to their ancestors, invited and brought from the Tamil district of Thanjavur-Chidambaram. They were to reciprocate this royal charity by praying for the Maharaja's

---

"Grandsons of the Sastrigals: Migration and Identity Transformation among Dharmika Brahmans of Travancore." In *South Asia 2,* papers from the Thirtieth International Congress of Human Sciences in Asia and North Africa, Mexico City, 1976. Graciela de la Lama, Susana Gonzalez Del Solar, and Benjamin Preciado Solis, editors. Mexico City: El Colegio de Mexico, pp. 29–61.

salvation. Unlike Brahmans in various parts of British India, those of Travancore continued to be supported in their traditional roles by their king right through the mid-1930s. Members of families which traced their ancestry back to the eighteen families that received the Maharaja's *danam* (gift), who continued to reside in the village, and study the *Veda*s and other religious works. Land records from 1905 show them dubbed with religious titles like *Shastrigal* (learned in the *Shastra*s), *Shrotigal* (learned in the *Sruti,* revealed writ, the *Veda*s), *Ganapadigal* (learned in the *ganapadi* metre of the *Veda*s), and *Vatyar* (teacher of the *Veda*s). Their genealogies show a variety of religious occupations held by ancestors besides those suggested by these titles. Some were *purohita*s (household priests), or *shivanpujan*s (priest in Shiva temples). Those who could not support themselves from their lands or who did not receive a religious education became officials, most commonly customs inspectors or teachers in the government of Travancore. They worked in the Malayalam language of Travancore or the Tamil of the Tamil migrants of southern Travancore. While they might be transferred frequently while in the Maharaja's service, they typically resided, wherever their assignment might take them in a Tamil Brahman (Iyer) *agraharam*. So they remained throughout life in the orbit of Smartha Tamil Brahmanism.

It was not until the 1920s that the Iyers of southern Travancore began migrating out beyond the borders of Travancore, Cochin, and Madras. Some went to Burma, Sri Lanka or Malaya and in the 1930s, some sons of Dharmarajapuram went to Calcutta and thereafter some went to Delhi, Bombay and to the many posts outside of southernmost India, as they were transferred in central government service.

Today, there are few men of the ancestral families in the ages between 20 and 50 residing in the village. It has become the pattern that young men, and increasingly young women, get a western-style education through high school or college, then take a course of typing, and possibly stenography, and then enter government or business "service" as white-collar workers – minor bureaucrats, secretaries, or clerks. In their occupations, they communicate in English. They have the additional challenges of Bengali or Hindi or Marathi or whatever is the language of the region where they find their job.

During the winter of 1973–74 I visited the sons and daughters of Dharmarajapuram who had migrated out and were now residing in Madras, Calcutta, Delhi, Kanpur, Bombay, and Cochin. I interviewed some two dozen of them, all representing the first generation of English speakers in their immediate families, and who had left their cultural homeland.

They are unusual in that they are so late in their entry into the modern English-speaking sector of Indian society. Brahmans in Maharashtra, Madras, and Bengal made such an entrance more than a hundred years ago. They are also unusual in their lot as repudiated by their non-Brahman fellow-citizens, once their non-Brahman subordinates. Their repudiation is part of the DK and DMK (Dravida Munnetra Kazhagam) politico-cultural movements. They all believed that it would be extremely difficult for them to obtain suitable positions of employment in their native Tamilnadu or in Kerala, because of such anti-Brahman sentiments and legislation.

There are a number of common features shared by the interviewees. All had spent their childhood and adolescence in Dharmarajapuram and its environs, typically attending the village school for the first few years, then attending schools in nearby villages or in the town of Nagercoil, then going on, in some cases to Scott Christian College in Nagercoil or South Travancore Hindu College in Nagercoil or for a few St. Joseph's College in Tiruchirappalli.

Although all are practicing Hindus, none had had any lengthy religious education, either in a *pathshala* (religious school), or with a *vatyar* (religious teacher). And, none wanted his or her children to become *purohitas* (household priests) or temple priests. All wanted their children to become more successful in the modern sector of the Indian economy than themselves. Thus, ideally, both sons and daughters should become engineers, doctors or MAs. In all families the children of school age had their feet firmly planted on the educational paths that lead to such secular western-style higher education. The parents whose children were showing signs of failure in this undertaking were very worried and anxious.

The effect of these ambitions on the family structure include heavier duties for the mother. As children's studies take precedence over household chores, children are largely excused from helping around the house. Since the mother, to boot, usually does not speak English, she also tends to be looked down upon by her educated children. She tends to become a glorified household servant. This pattern came out as we tried to interview migrant daughters of the village, whose children or husband would answer the questions for them, and whose children ridiculed the mother's naïve answers. It was very difficult to interview daughters of the village, because of the limitations upon their autonomy by husband and educated children, and in some cases, by other relatives in the household.

There was no youthful rebellion against parents, however. The exchange made across the generations is clearly recognized and accepted by both sides. The parents, namely, the father, pay for the children's education, but it is the obligation of the children to support the parents in their old age. The male interviewees were themselves helping to support their parents back in Dharmarajapuram. All interviewees accepted their own obedience to parents as an unquestioned norm.

All interviewees had had arranged marriage. In some cases, photographs had been exchanged or sent one way (from bride's family to groom's), or even a brief visit between prospective couple had occurred. But interviewees emphasized their acquiescence to their parents' wishes in the matter of marriage.

Male interviewees tended to speak of their duty to spend time with their children and presumably they do spend much time with children. Those whose children are beyond babyhood, however, tend to be nostalgic for "that old gang of mine," the group of age-mates from Dharmarajapuram who attended school together and played volleyball in the village threshing ground.

All tend to idealize the beauty of the village and its surrounding setting, emphasizing the healthiness of the area of southern Travancore. It is, surely, one of the most beautiful parts of India in which to live with palm trees, paddy fields against a blue sky and jagged mountains, the last petering-out of the Western Ghats. They vary, however, in their assessment of interpersonal relations in the village, and this assessment clearly seems to have influenced their own self-conception and ambitions.

All the men interviewed speak English well. Women had to be interviewed through Tamil, however. Men's Anglicization varies, as does their interest in the foreign regional cultures of Calcutta, Bombay, Delhi, wherever they find themselves.

Plate 15

A bridegroom's party, led by musicians, comes down the street of the Brahman *agraharam*, Dharmarajapuram, in Kanyakumari district, Tamilnadu. (Photo June 1980, by Pauline Kolenda. See the first three papers in Part II Kanyakumari.)

Almost all had gotten jobs through Tamil Smartha Brahmans, usually close or more distant relatives. Most had helped others get jobs. Their caste continues to be a resource and social network for them.

As white-collar workers, not professional men, some seemed to suffer from a certain frustration, for they had rather early, by their mid-thirties, reached the top of the mobility ladder upon which they climbed. I was struck by a certain psychological depression among many, stemming partly perhaps from job frustration and partly from cultural disorientation as they try to contend with their ambivalence toward their traditional role and status, with Tamil chauvinism, and with aspects of the regional cultures in which they find themselves.

Their adherence to customs of pollution varies. Some probably most, have given up birth and death pollution practices, but all continue some practices connected with menstrual pollution – a woman should not cook during her menstruation period.

A dominant note was their familism, and to a lesser extent their casteism. All live in a Brahman network of Iyers. Some stick close to migrant fellow-villagers. Others have made new Iyer friends in the northern cities. But all live in an Iyer context. Their familism is reinforced by their caste's religious tradition, as well.

The Cases of Mani and Subramaniam

Following Erik Erikson, we can see that these Tamil Brahmans migrated at an age when they were developing their own sense of identity. As the first generation of English-speaking western-educated sons of fathers and grandfathers who were learned Brahmans, or priests, or Travancore state officials and teachers, they have sought and sometimes made for themselves new identities.

I shall illustrate the process of finding a new identity by comparing two young men of similar age and background, both of whom migrated to Calcutta from Dharmarajapuram in the mid-1950s. They are Mani and Subramaniam. Both are of the same age, born in 1939. Both were strongly influenced by DMK beliefs in their adolescence. Both are anti-caste. Both are very devoted to their parents. Both send remittances to their parents monthly. Both work in British firms as typist-stenographers. Both wish to retire to Dharmarajapuram some day, after they have educated their children to become professionals.

They differ profoundly, however, in their search for a modern identity.

After looking at Mani and Subramaniam, we will look briefly at identities wrought by others of the sons of Dharmarajapuram.

Mani

We had gone late on a February afternoon to his office, located on the third floor of a shabby but modern Calcutta office building. It was a long narrow office, perhaps thirty-five feet by fifteen feet with big, many-drawered desks in a long row, at which men sat before typewriters. Mani was one of these typists, a man of thirty-five with a large, pleasant, very dark-skinned face. The face had a kind of bulging shape which made me think of the elephant-headed god – Ganesha. He wore a beige and white striped sports shirt and dark green slacks with a light pin-stripe, and the usual sandals. As so often happens, the tailor had economized and made trousers and shirt a bit too short and in Mani's case too tight, since, like Ganesh, he had a plump tummy pressing against the straining buttons of his shirt.

We explained ourselves and arranged an immediate interview. Since office hours were over – it was five o'clock – we went by taxi (one which Mani insisted on paying for, taking out a roll of ten rupee bills to do so) to Mani's home. We went up to his upper-floor flat, a series of bare small rooms with children's paraphernalia strewn about. He told my assistant to talk to his wife in the kitchen. He would talk to me alone. He and I sat on light metal chairs in a small bare room adjoining a balcony. His two small sons ran in and out, and, occasionally, he set a small son aside, indicating that he should not bother us. Mani also did not want his friend, Swami, when he arrived, to join us or even to overhear us. It was to be a completely private session.

Mani struck me as straightforward and sincere, calm, matter-of-fact, a solid, good person with somewhat limited vision and intelligence. He gave much thought to his answers, often putting his hand over his closed eyes, knitting his brows answering only after lengthy pauses. I felt Mani wanted very much to talk, as frankly as possible, that it was therapeutic for him to do so.

Mani was born in 1939. He lives at present in Baliganj. Calcutta, which he characterizes as the area in which most South Indians are living, "mostly Nayars and Iyers" (major South Indian castes: the Nayars are a dominant landed Shudra caste of Kerala; the Iyers are Tamil Brahmans). He works as a senior assistant in the office of an engineering company, earning Rs 850 per month.

He lived in Dharmarajapuram almost continuously from infancy through age 15. Between 15 and 17, he attended the Maharaja's College in Trivandrum, the capital of the princely state of Travancore, where he took a B.Sc. degree in chemistry.

Forebears

Mani's ancestry can be traced back to one of the original eighteen families which received the *danam*, the gift of land, from the Maharaja of Travancore in 1753. His father's father's mother's father was a descendant of one of these families. This great-great-grandfather's daughter married a landed Brahman in the village of Kuzhiturai. When she was widowed, she returned with her children to live with her brothers in her paternal village. Two out of three of her brothers were *vatyars* (teachers of the religious tradition); the other brother was a cultivator.

Thus, Mani's grandfather, his father's father, lived as a child in Dharmarajapuram. He sold the land he had inherited from his father in Kuzhiturai, to buy land in Dharmarajapuram. As an adult, however, this grandfather had to live elsewhere, in order to serve in a temple in the village of Munchirai. There he was a *shivanpujan*, performer of *puja* or ritualized offering to the great god, *Shiva*. This was in one of the twelve Shiva temples in Kanyakumari district maintained by the Maharaja of Travancore for his own welfare and long life. This grandfather's name included the title *Shrotigal* indicating that he was learned in the *Srutis* (the revealed tradition), the *Vedas*. That man's wife's father similarly was a religious specialist, *purohita* (a household priest) in the *agraharam* (Brahman village) of Vadiveeswaram.

The *shivanpujan* prebendary was inherited by the elder son, Mani's uncle. The younger son, Mani's father, had to seek some other livelihood. He had seven years of schooling, an unusually high amount at that time, 1914, so at the age of seventeen, he became a teacher. He was a school teacher for almost forty years, teaching in over a dozen different schools in Kanyakumari district.

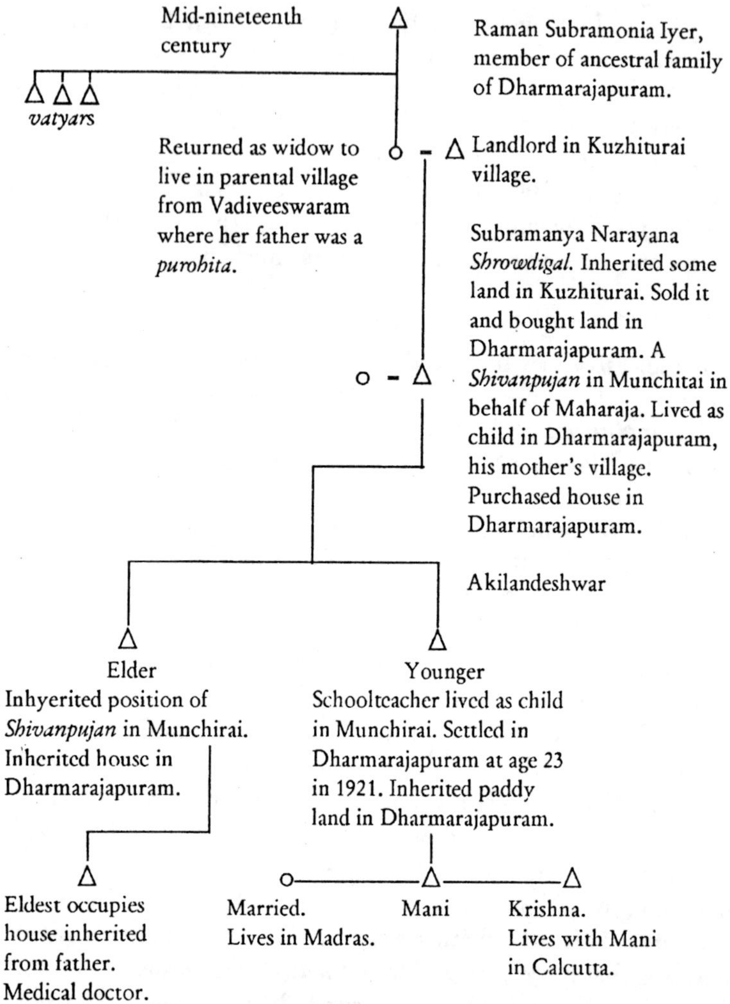

He had lived as a child in Munchirai where the *Astadanam* temple was located, at which his father had served. But, at the age of 23, in 1921, he settled for the first time in Dharmarajapuram. Here, he owned some land inherited from his father. (His elder brother similarly had inherited the house that had belonged originally to his grandmother and then to his father.) He lived on and off in Dharmarajapuram, whenever it was conveniently located with respect to his teaching assignment. He retired from teaching in 1954, to begin a second career as a postmaster in Dharmarajapuram, and to settle there permanently. He retired from that in 1969, and he now draws a postmaster's pension of fifty rupees a month. This is supplemented by his two sons in Calcutta who each send him fifty rupees per month. Out of a total income of 150 rupees, he pays twenty-five rupees per month for the house which he rents from a Brahman who lives in Bombay (Mani's father's photograph appears on page 143).

Mani's father taught in both the Tamil and Malayalam languages. He never studied English, and is not able to carry on a conversation in English. A sign of the times was that Mani's father's elder brother lost a position in the Travancore state government in the 1920s, because he could not speak English. So having suffered, this elder brother saw to it that his sons learned English. It was his English-educated elder son who was the first man of Dharmarajapuram to go to Calcutta. Three of his brothers, in turn, joined him there. It was these men, four of Mani's father's elder brother's sons, who advised Mani, and were his initial contacts in Calcutta. One of these is the principal figure in the essay just before this, "The Tamil Brahman Family as Affected by Out-Migration and Modern Occupations".

By Mani's generation, educated in the years right after the independence of India was established in 1947, virtually all of the sons of Dharmarajapuram studied English and had a modern-style education. After completing high school or college, they all then departed to scattered towns and cities to take up white-collar jobs away from home.

Childhood and Youth in the Village

Like several other of the Brahman men, Mani attended a number of different schools in the area around Dharmarajapuram. He attended elementary school in Dharmarajpuram for grades one and two. He described the school in Dharmarajapuram in those days (1940s) as:

> "a small hut in which some village man used to teach, where we used to study up to class 2. Some individuals studied only for two or three years there, and then went directly to St. Anthony's English High School for class 5."

Mani himself then attended four different schools in three different villages for two or three years each – third and fourth grades in Rampuram (two miles away), eighth in Suchindram (eight miles away), then ninth through eleventh at Saint Anthony's English High School in Kanyakumari again. The variety of schools reflects his village's closeness to other villages in a heavily populated rural area. The schooling in Suchindram reflects his family's residence there for a year while his father was teaching in the school there.

Mani pointed out that most Dharmarajapuram boys had been educated at St. Anthony's English High School in Cape Comorin. He said:

> There were a lot of very good teachers there also. Most Dharmarajapuram boys had their education there. In my class, there were about five students going from Dharmarajapuram. In all, there were fifteen or twenty students from Dharmarajapuram attending St. Anthony's -- including some girls.

Mani took his Intermediate degree by commuting the twelve miles from Dharmarajapuram by bus to Scott Christian College in Nagercoil. After attending these local schools, he went more then fifty miles north to Trivandrum, to take his Bachelor of Science degree at the Maharaja's College there, finishing in 1956, at the age of 17. He lived in Trivandrum with his mother's elder sister.

Mani grew up during a period when the DMK (Dravida Munnetra Kazhagam), a Dravidian regional chauvinistic political party, was in its early stages of development. It was characterized by an extraordinarily young leadership and membership (Barnett 1976: 188--89). There was a special issue for the party in Kanyakumari district, because it was a region in which the populace was largely Tamil-speaking. It had been part of the princely state of Travancore, and after independence, it was part of the territory of Travancore-Cochin. When a committee was appointed to reconsider the boundaries of the states constituting India, a movement sparked by the Nadars of Nagercoil began, with the purpose of making Kanyakumari part of Tamil-language Madras state, rather than being part of Malayalam-language Kerala state.

The DMK leadership, during the early 1950s when Mani was in high school, was extremely anti-Brahman. The famous movie -- *Parashakti* – written and directed by the DMK politician, Karunanidhi was released in 1952, and it showed several anti-Brahman scenes including one of a temple Brahman priest making sexual advance toward a female worshipper within the temple.

Mani (and as we shall see below, Subramoniam, also) was caught up in the DMK movement among the youth at St. Anthony's High School. The DMK was atheistic and anti-religion. The 1950s were a period when orthodox Hinduism was in defensive retreat.

Mani ties together his own minimal religiosity with his DMK commitment. He said:

> In my younger days, naturally, prayers and scriptures were in Sanskrit, and there were not many elders to teach you what the Vedas say and what is Hinduism. During my younger days, most people lost faith in God and in the Vedas. Other boys were also of that type. Nobody was keen on prayers or temples. They were just interested in playing. The DMK was just expanding its activities in those years between 1950 and 1956 [during the years of Mani's high school and college].

Mani explained his own attraction to the DMK as due to three facts: First, that the DMK was not at that time strongly anti-Brahman. The earlier DK party from which the DMK had seceded had been anti-Brahman, but not the DMK, Mani explained. Secondly, in those times, the Sanskritic Brahmanical tradition of prayers and scriptures was not being taught. Thirdly, the leaders of the group of youth to which Mani belonged were DMK, young men of non-Brahman castes.

> There were a lot of non-Brahmans there, and they taught against Hinduism. We have a lot of non-Brahman friends. Unfortunately, we had selected two of three persons who were DMK as leaders.

Because of his attraction to the DMK and the weakness of the Brahmanical teaching at the time, Mani claims not to have received much religious training.

> Actually, excepting for eating and playing, there were no activities in Dharmarajapuram. I never worked in a paddy field. I have not learned any *mantras*. I had *upanayanam* at age thirteen, and for a fortnight or so, I learned *mantras* from a pandit. Since I was influenced by DMK , I discontinued. I wore the sacred thread for my family's sake.

Part of the reform and revolution in the air among the DMK youth was criticism of the caste system and Mani accepted the DMK advocacy of inter-caste marriage.

Decision to Migrate to Calcutta

I finished my degree in September 1956. I came here (Calcutta) in May 1957. In between, I spent a few months in Dharmarajapuram just wandering about. We had a little property, a paddy field and coconut plantation, and I took some interest in gardening at that time. I did not want to be a cultivator. Most Brahmans are eager to be white-collared men, rather than cultivators. So, naturally, I also wanted to become a white-collared man. I had the idea of going to Calcutta, because a few of my cousins were here, and also they were in good position. So, quite naturally, I expected that I could get employed without any difficulty. People in a village always have some members of the family in some cities, so that another person going to the city goes to the particular city where these previous persons have gone. I had cousins here, so I came to Calcutta. Others might go to Bombay or Delhi. I showed some interest in coming to Calcutta to a cousin of mine who was visiting from Calcutta (a father's brother's son). I told him that in my family's poor financial position, it was essential that I do what I could to help.

One of my other cousins in Calcutta was against my coming. Perhaps he was afraid that I would become a burden on their family. We thought I should first master typing and shorthand. Otherwise, there would not be any betterment for me here. But my eldest cousin (a medical doctor with a clinic in Cape Comorin, and a resident in the ancestral house in Dharmarajapuram) was determined to send me, so he arranged it with one of his brothers in Calcutta.

Getting Established in Calcutta

I came on May 13, 1957 with barely two pants and two shirts, not even a suitcase. I had no *chappals* (sandals). My cousins arranged for *chappals* for me on that same day, and the next day, they asked me to go for an interview for a typist's job in the Indian Oxygen Company which was a good concern. During my college days, I had learned some typing at a typing institute where a friend was working. This helped me in getting the job.

But I was not very proficient at it. When I went for the interview, I typed for seven minutes and committed thirty-two mistakes. By a bit of luck, the typing examiner had written on the report 7/32. The Labor Officer misunderstood and thought I had typed for thirty-two minutes and had committed seven mistakes. He even asked me if that was so. Now, even though I had passed B.Sc., I could not speak English very well. I was just a village boy, very shy. So I simply nodded my head, and I got the job.

When I started work, I could not even insert the carbons (for copies) and quite a few times I failed. Fortunately, a lot of Bengali employees -- even though I am from a different state -- came to my rescue and typed many letters assigned to me. I stayed in that job for eleven days. I was then asked to quit. I was to keep in touch with them, and they would call me when a vacancy arose.

I remember one Bengali officer who was very nice to me. He taught me, "First deserve, *then* desire". I had been having a high opinion of my B.Sc. degree. He told me that if I was going for a typist job, I should be able to type, not mix acids and alkalis. So I went to a typing institute and learned typing. I was without a job for only five days and my cousin, with whom I was staying, put me in the same company where he was working. This job was as a file clerk. I used to finish all the filing within half an hour and then I used to sit quietly. Another man working there, who wanted to get extra pay because of so-called "pressures of work" advised me not to finish all the work in such a short time; otherwise, the manager might believe additional hands were unjustified.

Mani quarreled with the cousin with whom he was both living and working (they were working in the same office), so he moved out. He moved in with two men with whom he had attended St. Anthony's High School. One was his friend and neighbor from Dharmarajapuram, Swami. Through Swami's relative (his mother's father's brother's son), who was an accountant in the central government of India, he got a job in the engineering company. The exact resource network was as follows: Swami's relative (his mother's cousin -- her father's brother's son) had a son who had a friend, also from South India, who was the manager at an engineering company. Through this friend -- Mani's friend's mother's cousin's son's friend -- Mani got a job. The actual communication with this manager was done not by the son, but by his father's sister who also knew the manager. (She was also married to a man from Dharmarajapuram.) The manager said he needed someone from the South.

> It was the manager's preference. He thought Bengalis were not fit for typists' jobs. I had also learned a bit of stenography. I was used as a stenographer, though getting a typist's salary.

Mani got the job as an assistant paying Rs 150 per month. Over the subsequent sixteen years, Mani has become a senior assistant and his salary has increased to Rs 850 per month.

Mani has managed to get jobs in the office of the engineering company for both his younger brother and for the husband of a neighbor Iyer girl whom he knew in Dharmarajapuram.

Mani was married in 1963 after he had been in Calcutta for five or six years. The following year his brother, Krishna, came to live with him and his wife, and to work with Mani in the same office. Later his wife's brother also joined them. He also brought his mother's sister's son to Calcutta. He lived with Mani for two years. The couple has three children – a daughter aged ten, a son aged four, and another son aged two. The daughter is named for Mani's mother. The first son is named for his father, and the second son for his wife's father.

At the time of the interview in 1974 Mani's household was composed of his wife, three children, his own brother, and his wife's brother.

Ideology

In his ideological development over the years, Mani has become more conservative, tending to revert to cultural tradition and religious orthodoxy. He now wears the sacred thread by choice, not just to please his parents. He said, "Now I have got faith in God and am trying to learn *mantras.*"

Mani explained his reversion to more orthodox religion as due to a personal crisis that occurred when he was 25, probably the loss of a child, and to the unexpectedly religious milieu that he found to obtain in Calcutta.

> The turning point for me was age 25 or so. No, it was not like that. There has not been much of major development. Circumstances have entirely changed. When I came to Calcutta I found that the Bengalis were religious-minded. I had to change my opinion about people

> from the South. I was thinking that people who left that village left their faith in *mantras*. They may not even wear the sacred thread, I thought. When I came to Calcutta, I found that my impressions were wrong. Now I have also cultivated the habit of worshipping gods and goddesses and joined an association for these activities. My friend Swami was also influential in this changeover.

Mani's religious life includes attending the religious functions of a South Indian religious society – the *Shasta Samooham*. He also goes to a Kali temple once a month. He had a *purohita* (household priest) come a year and a half ago to celebrate the first birthday (*ayashahomma*) for his son. He also arranged for this *purohita* to come to the office at the engineering company where he works, to lead prayers on Fridays. Still Mani's activities are rather slight compared to the full religious life of Dharmarajapuram. He said:

> Apart from lighting a brass lamp and praying for a few seconds, there is not much I could say I do regularly. On evenings or Sundays, I used to read religious stories. Actually, all Brahmans are supposed to say *sandhya vandanam* three times a day. Because of the busy city life, it is not possible to do them every day. Whenever it is convenient, when I am free, I used to say them.

Mani would not like his son to be a *purohita* (a household priest. Nevertheless, he believes that Brahman priests will continue to be important. "As long as villagers give importance to temples, Brahmans will not lose their identity." He does not have sufficient leave from work to ever consider going on a pilgrimage himself, however.

So we find Mani having reverted from militant atheism or anti-religiosity to a kind of perfunctory orthodoxy.

Mani similarly gave up his reformist ideas about intercaste marriage. He explained:

> Those people [DMK political party] have come to power, and they require the help from everybody, so they cannot do much harm, so long as they are in power. Earlier I had also the idea of mixed marriages, marriages between different castes. I also wanted to marry a non-Brahman girl only, and even though when I married, my parents could not say anything against it – I was not taking expenses

> or finance from my parents; to the contrary, they were dependent on me, taking money from me – so I could have married a non-Brahman. I had a changeover. And I have not done that. I married a girl selected by my parents, even without seeing her.
>
> When I was influenced by DMK I wanted to do away with casteism, but even among the non-Brahmans they organize for themselves, the Thevars -- the Maravars – they organize to help each other. I am still against casteism, but I now feel it cannot be changed so easily.

His limited linguistic ability perhaps accounts in part for his immunity to Communist politics so strong in Calcutta. His friend, Swami, does consider himself to be a Communist, but Swami speaks Bengali, has a Bangali Communist friend, and takes a great interest in Calcutta politics.

Mani does not feel that anti-Brahmanism is strong in Calcutta. He also suggests that the DMK back in Tamilnadu cannot be too anti-Brahman in its policy, because it needs everyone's vote. Because of anti-Brahmanism, however,

> "I was not trying for a job there or trying to do some business there. Then I would have felt it. There is no anti-Brahmanism here."

Hopes for Children

Mani's children speak Tamil, and his older son and daughter go to a Tamil school. Mani finds that the costs of education are not excessively high in Calcutta, so he believes he will be able to afford to educate all three children. He recognizes that entrance to institutions of higher education is highly competitive. He hopes the sons will become doctors or engineers, and that his daughter will study through the B.A., but will never work. He also intends to arrange their marriages, hoping already that his daughter will marry one of his sister's sons (thus, a South Indian cross-cousin marriage).

Mani finds his outside activities limited by family life, saying that he has few other activities. Aside from work, "I play with the children and try to educate them."

Social Network

Mani himself commented on the ethnicity of his circle of acquaintances, almost all Iyers form the Kanyakumari area.

> We move closely only with people from our place, and especially with Iyers. Only two or three Bengali houses are known to us.

Mani has four patrilateral cousins (father's elder brother's sons) in Calcutta, and he visits them every two weeks or so. One lives in the same apartment house with him. The others live within a ten-minute walk. Another cousin, his mother's sister's son, is also in Calcutta. His classmate and close friend, Swami, also lives within a ten-minute walk. He has friends who are Iyers from Kerala (Palghat and elsewhere) whom he knew as a bachelor when groups of Iyer bachelors shared rooms and apartments.

Mani has rather limited activities outside of family and work. He attends the religious functions of the *Shasta Samooham*, and he plays bridge with his office colleagues after lunch and between five and six in the evening after office hours. He goes to cinema two or three times a year.

Homesickness, Nostalgia, and Regret

Mani came to Calcutta in order to help his aged and poor parents. He is very devoted to them. He said wistfully:

> If my father had had any property at all, I would not have left. But when you are hungry and you have education, all you can think is, "I must get out and earn." I was ashamed of doing cultivation. If I had waited two years, I could have gotten something. I only wanted to be a teacher, a teacher at St. Anthony's School. It is such a beautiful place. I miss my parents so. Here, the language is a barrier. Once married, friendships fall off. I only see my friends once in a while. One's family becomes most important. If I had stayed there, I could have had a social life, and lived among my own people. I am quite happy to work in Calcutta since I find not much bossism in the office and Bengalis are very cooperative. But only because I am far away from my parents. That is the only thing I mean, even though we mingle with Bengalis. I always want to go south and settle in my village only as quick as possible. But I am not sure whether I shall be able to go and settle in Dharmarajapuram since the income I may be able to save may not be sufficient to buy a house or buy paddy fields. After spending for my children's education and also after giving my daughter in marriage, I have to depend upon my sons who may get employment anywhere. I will stay with them only.

He expects that Dharmarajapuram will become a more cosmopolitan place in the future.

When I asked Mani about going on pilgrimages, he said:

> I am not opposed to going on pilgrimages, but I get leave only once in two years or so, so I definitely have to go to see my parents which is better than any pilgrimage.

On balance, Mani is sorry to have left Dharmarajapuram. He feels that it is a mistake to have left.

Subramaniam

Subramaniam was born in 1939. He lives in Old Rajindranagar, a new, middle-class, section of Delhi. He works as a personal secretary to the branch manager of a British firm. His move from Calcutta to Delhi represents for him a promotion within the firm. He came to Delhi a little over a year ago. Between 1959 and 1972, he worked in Calcutta at various white-collar jobs.

He was born in Dharmarajapuram and lived the first seventeen years of his life there. He holds an Intermediate degree from South Travancore Hindu College, Nagercoil.

Subramaniam is a pock-marked, rather heavy-faced man with the compact figure of a man younger than his 35 years. His wife is a sweet round-faced girl of 25 whose parental home is Trivandrum. They have a one-year old son, a tiny fellow dressed, on the day we called, in brand new clothes – a red woolen bonnet, a sweater, shorts, and a tiny pair of pointed Jaipuri slippers. He very much liked to sit on his father's lap.

The couple's home is new. They had only recently moved in. The room in which we visited them contained all new furniture. At the far end of the room were two single beds covered with bright, striped handloom spreads of modern design. These stood before large paneled cupboards. Near the door were two new couches, covered in a grey plastic fabric. Between them was a coffee table also covered with a gaily-colored plastic which matched the plastic on the head-boards of the beds. A new wooden table with two Danish-style chairs with string seats and plastic fabric covering were against one wall. Against another wall was a shining wooden bookcase decoratively filled with a copper Lakshmi figure, two carved wooden elephants, two carved wooden fauns, a radio, and a clock.

This was the most tastefully arranged and furnished Iyer house we had been in. We learned later that the family rents the entire house for Rs 500 a month. They rent out the other half of the house to a Punjabi family with four children. They themselves have the one room where we visited, which serves as bedroom, dining, and sitting room. In a central courtyard beyond were wash bowls, toilet rooms, and a small kitchen.

My assistant talked to his wife at the other end of the room while I talked to Subramaniam. He liked having his words taken down and at times, he gave much thought to what he was saying. Subramaniam struck me as self-confident, even a bit egotistical. He hinted that he had dreams of being a politician. He pronounced the interview a good experience "in case I go into politics".

Forebears

Subramaniam's mother and mother's mother moved to Dharmarajapuram when he was a small child. His mother's mother had been born in Cape Comorin, two and a half miles from Dharmarajapuram. She lived there until the time of her marriage, at the age of twelve, when she joined her husband in northern Travancore. Both her parents came from Cape Comorin. Her father had been the headmaster of a government school in Tamil and Malayalam media there.

Subramaniam's father came from Kottayam, Kerala; he worked in a bank in Trivandrum. So, his father's line was not associated with Dharmarajapuram. It is conceivable that his mother's line might be related to one or another of the ancestral families in Dharmarajapuram, since her mother's forebears of Cape Comorin might well have intermarried with people of Dharmarajapuram, as Cape Comorin Brahmans still frequently do today.

Subramaniam's father died soon after Subramaniam was born. His mother's mother had her widowed daughter and her three children come to settle in Dharmarajapuram. The money his father had left for her, his mother invested in four acres of paddy field nearby. The cultivation of this land was done by a Nadar (low caste toddy-tapper) sharecropper for over thirty years. Recently, some of the land was sold.

The family seems to have no relations with Subramaniam's father's kin.

The two women, Subramaniam's mother, and his mother's mother, live alone together in Dharmarajapuram. They are quite comfortably well-off, due to the income from the land. Nevertheless, each of the two sons send them Rs 25 a month.

Childhood and Youth in the Village

Subramaniam was educated in schools in and around Dharmarajapuram. He went through the first five grades in Dharmarajapuram. Then grades 6 to 8 at St. Anthony's, 9 to 10 at Rampur, and finally he took the Intermediate degree at South Travancore Hindu College in Nagercoil. He also studied typewriting in Rampuram.

Subramaniam explained that he did not like Dharmarajapuram when he was a boy, because the villagers took advantage of the absence of an adult man from his family. His father was dead. He said:

> ...it was the general nature of the villagers to harass the weakest, and due to the unfortunate fact that my father was not alive, they harassed and teased me... They would tease anyone from outside. Such high-handedness and harassing has now ended. See, in those days the trustees had such power that whatever their whim, it went. And their children took advantage of that. But all those old vanguards are no more. Their sons are more cultured and civilized.

Not only did his family have low status, with the resulting hazing which Subramaniam complained of, but he was a rebellious boy, a "DMK fanatic". He said:

> When I was in the village, I was anti-religion. I was against even wearing the sacred thread. At the time of my sister's marriage, my mother thought she would do my thread ceremony at the same time without extra expense. On the second day, I turned on the priest. He was teaching us the *sandhya vandanam* – telling us how to perform, so we would do it ourselves. I was not liked by the villagers when I was young, because I was too rational for a conservative Brahman society. People didn't like my smoking, considering it to be a sin or a crime. So I was very keen on leaving the village when I was young. Now having left, I suddenly have found some affection toward that

> village. Probably I visit it every year now. There is nothing else to say about it.

Already as a boy studying for the Intermediate degree, he read English literature. His favorite author during this period, he said, was Dickens. "I read David Copperfield, and then I read all of Dickens."

Decision to Migrate to Calcutta

Subramaniam said that it was the pattern for young men to migrate from Dharmarajapuram at the age of 17 or 18. In his own family, his sister married (she presently lives in Madras), and both he and his elder brother left at the age of 17. Since Subramaniam's brother, Swami, is two years older, he was already in Calcutta when Subramaniam came to join him. Swami is also the friend of Mani of Calcutta, mentioned on p. 180.

Getting Established in Calcutta

Subramaniam claims that he found his first job in Calcutta himself. He said:

> No, I found a job on my own, as a dispatch clerk in a trucking company. That was in 1959. I learned stenography after hours. Then I was a stenographer with a bad temperament. I worked in three dozen firms, more than three dozen.

His brother disapproved of his frequent change of jobs, as well as of his chronic indebtedness to friends for small sums of money, for his smoking, and for his staying out late. The brother would become impatient and angry and ask him to leave. Then, after some time, he would invite the younger brother to come back.

During this period, he said he was like the American hippies who also do not like to work. He preferred to stay at home reading rather than working. During 1960–61, when he had a renewed interest in religion, he read religious books like Vivekananda and Swami Simiyananda and Ramakrishna books. From 1961 to 1968, it was Tolstoy, Dostoeyevski, Maxim Gorky, the *Dialectic of Materialism* by Maurice Conforth, Lenin, Marx, Communism, and Mao. Since his marriage in 1969, he reads "easy fiction" like Harold Robbins, murder stories by Agatha Christie, Somerset Maugham's *Razor's Edge* and *Of Human Bondage*, Pearl S. Buck's *Good Earth*, A.J. Cronin, and Mary Corliss' *Vendetta*.

In 1963, he considered returning to Dharmarajapuram to become a cultivator. He explained:

> I would very much like to have worked on the land. I never wanted to be a landowner and enjoy the crop without actually working on it. That is a sort of feudalism. I firmly believe in the class struggle, and these Pariahs were really proletariat, and the village was bourgeoisie. I went once in 1963. I resigned my job at Calcutta and went to Dharmarajapuram. When I told my mother my proposal to work in the fields instead of giving the land out to the tiller, my mother totally rejected it saying, "Get back to Calcutta and do white-collar work". One thing I have not done is turn down my mother's request. That was in 1963. In 1969 after my marriage, I gradually was getting attracted toward city life, or I should confess my share in armchair bourgeoisie. I was married in June 1969. That was the turning point. Before that, I never worked in any firm for more than six months. After marriage, I thought only of promotions and other material comforts. I suddenly became very selfish. I don't want to blame my family. Suddenly I became selfish. I don't know the reason, unless it is because of my love toward my wife and my anxiety to give her proper protection.

Subramaniam resisted getting married. He married only because his mother insisted. She arranged the marriage. At first, when his mother sent a photo of a proposed bride for him to see, he wrote back: "No leave. I have no intention of marrying." Subsequently, when he went home to see his mother, it was thrust upon him. He explained:

> Even my seeing the girl was only a formality, because my mother had decided before my meeting her that I must marry her. And as opposed as I had been to the dowry system all along. I received a handsome dowry. But after marriage, I was very shy about taking a single copper from my in-laws – even as a gift. I try to reciprocate the gifts.

Ideology

> Probably, between the ages of 15 and 22 is the time of character-building. Invariably at 17 or 18 people leave that village.

> Then, it all depends upon the environment they are in. All in my family left at 17. In the village, the DMK influenced me in those days. I was a great Tamil fanatic. Later I changed my mind, and I spoke in a symposium in favor of wearing the sacred thread. That was in Calcutta in 1960. I regretted not having performed those things.
>
> In Calcutta, after one or two years, I suddenly was interested in religion and was a member of the *Shasta Samooham*. I started gong to the Kali temple and all, and to the United Lodge of Theosophy – Blavatsky and all.
>
> Then, in 1961 or 2, somebody left by mistake a copy of the Manifesto of Marx, and that turned me mad. Since then, I was seriously interested in Marxism. That was after reading religious books. I was not interested in ritual. I even read an English translation of the Veda, which I must confess I found full of contradictions, except for the Vedanta – the end. That is in harmony with the best Advaita philosophy. Sankara must figure among the best philosophers the world has ever produced. I accept only Advaita philosophy of Sankara. Probably, many Hindus, including the elite, would not know that. Iyers would not know Sankara's philosophy of *paramatma* and *jivatma* being one and the same. It is a clear indication of universal brotherhood and goes against the caste system.

Subramaniam thus indicated the pendulum swings in his ideology from DMK politics to orthodoxy Hinduism, then Theosophy and Vedanta, back to communist politics, and, as we shall see, then a swing back to orthodoxy.

Subramaniam still believes that the DMK and non-Brahmans in Tamilnadu are strongly anti-Brahman. He said that the DMK leaders believed that Brahmans had voted against them in the 1971 elections and were since taking revenge. The extreme of non-Brahman anti-Brahmanism, he comments upon as follows:

> E.V. Ramaswami Naickar's ideas have gotten so deeply into the blood of the Tamil, whatever may be his politics, that the non-Brahman is basically anti-Brahman.

Subramaniam himself believes that it was wrong for Brahmans to "exploit" people by teaching them that they would gain merit by feeding and gifting Brahmans. If, however, they performed their role by "imparting knowledge to all men and women irrespective of caste," or in listening to their personal problems as a psychiatrist would, then they were good for the people, i.e., the non-Brahmans. Consistent with this opinion is his position that the Maharaja's gift of land to the Brahmans of Dharmarajapuram was wrong if it was only to gain merit (*puniya,* good *karma* in some supernatural account). But it was right and good if it was to support the Brahmans so they could carry out their duty of "imparting of knowledge". As he expressed these views, he said:

> I am not against Brahmanism, but certain developments in later stages...They exploited people by spreading stories of *puniya*s (merit), the necessity of feeding Brahmans. If, to the contrary, the Maharaja had given the gift (of land in Dharmarajapuram), because he considered it the foremost duty of Brahmans to impart knowledge, and to gain knowledge. And by giving the gift, he provided a basic annuity, to free life for them, to lighten their family burden, then it would have been all right. But if he gave it because of *puniya*, that is exploitation.
>
> I do not have very good knowledge about the old traditions. But I am sure that although there were restrictions on certain *mantras* not being told to non-Brahmans, still Brahmans imparted knowledge to all men and women irrespective of caste. Thus, the Brahmans of Dharmarajapuram imparted knowledge to the non-Brahmans of B. Hamlet nearby. It is quite likely that these people would have taken advice from Brahmans in the good old days. And if they did not teach them, then they must have helped them with any personal problem, more as a psychiatrist would – giving them mental advice.

So, Subramaniam seems to reinterpret the traditional system from one in which Brahmans exploited non-Brahmans in order to be fed and supported by gifts, to one in which Brahmans were *gurus* or "psychiatrists" to non-Brahmans. He admitted that he saw this reinterpreted system as one that was benign.

Despite his benign interpretation of the behavior of his Brahmanical forebears, Subramaniam is not very religious today. He does not perform daily *sandhya vandanams*, although he did in 1960–61 in a period of religiosity. He described his activities as follows:

> In Calcutta I went to the Kali temple before 1961 and after 1969. Between 1961 and 1968, I was a strong Marxist. After marriage, a concept of fear has come into me as a confused person taking consolation in illusion. Once I had preached against it as an insult to human dignity. I went to the temple, because I lost my first son... That made some impact on me and subsequently when my wife was pregnant, I started thinking in terms of bribing the goddess with a *sari* to bless my child with a long life. From 1961 to 1968, I was a man of conviction. I was never hypocritical. After 1969, I started living on compromises. The only time I have gone on pilgrimage was in 1973 when I went to Guruvayur, we had the first food ceremony (*annaprashana*) for my child, because I wanted him to live.

Subramaniam opened the paneled cupboard door, revealing inside the *puja* shelf, containing pictures and images of Hindu gods. He said:

> We do *namaskars* (hailing the gods) here. There is not enough space here, but these are our accommodations in the way of tradition. It makes me think we live on compromises. "Necessity knows no laws." That is a Sanskrit saying. When Lord Vishwamitra ate the flesh of a dog, he did it in order to survive, and he said, "Necessity knows no laws."

With respect to his religious and political beliefs today, Subramaniam says:

> I am still a confused man. From the economic point of view, I look towards Marx for a solution in India. And, in spite of my rational thinking and convictions, I still sometimes worry about things that are considered to be bad omens – everything which my intelligence has rejected. I don't have faith, but if there is a bad omen, I stop. One should sit still, and the effects of the bed omen will go. I know that is bunkum. Yet the philosophy of 2000 years in there in me. I know it is wrong.
>
> I do not worship today, but my wife does something, and I stand there. My family is not religious compared to others. She is lightly religious. She does not do daily *puja* (offerings made to God). All she does is light the lamp and make two or three *namaskarams* (greetings to the gods) in the morning after bathing. I am very different from others in my family. My brother is very religious and pious. He grew

> up in a different way. He is very interested in rituals. Swami Ranganand is the only one whom I have heard preach who was not confused. He is in the United States. He preaches Advaita Vedanta, the *jnana marg.* I myself can only follow the *bhakti marg,* because it is the easiest. I do not and could not do all the rituals for *karma marg.* I do not have the time for contemplation and concentration of *jnana marg,* so I can try to love one being devotedly. I have not attained that yet, however.

Subramaniam dubs his ambivalence concerning religion as his "split personality".

Subramaniam greatly prefers the intellectual atmosphere of Calcutta to the pragmatism of Delhi.

> I do not like Delhi at all. Of all the places I have lived. I like Calcutta the best. I found people in Calcutta having some element of affection, some human values, which, if I am right, people in Delhi lack completely. During my stay in Calcutta, the Marxist thought greatly influenced me. Any intelligent discussion in Delhi with the common man is impossible. People do not have a political conscience, nor are they interested in serious subjects. All they wish to talk about is rationing and other petty things. The common man in Calcutta has political ideology and political conscience. The reason, I presume, is that Bengali literature is more realistic than the high imaginativeness of other Indian literature -- with the exception of Malayalam. Another reason is that revolutionary thoughts were very much in Bengal even before independence, whereas the rest of Indians were concerned with fate and Gandhian philosophy. That's what I think. Gandhian philosophy, I think, is utopian. *Ahimsa* (non-violence) is a utopian theory. I even doubt that India won independence by non-violence at all. The revolutionary upsurge plus the Indian interest in the army were the main reasons for the British to quit. There were many Indians in high offices in the military. Then, there were the trials of the Indians National Army. The British could not have continued British administration of India. They felt the days were not far off when they would be forced to quit. The Labour Party and Attlee were very much in favor, apart from the Americans who also very much favored Indian independence. You must see in making a study of Dharmarajapuram that a boy from Dharmarajapuram could have knowledge of history and politics only

> from close association with Bengalis. I would not have the knowledge I have, had I not come to Calcutta. In any other city, I would not have gained that knowledge.

Subramaniam's is critical of the Bengali, however, he finds them to be:

> very emotional. They are an intelligent race, and I must say, they are lethargic. Bengal is a place unfit for Communism, because of their negligence toward duty. They are inclined not to work very much there. The preachers of communism are mostly white-collar workers. Even in the trade union movement, they are more interested in quantitative demands than in changing society. Again, the trade unions are dominated by white-collar clerks or *babus*, and in drawing up charters of demands. They look towards the interest of office workers more than factory workers.

Hopes for Son

Subramaniam believes that anti-Brahmanism will intensify even further in South India, so "however efficient," his son might be, he will not be given a "due place" in either Tamilnadu, or Kerala. Although Kerala is not anti-Brahman as Tamilnadu "there also Brahmans were not liked by other castes". In northern India, he expects that "provincial and parochial feelings" will also grow, so his son will also "not find it easy to move smoothly in North India." His hopes for his son, he voiced saying:

> I want good health for my child, and the best possible education. I would like to make him a professional man and nurse him to meet any eventuality. If a man can make his son to study what the father thinks, I will see my son become an expert in computer science, computer programming. I would be happy if when my son grows up, he leaves India and settles anywhere else, but in India -- except in Africa.

So Subramaniam is prepared to encourage his son to leave India, with nary a thought about his own needs in his old age.

Social Network

Subramaniam did not associate with people from Dharmarajapuram when he lived in Calcutta, except for his brother.

> I did not move with people of my village – with the exception of my brother. The main reason for that was that I felt people from my village were very hypocritical. If I were to tell them the truth about myself, they would brand me a bad character. And I have never wanted to hide anything about myself from any good friend of mine. If I were to smoke, they would brand it a sin. If a rich man smokes, they call it aristocracy. If I wear good clothes, they brand it lavishness; if a rich man does it, they call it modern living. I am not satisfied with my own answer. It is not exactly hypocrisy.

Although Subramaniam learned to speak Bengali readily, and he says he had friends from Kerala and Bengal, the three friends in Calcutta whom he greatly misses are all Iyers from Kerala. Two presumably are white-collar workers in businesses; the third is a social worker. These three men gave Subramaniam money in his bachelor days. With them he can carry on lively conversations on politics, literature, and films.

In Calcutta, Subramaniam belonged to the South Indian Club, and to the Friends Forum where they had "social meets and intellectual talk". He was editor of a newspaper, the *Educator*, for one of these organizations, for some time. At the South Indian Club he also played rummy for stakes, as well as bridge and table tennis.

While I was interviewing Subramaniam, two couples, one with a small child, came in. These were his wife's brother and his wife, plus their friends, a man, wife and small child. All were from Kerala. Subramaniam joked with these visitors, saying that his best friend in Delhi was the friend's wife.

Subramaniam sees his married sister who lives in Delhi at least twice a week. He stayed with her family for four days when he first came to Delhi, before finding a place to live. He already knows two of the neighbors, although he has been in this new house for only a short time. One of the neighbors is a Nayar from Kerala, the other an Iyer from Kerala. He says, however:

> I have no plans to expand my friends, because I am very fond of playing with my child when I come back from the office.

Living nearby is his closest friend, an Iyer from the Vadiveeswaram *agraharam*, a dozen miles from Dharmarajapuram.

The Cosmopolitan Rejecting Home

As we have seen above, Subramaniam believes that the Calcutta milieu liberated his intellect, provided him with a knowledge of the great world. He said:

> Had I lived and married in Dharmarajapuram, I would have continued to be a fanatic Tamilian, thought Shivaji Ganeshan was the greatest actor in the world, thought that Tamil was the greatest literature in the world, been movie crazy, been a strong supporter of the DMK. The difference is that now I hold the view that contemporary literature in Tamil is zero, if not negative. S.G. overacts. Tamil movies lack realism. And the Naxalbari movement is the only political movement after independence, when all the rest of the people in politics are political opportunists or careerists.

In Dharmarajapuram, he would have had fewer clothes to wear, but better housing and food than he has in Delhi. He would have suffered from lack of cash for cigarettes and recreation.

> In Delhi, now I feel. When will I be able to have a small flat of my own? When will I be able to buy a fridge and TV?

Subramaniam predicts that the future of Dharmarajapuram will be that of a retirement village. Most of the land will be sold off by the Brahman owners.

> The owners are very few; in days to come, there will be none. There will be only pensioners in hired houses or bought houses who will spend their old age there. I will definitely live there only. I am contemplating buying a house there. I'll go there upon retirement. Of all place, I have affection toward Dharmarajapuram, although I have liking for Calcutta, because of my many friends there. Note the difference between affection and liking.

A Comparison of Mani and Subramaniam

Differences

In comparing the adjustment of the two men, we may note a number of factors that seem to have affected them. *First*, the standing of the two men's families differed in their home village. Mani's ancestry goes back to the original families. His father's father's mother was a native, and his father's brother married a woman of an ancestral family. Thus, although his father was poor, the family was accepted by the ancestral families as having a right to live in the village. His father's father's home is still known as such, and is occupied by his father's eldest brother's son. With such solid community standing, Mani left Dharmarajapuram only reluctantly, motivated by the expectation that he should help his impoverished family.

Subramaniam's family, on the other hand, was prosperous, but it had only marginal status, because its ancestry did not stem from the original Dharmarajapuram families. His mother's mother had bought a house in the village; she herself was a native of the Cape Comorin *agraharam* a few miles away. Her daughter and children came to live with her, after the daughter was widowed. Subramaniam felt unwelcomed in the village. The fatherless children were treated badly in their childhood, he recalled, as villagers pressured the family to sell its land and to leave. His non-conformism exacerbated the lack of welcome he suffered because of his family's status as intruders. Subramaniam was eager to leave Dharmarajapuram.

Second, the two men differ in their linguistic abilities. Mani could not speak English well when he first arrived in Calcutta. Subramaniam already had developed a taste for English literature when he was studying for his Intermediate degree. It was then that he read "all of Dickens". One suspects that the ease with which he got new jobs, one right after the other, is to be explained by his proficiency in English. Mani has lived in Calcutta for eighteen years, but still complains of the language barrier, the Bengali spoken in Calcutta. Subramaniam prided himself in having learned Bengali quickly.

Third, Subramaniam seems to have prepared himself for work in Calcutta more realistically than Mani, first taking a job as a dispatch clerk, while studying stenography at night. Knowing that he was not a proficient or even a passable typist, Mani, nevertheless, took a typist's job. Mani got his job through relatives; Subramaniam got his own.

Fourth, Mani stays within a circle of relative and neighbors who have migrated to Calcutta, both at the office and in his neighborhood. Subramaniam avoided co-villagers living Calcutta, and made new friends less critical of him and more intellectually-stimulating. They also were Iyers, however. Subramaniam reached out to imbibe the ideas in the Calcutta milieu to a greater degree than Mani.

While both men indicate the importance of their ties to their parents, Mani seems to yearn for the psychological support his parents can give him, while Subramaniam takes a stance of humoring mother and grandmother, using his "obedience" to them as an excuse for conforming to the norm of doing "white-collar" work, and accepting an arranged marriage. For Subramaniam, devotion to his wife binds him to his family of procreation. Mani has not made such a substitution, being still bound to his parental family, perhaps overwhelmed by the responsibility of supporting three small children on his modest salary.

Fifth, Subramaniam married at the age of 29 and spent several years in his twenties as an ideological Marxist. During that time, he read serious works, and engaged in intellectual discussions with new but close friends. Mani married at 25, so he had four years less time to imbibe what Calcutta had to offer or to make deep new friendships. He did not indicate, in my interview with him, any interest in reading or in intellectual matters. At 35, he has three children to worry about, while Subramaniam has only one toddler. In Erikson's terms, we may say that Subramaniam had a longer psychological moratorium between adolescence and adulthood in which to find his identity.

Subramaniam is the intellectual. Mani in the frustrated would-be scientist. One has been able to follow his bent; the other has not. But Subramaniam is also more out-going. Although he has just moved to a new flat in Delhi, he already knows neighbors, both South Indian and Punjabi, after only a few days. Mani limiting himself to family and work, complains about friendships deteriorating after marriage.

Mani looks forward to his retirement in twenty years. He would like to settle in Dharmarajapuram, but assumes he will not be able to do so, because he will be dependent then upon his sons and will live where they do. Subramaniam hopes to settle in Dharmarajapuram, and to do so, is trying to buy a house there now. Meanwhile, however, he dreams of becoming a politician. He hopes his son will go abroad. He indicates no intention of living with his son when he is older.

Subramaniam has tried on various identities between the ages of 15 and 35 – that of the DMK fanatic, the angry Marxist, the village agriculturalist, the lover of English literature, the religious fanatic, and now he toys with a new one, as politician. Mani, on the other hand, became disillusioned with his DMK identity and reverted to a rather unsatisfactory, superficial and empty conformity to tradition, without trying out some other new ideology or new identity.

Subramaniam as the Modern Man

Sociologists who have tried to understand processes of modernization have suggested that the modern man is open to new experiences and believes in his own efficacy, his own ability to accomplish things himself effectively (Inkeles and Smith 1974). He is empathic (Lerner 1958), able to project himself into the roles and situations of others at a distance – people like political leaders. It seems in our comparison of Mani and Subramaniam that Subramaniam is more open to new experiences. He has learned Bengali, has learned about Marxism, has read serious political philosophical literature, as well as English novels. He reaches out more readily to meet new people, and to seek out and spend time with others who share his interests. Mani is more formally educated than Subramaniam, having a B.Sc. degree, while Subramaniam has only the Intermediate degree, but he is not as open to new experience and new learning. Perhaps in part, this is because the kind of education he had, a science education, has no applicability in the milieu in which he works. Subramaniam is, then, the more "modern" man.

Similarities

Inkeles and Smith (1974) say that the traditional man is not only passive and fatalistic, but also obedient to elders. Neither Mani nor Subramaniam can be said to be free from strong parental influence. Mani quite willingly states his yearning to continue to be dependent upon them. Subramaniam made some protest to his mother and mother's mother concerning both his work (when he came back to the village determined to be a cultivator) and his marriage (he wrote them that he did not want to marry), but in the end he obeyed them – returning to Calcutta to be a white-collar man instead of a cultivator, and allowing them to arrange a marriage for him.

Both men are alike in their return to orthodox religion due to the death of a first child. Mani seems to feel betrayed, because the Iyers in Calcutta are quite orthodox, rather than being liberated from religion.

Subramaniam is "confused", because such "superstition" is inconsistent with the atheistic Bengali Marxism to which he was attracted.

The modern man is above all politically modernized. Both Subramaniam and Mani were very much influenced by the activities of the DMK party in their high school years. Subramaniam continued this political interest, but shifted it from the DMK to Marxism, at the same time reinterpreting the traditional Brahman role to make it more acceptable and congruent with his modern beliefs. He prefers to see it now as imparting knowledge to everyone, a kind of democratization of Hinduism (Singer 1972: 149, 162, 188). Mani became disillusioned with DMK ideology, finding it did not fit in the sub-culture of South Indians in Calcutta.

The Meaning of Migration

Migration to Calcutta and North India has meant rather different things to the two men. Mani, to the extent he can, stays within his village and *jati* network. His close associates at work, at home, and in his neighborhood are close relatives from Dharmarajapuram, and from southern Tamilnadu and Kerala, persons from his own *jati* network. Subramaniam used migration as a means to escape from the village and confines of southern Tamil Iyer culture. He is willing to reach out to Bengali and English cultures, and to be influenced by them. He is more modern than Mani, but also more alienated from his own micro-community.

In speaking about Tahitian migrants, Robert Levy has also contrasted the locally oriented migrant and the escapee migrant.

> There are perhaps two basic types of emigration. The majority, even though they had moved to another place, were still part of the interlocking series of rural communities of which Piri (village of study) was, for them, the center. Even when these people moved to Papeete (the city) they lived in "rural" Papeete, in neighborhoods and in activities which kept them in close contact with Leeward Island affairs and visitors, and from which they could easily return to Piri, having seen the big city life very much from the outside. For a small minority of others, emigration from Piri was an attempt to escape the whole system (Levy 1973: 65).

Migration to Calcutta for Mani and Subramaniam was not traumatic, eased as it was by the presence of relatives and a Tamil Iyer sub-community. South Indian institutions have been transported – the *Shasta Samooham* and other South Indian religious organizations, and the Tamil schools for the migrants' children. Then, Tamil wives join these men, as marriages are arranged by parents or relatives still at home.

Migration for the youth of Dharmarajapuram is not a matter of selectivity of a few pioneers, even though it might once has been. It is a matter of "mass migration". All youth leave now for jobs outside their village and region. It is an "environment of mobility", one in which it is taken for granted that a boy will be educated and take up a non-manual occupation, that his parents will make the sacrifices necessary for that education. It does not even seem to involve upward social mobility, in that the jobs taken by the young men are not clearly more prestigeful than those of their fathers as officials and teachers in Travancore. It is a migration required by history – population pressure, the disappearance of the state of Travancore, and the anti-Brahmanism of the new era in Tamilnadu.

Migration is not a new development. Their forefathers moved readily to priestly, religious, or bureaucratic jobs in Travancore. What is new is the distance, and the foreignness of the clime – whether Bengali, Hindi or Marathi, plus the new constant, the English language. Ease of migration depends heavily upon an individual's capacity for languages and his readiness to learn languages.

One can even argue that migration is traditional with Brahmans. After all, the eighteen families who found Dharmarajapuram came considerable distances to a strange country, presumably to better themselves. The taking up of a strange language is merely part of the traditional Brahman effort to remain the supporters and close associates of rulers, whether as priests or as councilors.

The ideological challenge for Subramaniam and Mani and men of his generation is the repudiation of Brahmans. Their inherited centuries-old role is no longer valued in either Tamil society or society elsewhere. As youth, they accepted the DMK criticism of traditional Hinduism, and by implication, the criticism of their own inherited roles as Brahmans. In Calcutta, both have discarded the DMK ideology. Mani has weakly returned to orthodox Brahmanism.

Subramaniam reluctantly depends on what he considers to be old Brahman superstition, ambivalently leaning still on the Marxism which he put in the place of the DMK ideology, and admitting that he is a "confused man". The challenge for both these men is to find in their mid-thirties, a new life ideology.

As Erikson has pointed out, identity crises in the individual's life cannot be separated from contemporary crises in historical development, because the two help to define each other and are truly relative to each other (Erikson 1968:23). At the same time, self-identity and ideology are aspects of the same process, necessary for "further individual maturation" (*ibid.* 189).

Other Men, Other Identities

How do these two men compare with other male migrants from Dharmarajapuram? What other kinds of identities have they developed? There were some others who, like Mani, seem to have settled for a rather constricted life of work and family. In some cases, the men in question were very successful on the job, but they seem to suffer from a psychological depression from the absence of other meaning in their lives.

With some older men, a greater Anglicization proceeded in their youths before independence. In the case of two men who had worked for the national government, their true cultural home lies in the English language newspaper and in English novels. One 52–year old man, resident in Delhi, regularly borrows books at the British Cultural Center. Another man, aged 73, and now retired in Dharmarajapuram, has read all of the English language books in the Nagercoil library, and he spends much time reading his daily English newspaper and listening to cricket matches on the radio. He has never joined in village religious and lifecycle rites, feeling isolated except for a feeling friendship with a retired professor who lived in the village for a few years – another Anglicized gentleman who told us that he had never learned to read and write Tamil, that Tamil culture was not recognized as existing in the 1930s when he was growing up.

The Anglicized find enjoyment in their English novels, but suffer social and cultural isolation.

A more successful identity was that adopted by two of the men interviewed. One is a classmate of Mani's residing in Kanpur where he is a high officer in his company's union. In interviewing him, I had the impression that he was so deeply involved in his union organization's activities that he seldom thought about Dharmarajapuram. He was hard put to remember the details of his youth there – in contrast to Mani who seems to be living his youth there still.

Another man, now aged 52, had a successful career as a labor union official, but now looks forward to living in retirement in Dharmarajapuram. He fully intends to organize the village for progress and betterment. He is implementing his plans for this, by buying three houses there, and by arranging a marriage for his nephew with a daughter of the most prominent ancestral family in the village. His efforts at leadership are likely to be furthered by the fact that both he and his wife have ancestral connections in the village, and ties with four or five of the ancestral families.

In the case of the labor union leaders, the seemingly natural leadership ability of the Brahmans is brought into play, and their repudiation by the non-Brahman citizenry is overcome by their service to men of all castes who belong to their unions. Such men seem to have relatively little interest in traditional Smartha Brahman religion.

Another successful identity was developed by the first male migrant from Dharmarajapuram to Calcutta. He came in 1932 when there was no South Indian Brahman community to join. He pictures his situation as one of "sink or swim". He could not be finicky about food pollution, because he had to eat in Bengali restaurants. He had to learn Bengali (which he did rapidly), because no one spoke Tamil. This gentleman, aged 56, has educated his children successfully, including a son who is a doctor, and holds a responsible custodial job in his company. His meaningful identity, however, that has given completion to his life, is as a clubman, one belonging to a large number of different community organizations, some all Tamil Brahman, some quite cosmopolitan, like the Rotary and Lions. He now says he is deluged with requests to be on boards of directors of philanthropic organizations. When we went to interview him, we had to wait while he finished his conversation with a leading Calcutta politician. Again, his predisposition to lead and to have high status has been met in a non-religious and non-caste context, where non-Brahmans can accept his ascendancy.

Conclusion

In this paper, I have tried to look at the dilemma facing Brahmans newly emerging from generations as learned religious specialists into an India no longer willing to confirm their once god-given superiority. Repudiated in their homeland, they migrate out seeking new lives and new identities.

References

Balan, Jorge, Harley L. Browning, and Elizabeth Jelin (1973), *Men in a Developing Society*, Austin: University of Texas Press.

Barnett, Marguerite Ross (1976), *The Politics of Cultural Nationalism in South India*, Princeton, New Jersey: Princeton University Press.

Erikson, Erik II (1968), *Identity: Youth and Crisis*, New York: W.W. Norton & Co.

Inkeles, Alex and David II Smith (1974), *Becoming Modern*, Cambridge. Massachusetts: Harvard University Press.

Lerner, Daniel (1958), *The Passing of Traditional Society*, Glencoe, Illinois: The Free Press.

Levy, Robert I. (1973), *The Tahitians*, Chicago: University of Chicago Press.

Singer, Milton (1972), *When a Great Tradition Modernizes*, New York: Praeger.

8

Foxes, Lions and Bears

The Circulation of Landownership in Southernmost Tamilnadu

Is a transition taking place in the rural social structure of India from caste to class – from a caste system organized on a local basis to a system of stratified social classes, also organized on a local basis? Andre Béteille doubts that the process of change taking place represents a shift to social stratification in terms of social classes, especially if social classes are defined as interest groups in conflict with one another. He observes:

> It is frequently argued that in countries like India the older system of inequalities based on caste is being replaced by a class system not only in the cities but also in the rural areas. If caste stands for a system of inequality in which groups are sharply differentiated and at the same time organically related, then clearly there is evidence of the decline of caste. If, on the other hand, class stands for a system of antagonistic groups based on the polarization of consciously organized interests, there is no general evidence that this kind of structure is emerging throughout the country: the predominant impression is one of amorphousness rather than structure (1974: 110).

Can we advance beyond Béteille's impression of amorphousness? Joan Mencher, in her book *Agriculture and Social Structure in Tamilnadu*, divides the rural land-cultivators of Chingleput district into six socioeconomic classes: the landless, those with 1–2.5 acres, those owning between 2.5 and 7.49 acres, those owning between 7.5 and 15 acres, those owning between 15 and 30 acres, and those owning

---

over 30 acres (1978: 161–68). Taking a Marxist-inspired orientation, Mencher has defined class "in relation to the productive process and the access which a family has to the means of production" (ibid: 160). She admits, however, that there are "forces at work which tend to mask or blur class distinctions, or to create conflicts within the same social class (in the Marxian sense, *i.e.*, people who share the same position in relation to their control over the sources and means of production)" (ibid: 190). Mencher has certainly advanced beyond Béteille's 'amorphousness', but we can only say that we are *beginning* to approach a conceptualization, not that we have arrived.

In this paper,[1] I would like to look at land transference as an index of transformation going on in a local society still operating very much in terms of caste-communities. Since 1967, I have made fourteen short field trips to Kanyakumari district in southernmost Tamilnadu.[2] There I have tried to look closely at the processes of change taking place in half a dozen hamlets mostly in Agasteeswaram taluk, the area around Cape Comorin and Nagercoil. In this paper, I shall look at the land transferences affecting the people of five hamlets. Three of the hamlets adjoin one another; the fourth is about half a mile away from the threesome; the fifth is perhaps three-fourths of a mile away from the threesome and about one-fourth of a mile away from the fourth. Of the three adjoined hamlets, two are composed of Nadars (toddytappers and cultivators of low Sudra rank); the other is multicaste, composed of Vellalas (high Sudra cultivators), Asaris (goldsmiths and carpenters), and Thevars (traditionally military and local guardsmen). The fourth hamlet is composed of Sambhavars, untouchable Parayas who used to be agrestic slaves to the Brahmans of the fifth hamlet.

What makes the location for this exercise in the relationship between land transference and change in social structure more than just one of convenience is that these hamlets represent a sample from one of the most literate rural districts in India; it is also a region in which land has been a saleable commodity and a form of private property for more than a hundred years. Here we may see the results of a long-term experiment in an Indian setting of land having been defined legally and in action treated as a freely-moving commodity.

The questions I ask are these: (i) What have been the trends in land transfer? From which castes to which castes? (ii) What are the people's own views of these changes? How do the inhabitants in Agasteeswaram taluk describe and explain them? (iii) Why have these trends taken place? Granted that, as Mencher says, "much of the dynamics which one can see on the ground is hard to capture..." (1978: 194), what causes can we, as outside observers, specify? (iv) What kind of changes in social structure have taken place by virtue of these land transfers? (v) How can we conceptualize the emerging social structure?

The paper will be in six parts:

1. some remarks about Agasteeswaram taluk, Kanyakumari district, and the five hamlets;
2. some comments on important nineteenth- and twentieth-century happenings of relevance;
3. a consideration of who has amassed land;
4. and who has lost land;
5. a summary of these trends; and
6. a consideration of how we can conceptualize this dynamic social structure.

What if land were easily saleable everywhere? What effects upon the caste structure would there be? What kind of social structure would emerge? In southernmost Tamilnadu, we may begin to get some answers.

District, Taluk, Hamlets

Kanyakumari district dots the southernmost apex of the inverted triangle that is South India. According to the 1981 Census of India, the literacy rate in Kanyakumari district is 64 percent *(Kanyakumari District Census Handbook* 1981: 4, hereafter KDCH 1981), as compared to an all-India percentage of 36 percent (*Statistical Abstract India* 1986: 538–39), giving it one of the highest literacy rates in India; among the highest for an almost entirely rural district (83 percent of its population). Although some timber and rubber are produced, the district is primarily food-producing, its main crops being wet rice, tapioca, pepper, pulses, mangoes, palmyra, coconuts, cashewnuts, peanuts, vegetables and plantains. Kanyakumari district has a long coastline; therefore, some commercial fishing is done. The main cash crop is coconut, the fiber from the coconuts being used as coir in rope-making.

Only 12 percent of the district's 1,423,399 people live in the one big town – Nagercoil – which has two major 'industries', namely, education and medical treatment. The 1981 Census listed 32 primary schools, 22 middle schools, 26 high schools, and five colleges in Nagercoil, as well as four hospitals, two dispensaries, and one family planning clinic (KDCH 1981: 80); in addition, there are more than a score of nursing homes. The Tamilnadu government has characterized Kanyakumari as a district 'backward' in all respects except for literacy (Tamilnadu Government 1973: 1, 12).

The high rate of literacy results from a combination of missionary activity which began in the early nineteenth century, which had the founding of schools as one of its primary achievements, and the encouragement of and support for such objectives by the Maharajas of Travancore throughout the nineteenth and the first half of the twentieth centuries when Travancore was often rated as the most progressive of the princely states. Kanyakumari district was part of Travancore State up until independence, and since its population was Tamil-speaking, it became part of Madras State (later Tamilnadu) after states reorganization in 1956. Though now part of Tamilnadu, Kanyakumari's pre-1956 history must be understood within that of the former princely state of Travancore.

The hamlets, whose lands I shall focus on, are in Agasteeswaram taluk, the southernmost of the four taluks composing Kanyakumari district. Agasteeswaram taluk is divided into 19 villages (KDCH 1981: 59); it should be understood that here 'villages' refer to revenue divisions. Each 'village' has an average of over 11 thousand people, and, though covering a continuous territory, each is dotted with scores of hamlets. The largest caste of the taluk is Nadar. Other numerous castes include Brahmans, Vellalas, Asaris, Thevars, and Sambhavars.

Before turning to the land transactions of these three hamlets, let me make four points about the land history for this region.

Four Points Concerning Travancore and Agasteeswaram Taluk Land History

Travancore emerged with the unification of a number of small principalities conquered by Maharaja Martanda Varma during the 1720s. The territories conquered were owned directly by Travancore State, so that by the mid-nineteenth century, 80 percent of the cultivable land belonged to the state itself. This is a first point of importance in the land history of Travancore. In contrast to many other parts of India where there were a series of intermediaries between the top government and the tiller of land, in Travancore, from the eighteenth century through mid-nineteenth century, most of the land was tilled by the cultivators *directly* for the state owners (Varghese 1970: x).

A second important point in Travancore land history was the 'Magna Carta of Travancore', as it was called, actually a royal proclamation made in 1865. Previously, the *pandara pattom* lands, the lands of the king, were given on more or less permanent lease to tillers in exchange for a kingly share in the produce. Such *pattom* lands could not be transferred to anyone else without permission. But, the proclamation of 1865 changed all that. Lands were transferred as private property to the tillers or former *pattom*-holders who could now transmit them to relatives or to others by testament or registration of transfer, and they could now sell or mortgage the land (*Travancore Land Revenue Manual* IV: 375).

T.C. Varghese, in his fine history of land tenures in Kerala, assessed the effects of the 1865 Magna Carta Proclamation, writing as follows:

> This action, in effect, meant the release of these lands from State-landlordism, and their distribution among cultivators. Ownership of land was, in the process, diffused among all castes and groups connected with agriculture. By allowing free-transferability in land, the most valued asset in the economy was made a commodity in the market...it caused a spurt in transactions revolving around land, and this paved the way for expansion in economic activities.
>
> The Administrative Report of Travancore for the year after the Proclamation observed that, in the course of that year, lands valued at about Rs 475,000 were sold among the cultivators. A spurt in the reclamation of waste lands followed suit (1970: 65).

So, the second point concerning the land history is that land was transformed into private property by the proclamation of 1865; it became a freely-moving commodity. As my friend and informant of the multicaste hamlet under study, Chidambaram Pillai, put it: "Land goes round and round and round." In other words, land tends not to remain in any one owner's hand for many years.

The third point in land history is the increase in productivity and the consequent value of land brought about by the Travancore State irrigation projects. Of especially great importance to Agasteeswaram taluk was the Kodeyar Dam Project, located 28 miles north of Nagercoil, completed in 1906.

Rainfall at this, Indian land's end, is especially sparse. Before the building of Kodeyar system of canals, mostly dry crops were grown in Agasteeswaram. The Brahmans were fortunate to have a large tank on the lands granted to them by the Travancore Maharaja in 1753. Its waters irrigated the lands of the Brahmans and their Sambhavar slaves. The Asaris, Vellalas, and Thevars had various craft and service occupations and owned some dry land. The Nadars depended heavily for their livelihood upon palm sugar and toddy-making from the sap of palmyra palm trees which grew on dry land. With the increase in irrigation facilities around 1906, the value of rather poorly producing dry land was suddenly enhanced. Improvement in irrigation facilities has been made from time to time, especially by the construction of more channels from the main arteries, which have benefited Agasteeswaram farmers.

A fourth point about land is that none of the major crops in southernmost Kanyakumari have enjoyed a recent production revolution, even though Chidambaram proved that rice production in Agasteeswaram taluk could be increased ninefold through the use of improved seed and chemical fertilizer, a story that will be alluded to later. (He won an all-Madras State prize for his accomplishment in the mid-1960s.) Neither at the time of writing this paper in 1980, nor while making minor revisions in it in 1989–90, has rice or any other crop in Agasteeswaram taluk enjoyed an increase in yield that could be called a 'green revolution'. Mechanized agriculture is not yet popular; work continues to be done by hand by coolies. This is a fourth point – that there has been no remarkable increase in agricultural production in southern Kanyakumari since the mid-1960s, as there has been in the Punjab and other parts of India.

Who can Amass Land?

Since the improvement in irrigation in 1906, the rural population of Kanyakumari district has more than quadrupled (333,466 in 1901 to

1,423,399 in 1981). Such increase is partly natural, but largely due to immigration of people from neighbouring Tinnevelly district, formerly part of the Madras Presidency, administered directly by the British; these people were attracted to Kanyakumari by the newly wet land. Density of population in 1981 was recorded as 845 per square mile as compared to an average for Tamilnadu of 372 (KDCH 1981: 3). Population is unusually dense in rural Agasteeswaram taluk.

Where did the population come from? Starting with the earliest traditions, at least some Nadars seem to be indigenous to the area; many others have moved in from Tinnevelly district, in the past century. Originally 18 Brahman families were granted 200 acres, along with a tank and 18 families of Sambhavar slaves, in 1753 by the Maharaja of Travancore; the land and the tank were part of the holdings of the Kanyakumari temple which became his when he acquired the area from the Nawab of Arcot.

The tradition among the Brahmans is that the founding families of their *agraharam* came from the temple community at Chidambaram, also located in Tinnevelly district. The Asaris seem to have come into the area about the same time as the Brahmans; they were brought in for stone construction for the Maharaja. The Thevars may have been brought in at the same time to guard over the ongoing construction. While these caste groups speak Tamil and, thus, it seems likely that they originally came from Tinnevelly district, the oral tradition among the Asaris holds that at least some of their families came from further north in Travancore – a Malayali-speaking region. Such groups were given land to support themselves, and it is likely that they became owners of this land through the proclamation of 1865.

Most of the present-day Vellalas are descendants of the two customs officials who served at a post on the boundary between Travancore and the Madras presidency of British India, to the northeast.

Of the Brahmans, only about half are descendants from the original 18 families granted land by the Maharaja; others are tenants in houses belonging to absentee owners, most of whom are also descendants of the original grantees. Unlike any of the other caste-communities of our study, the Brahmans have migrated out. Under the Maharaja, they were either temple priests or scholars of classical Hinduism, or they were school teachers and officials within

Plate 16

A street in the multi-caste Kanyakumari village. (Photo: Spring 1967, by Konstantin Kolenda)

Plate 17

A Saiva Vellala farmer in the Kanyakumari multi-caste village with his wife, one of his three children, his brother's wife, his brother's three children, and the two brothers' widowed mother. The brother absent from the photo is a minor government official. The two brothers' grandfather, a customs officer on the border between Travancore and the Madras presidency, bought about 50 acres of dry land from lower-caste farmers in the 1880s. Fifty acres is considered a large land-holding in southern Tamilnadu, but it was divided among the grandfather's four sons and ten grandsons. In waiting are at least fourteen great-grandsons and 5 great-great-grandsons. (Photo: August 1978, by Pauline Kolenda)

Plate 18

A Nattatti Nadar landowner in front of his house. Out of the 43 households among the Nattatti Nadars in the multi-caste Kanayakumari village in 1969, this man ranked tenth in landownership, with almost 27 cents of dry land and more than 14 cents of wet land (There are 100 cents in an acre). Over the years, this man paid for the education of his three sons who are all in professional jobs and married off his three daughters in good style. (Photo: August 1978, by Pauline Kolenda)

the princely state. Beginning in the 1930s, when one Brahman high school graduate left to work as a clerk in a business in Calcutta, increasing numbers of youths went out, so that in the 1970s virtually all young men finished high school and a stenographic-typing course and then left to work in businesses in Madras, Calcutta, Kanpur, Bombay, and Delhi. Some of the Brahmans became officials in the national government, some in the state government; but most worked as office personnel in urban business firms.

Now residing in the Brahman hamlet are their elderly parents and collateral elderly kin. There are, as well, some younger and older tenants who are Brahmans from elsewhere, people now working in the area who need housing accommodation. While once the ancestral owners of the village land together owned 200 acres, now few own more than a house and an acre of land. Over the years land was sold to pay for expenses of seeing sons through high school and for dowering daughters. Brahmans typically have had large families of four or more children, although they are not the only ones to do so.

Among the other communities, there has been relatively little education – among the Vellalas, one or two men have finished high school; among the other communities, almost none have gone so far in school. The Sambhavars, however, like the Brahmans, have migrated out in large numbers, their bondage to the Brahmans having been broken by the 1880s. Their destination has been the tea plantations of Kerala to the north. There has been relatively little out-migration of Thevars and Nadars. A few Asari goldsmiths have moved out to set up shops in the nearby town of Nagercoil.

Landownership is not highly concentrated in Agasteeswaram. There may be one or two families in the taluk who own over 100 acres, another handful of families own over 60 acres, perhaps 2 or 3 percent of the total own over 5 acres, 35 percent own between 1 and 4.9 acres, and 62 percent own less than 1 acre (KDCH 1961: 203). In land transferences, land is measured in cents and even in hundredths of cents, called square links. Thus, the 'richest' family among the Nadars of the two hamlets owns 1 acre 44 cents and 765 square links of dry land and 1 acre 33 cents and 750 square links of wet land, while the poorest of the 36 families of the two Nadar hamlets owns less than a house plot. Twenty-five percent of the families own no wet land and less than 4 cents of dry land.

Land is widely dispersed in small and tiny fragments. The pattern is similar for the other caste-communities. Almost every family has at least a smidgen of land, and what is considered to be a 'large holding' by the standards of these hamlet residents – 2 acres – is very modest, indeed, from a world comparative perspective. In 1978–79, Kanyakumari district had 301,308 operational agricultural holdings, most of which were less than half a hectare (KDCH 1981: 11).

Who are the community members who have been successful in amassing and acquiring land? Let us look at the family of Chidambaram Pillai, known as the family of the hamlet's *paNNaiyaar* or 'big man'. This family is Saiva Vellala and at its height owned 50 acres of paddy land, as well as some coconut gardens. Its founder was a customs official at the checkpoint between Kanyakumari and Tinnevelly districts. The story of the establishment of this large landed family is as follows: The founder whom I shall call Gopalramakrishna (hereafter GRK), was left fatherless at the age of seven. He was born probably about 1839. His father was from further northwest in Travancore, a place called Mayvelikalay, although they were Tamil Saiva Vellalas, not Malayalis, native to Kerala. He was probably one among the group of Tamil Vellala officials – descendants of those brought in by a Maharaja of Travancore to serve him, on the principle that foreigners make more honest and loyal bureaucrats. GRK's father had been the customs inspector at the Kanyakumari-Tinnevelly checkpoint nearby, and his son was allowed to inherit his father's job. The widowed mother and her children came to reside in one of the multicaste (MC) hamlets of my study. GRK was able, through his earnings as a customs inspector, to buy land from the *kiR jaadiis* (lower castes).

Subramoniam, GRK's son, a man in his seventies when I interviewed him in 1967, said that his grandfather, the first customs inspector, had bought land worth Rs 1,000, but his father, GRK, bought land worth Rs 10,000. My notes report him as saying:

> All the land here then was wasteland. There were no tanks and no plots. It was during my father's time that the tank was dug and the fields made. Before 1906 and the Kodeyar Project, the lands were wastelands. He bought those wastelands from Asaris, Thevars and Pillaimars.

GRK's younger relatives take a dim view of him. His grandson, my informant Chidambaram, told me that his grandfather got land 'by tricking the ignorant', and one of his grandsons' wives, a woman in her forties, told me this in 1967:

> My *taattaa* (actually her husband's father's father) got his land by cheating. Most of his land belonged to some women of *kiR jaadiis,* and he got the land by promising money and not delivering.

Such stories of the literate cheating the illiterate in earlier times are fairly common. Thus, a Nadar informant, a young man in his early thirties in 1969 when he told me this, claimed that his grandfather had been cheated out of five acres of land by the gift of a *veeshTii* (a waist cloth), again presumably before the Kodeyar dam was built which brought irrigation waters to the dry lands of Kanyakumari.

According to Subramoniam, when his father, GRK, bought land, there were three Saiva Pillaimar families already in the MC hamlet. All three families seem to have been headed by men who were specialists in religion; two were temple *puusaariis;* the other was a family of temple dancers and garland makers. It seems likely that their land may have been granted to them to support their temple services.

That customs officials commonly invested in land is indicated by the fact that another of the Saiva Vellala families of MC hamlet is headed by an elder whose father was also a customs official who bought land locally.

GRK had a sororal polygynous marriage. He married his father's sister's two daughters from a village near Tinnevelly. He had four sons, one by the elder sister, and three by the younger. He had 10 grandsons from these four sons, five of whom still live in the MC hamlet, while five live outside. He had at least 14 great-grandsons – sons of the 10 sons' sons. Of these 14, seven are in the MC hamlet, and seven are outside. He had at least five great-great-grandsons in the male line, all of whom are in the MC hamlet. He has had at least 28 female descendants, with a total of at least 64 descendants over four generations. The decline in the family fortunes, the second part of this family saga, was due to the dispersion of the 50 acres, as it was fragmented among the myriad descendants.

As that is a tale of losers of land, it will be told in the next section of the paper. Here I am concerned with the winners.

Another individual who amassed land was a Thevar of MC hamlet. This is Suppayya, reputed to be the richest man in MC hamlet at present. I do not know the exact extent of his holdings, but this interview I had with Suppayya on 1 May 1967 will give some idea of how he operates:

> Suppayya explained the chit fund to us. He runs one with 12 members, to which each gives Rs 500 every six months, and it runs for six years. For the first month, the lowest bidder gets the money. Thus, a man may bid Rs 5,000 and be the lowest bidder. Then Suppayya, as chit fund organizer, takes a commission of Rs 300, and the other Rs 700 are divided among the 10 others (leaving out the lowest bidder and the organizer), so each of these is given back Rs 70 as a kind of profit. The second month, the Rs 6,000 go to Suppayya. Then after that, each member in turn bids on Rs 5,700 each month (since Suppayya, the organizer gets Rs 300 out of the 6,000 every month). Each person who has had a turn continues to deposit Rs 500 every six months. The last person benefits by receiving the entire Rs 5,700. Any chit fund taking more than Rs 100 from each member is supposed to be registered with the government registrar. The government has been regulating chit funds for as long as Suppayya can remember. He himself had started out with small chit funds before moving on to higher ones. He knows of chit funds running as high as Rs 10,000 which are not registered, but in such cases the members have no recourse in case they are cheated. When the chit fund is registered, the organizer also has to pay Rs 10 per 1,000 of the fund to pay for its books that are audited each year. The organizer must also put up property in bond; in Suppayya's case, it is the equivalent of Rs 18,000. Each member further gives Suppayya a document stating certain terms of security; at a maximum, the member may have to pledge property worth Rs 6,000. If a member is unable to pay his Rs 500, Suppayya may advance him the money and collect it later. Collections take place after harvest. The individual who does not pay can be taken to court and the pledged land sold. Then the amount owed the chit fund organizer and the other members will be deducted from the price collected from the sale of the land by the court. In the same way, if Suppayya is untrustworthy, the members can bring a case against him and get the proceeds from the sale of his Rs 18,000 worth of land.

All 12 members of his chit fund are cultivators in the area and include Vellalas, Nadars, Asaris, and at least one Sambhavar. Suppayya has been running the chit fund for 18 years and has never taken anyone to court. If times are bad for everyone, they suspend the chit fund for a period. The sum taken by a member may be used to clear debts on which he has been paying interest, or may be used to pay for a wedding. We asked if it might be used to buy land. He did not say it was.

Suppayya said that it was his grandfather who came here from Tinnevelly district. In those days if a man could not pay his land revenue for a year or two, even though it was an extremely dry area dependent upon rainfall, he was beaten in full view of the entire community, as directed by a British official. His grandfather and two of his brothers settled here.

Suppayya was waiting for the arrival of his son who is studying for his MA in Madras. Only one of his seven sons had not been educated, and that son, who only studied up to pre-university, carries on the agriculture for the family in the village. Suppayya himself has studied up to the fifth class. He was now planning to arrange the marriage of his son. He would search among relatives in Tinnevelly for a bride. Since the son is an MA the girl should also be educated.

Suppayya said that Thevars had given up *kaaval* (guarding of private homes and property) 30 years ago. We asked if it had been outlawed by the government. He said, "No, people just stopped giving Thevars six-monthly payments." Suppayya denied knowing much about *kaaval* since he had never done it. However, he explained that the guard was responsible for catching any thieves. The Thevars of MC were guards for the whole area around.

In both the positions, of customs official and chit fund organizer, a man could make money in Agasteeswaram taluk. Of course, both positions required some education. Suppayya had been through fifth grade. We can probably safely assume that Chidambaram's grandfather, GRK, had not had any more education than that. To make money, one handles money. That the customs official, like the chit fund organizer, was in a favourable position to make money may be suggested by this story told by a Brahman of the Brahman hamlet:

> B said his grandfather had been an excise officer, that when he started out he had not intended to take bribes, but there was a regular system going. Out of 100 jackfruits, the excise officer might keep 10. The checkpost officers also used to wet the areca nuts being taken out in order to make them weigh more, then they pocketed the difference in customs paid between the true dry weight rate and the wet rate. When his grandfather had not wanted to take such bribes, the other men gave his grandmother her husband's share in the bribes. Thus, they perhaps made wealth which was, in turn, put into the land. He indicated that the position of excise inspector was not one of which one was exactly proud. One had to do rough work with business men and others trying to smuggle things across the border from the Madras Presidency. There were always things that were cheaper on one side of the border than the other.

Are there other ways to amass land besides these foxy ways? There are two other ways, also a bit foxy, the other less so.

One way is to marry well. The preferred marriage in Agasteeswaram taluk is between the mother's brother's son and the father's sister's daughter, but any 'cross-relative' of the appropriate age is proper *(urrimae)*. However, though marriages are arranged, an enterprising couple may manage to elope and have their relatives accept the marriage, especially if they are *urimaipen* and *urimae maappiiLLai* -- a properly related bride and a properly related bridegroom.

So, two brothers, Narayan and Krishna, managed to make off with their distant cross-cousin, Bagavati. She was already engaged to her distant cross-cousin through her father; Narayan was a distant cross-cousin through her mother; but I will not here go into the exact details of these relationships. The two brothers drove off with the bride in a taxi (this must have taken place at least 40 years ago) to another village where they stayed with relatives. While there, Narayan tied the *taalii* (wedding pendant). Krishna had actually 'borrowed' his own wife's *taalii* to do the deed. Narayan said, "That was very wrong – to take the *taalii* of a living person. No one told me it was improper." The attraction of this particular cross-cousin was her status as the only daughter of a landed father. She could be expected to inherit that land.

Elopements are fairly common; it takes a young man who sees his main chance and a potentially better-off female cross-relative willing to accept his blandishments.

Of course, being the only heiress to parents' property is a matter of luck in the game of demographic roulette. Just as the reader can already see that the 64 descendants of GRK are going to have to divide up his 50 acres beyond what is economically feasible for any one of them – an unlucky turn of the demographic wheel – so demographic roulette can also work the other way. For example, the second wealthiest man among the Nadars of the two Nadar hamlets, owner of 12 cents of dry land and 1 acre 89 cents of paddy land, has so much land (by Nadar-hamlet standards), partly because he was able to buy some of GRK's land when it inevitably, but gradually, went on sale; and partly because his three sisters (there were no brothers besides the heir), all of whom were married, were all childless, and they all gave their land to their brother. So he won at demographic roulette.

So, these are three ways to amass land. Probably, only the first way results in amassing land; the other two ways make possible only small acquisitions. Land can be amassed through being in a business where profits can be made -- like being a customs official or running a chit fund. I have not given an example of someone who has made it as a land broker, but I am sure that the reader can imagine the scenario quite accurately. A second way is to marry well, and a third way is to win at demographic roulette.

Who Loses Land?

It is possible by pouring earnestly over land records to trace the disposition of GRK's lands. By 1952, the 50 acres of paddy land had shrunk to 22 acres. In 1967, more than 8 acres of the 22 acres had been sold. Similarly, the dry land of GRK's family was being sold. Almost half of the paddy land was purchased by various Nadars, and the largest proportion by Nadars from the two sample hamlets. This is not too surprising since the two Nadar hamlets adjoin the MC hamlet where Chidambaram and other descendants of GRK reside. Nadars also bought 43 percent of the dry land sold from this estate between 1952 and 1967. The other large buyer was a Brahman family (from the sample hamlet of Brahmans) that bought about one-fourth of the paddy land and 43 percent of the dry land.

The descendants of GRK seemed to be trying to make the transition from being landholders, for whom Nadars and Sambhavars did the farm work, to being businessmen. Chidambaram, for example, tried to establish a cinema in the next village. To do so, he borrowed Rs 4,000 on his land, and when the cinema did not attract sufficient attendance, he lost it all. Other members of his family made similar unsuccessful ventures into the world of business.

The Vellalas have undoubtedly suffered from the demise of the Travancore State and the annexation of Kanyakumari district to Tamilnadu. Under the Maharaja, Vellalas were favoured as accountants and officials, as, of course, were Tamil Brahmans. Chidambaram's uncle, his father's eldest brother, belonged to the Travancore Assembly in the 1930s; in contrast, the best Chidambaram can do is to be a minor official in the Community Development Programme, and he is not in a position where he is likely to receive any special emoluments.

The Nadars, on the other hand, have been in a better position since they have sizeable numbers, and the Nadar community of Tamilnadu is fairly powerful in politics. The national prominence of Kamaraj Nadar in the Congress party in the 1960s helped the caste generally in the state of Tamilnadu. The Nadars, as one hears everywhere in Agasteeswaram taluk, are coming up in the world. The credit for this is attributed firmly to their outstanding personal character.

The prevailing local view, one shared by Thevars, Vellalas Christian Nadars, Nanjinad Vellalas and others, is that the Vellalas are losing land in Agasteeswaram while the Nadars are acquiring it. A Thevar petty official assessed the two caste-communities thus:

> Vellalas are lazy. They just want to sit at home and eat without working. Nadars work in heat and rain. It isn't that the Maharaja used to favour the Vellalas and they are favoured no longer; it is that the majority don't work.

The local Block Development Officer, a Nanjinad Vellala himself, looked at it more analytically:

> Nadars have more land than Vellalas, because they actually work the fields, while Vellalas, if they have fields, engage people to work for them. Vellalas are lazy; it is below their dignity to do manual work.

> Nadars are not only very hard workers, but they spend very little for their maintenance, so they save a lot.

A member of the state legislature and a newspaper journalist, the first a Nanjinad Vellala, the second a Nadar Christian, added in factors such as the costly, refined lifestyle of the Vellalas, so that Vellalas were spending not only on the wages of the field coolies but on high living standards during periods when the price of paddy was poor, while at the same time traditional Nadar crops, palmyra products and coconuts, were priced advantageously. The Christian newsman observed:

> For an illiterate having nothing but his body (with which he climbed palmyra palms to tap the tubers giving the sap), the prices for jaggery (palm sugar) were very good, and the toddy shopkeepers engaged climbers to tap for toddy alone. There are families whose forefathers were climbers who are well-off now.

I did not, in fact, find such Nadars in the two hamlets. But some Nadars do manage to be losers. There is the case of Dharmalingam, the only son of a *paNNaiyaar* (a 'big man') of the Nadar hamlets. Not only is he an only son but his sororal polygynous marriages involved considerable wealth that belonged to the two sisters who are his wives who had no brothers. His mother told us that Dharmalingam had inherited 10 *kooTaa* of paddy fields, 20 cows and bullocks, and coconut groves. Dharmalingam's father had been lucky because he owned considerable land when the Kodeyar Dam Project came in, and was able to convert it into paddy land.

When we interviewed Dharmalingam's mother in January 1974, she had just sold her house to Nadars of a neighbouring hamlet and was living in a palm-frond shed. She lamented that her son had spent at least Rs 30,000 during his political career. He had twice been elected to the government-sponsored panchayat and twice had been made president of the panchayat. Between election expenses and entertaining his political associates lavishly, Dharmalingam seemed to have ruined himself; unfortunately, he also lost his last election.

That political glory may entail financial disaster is also illustrated by my Vellala friend, Chidambaram, who in 1965 won the All-Madras State Award for growing paddy. He grew more paddy on his demonstration plot than any other cultivator in the entire state. His modest prize money came nowhere near the over Rs 20,000 he subsequently had to spend in court battles with his cousins, also descendants of GRK, who claim that the land on which he sowed his bumper crop was the family's temple land and did not belong to him! The levelling mechanism of the high cost of a court case can be very effective.

The temptation of community temple land is not limited to the Vellalas' case against Chidambaram. Although the ancestral land of the Brahman community was almost all sold long ago to educate the many sons, there are still a few acres which belong to the community as a whole, as it was given to support community worship or was the land of what was once a community tank. A temple trust committee supervises this land, and rumor in the Brahman hamlet has it that the trustees fill their own granaries with the paddy that should be devoted to worship or to equal division among the families descended from the village ancestors.

Like Chidambaram, a Sambhavar land broker is also similarly embroiled in several court cases as his jealous rivals effectively force him to expend his resources on lawyers, judges, and witnesses, all of whom, no doubt, use the money received to invest in land.

There are more humdrum ways to lose land, of course. It is common to have to sell land just to make ends meet; more prevalent is the gradual selling of land to educate sons and to dower daughters. Land is often transferred as a gift to a daughter upon marriage. Part of the tragedy of the high unemployment among educated young people is the bankruptcy of many families who have invested so much in educating the now unemployed degree-holder although more tragic are those who simply cannot pass the SSLC (Secondary School Leaving Certificate), PUC (Pre-University Course) or BA examinations.

With a good job, the hope is that the cycle can begin again. Salary can be invested in land and the land which a father had to sell to pay for his sons' education may be recouped when the successful sons buy land.

There are other usual tragedies like early death of an earning household head, or severe illness. Medical expenses can destroy a family's resources.

Losing land is easy. There is demographic roulette by which to lose – too many children, too many sons to educate, too many daughters to dower, too many mouths to feed, too few earning family members. One can lose in court cases filed by jealous neighbours and relatives or more distant rivals. One can blow it all in politics. Or have your business fail.

As always, losing is more depressing and less interesting than winning.

Summary of Trends

In this situation, one can win land in a small way by being lucky at demographic roulette, or by marrying well, which means marrying a husband or wife who happens, usually, to have won at demographic roulette. Otherwise, one must get oneself into a position where usury, bribery or graft are possible.

This is a rural economy with so little opportunity in it for the individual, so little potential for expansion, that success has been possible only by parasitic means. But does the near-sighted focus on these three hamlets blind us or make it hard for us to focus with a far-sighted gaze? Is there outside exploitation? Does this explain this eking-out economy? The traditional exploiters, the so-called dominant castes of the area are, in fact, in the process of departing. In the case of the Brahmans, since the 1950s, their sons have routinely been leaving for cities, often in far-away places, at the age of 17 or 18. The Vellalas, similarly, have been trying to make this transition, as have the better-off Nadars. The departure of the traditional dominants has actually loosened the land ties; much Brahman and Vellala land has been sold to the lower castes, the Nadars and Thevars, for example. The land which they retain must be tilled, and it is usually tilled by Nadar, Thevar or Sambhavar leasers.

This departure of the dominants is taking place in many parts of India, as the Brahmans and others have left for the city and/or the modern sector (government, schools, universities, business firms), so it has been noted by several social scientists that middle castes are now becoming dominant in the rural areas (Béteille 1965; Bhatt 1978; Singh 1978).

Does the answer lie in that wealth cannot be made in the twentieth century in this rural area, given traditional food-producing methods and rapid population growth, except on the margins, by usury or by graft? The dream of every person with even few means is to educate sons who will get good jobs and then live well and later perhaps invest in land, or marry a wife who brings money or land. Is this just a dream, or does it really happen? There is one instance of a young Nadar man who is buying land through his salary from working at a municipal service company in Nagercoil. And, there is ample sign in the sky-rocketing price of land in the area of recent years, that land is wanted very much as an investment by the rich doctors in Nagercoil, or by the occasional man successful there in business. These townsmen, of course, have made their money from the rural folk who use their hospitals and nursing homes, or ride their buses, or come in to view their cinemas. So, the earnings of the countrymen enrich the townsmen who then buy up the land. Perhaps that is the next part of the scenario. Are those who give the cinemas and the medicine and the bus rides the new men to amass the land? And will these new wealthy, still making money at the margins of the economy, be new dominants? Will they buy up all the land? To what extent will the educated sons of the rural folk be among them? No wonder a bridegroom who is a medical doctor requires a dowry of Rs 200,000!

Conceptualization of this Dynamic Social Structure

A Marxist model does not seem to fit these Agasteeswaram taluk hamlets. The villains of the piece do not seem to be exploitative dominant castes or those who control the main means of production – the land. The land, in fact, seems to be widely distributed; it is just that it is distributed in very tiny dribs and drabs. The villains of the piece are population growth and a stagnant economy. The model provided us by Vilfredo Pareto seems to fit better than the model provided by Marx which refers to a productive economy or one in which there is some profit. There is very little profit to be made in this agricultural economy. Pareto talked about the circulating elite, consolidating elite, and innovating elite. One succeeds the other often with a religious ideology followed by a secular ideology – when consolidating elites are in power, religion is strong; when an innovating elite is in power, secularism is promulgated. Pareto, however, assumes a struggle between the old elite and the new elite. The consolidating elite uses force to *maintain* its position; the innovating elite uses fraud to *gain* its position. Pareto called consolidators 'lions' and innovators 'foxes'. Doesn't Pareto's model fit better here than Marx's?

Perhaps it would if the consolidators, the traditional elite, had not all, more or less, decamped, or at least had not lost interest in consolidating their rural position. They vacate the top positions and the innovators move in. They are less 'lions' defending their territory than 'bears' who have gone "over the mountain to see what they can see." They have migrated out, or are in the process of preparing to leave. While their going may seem to make it easy for others to take their places, in fact, it only seems to be very clever 'foxes' who can move in to accumulate much land. The kinds of innovation that will work are rather limited. One must be a usurous or grafting fox in the rural world itself. Otherwise, one must move to town where perhaps one can make a profit as a bus company owner or a doctor who serves the rural poor (but not for charity) and be the town fox. How can one innovate *productively* in the stagnant economy?

Do we see the DMK of the 1950s as providing the ideology, the secular ideology of the innovative rising elite? Possibly.

Conclusion

At the beginning of this paper, I have asked some questions about the emerging social structure in rural India. A process of the following type seems to have taken place in this part of India, but there is considerable evidence that it has taken place in many other parts of India as well. The old established dominant castes have largely left for the city. This is certainly true of the Brahmans of the hamlet of this study, but others (Béteille 1965; Sivertsen 1963; Gough 1955; Mencher 1972) have found this true for Chingleput and Tanjavur districts of Tamilnadu further to the north. Their departure has made room for the new landowners. And, in Tamilnadu, these have been various non-Brahman caste communities such as Thevars, Kallars, and Nadars. In Kanyakumari, many Vellalas have also opted for education and white-collar jobs and business ventures. Asaris also have left in some numbers for towns. In other words, the urbanization and modernization of India, especially the growth of modern western-style education, has opened up many occupations of a white-collar, largely non-manual sort. In a rural area like Kanyakumari, no new dominants have emerged. The traditional coolies working on the fields, the Paraya Sambhavars, have also left in large numbers for the tea plantations lying to the north. Very few of the Sambhavars or Nadars of the area have taken up modern education and then moved out, although there are some families such as that of one of the older Nadar *paNNaiyar* families and that of the Sambhavar land broker who have been able to educate their sons. The emerging modern middle class then uses some of its money to buy up land, their parents having sold the land in order to educate their sons and marry their daughters off to educated boys.

Success, in other words, takes place very largely outside of the villages; sons who manage to get jobs at salaries which provide some surplus, buy land. In the Kanyakumari area, it is professionals, especially medical doctors and others who have done well in business in town, who are buying land. Whether they will become commercial farmers is yet to be seen.

We, thus, have the picture of a society which continues to operate in terms of caste communities if not in terms of a caste system in the rural areas, and which operates increasingly in terms of middle-class men with modern occupations in towns and cities. In neither rural nor urban areas does the old self-sufficient caste system operate, but castes persist as residential locations and as organized communities in the rural area. Middle-class men with modern occupations are undoubtedly enmeshed in networks of caste, kin and affines, although they may or may not live in caste residential localities. The networks in which they move most probably include people of a variety of occupations, especially if they are non-Brahman, since such castes include men of occupations both high and low.

This seems to indicate that there is relatively little organization in the middle class. Members of the middle class are likely to live in the more fashionable residential sections of towns and cities where their neighbours may be of various castes. However, from a land perspective, this group does operate as a social segment, since it is this group which has the capital to invest in land, it would appear that as the middle class becomes more entrenched in the countryside from which most originally came, the rural social structure may become rentier type with many absentee landlords and yeoman tenants who take the entire responsibility for the agricultural enterprises. This is already fairly common in parts of Tamilnadu. Such agricultural enterprises are likely to be considerably less exploitative of labour than were those of the dominant castes of the past. However, such enterprises may well employ fewer people and represent developments that leave many rural folk unemployed.

Notes

1. An earlier version of this paper was read at the Society for South India Studies Symposium, held at the University of Pennsylvania, Philadelphia, 17–19 March 1980. Professor Srinivas was in attendance at that meeting and gave the author some valuable insights. I owe thanks to David Ludden, Polly Hill and others who joined in the discussion of that presentation.
2. The author carried out fieldwork for about 32 months between 1967 and 1997. This paper, however, was written in 1979--80, so was based on data gathered in 1967, 1969, 1971, 1974, 1978 and 1980. Some revisions were made in 1989--90.

References

Bhatt, Anil (1978), Dominant Caste and Political Process. In M.N. Srinivas, S. Seshaiah and V.S. Parthasarathy (eds.), *Dimensions of Social Change in India* Columbia, Missouri: South Asia Books.

Béteille, Andre (1965), *Caste, Class and Power,* Berkeley and Los Angeles: University of California Press.

---- (1974), *Studies in Agrarian Social Structure,* Delhi: Oxford University Press.

Gough, E. Kathleen (1955), Caste in a Tanjore Village. In E.R. Leach (ed.), *Aspects of Caste in South India, Ceylon and North-West Pakistan,* Cambridge: Cambridge University Press.

Kanyakumari District Census Handbook 1961. Census of India, 1961, Volume IX. Madras, Part X-XII, Madras: Director of Stationery and Printing.

--- (1981), Census of India, 1981, Series 20, Tamilnadu, Part XIII (A and B) Village and Town Directory and Village and Township Primary Census Abstract, Madras: Government of Tamilnadu.

Mencher, Joan P. (1972), Continuity and Change in an Ex-Untouchable Community of South India. In J. Michael Mahar (ed.), *The Untouchables in Contemporary India,* Tucson, Arizona: University of Arizona Press.

---(1978), *Agriculture and Social Structure in Tamilnadu,* Delhi: Allied.

Pareto, Vilfredo (1968), *The Rise and Fall of the Elites,* Totowa, New Jersey: The Bedminster Press. Originally published in Italian.

Singh, Yogendra (1978), The Changing Pattern of Social Stratification in India. In M.N. Srinivas, S. Seshaiah and V.S. Parthasarathy (eds.), *Dimensions of Social Change in India,* Columbia, Missouri: South Asia Books.

Sivertsen, Dagfinn (1963), *When Caste Barries Fall,* London: Allen and Unwin.

Statistical Abstract India (1986), Delhi: Central Statistical Organisation, Department of Statistics, Ministry of Planning, Government of India.

Tamilnadu Government (1993), *Toward an Affluent District Economy: A Prospective Plan for Kanyakumari District.*

Travancore Land Revenue Manual (1915), Trivandrum: Travancore Government Press.

Varghese, T.C. (1970), *Agrarian Change and Economic Consequences: Land Tenures in Kerala 1850--1960,* Bombay: Allied.

Part III

Joint Families in Rajasthan

9

The Joint Family Household in Rural Rajasthan

Ecological, Cultural and Demographic Conditions for its Occurrence

One of the most characteristic social institutions of Rajasthan is the rural joint family household. Often considered to be one of the most characteristic social institutions in India as a whole, the joint family takes its place beside caste and the arranged marriage as close to universal in India. The 1961 Census of India was one of the first to collect data on household composition, enabling comparative analysis of family household structure between different states, regions and districts. A comparison of the 1961 household composition tables for 326 districts and territories was reported in an earlier paper (Kolenda and Haddon 1987). Mapping of various measures of the occurrence of joint family household revealed that in proportion to the population, there were more rural joint family households in Rajasthan than in any other state (ibid.: 227–38; see also Maps 1 and 2 in this paper).

What accounts for this high occurrence of joint family households in Rajasthan? That is the problem that I try to solve in this paper. I draw on three kinds of data – cultural, derived from ethnographies of various villages in Rajasthan, most done by census ethnographers, some by other anthropologists and by myself; demographic, namely, statistics derived from a variety of tabulations in the 1961 Census; and ecological, derived from Census District Gazetteers, geographical works, and especially important, from

---

mapping done by A.K. Sen of the Central Arid Zone Research Institute (CAZRI) in Jodhpur, Rajasthan.

The Concept of Joint Family Household as Used in the Census of India

There are two aspects to the definition of the joint family household, that of composition – who belongs to a joint family? – and that of location and boundaries – how does one locate a joint family and distinguish it from other families and other social units? There has been much more agreement about the functional location and boundaries of the family than about its composition. The problem of definition of family structure is one I addressed in the past (Kolenda 1968: 344–49; see also Kolenda 1987: 8–16); the conclusions of that effort are briefly stated here and are used in the present analysis.

The functional definition of the joint family established by the Census of India more than a hundred years ago is relatives who eat from the same kitchen (*chulha* in Hindi), or the 'hearth-group'. This definition has been used by many social scientists, as well as the census, and its use has made for consistency, enabling comparability between studies. This is not the ideal definition of joint family for all research purposes, as a *chulha*-group is almost always linked socially and economically to others, and it is a wider *set* of *chulha*-groups that functions in many contexts as the joint family. The household in the C-I tables of the Census of India, central to this study, are *chulha*-groups however, and the ethnographers who studied hundreds of villages in the 1960s for the census also used that functional definition. Thus, the problem of this paper more precisely is: why were there, in proportion to the population, more joint family hearth-groups in Rajasthan according to the 1961 Census of India, than in other Indian states?

As for the composition of the joint family household, while Indians are often inconsistent in their use of the term 'joint family', they are usually referring to a household consisting of two or more related couples. Usually, a joint family is composed of parents and one married son, his wife and their children (the patrilineal joint family), but there can also be more than one married son (the patrilineal-collateral joint family). Consistent with my previous work

(1967, 1968, 1987: 1–154; Kolenda and Haddon 1987), I will follow the above definition: a joint family is a household composed of two or more related couples. While anthropologists might consider the Indian joint family to fall under their more general rubric of 'extended family', I prefer to be consistent with Indian usage here.

While English-speaking Indians generally use 'joint family', there are various terms in Indian languages for it. The villagers in the village I studied in Jaipur district used the expression *puna parivar* (literally, 'the complete family').

While most Indians trace their descent and structure their families along the father-son line, the culturally prescribed structure among some communities in the northeast and southeast is along the mother-child line (the matrilineal joint family). In Rajasthan, the norm is the patrilineal joint family.

Household Tables in the 1961 Census of India

The 1961 Census examined a 20 percent sample of all households (hearth-groups) within every district and territory of India, tabulating their composition under the rubrics of head, spouse of head, other married relatives (sons, other males, other females), unmarried relatives (never married, widowed or divorced, separated) and unrelated persons. The data are presented in the C-I tables of the census, entitled 'Composition of Sample Households by Relationship to Head of Family Classified by Size of Land Cultivated'.[1] That table divides each district or territory's population into rural and urban. In this paper, I am concerned only with the statistics for rural populations. Since over 80 percent of the Indian population lived in rural areas in 1961, we are concerned with the households of the vast majority of Indians at that time.

The reader may ask why I report a study done with data from the 1961 Census rather than the 1981 Census. One answer is that conditions in Rajasthan a generation ago were probably closer to those which fostered joint family households in past centuries than are the changed conditions of the 1980s. For example, land reform, which began in Rajasthan in 1952, significantly affected household structures, at least as these were reported to census-takers in 1961, and it is likely that it continued to stimulate changes for a decade or more. While it would add significantly to this study to compare the 1961 figures with those of 1981, this study involved references to scores of different volumes of the 1961 Census of India, and sufficient comparable volumes from the 1981 Census have only recently become available in United States libraries. It might be possible at present to replicate this study with 1971 Census data if the enterprise proved worthwhile. The 1961 analysis should, in any case, serve as a 'baseline' against which to compare changes in household distribution in 1971 and 1981 and in subsequent censuses.

The 1961 data showed marked regional differences in family structure. These were revealed by mapping two indices derived from the C-I tables. By dividing the total rural population in the 20 percent sample of all households in a district into the number of married sons residing with the heads of those households, the resulting percentage was used as an index of the prevalence of the patrilineal joint family, as one can expect that where a larger percentage of the persons in the sample households are married sons of the household head, there are more patrilineal joint families. In the same way, the total number in the 20 percent sample of households was divided into the total for other married relatives (excluding the spouse), as one can also expect that where a larger proportion of the persons in the sample households are other married relatives, there is a larger proportion of lineal, collateral, lineal-collateral and other types of joint families (Note, of course, that one kind of other married relative is the married son).

The method used for mapping these two variables and others based on census data depends upon ranking all districts and territories on the variable and then dividing them into quintiles. The 326 districts and territories of this study[2] are divided into four quintiles of 65 districts each, and one quintile (Quintile 3) with 66 districts. The districts with the highest value on a variable are in Quintile 1, those with the lowest in Quintile 5. Thus, Maps 1 and 2 show the districts in Quintile 1 and Quintile 5 for the two measures of joint family, the *proportions of married sons* and the *proportions of other married relatives* in the household sample populations. Mapping of these two indices of joint family should be a reasonably sound guide to those regions where joint families occur with high frequency and those where they are more rare.

Looking first at Map 1, we see that districts in Quintile 1 on proportions of married sons, indicating high proportions of patrilineal

Map 1

Proportions of Joint Families in India from Census of India 1961 as Measured by Proportions of 'Married Sons' in 20% Sample of Households

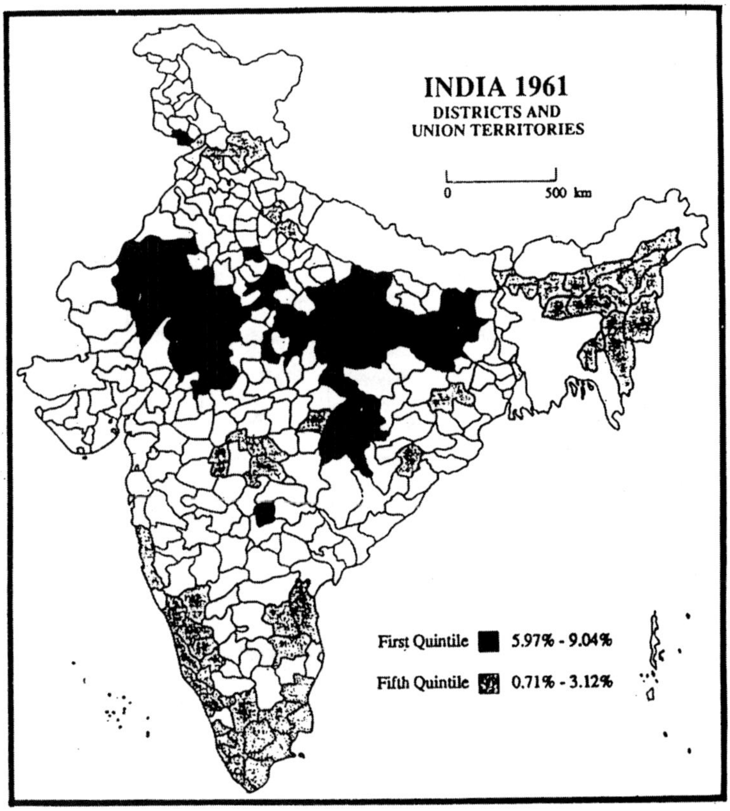

joint families from a belt of 62 districts across northern India – 15 in Rajasthan, contiguous with 14 in Madhya Pradesh, 25 in Uttar Pradesh, and eight in Bihar. Districts in Quintile 5 cluster in two blocks: one in the northeast, composed of all the districts of Assam, some territories beyond Assam, and some of the districts of West Bengal, and the other in the southwest, composed of Kerala and parts of Madras, Andhra Pradesh and Mysore. Map 2, showing quintiles based on other married relatives, indicating high proportions of all types of joint families, shows a similar pattern of a Quintile 1 belt

Map 2

Proportions of Joint Families in India from Census of India 1961 as Measured by Proportions of 'Other Married Relatives' in 20% Sample of Households

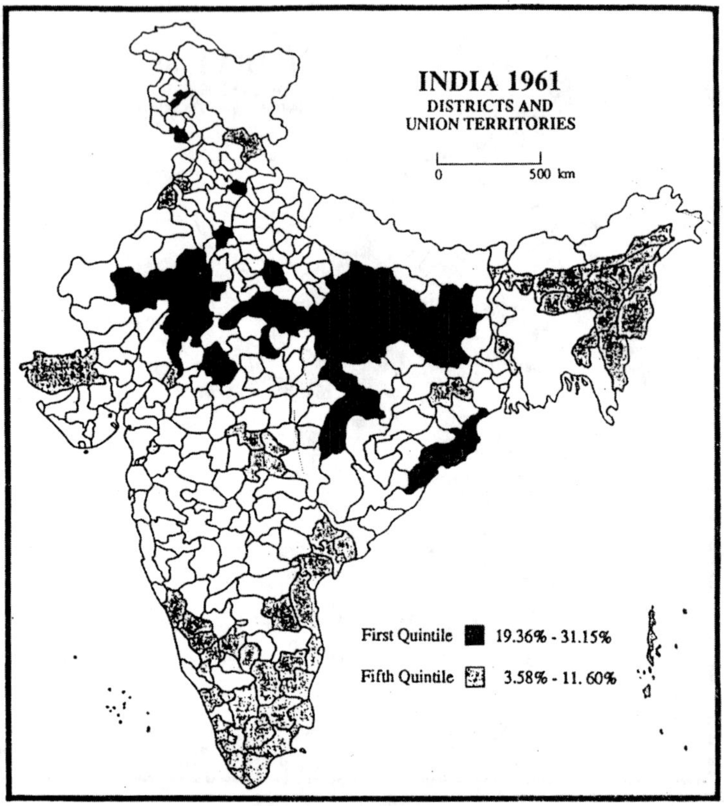

across the waist of India and two Quintile 5 clusters, one in the northeast and one in the south, with a few Quintile 1 and Quintile 5 districts scattered elsewhere.[3]

Map 3 shows the 15 districts out of Rajasthan's 26 which fall in Quintile 1 on married sons – an index of the occurrence of the patrilineal joint family. This is the highest proportion of Quintile 1 districts for a single state (58 percent), as compared to 25 out of 54 districts (46 percent) for Uttar Pradesh, 14 out of 43 (33 percent) for

Map 3

Joint Family Districts in Rajasthan as Measured by the First Quintile Rankings on Proportions of Married Sons in 20% Households Sample (Census of India 1961)

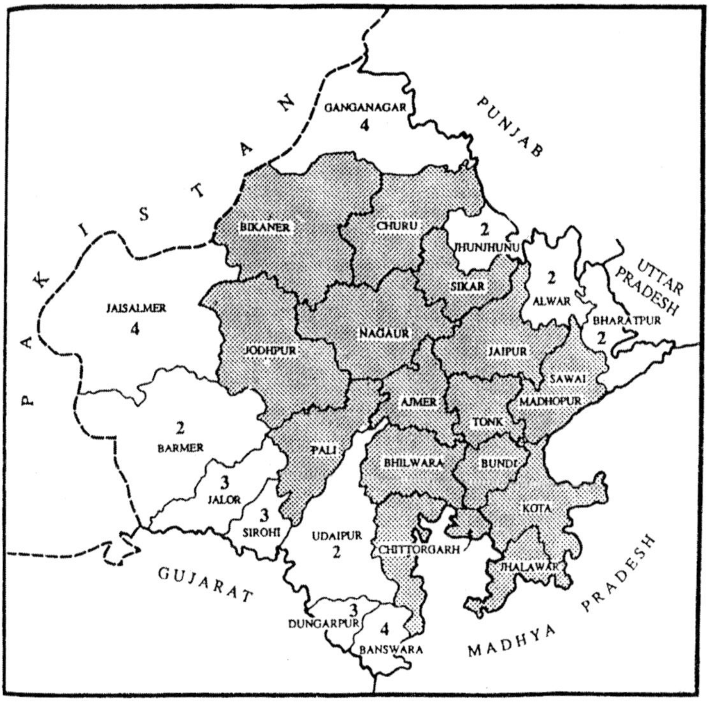

Madhya Pradesh, eight out of 17 (47 percent) for Bihar, one district each for Jammu & Kashmir, Andhra Pradesh and Himachal Pradesh, and no districts in the other eight states and nine territories. On Map 3 and on subsequent maps, each district outside Quintile 1 has within its outline the quintile number to which it belongs. In addition to the 15 districts of Rajasthan in Quintile 1, there are five in Quintile 2. Thus, 20 out of Rajasthan's 26 districts (76 percent) are above average in frequency of joint family households in the all-India perspective, since Quintiles 1 and 2 are together the upper 40 percent of all districts and territories. Three of the remaining districts in Rajasthan are in the third or 'average' quintile, and three in the fourth, a below average quintile; none are in Quintile 5, the lowest.

Map 4

Joint Family Districts in Rajasthan as Measured by the First Quintile Rankings on Proportions of Married Relatives in 20% Households Sample (Census of India 1961)

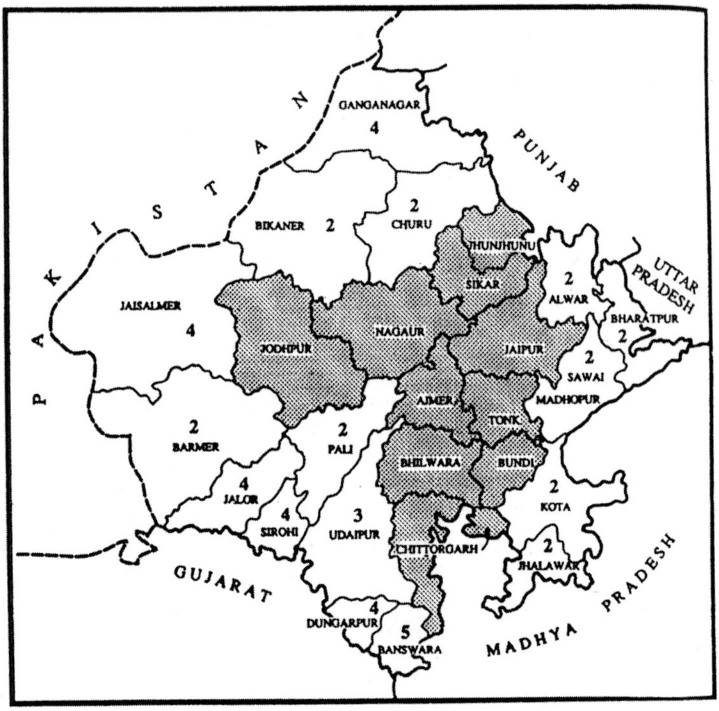

Map 4 shows the 11 districts in Rajasthan which fall in Quintile 1 on other married relatives, and eight other districts that are in Quintile 2. Thus, 19 out of Rajasthan's 26 districts (73 percent) are above average in joint family households as indexed by other married relatives. Of the remaining districts, one is in Quintile 3, five are in Quintile 4, and one is in the lowest, Quintile 5.

Thus, according to the figures of the 1961 Census, there were at that time more rural joint family households (hearth-groups) in Rajasthan in proportion to the population than in any other state of India. What accounts for this high proportion? The remainder of this paper is devoted to exploring this question through an analysis of demographic, cultural and ecological factors.

Ethnographic Fieldwork in Rajasthan

My own ethnographic fieldwork in Rajasthan was guided by preliminary, incomplete versions of Maps 1 and 2 that I prepared in the summer of 1966, using the 1961 Census volumes then available. On the basis of these maps, I chose six districts in various parts of India to do fieldwork. One of them was Jaipur district in Rajasthan. By observation of families in their villagers, I hoped to discover the essential conditions for joint family structure. In this paper, I draw on my field notes and published and unpublished articles (Kolenda 1978a; 1987; 178–213) concerning the linked villages of Maharajapur-Kishanpur, 13 miles west of the city of Jaipur, where my research assistant, Indira Sapru, and I worked for five months in 1966–67. Mrs. Sapru has gone back to Maharajapur-Kishanpur several times to gather further data, and we have worked there together for brief periods in 1969, 1974, 1978 and 1985.

In Maharajapur-Kishanpur (henceforth M-K), with a population of 367 in 1966, consisting almost entirely of two well-known Rajasthan ethnic groups, Jats (63 percent of the population) and Minas (25 percent), I expected to find high proportions of joint families. There were indeed high proportions -- 31 percent of the Jat families and 49.5 percent of the Jat population lived in joint families, as did 21.5 percent of the Mina families and 46.5 percent of the Mina population (see Tables 9.1 and 9.2 for the full distributions).

Table 9.1

Family Structure among the Jats of Maharajapur-Kishanpur

Type of Family	*Families*		*Persons*	
	No.	*%*	*No.*	*%*
Joint	12	31	131	49.5
Supplemented nuclear	9	25	66	24
Nuclear	12	31	51	20
Polygynous	1	3.25	6	3
Supplemented sub-nuclear	1	3.25	3	1.5
Sub-nuclear	1	3.25	3	1.5
Single-person	1	3.25	1	0.5
	37	100	267	100

Source: Kolenda 1978: 243; 1987: 179.

Table 9.2

Family Structure among the Minas of Maharajapur-Kishanpur

Type of Family	*Families*		*Persons*	
	No.	%	*No.*	%
Joint	3	21.5	39	46.5
Supplemented nuclear	3	21.5	22	26
Nuclear	5	35.5	19	22.5
Single-person	2	14	2	2.5
Other	1	7.5	2	2.5
	14	100	84	100

Source: Kolenda 1969: 29.

An unexpected factor emerged, one not previously highlighted in Indian or other ethnography: the existence of very high proportions of sibling-set and collateral-set marriages. This was the custom of a set of two or three brothers marrying a set of two or three sisters or 'cousin-sisters' (father's brother's daughter to each other), or other sets of women who were close relatives.[4] The male set might be 'cousin-brothers' (father's brother's son to each other) or other sets of men who were close relatives. Almost two-thirds (63 percent) of M-K Jat daughters were married in sibling- or collateral-sets (Kolenda 1978a: 253; 1987: 190), as were 60 percent of Mina wives (Kolenda 1969: 53). This very strong marital pattern double-bonded the joint families of M-K, so that not only were the adult males of a family brothers, but the adult females were sisters or cousin-sisters as well as sisters-in-law (brothers' wives). A newly in-married woman would not be entirely among strangers, because her older sister might be in the same household; her aunt (father's sister) might live in a household nearby, as might other women from her village. She could thus, presumably, make an easier adjustment to her life as a married woman and be less likely to develop hostile relations with her sisters-in-law. Such double-bonding might ensure greater harmony between women and, hence, a joint family would be less likely to fragment into its component nuclear units.

The villagers themselves did not emphasize joint family double-bonding through sibling-set or collateral-set marriages; rather, they emphasized the economy in affinal ties thus established. The

Plate 19

Some houses in Maharajapura-Kishanpura, Jaipur District, Rajasthan. (Photo December 1978, by Pauline Kolenda)

Plate 20

A Jat farmer on his well, emptying water into a channel that takes it to his field, in Maharajapura, Jaipur District, Rajasthan. (Photo Spring 1967, by Konstantin Kolenda)

expenses of the wedding and of subsequent gift-giving and hospitality are indeed curtailed if two married daughters share the same set of affinal kin, or two daughters-in-law share the same set of natal kin. Furthermore, the difficulty of seeking bridegrooms for daughters is less if two or three marry into the same family. Despite the villagers' ability to cite some instances of sisters married into the same family who quarreled, my comparison of Jat joint families in M-K indicated that families in which sisters or cousin-sisters were sisters-in-law endured longer (Kolenda 1978a; 1978b: 265; 1987: 201; see also Rosin 1987: 26).

Other anthropologists have noticed sibling-set marriage. Brij Raj Chauhan (1967: 212), in his book on a village in Chittorgarh district, mentions that it is "permissible in southern Rajasthan, to find two brothers marrying two sisters". Drs. Anandlaxsmi and Carol Henderson have mentioned to me the prevalence of the custom in the villages they have studied in Jaipur and Jodhpur districts, respectively (personal communication). Bhargava and Gupta (1965c: 20), writing about Rangmahal village in Ganganagar district, refer to the Scheduled Caste (SC) Meghwals and Nayaks (together composing 54 percent of families) "among whom younger sisters of a grown up girl are sometimes married along with her. This is done with a view to economise". Similarly, writing about Mudh village (in Bikaner district), a multi-caste Hindu village in which 31 percent of the population was Scheduled Tribe (ST) Meghwals, the same authors say that "a person having more than one daughter may arrange their marriages simultaneously in order to effect economy. In such cases girls even of tender age might be married along with his elder daughters" (1965a: 22). Thomas Rosin (1978: 490) mentions that "the high frequency of sibling- and cousin-set marriages strengthens joint family family solidarity", in the Nagaur village he studied.

Rosin (1987), in the only other analysis of sibling-set and collateral-set marriages in Rajasthan, found that 24 percent of all married couples in Undhyala village in Nagaur district were married in sibling- or collateral-sets in 1964–65. This proportion of such marriages is much lower than the three-fifths or more of such marriage among the Jats and Minas of M-K. This comparison raises the question of why there were higher proportions of sibling- and collateral-set marriages in the one village rather than the other. Similar to M-K, Undhyala Jats, the largest caste group in the village (2 percent of the total population), have: (i) relatively high proportions (40 percent) of such marriages (ibid.: 3, 19), (ii) their joint families composed of such sets tend to endure (ibid.: 26), and (iii) their motivation for such marriages is 'cost cutting' in performing weddings (ibid.: 25). Sibling- or collateral-set marriages occur in Undhyala among all the larger castes (ibid.: 11). Rosin is especially concerned with the relationship between sibling- and collateral-set marriages and the endurance of joint families. When his analysis is ready for publication, it will undoubtedly shed much light on this relationship.

In Jaipur district (Agrawal and Gupta 1965: 16) and other parts of Rajasthan (Rosin 1987: 4 for Nagaur district; Singh and Pendharker 1967: 15 for Jodhpur district), it is customary to hold all weddings on only a few specific days during the year. In M-K, the two wedding days were Akha Tij (the third day of the bright half of the month of Baisakh) and Pipal Purnima (the full-moon day in Jeth). In 1967, Akha Tij fell on 12 May, when there were five weddings of M-K children and, according to newspapers, thousands in and around Jaipur city, and Pipal Purnima fell on 22 May, when there were four weddings of M-K children.

As a result of this custom, a wedding guest invited to more than one wedding has to stay at each wedding only briefly or else must choose among his invitations. The many weddings occurring on the same day in a region therefore helped save on wedding costs by limiting the number of guests. The reason villagers gave for having weddings only on these two days – that they were auspicious and hence one did not have to consult a Brahman pandit to find an auspicious date -- appears to be another economy measure.

In addition, there are many double or triple weddings. In M-K, there have been as many as seven weddings taking place together. Sisters and/or cousin-sisters are often married at the same time.

One cannot reconstruct a precise composition of families from the C-I tables of the census, and it is therefore not possible to find sibling-sets or collateral-sets in joint families there. However, as we will see later, the factor with which the census measures of joint family ('married sons' and 'other married relatives') correlates most strongly is young adolescent marriage. As Bhargava and Gupta (1965c) suggest, and as I have found in M-K, the practices of sibling-set and collateral-set marriages and of multiple weddings on the same day tend to encourage the marriage of much younger girls along with their older sisters or cousin-sisters. The matching bridegrooms are often similarly apart in age. Thus, these customs contribute to the high proportions of married young adolescents in Rajasthan. Young adolescent marriage, in turn, contributes to the high proportion of joint families in Rajasthan, as the high correlations between the indices of joint family structure and the proportions of males or female aged 10–14 who are reported as married show.

Young adolescent marriage or even child marriage is prescribed by some influential Hindu law books. Some speak of brides as young as 6 (Kane 1958: 614), 8 and 12 (Buhler 1886: 355). A frequent prescription is that a daughter should be married before or immediately after her first menstruation (Kane 1941: 438–47). As Kane points out, with respect to the recommended young ages (6–12) for brides: "There was no question of consummation which took place only after puberty" (ibid.: 446), and some law books prescribe celibacy for the married couple for some time after marriage (ibid.: 441), which is consistent with the continuing physical immaturity of one or both members of the couple for some time after the wedding.

Traditionally, Rajasthani Hindu custom has tended to be consistent with the law books. In the mid-1960s it was customary in M-K and in surrounding villages for marriage to be celebrated by two major sets of ceremonies, usually a year or more apart, the *shadi* and the *muklava*. The first established an alliance between the two families, and often took place before a girl reached puberty. The second usually took place one or more years later, usually after the bride had reached puberty, and preceded the couple's commencement of sexual relations.

Among the Jats of M-K, the custom was for the *shadi* to take place before the age of 12 for both sons and daughters, and for the *muklava* to take place one to seven years later; exactly how soon after the *muklava* a bride began to live with her husband and his family depended upon her age and physical maturity. For example, one Jat wife who had come to live with her husband four years before told us that she had been married at the same time as her older sisters, 15 years before, and the *muklava* for both had been one year later. While the older sister came to live with her husband's family immediately, our informant, married at age 5 or 7, did not come until 11 years after the *muklava*. We may guess that the older sister was 11 or 12 at the time of the *shadi* and 13 at the time of the *muklava*, and that her younger sister probably did not come to reside with her marital family until the age of 16. Another girl of about 12 had still not gone to her mother-in-law even though she had had her *muklava* four or five years earlier, again as the junior bride in a double sibling-set marriage with her sister. True to their proclivity for economizing, many Jats dispense with the *muklava* ceremonies entirely and allow one or more men from the groom's family to come and escort the bride to her mother-in-law when she is mature, or if the bride is already mature at the time of the *shadi*, the *muklava* takes place immediately after the *shadi*, before the bride departs with the new husband and his party for his village.

Lushington (1833: 294–95) wrote about the weddings of the royal Jats of Bharatpur:

> On the expiration of her three days residence at the home of her lord and master, the bride returns to her relations for a period of one, three or five years, and she is then brought home by the bridegroom to assume the duties of the married state. This second bringing home of the wife is termed *gona* or *gaman*, and is usually the consummation of the marriage; but the *gaman* may be altogether dispensed with by the performance of *phir-pattah*, or changing the stools of the bride and bridegroom, when the *hom* is celebrated.

The customs Lushington described for royal Jats are consistent with those followed by M-K Jats 133 years later.

Thus, both Hindu domestic law and long tradition support the M-K Jats in their child marriages. Since there is no real lower limit in age for marriage, and a considerable feeling that there must be something wrong with an unmarried person who is over the age of 16 (for girls) and 20 (for boys), the custom of sibling-set or collateral-set marriages for children several years apart in age makes good sense, especially in the context of Jat penury and adherence to Brahman advice. I should add that some families are so poor that sons among them may not marry until they are mature, when a man can earn enough to pay a brideprice himself.[5] We attended one Jat wedding in M-K at which the bride appeared to be 12 and the groom 25 or 30 years old. There are some men who get only a levirate bride when a brother dies; some men never marry.

Among the Minas, on the other hand, there appeared to be two patterns. Among the wealthier Minas, the grooms tended to be 17 to 20, and the brides 15 to 16; among poor Minas, grooms tended to be 25 to 30 and brides 10 to 14. Among both Jats and Minas, the marriages of men in their twenties to young girls were likely to be brideprice marriages in which a very poor man gave his daughter to a bachelor, also from a poor family, who had managed to raise enough money (about 2,000 to 4,000 rupees in the mid-1960s) to pay the brideprice. Especially important in evaluating a bridegroom's status was whether his family owned land and how much land, and whether the men of the family had outside jobs from which they earned money.

The first factor discovered to be related to joint family households, then, was sibling-set and collateral-set marriages, and the second was child or young adolescent marriage. Both are facilitated by the Rajasthani custom of holding multiple weddings on the one or two days a year deemed by astrological almanacs to be auspicious for them to take place. A third factor was one often mentioned by anthropologists: the joint family as work-team. This was a factor I was aware of from writings about Japanese families (Johnson 1964: 846; Nakane 1967). In M-K, the joint family functioned as a well-team consisting of two adult men, who were almost always related, either as father and son, or as brothers, plus one of their wives and some of their older children. I described the system as follows:

> ...an incline is built in front of a well down which a pair of bullocks is driven, their downward movement pulling a leather pouch (*charas*) full of water from the well. One man drives the bullocks, a second man empties the pouch of water into a sink from which it drains along dried-mud channel-bunds built above the fields. A third person, often a woman or older child, releases the water from the channel at the desired point to enter the fields.... Almost three-quarters of the Jat well-teams (74 percent) – seventeen out of twenty-three – are composed of patrilineally-related men. Two-thirds (65 percent) -- fifteen out of twenty-three -- are composed either of brothers or of father-son combinations. Thirteen, 56 percent, are composed of brother or of father-sons who share the same house and eat from the same kitchen. There is thus a majority tendency for Jat

men who compose well-teams to be members of the same commensal extended families.

Jat women not only work in the house caring for children and cooking for the family, but they work in the fields irrigating the patches of garden. They also harvest and winnow grains such as *bajra*, and vegetables such as *moth*. They cut and carry thorn bushes used for barriers. They gather foliage for fuel. They cut, carry, and chop fodder for animals. They water and feed the animals as well. Jats and Minas have herds of sheep and goats. They and villagers of other castes have some cows and buffaloes. It is the children who are in charge of herding.

Joint families make possible a division of labor among the members. One wife can care for small children, while another works in the field or collects and chops fodder. It makes possible a division of labor among men, as well, either on the well -- one driving the bullocks, the other emptying out the water pouch – or by some men doing agricultural work in M-K and others working outside. Older children similarly can be assigned different tasks -- some in the fields, or herding, or caring for the babies, some attending school (Kolenda 1978b: 248–49; 1987: 183–85).

This Jat and Mina pattern illustrates the hypothesis of Pasternak, Ember and Ember (1976) that joint families often occur in pre-industrial societies where and when an adult has incompatible tasks to perform. The incompatibility is solved by having more than one man or more than one woman to do the tasks which would be incompatible for one man or for one woman alone to do.

Also related to the joint family as a work-team was the paucity of agricultural labor employed by the landholding Jats and Minas. Only at peak labor times, as when the sowing of the winter crop was taking place at the same time as the harvesting of the summer crop, did they employ untouchable Balais to help them in the fields. Map 5 shows the distribution of SCs by district in rural Rajasthan in 1961. These communities, who often serve as agrestic servants, were not heavily concentrated in the high joint family districts; of the 11 Quintile 1 districts shown on Map 4, only one, Tonk, had more than 20 percent of its population among the SCs. The correlation coefficient between married sons and SCs was +0.22, that between other married relatives

Map 5

Population of Scheduled Caste People in Each District of Rajasthan (Census of India 1961)

and SCs was +0.28, both low relationships. The most economical way that the Jats and Minas of M-K knew of to farm was to have all work in the fields done by family members. Thus, there were only two extended families of Balais, and very few members of the five other artisan or serving castes living in the village; only 3 percent of the population of M-K were not Jats or Minas. Among the Jats and Minas, agricultural work was done by the women and children rather than by agrestic servants of low caste. Women and children were thus vital members of the family work-team, both in the house and field.

Well-teams and, more broadly, joint families as work-teams, were also affected by the rather large proportion of men in M-K who worked outside the village in factories, foundries and services in the city of Jaipur, or on commercial farms nearby, or in public or private

Map 6

Location of 24 Villages Surveyed by the Census of India 1961 in Rajasthan (Used for Comparative Purpose in Studying Family Structure)

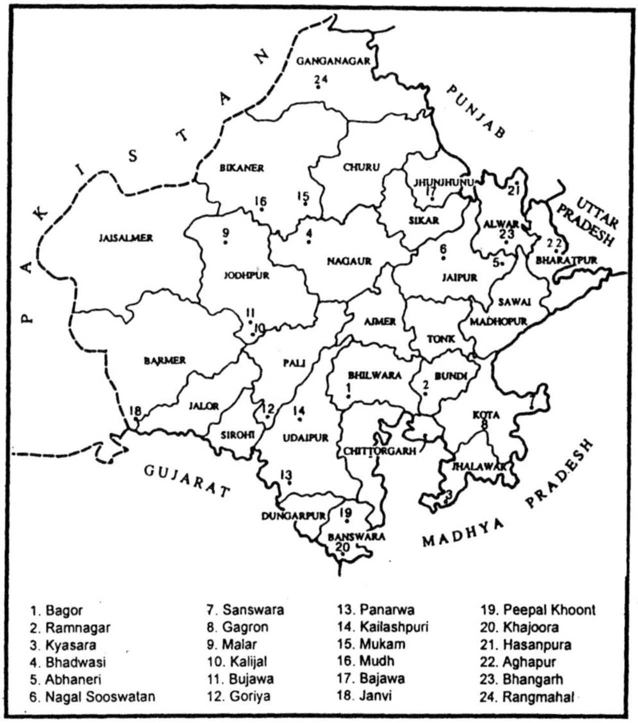

construction projects. Almost one-third of the adult Mina men who were not too old to work (six out of 19) worked outside the village. Among the 73 Jat adult men, 50 (68 percent) worked on the land, 10 (14 percent) worked outside, and 13 (18 percent) were retired. The usual pattern was for at least one man of a joint family to work outside, contributing his cash income to the joint family pool of resources. Because of the absence of brothers who were working outside, the men who composed well-teams were sometimes more distantly related than as brothers or were unrelated (although over 90 percent of the teams were composed of men who were both Jats) (see Kolenda 1978b: 249; 1987: 185), and hence the correlation between joint family households and well-teams was less than it might have been if all brothers worked in the village.

Sibling- and collateral-set marriage, young adolescent/child marriage and work-team requirements thus all supported the organization of joint families in M-K. A fourth factor was the role of the former *jagirdar* (hereditary estate-holder), *inamdar* (rent-free landholder), and the *mahant* (head priest) of the Krishna temple in Kishanpur in influencing household structure before the implementation of the Rajasthan Land Reforms and Resumption of Jagirs Act of 1952. Maharajapur had been a *khalsa* village (a village belonging to the Maharaja of Jaipur), while Kishanpur had been partly an *inamdari* and partly a *jagirdari* village. Most of its lands had belonged to the Krishna (locally, 'Kishan') temple. The former *mahant* told us that his predecessors had tried to encourage cultivation by tenants by building houses and wells for them, or else they would give tenants wood or lend them money toward the cost of building houses. But he also stated that "during *jagirdari* days the cultivator's life was very unstable, because *jagirdars* threw cultivators off the land whenever they pleased. Therefore, no cultivator could build a *pakka* (fired-brick) house" (field interview by Indira Sapru, 1 April 1968). Since building new houses was by permission of the *jagirdar*, *inamdar*, or Maharaja's official, tenants may not have built houses quite as soon as they felt they were needed for their expanding families. There is thus the possibility that more families lived in a house or shared a *chulha* in the past than might have chosen to do so.

That the requirement of the village landlord's permission to partition joint households may have considerable impact upon the pattern of family structure among tenants or agrestic servants is indicated by Peter Czap's study (1983) of serf households in Mishino, Russia, between 1814 and 1858. Among the serfs, 75 percent of households were joint (Hajnal 1983: 91), and as much as 65 percent were composed of three or more generations (Czap 1983: 133).[6] It was part of the authority of the *seigneur* to inhibit household fission (ibid.: 122, 136), possibly from a belief in the benefits of the large family system either for their members or for the estate management. The role of the *jagirdar*, *inamdar*, or royal official in Rajasthan may have included a similar inhibition.

Evidence of the unwilling persistence of some joint families in M-K is indicated by the fact that some of eldest brothers of Jat and Mina families left their joint family household in Maharajapur to build separate houses in Kishanpur or elsewhere as soon as land reform permitted it (Kolenda 1987: 181) (Eldest sons are likely to have the largest numbers of children first in the joint family's development, and hence may feel crowded earliest). By the Land Reform Act, Kishanpur land went to the Minas who had previously tilled it, while Maharajapur land went to the former Jat tenants of the Maharaja. After almost all the Minas had left Maharajapur to live in Kishanpur, some of the eldest sons of Jat joint families moved into the vacant houses, establishing separate *chulhas* there. Since so much building of new houses and moving out had taken place in the eight years since land reforms (1958–1966), the proportions of joint families and the number of people in them may well have been higher in M-K prior to that time. The fact that none of the former tenants of the former *jagirdar* and *inamdar* of Kishanpur lived in Kishanpur until after land reforms raises the question: Did the *jagirdar* and *inamdar* forbid their tenants to live near the fields they tilled? This was possible since the Kishanpur tenants were Minas who had supported themselves as 'protectors' of the Jats of Maharajapur and thus lived in Maharajapur, until an epidemic in Kishanpur in 1928 motivated the *mahant* and the *jagirdar* to take them on as tenants. The *mahant* and the *jagirdar* could thus insist that the Minas continue to reside in Maharajapur rather than move to Kishanpur.

The fieldwork conducted in M-K thus suggests four major factors contributing to the occurrence of joint families: (i) sibling-set and collateral-set marriage, (ii) young adolescent/child marriage, (iii) well-teams composed of members of the same joint family, and (iv) the need, in the past, for permission from *inamdars*, *jagirdars* or other officials in order to build houses. Sibling-set and collateral-set marriages serve to strengthen the joint family by bringing together as daughters-in-law, women who are sisters or cousin-sisters; hence quarrels between co-daughters-in-law are less likely to be serious enough to lead to demands on their part for dissolution of their common joint family. The need to economize in wedding expenses, along with Hindu teachings on the desirability of marrying daughters before puberty, encourages these sibling- and collateral-set marriages, as do multiple weddings and a very young age of marriage for brides and grooms – a crucial factor which will be taken up again later. The well-team/work-team formed by the joint family serves as a functional cause for the persistence of the joint family. Finally, the former requirement that tenants get permission from their landlords to build new living quarters is an oppressive cause of joint family households: people shared house and *chulha* because of a shortage of living space. Since land was allotted to the former tenants in the 1950s, a landlord's permission is no longer necessary in M-K, but the cost of building a new house or even adding on to an existing house may still be prohibitive enough for some joint families to continue to live together despite their preference for division into separate households.

Family Structure in the 1961 Census Village Surveys of Rajasthan

As part of the 1961 Census, representative villages were surveyed for every state and territory of India. For Rajasthan, 36 village surveys were done, of which 24 were obtained for this study.[7] These are listed in the bibliography. Map 6 shows the location of the 24 villages. In the surveys, four types of families were tabulated: simple, intermediate, joint, and other. Two of the census ethnographers, Gupta and Pendharker (1969: 27), define these as follows:

> A simple family consists of husband, his wife and unmarried children; an intermediate one consists of a married couple and unmarried brother, sister or one of the parents; whereas the joint family consists of a married couple with married sons/daughters, or with married brothers/sisters. The types of families not covered by any of the above have been classified as 'others'.

Given these definitions, it is reasonable to equate the census categories of simple, intermediate and joint with those of nuclear, supplemented nuclear and joint as I have defined them in my earlier works (Kolenda 1967: 346–47; 1987: 11–13). Table 9.3 shows the proportions for the four types of families in the 24 village surveys, as well as quintile rank on proportion of married females aged 10–14 and married males aged 10–14.

In my 1968 comparative study of the Indian joint family, based on a comparison of 26 studies from 14 different states of India, I developed a principle of what constitutes high, medium, and low proportions of joint family households in India. A proportion of 30 percent or more is high, 20 to 29 percent is medium, and 19 percent or

Table 9.3

Figure on Joint Families from 24 Village Studies in Rajasthan (Census of India 1961)

1.	Bagor		Mandal Tehsil		Bhilwara District	1-1
	(p. 26)	43 S (81%)	3 I (6%)	7 Jt	(13%)	
2.	Ramnagar	Kanjar Colony	Bundi Tehsil		Bundi District	1-1
	(p. 30)	168 S (93%)	12 I (7%)	0 Jt		
3.	Kyasara		Dag Tehsil		Jhalawar District	1-1
	(p. 39)	31 S (33%)	20 I (21%)	37 Jt	(39%) 6 O (6%)	
4.	Bhadwasi		Nagaur Tehsil		Nagaur District	1-1
	(p. 27)	35 S (61%)	1 I (2%)	21 Jt	(37%)	
5.	Abhaneri		Baswa Tehsil		Jaipur District	1-2
	(p. 30)	66 S (41%)	50 I (31%)	41 Jt	(27%) 1 O (1%)	
6.	Nangal Sooswatan		Amber Tehsil		Jaipur District	1-2
7.	Sanwara		Shahbad Tehsil		Kota District	1-2
	(p. 31)	24 S (55%)	5 I (11%)	15 Jt	(34%)	
8.	Gagron		Kanwas Tehsil		Kota District	1-2
	(p. 26)	23 S (40%)	7 I (12%)	19 Jt	(33%) 8 O (14%)	
9.	Malar		Palodi Tehsil		Jodhpur District	2-1
	(p. 35)	77 S (55%)	25 I (18%)	39 Jt	(28%)	
10.	Kalijal		Jodhpur Tehsil		Jodhpur District	2-1
	(p. 28)	55 S (48%)	23 I (20%)	36 Jt	(31%) 1 O (1%)	
11.	Bujawa		Jodhpur Tehsil		Jodhpur District	2-1
	(p.36)	16 S (44%)	9 I (25%)	11 Jt	(31%)	
12.	Goriya		Bali Tehsil		Pali District	2-1
	(p. 33)	94 S (69%)	8 I (6%)	35 Jt	(25%)	
13.	Panarwa		Phalasia Tehsil		Udaipur District	2-1
	(p. 32)	18 S (58%)	1 I (3%)	9 Jt	(29%) 3 O (10%)	
14.	Kailashpur		Nokha Tehsil		Udaipur District	2-1
	(p. 25)	119 S (66%)	21 I (12%)	27 Jt	(15%) 13 O (7%)	
15.	Mukam		Nokha Tehsil		Bikaner District	2-2
	(p. 32)	41 S (63%)	14 I (22%)	10 Jt	(15%)	
16.	Mudh		Kolayat Tehsil		Bikaner District	2-2
	(p. 41)	38 S (49%)	0 I	39 Jt	(51%)	
17.	Bajawa		Udaipurwati Tehsil		Jhunjhunu District	2-3
	(p. 31)	16 S (59%)	1 I (4%)	8 Jt	(30%) 2 O (7%)	

Contd...

Contd...

18. Janvi		Sanchore Tehsil		Jalor District	3-2
(p. 58)	72 S (53%)	23 I (17%)	39 Jt	(29%) 1 O (1%)	
19. Peepal Khoont		Ghatol Tehsil		Banswara District	3-2
(p. 49)	129 S (77%)	17 I (10%)	17 Jt	(10% 5 O (3%)	
20. Khajoora		Kushalgarh Tehsil		Banswara District	3-2
(p. 31)	18 S (51%)	5 I (14%)	8 Jt	(23%) 4 O (12%)	
21. Hasanpur		Tijara Tehsil		Alwar District	3-2
(p. 25)	68 S (80%)	9 I (11%)	8 Jt	(9%)	
22. Aghapur		Bharatpur Tehsil		Bharatpur District	3-2
(p. 33)	64 S (54%)	27 I (23%)	25 Jt	(21%) 3 O (2%)	
23. Bhangarh		Rajgarh Tehsil		Alwar District	3-2
(p. 34)	33 S (55%)	10 I (16%)	16 Jt	(26%) 2 O (3%)	
24. Rangmahal		Suratgarh Tehsil		Ganganagar District	4-3
(p. 33)	63 S (76%)	10 I (12%)	9 Jt	(11%) 1 O (1%)	

(Key: S = Simple, I = Intermediate, Jt = Joint, O = Other. Hyphenated pair of numbers at the end of lines, 1-1, 2-1, etc., refer to the quintile rank on proportion of females 10–14 who are married and quintile rank on proportion of males 10–14 who are married.)

less is low (Kolenda 1968: 375; 1987: 57). By this principle, nine (38 percent) of the Rajasthan villages considered here were high (with Mudh, Bikaner district, a largely SC village consisting mostly of Meghwals, the highest, at 51 percent), eight were medium, and seven were low. Thus, 17 out of 24 (70 percent) villages showed medium and high proportions of joint families, confirming the district statistics for Rajasthan presented earlier and showing that the state has a higher than average proportion of joint family households.

Two of the 'low' villages, Ramnagar Kanjar Colony (Bundi district) and Bagor (Bhilwara district), were composed almost entirely of Kanjars, an erstwhile nomadic criminal tribe which the government had tried to sedentarize. The ethnographers of Ramnagar Kanjar Colony, Sharma and Gupta (1967a), explained the absence of joint families as customary:

> The reason is that it is customary among the Kanjars for a boy who is about to be married to receive a separate piece of land, a residential house and other necessary articles for his maintenance from his parents. After the marriage the newly married couple lives in a new house, and not with the parents (1967: 30 see also p. 12).

According to them, the age of marriage among the SC sedentarized Kanjars of Ramnagar Kanjar Colony was 20--29 for males and 15–24 for females. While they did not specify the connection between the couple setting up their own house immediately upon marriage and the older age of marriage among these Kanjars as compared to other Rajasthani communities, it would appear to be much easier for a couple to run a household if they are older.

Concerning the Kanjars and Sansis (another former nomadic criminal tribe) who composed Bagor village, Bhargava and Pendharker (1968: 26) write:

> The preference for simple type of family is a natural consequence of the settlement of the communities on land. Separate families were allotted separate holdings and it was advantageous for the settlers to claim to belong to separate rather than joint family type.

According to this explanation, the low proportion of joint family households in Bagor was not due to either custom or older age of marriage, but to the recent redistribution of land under the Land Reform Act, as a result of which the Kanjars and Sansis found it advantageous to maximize the number of families among them in order to qualify for the most land possible. In fact, it is clear that at the time of the survey young adolescent marriage for girls prevailed in Bagor. According to Bhargava and Pendharker (1968: 24), there were no unmarried females over the age of 14 among the Kanjars, and the usual age of marriage was 15–16 for boys and 12–13 for girls (ibid.: 12).

The influence of land redistribution on family composition, encouraging the maximization of nuclear families, may well have taken place in the low joint family village of Kailashpuri (Udaipur district) as well, where Bhil cultivators had recently been allotted former Eklingji temple lands.

The village with the lowest proportion of joint family households (9 percent) was Hasanpur (Alwar district), where almost two-thirds of the population (63 percent) were Muslim Meos. The explanation offered by Sharma and Pendharker (1969: 25) was that "the large number of families of the simple type is due to the fact that landholdings are small and they cannot bear the burden of joint families". This explanation is questionable, because as will be seen later in Table 9.10 showing types of families among landless Chamars, those represented in the Rajasthan villages surveyed had high proportions of joint families. Since some proportion of Hasanpur's population had departed for Pakistan at the time of partition in 1947 (Sharma and Pendharker 1969: 23), it is more likely that joint families had been fragmented by out-migration of one or more of their nuclear family components. Out-migration may also have been important in the low joint family village of Mukam (Bikaner district), a pilgrimage centre for Jambheswarji (the founder of the Bishnoi sect), composed only of Bishnois and their Meghwal servants. Mukam had little agricultural land, so that some Bishnoi cultivators tilled land in nearby villages, and many other Bishnois had migrated out.

In the cases of both Hasanpur and Mukam, it is likely that entire nuclear families migrated out, and not just male members. It is a common pattern in many rural areas of India for men to work outside the village for months or years at a time, leaving their wives and children on the land or in the house owned there, sometimes in the care of the remaining men of their joint families, the man returning to live with his family upon his retirement from his work outside. (For an example of such a pattern, see Dandekar 1986 for a village in Maharashtra.) While such out-migration may have occurred in Hasanpur and Mukam, it also seems likely that entire nuclear families or components of joint families migrated out permanently.

Rangmahal (Ganganagar district) and Peepal Khoont (Banswara district), two other villages low in joint families, were in districts ranked in either the fourth or fifth quintile on 'married sons' and 'other married relatives'. Their low (12 percent and 10 percent) joint family households were consistent with their districts' low quintile ratings on measures of joint family living (to be discussed later).

Thus, alongside the factors *encouraging* joint family living (sibling- and collateral-set marriage, young adolescent/child marriage, well-teams/work-teams, and need for official permission to build new homes), there are two factors (land reform and permanent out-migration) that tend to *fragment* joint families and reduce their proportion in a village. Of the villages low in joint family households, two were in districts of Rajasthan with below average quintiles on joint family measures, but three seemed to have a low proportion of joint families because of government land redistribution, and two seemed to have been disrupted by departure, permanent out-migration. In only one was there clear evidence that the custom was for marriage to be at an older age, with the couple occupying their own new house immediately after marriage.

Caste or Tribal Preference for Joint Family Living

A popular hypothesis concerning joint family living is an ethnic one – that joint families are preferred by certain communities (in Rajasthan, by Rajputs and Jats) and rejected by others (in Rajasthan, by Bhils and other tribals). The ethnographic material in the 1961 Census village surveys provides an opportunity to test this hypothesis. Though a few of the 24 villages were populated by a single ethnic community (nos. 2 and 17) or by two (no. 15), most were multi-caste communities (see Table 9.4 for caste composition of the 24 villages of Rajasthan).

Table 9.4

Castes in 24 Villages of Rajasthan (Census of India 1961)

1.	Bagor	Mandal Tehsil	Bhilwara District
	Castes: Sansi 32; Kanjar 21 (Nomadic criminal tribes)		
2.	Ramnagar, Kanjar Colony	Bundi Tehsil	Bundi District
	Castes: Kanjar 180 (a scheduled caste, formerly nomadic, dacoits and prostitutes)		
3.	Kyasara	Dag Tehsil	Jhalawar District
	Castes: Rajput 46; Nath 18; Chamar 12; Brahman 4; Suthar 3; Teli 1; Nai 2; Balai 2; Darzi 2; Dholi 2; Bania 1; Kumhar 1		
4.	Bhadwasi	Nagaur Tehsil	Nagaur District
	Castes: Mali 23; Rajput 10; Jat 10; Nayak 7; Bhambi 4; Muslim 3		
5.	Abhaneri	Baswa Tehsil	Jaipur District
	Castes: Brahman 69; Gujar 35; Kumhar 16; Mali 11; Chamar 8; Mahajan 4; Nai 4; Rajput 3; Koli 3; Jain 2; Khati 2; Mina 2; Bhangi 2; N = 161		
6.	Nangal Sooswatan	Amber Tehsil	Jaipur District
	Castes: Mina 87; Balai 13; Mali 6; Khati 5; Brahmbhat 7; Brahman 4; Mahajan 1; Dholi (Rana) 2; Jogi 1; N = 126		
7.	Sanwara	Shahbad Tehsil	Kota District
	Castes: Sahairya 32; Ahir 10; Brahman 1; Muslim 1; N = 44		
8.	Gagron	Kanwas Tehsil	Kota District
	Castes: Muslim Rajput 25; Rajput 5; Brahman 2; Bhil 6; Mali 7; Chamar 7; Moghia 3; Bhangi 2; N = 57		
9.	Malar	Palodi Tehsil	Jodhpur District
	Castes: Pushkarna Brahman 121; Sewak Brahman 3; Darzi 5; Suthar 1; Nai 3; Bhil 3; Bawari 2; Bhambi 3		
10.	Kalijal	Jodhpur Tehsil	Jodhpur District
	Castes: Jat 51; Rajput 33; Rebari 10; Bhil 8; Bhambi 7; Suthar 3; Sadh 1; Daroga 1; Bhangi 1		

Contd...

Contd...

11. Bujawa	Jodhpur Tehsil	Jodhpur District
Castes: Rajput 21; Raika 4; Bhambi 4; Sadh 3; Suthar 2; Darzi 1; Nai 1		
12. Goriya	Bali Tehsil	Pali District
Castes: Girasias 104 (a scheduled tribe); Bhil 28; Lohar 2; Kumhar 1; Hargada 1; Muslim 1		
13. Panarwa	Phalasia Tehsil	Udaipur District
Castes: Bhil 13; Rajput 7; Daroga 6; Girasias 5		
14. Kailashpur	Nokha Tehsil	Udaipur District
Castes: Bhil 96; Brahman 55; Mali 18; Darzi 2; Rajput 3; Muslim 1; Nai 2; Jogi 1; Manihar 1; Jat 1		
15. Mukam	Nokha Tehsil	Bikaner District
Castes: Bishnois 58; Meghwals 7		
16. Mudh	Kolayat Tehsil	Bikaner District
Castes: Meghwal 21 (scheduled caste); Darzi 15; Kumhar 11; Nayak 10; Sadh 6; Nai 2; Lohar 4; Dholi 1; Khati 2; Muslim 1; Paliwal 1; Sunar 1; Rajput 1; Pushkarna Brahman 1; N = 77		
17. Bajawa	Udaipurwati Tehsil	Jhunjhunu District
Castes: Chowkidari Mina; 27		
18. Janvi	Sanchore Tehsil	Jalor District
Castes: Bishnoi 2; Rajput 23; Kalbi 16; Daroga 12; Bhambi 9; Rebari 7; Brahman 4; Bhil 5; Mahajan 3; Garuda 3; Ghanchi 3; Suthar 2; Koli 3; Swami 3; Mirasi 2; Jat 2; Sadh 1; Honi 1; N = 135		
19. Peepal Khoont	Ghatol Tehsil	Banswara District
Castes: Bhil 131 = 92% population. Remainder are Bhoi, Jogi, Chamar		
20. Khajoora	Kushalgarh Tehsil	Banswara District
Castes: Bhil 34; Gasa 1		
21. Hasanpur	Tijara Tehsil	Alwar District
Castes: Meo 53; Chamar 23; Sindhi 4; Bhangi 3; Faqir 1; Mahajan 1		
22. Aghapur	Bharatpur Tehsil	Bharatpur District
Castes: Gujar 43; Kachhi 19; Jat 15; Banjara 15; Brahman 10; Sikh 6; Kumhar 3; Nai 3; Lodha 2; Gadariyia 1; Kadera 1; Bhangi 1; N = 119		
23. Bhangarh	Rajgarh Tehsil	Alwar District
Castes: Jogis 10 (Kanphata); Kolis 24; Brahman 10; Chamars 5; Mina 4; Khati 1; Nai 1; Banjara 6; N = 61		
24. Rangmahal	Suratgarh Tehsil	Ganganagar District
Castes: Nayak 27; Jat 18; Meghwal 18; Baori 10; Jogi 5; Kumhar 4; Braham 1; Nayaks, Meghwals and Baoris are Untouchables.		

The village surveyed included 65 different castes and tribal communities. The fragmentation of the caste system is such that only seven out of these 65 had members in as many as six different villages. Jats, Chamars and Kumhars appeared in six, Nais in eight, Bhils in nine, Rajputs in 10, and Brahmans in 12. The possibility of comparison of members of the same caste or tribal community living in different places is thus limited. Such comparison is further limited by the absence, in some of the surveys, of reports or tables showing the breakdown of household types by caste and tribal community. Comparisons for Nais and Kumhars are precluded by the very small number of families of each in any one village. It has been claimed that Rajputs prefer to live in joint families. The data from the village surveys can be examined to test this, as Rajputs were to be found in 10 of the villages, ranging from one family (in Mudh, Bikaner district) to 23 (in Janvi, Jalor district). Unfortunately, the breakdown of family types by caste is not provided for these of the villages (nos. 10, 14, 16). But, for the other seven villages, the proportion of Rajput families which were joint ranged from 0 to 100 percent (see Table 9.5).

Table 9.5

Rajputs' Family Types in Seven Rajasthan Villages

Village	*No. of Families*	*Simple*	*Inter*	*Joint*	*Other*
3 Kyasara, Jhalawar	46	10 (22%)	15 (33%)	18 (39%)	3 (6%)
4 Bhadwasi, Nagaur	10	5 (50%)	1 (10%)	4 (40%)	
5 Abhaneri, Jaipur	3	0	0	3 (100%)	
8 Gagron, Kota	5	2 (40%)	2 (40%)	1 (20%)	
11 Bujawa, Jodhpur	21	6 (29%)	7 (33%)	8 (38%)	
13 Panarwa, Udaipur	7	3 (43%)	0	3 (43%)	1 (14%)
18 Janvi, Jalor	23	20 (87%)	3 (13%)	0	

Applying the principle that if the proportion of joint families is 30 percent or more in an Indian village, it probably means that about half the people live in joint families. We see that in five out of the seven villages, most Rajputs lived in joint families, but that in two villages (Gagron in Kota district and Janvi in Jalor district) they did not.[8] The figures for Janvi, showing that none of the 23 Rajput families there was joint, are puzzling, as the proportion for total number of families in the village (135) was 29 percent joint. Janvi included 18 different ethnic communities. The largest caste, the Bishnois, had 50 percent joint families (18 out of 36 families), as did the Brahmans, Kalbis, and Suthars. Why, then, were there no joint families at all among the Rajputs – the second largest ethnic group of Janvi?

The answer once again seems to be the effect of land reforms. The *bhumichara jagirdari* (jointly held estate) land owned by the Rajputs in the past had recently been redistributed. Sixty percent of the land had gone to Bishnois (the former tenants of the Rajputs) and members of other castes, and 40 percent had been subdivided among the former Rajput joint owners. It may well have been beneficial for the Rajputs to maximize the numbers of their families when it came to this redistribution of land. In addition, a number of the Rajput young men of Janvi had become sufficiently educated to become office workers in the town of Sanchore, and some Rajput men had gone into business. Thus, it seems plausible that the breaking up and partial loss of the *jagirdari* previously shared by the Rajputs of Janvi removed the support that had existed for joint family living among them (Singh and Gupta 1966b: 48--49, 58, 60). Unfortunately, we do not have the distribution of household types among them before land reforms, so we can only postulate that there were more joint families earlier.

A further characteristic of the Rajputs of Janvi that militated against joint families was the late age of marriage reported for them – 18--20 for boys and 14--18 for girls. There were much higher ages than those for Bishnoi and Kalbi children, who were reported to marry boys as young as 5 and girls as young as 3 (Singh and Gupta 1966b: 32). This factor of child marriage will be taken up in greater detail later.

The other village lacking a high proportion of joint family households among Rajputs (Gagron, Kota district) had a medium proportion of 20 percent -- one out of five families. The number of persons in each category of family was not given in the Gagron survey report, so it is not possible to say what proportion of the 29 Rajput individuals in the village belonged to the one joint family. This, of course, is also a small population with a small number of families.

Before land reforms, 30 to 100 percent of the land in five of the seven villages (nos. 3, 4, 8, 11, 18) had been controlled by the Rajputs. The Rajputs in the other two village (nos. 5 and 13) were few in

Table 9.6

Numbers and Proportions of Permanently Unmarried Persons (Bachelors, Widows and Widowers) in 24 Rajasthan Villages

	Village	No. of Unmarried Males	No. of Widowers	No. of Widows	Pop. Size	Total Unmarried	% Unmarried
1.	Bagor (Bhilwara)	2	5	4	229	11	5
2.	Ramnagar (Bundi)	many	7	20	655	27	?
3.	Kyasara (Jhalawar)	3	12	41	514	56	11
4.	Bhadwasi (Nagaur)	4	4	3	363	11	3
5.	Abhaneri (Jaipur)	26	34	31	1005	91	9
6.	Nangal Sooswatan (Jaipur)	3	9	36	708	48	7
7.	Sanwara (Kota)	1	2	5	222	8	4
8.	Gagrom (Kota)	3	15	11	282	29	10
9.	Malar (Jodhpur)	15	17	41	648	73	11
10.	Kalijal (Jodhpur)	5	14	35	689	53	8
11.	Bujawa (Jodhpur)	6	5	17	229	28	12
12.	Goriya (Pali)	1	7	8	782	16	2
13.	Panarwa (Udaipur)	0	1	3	146	4	3
14.	Kailashpuri (Udaipur)	3	8	33	664	44	7
15.	Mukam (Bikaner)	8	13	12	298	33	11
16.	Mudh (Bikaner)	1	11	20	298	33	11
17.	Bujawa (Jhunjhunu)	3	2	7	149	12	8
18.	Janvi (Jalor)	1	11	23	695	35	5
19.	Peepal Khoont (Banswara)	3	14	35	830	52	6
20.	Khaipora (Banswara)	4	3	7	206	14	7
21.	Hasanpur (Alwar)	1	5	9	356	15	4
22.	Aghapur (Bharatpur)	34	20	19	599	73	12
23.	Bhangarh (Alwar)	3	13	12	341	28	8
24.	Rangmahal (Ganganagar)	6	8	9	355	23	6

number, living in villages controlled by other dominant castes. Here again is the suggestion that large landholdings encourage a joint family structure.

A feature of Rajput life that is important in terms of family structure is that, along with Brahmans, Mahajans (Hindu merchants and bureaucrats) and Bishnois, they forbid the remarriage of widows. This tends to create a category of dependent women to be cared for by some family. Rajputs also tend to have especially distorted sex ratios (see Table 9.11)[9] which leads to some adult men remaining bachelors throughout life, another category of dependents to be cared for by some family; it does not seem to be a common Rajasthani custom to permit a single person to live alone, or more precisely, to eat from her or his own kitchen. The two factors, prohibition of widow remarriage and the greater number of males than females, may result in a sizeable number of permanently unmarried people of both sexes to be included in 'intermediate' or 'joint' families. The latter are equivalent to my terms, supplemented nuclear, and lineal-, collateral-, and lineal-collateral joint families. Of course, the addition of a single adult to a family cannot make it a joint family, since, by definition, a joint family consists of two or more related married couples. Thus, by definition, the addition of a permanently unmarried adult to a joint family can only 'supplement' it and increase its size, but such an addition does convert a nuclear family into a supplemented nuclear family/intermediate family.

When the 24 village surveys are compared on the proportions of their population which fall into the categories of unmarried males over the age of 25, widowers, and widows (see Table 9.6), we find high proportions (10 to 20 percent) in seven villages. Three of these were dominated by Rajputs – two by Hindu Rajputs (nos. 3 and 11) and one by Muslim Rajputs (no. 8). Two were dominated by Hindu religious specialists – one by Brahmans (no. 9) and one by Bishnois (no. 15). The other village with a high proportion of unmarried adults (Aghapur, Bharatpur district) was predominantly Gujar and Jat. According to its ethnographers, Agarwal and Gupta (1969: 32),

> the presence of 19 unmarried males in the age group 25–29 and the age group 30–34 is perhaps due to the fact that the economic position of the households is not strong enough to pay the high bride-price demanded by the parents of the girl.

Aghapur's high proportion of single adults seems to have been composed largely of unmarried adult males (34 out of 73), rather than by the widows so characteristic of villages with large Rajput or other high-caste populations.

The village with the lowest proportion of its population in these permanently unmarried categories was Goriya, in Pali district, in which three-fourths of the population were members of the SC Girasias. The sex ratio was also less unequal (52 percent male, 48 percent female) than in half the other villages. Among the Girasias, the common form of marriage is elopement, after which the bridegroom pays some brideprice; exchange is also allowed, requiring neither brideprice nor dowry; both widows and widowers are allowed to remarry, and extra-marital relationships are not "much looked down upon" (Gulati and Gupta 1966: 32, 16). These Girasia tribal norms seemed to result in few adults remaining unmated, hence a lower proportion of permanently unmarried adults and fewer intermediate families. Conversely, the high proportions of permaneunmarried adults among Rajputs and other high castes help account for the high proportions of 'intermediate' families among them.

Table 9.7

Jats' Family Types in Four Rajasthan Villages

Village	*No. of Families*	*Simple*	*Inter*	*Joint*	*Other*
4 Bhadwasi, Nagaur	10	7 (70%)	0	3 (30%)	
18 Janvi, Jalor	2	2 (100%)			
22 Aghapur, Bharatpur	15	8 (53%)	1 (7%)	5 (33%)	1 (7%)
24 Rangmahal, Ganganagar	18	12 (67%)	5 (28%)	0	1 (5%)

What about the other major castes and tribes in the village surveyed – the Jats, Brahmans, Bhils, and Chamars? Tables 9.7, 9.8, 9.9, and 9.10 show the distribution of family types in the villages in which each community was to be found. A persual of these tables indicates that there was no consistent pattern for Jats, Brahmans or Bhils. There were both high and low proportions of joint families among each of these ethnic groups. Clearly, therefore, Jats and

Brahmans do not have consistently high proportions of joint families, nor do Bhils have consistently low proportions. Thus, the popular idea that Jats and high castes have high proportions of joint families, and that tribals do not, is not sustained by these village surveys.

Table 9.8

Brahman Family Types in Eleven Rajasthan Villages

Village	*No. of Families*	*Simple*	*Inter*	*Joint*	*Other*
3 Kyasara, Jhalawar	4	3 (75%)	0	1 (25%)	0
5 Abhaneri, Jaipur	69	40 (58%)	25 (36%)	5 (7%)	
6 Nangal Sooswatan, Jaipur	4	0	1 (25%)	3 (75%)	
7 Sanwara, Kota	1	0	1 (100%)	0	
8 Gagron, Kota	2	0	0	1 (50%)	
9 Malar, Jodhpur	124	69 (56%)	23 (33%)	32 (26%)	
14 Kailashpuri, Udaipur	55	35 (64%)	6 (10%)	7 (13%)	7 (13%)
18 Janvi, Jalor	4	0	2 (50%)	2 (50%)	
22 Aghapur, Bharatpur	10	2 (20%)	2 (20%)	4 (40%)	4 (40%)
23 Bhangarh, Alwar	10	4 (40%)	1 (10%)	3 (30%)	2 (20%)
24 Rangmahal, Ganganagar	1	1 (100%)	0	0	

Table 9.9

Bhils' Family Types in Eight Rajasthan Villages

Village	*No. of Families*	*Simple*	*Inter*	*Joint*	*Other*
8 Gagron, Kota	46	10 (22%)	15 (33%)	18 (39%)	3 (6%)
9 Malar, Jodhpur	3	2 (67%)	0	1 (33%)	
12 Goriya, Pali	28	20 (71%)	0	8 (29%)	
13 Panarwa, Udaipur	13	8 (62%)	0	4 (31%)	1 (7%)
14 Kailashpuri, Udaipur	96	65 (68%)	10 (10%)	15 (16%)	6 (6%)
18 Janvi, Jalor	23	20 (87%)	3 (13%)	0	
19 Peepal Khoont, Banswara	155	120 (77%)	15 (10%)	15 (10%)	5 (3%)
20 Khajoora, Banswara	34	18 (53%)	5 (15%)	7 (20%)	4 (12%)

Any suggestion that joint family living is most characteristic of high castes is belied not only by the figures for Bhils in Table 9.9, but also by the figures in Table 9.10 for the low caste untouchable Chamars. Consistently, Chamars had high proportions of joint families, as high as 88 percent (Abhaneri, Jaipur district) and 80 percent (Bhangarh, Alwar district). The number of Chamar families in each village was small, however, between five and 12 families. Moreover, it should be noted that both Abhaneri and Bhangarh are well-watered villages on the Sanwar river, and that the Chamars there were agricultural labourers living in one-room house (Agarwal and Pendharker 1965: 3, 9, 20; Gulati and Pendharker 1965c: 11, 21). Possibly, then, the Chamars' high proportion of joint families was not entirely the result of choice, but also of lack of resources to build more housing. Thomas Rosin has pointed out to me (personal communication) that possibly the Chamar joint household may also be a work-team when it pursues the Chamars' traditional leather craft. He writes: "The jointness of leather worker's families also has struck me, but their structure seems consistent with their elaborate activities in hauling, flailing, tanning, and crafting leather." The importance of the joint family as a work-team was mentioned for Maharajapur-Kishanpur earlier, and will be discussed in greater detail for Rajasthan as a whole later.

Table 9.10

Chamar Family Types in Five Rajasthan Villages

Village	*No. of Families*	*Simple*	*Inter*	*Joint*	*Other*
3 Kyasara, Jhalawar	12	5 (42%)	1 (8%)	4 (33%)	2 (17%)
5 Abhaneri, Jaipur	8	0	0	7 (88%)	1 (12%)
8 Gagron, Kota	7	0	1 (14%)	4 (57%)	2 (29%)
9 Peepal Khoont, Banswara	7	3 (43%)	0	3 (43%)	1 (14%)
25 Bhangarh, Alwar	5	1 (20%)	0	4 (80%)	

Comparison of a caste's family structure in different Rajasthani villages thus suggests variation within the caste. In the village surveys examined here, only the SC Chamars showed consistently high proportions of joint family living, followed by the high-caste Rajputs. While the high proportions for Rajputajputs m(4Ubeen the result of large landholdings in the past, those for Chamars may have been due to crowded housing. The common beliefs about the relationships between ethnicity and family structure in Rajasthan are sustained by these census village survey data only with respect of Rajputs, and not with respect to Jats or Bhils.

Table 9.11

Sex Ratios for 24 Villages Studies Done in Rajasthan (Census of India 1961)

1.	Bagor		Mandal Tehsil	Bhilwara District	1-1
	Sex ratio:	124 M (58%)	105 F (42%)	(p. 2) total: 229	
2.	Ramnagar	Kanjar Colony	Bundi Tehsil	Bundi District	1-1
	Sex ratio:	380 M (58%)	275 F (42%)	(p. 27) total: 655	
3.	Kyasara		Dag Tehsil	Jhalawar District	1-1
	Sex ratio:	264 M (51%)	250 F (49%)	total: 514	
4.	Bhadwasi		Nagpur Tehsil	Nagpur District	1-1
	Sex ratio:	201 M (55%)	162 F (45%)	total: 363	
5.	Abhaneri		Bawa Tehsil	Jaipur District	1-2
	Sex ratio:	546 M (54%)	459 F (46%)	total: 1005	
6.	Nangal Sooswatan		Amber Tehsil	Jaipur District	1-2
	Sex ratio:	369 M (52%)	339 F (48%)	total: 708	
7.	Sanwara		Shahbad Tehsil	Kota District	1-2
	Sex ratio:	106 M (48%))	116 F m 5.2Utotal: 222		
8.	Gagron		Kanwas Tehsil	Kota District	1-2
	Sex ratio:	161 M (57%)	121 F (43%)	total: 282	
9.	Malar		Palodi Tehsil	Jodhpur District	2-1
	Sex ratio:	352 M (54%)	296 F (46%)	total: 648	
10.	Kalijal		Jodhpur Tehsel	Jodhpur District	2-1
	Sex ratio:	372 M (54%)	317 F (46%)	total: 689	
11.	Bujawa		Jodhpur Tehsil	Jodhpur District	2-1
	Sex ratio:	128 M (56%)	101 F (44%)	total: 229	
12.	Goriya		Bali Tehsil	Pali District	2-1
	Sex ratio:	406 M (52%)	376 F (48%)	total: 782	
13.	Panwara		Phalasïa Tehsil	Udaipur District	2-1
	Sex ratio:	79 M (54%)	67 F (46%)	total: 146	
14.	Kailashpuri		Girwa Tehsil	Udaipur District	2-1
	Sex ratio:	348 M (52%)	316 F (48%)	(p. 2) total: 664	

Contd...

Contd...

15.	Mukam		Nokha Tehsil	Bikaner District	2-2
	Sex ratio:	p. 1: 167 M (56%)	131 F (44%)	total: 298	
16.	Mudh		Kolayat Tehsil	Bikaner District	2-2
	Sex ratio:	p. 4: 213 M (51%)	206 F (49%)	total: 419	
17.	Bujawa	Udaipurwati Tehsil	Jhunjhunu	(Shekhawati)	2-3
	Sex ratio:	p. 28 70 M (47%)	79 F (53%)	total: 149	
	Chowkidari Minas	102 M (54%)	88 F (46%)		
18.	Janvi		Sanchore Tehsil	Jalor District	3-2
	Sex ratio:	p. 4: 343 M (50%)	342 F (50%)	total: 685	
19.	Peepal Khoont		Ghatol Tehsil	Banswara District	3-2
	Sex ratio:	p. 46 430 M (52%)	400 F (48%)	total: 830	
20.	Khajoora		Kushalgarh Tehsil	Banswara District	3-2
	Sex ratio:	p. 1: 103 M (50%)	103 F (50%)	total: 206	
21.	Hasanpur		Tijara Tehsil	Alwar District	3-2
	Sex ratio:	p. 6: 192 M (54%)	164 F (46%)	total: 356	
22.	Aghapur		Bharatpur Tehsil	Bharatpur District	3-2
	Sex ratio:	p. 7: 345 M (58%)	254 F (42%)	total: 599	
23.	Bhangarh		Rajgarh Tehsil	Alwar District	3-2
	Sex ratio:	p. 3: 185 M (54%)	156 F (46%)	total: 341	
24.	Rangmahal		Suratgarh Tehsil	Ganganagar District	4-3
	Sex ratio:	194 M (55%)	161 F (45%)	total: 355	

Early Adolescent Marriage and the 'Protective Joint Family'

In the late 1960s and early 1970s, Lorraine Haddon, a graduate student at the University of Houston, calculated measures of over 60 variables in the 1961 Census. These measures fell into three groups: variables related to family, variables taken to be indices of modernization, and other social-cultural variables such as religion, occupation, and caste or tribe membership. Only a few of these variables were found to have strong (positive or negative correlations of +/-0.60 or better with the indices of joint family living discussed above (married sons and other married relatives).[10] On an all-India basis, negative relationships were found between proportions of joint families and various educational variables and measures of modernization (Kolenda and Haddon 1987: 276, 279–86). These negative relationships were not found in Rajasthan, however, probably because the districts of Rajasthan in which there were low proportions of joint families (the Gujarat border districts, Jaisalmer and Ganganagar) were not highly modernized and did not have, except possibly in some towns and in some of the more modernized parts of Ganganagar, especially good educational facilities. The largest number of schools with the maximum number of school-going children are in the districts east of the Aravallis, the very districts which are high in joint families.

The variables with which the indices of joint family were found to be most strongly related were the proportions of females and males aged 10--14 reported as married. The correlation coefficients between the proportion of married sons and the two measures of adolescent marriage were +0.912 for females and +0.856 for males; the same relationships for proportion of other married relatives were +0.848 and +0.761. These two variables of adolescent marriage were also highly interrelated, with a correlation coefficient of +0.90.

Maps 7 and 8 show the districts in Rajasthan in Quintile 1 on proportions of married females and males aged 10–14. The nine districts shown on Map 7 ranged between 63.92 percent (Bhilwara district) and 42.26 percent (Jaipur district) for females aged 10–14 reported as married; 10 other districts were in the second quintile. Thus, in 19 districts of Rajasthan, the proportion of females aged 10--14 reported as married was well above all-India averages. In addition, six districts were in the third quintile and one in the fourth; none was in the fifth quintile.

Map 8 shows 11 Rajasthan districts that fell into the first quintile on proportion of married males aged 10--14, ranging from 32.48 percent (Bhilwara district) to 13.69 percent (Udaipur district). Moreover, with 12 districts falling into the second quintile, 23 of the districts of Rajasthan were well above average in proportion of married males 10–14. The other three districts fell in Quintile 3.

A comparison of Maps 3 and 4 with Maps 7 and 8 indicates that young adolescent marriage is more characteristic of Rajasthan than is that of joint families. That is, more districts fall above the all-India average on the two measures of adolescent marriage than on the two

Map 7

Rajasthan Districts in First Quintile on Proportions of Females Aged 10--14 Reported as Married (Census of India 1961)

measures of joint family. Map 9 shows seven districts which rank in the first quintile on all four measures. Spatially contiguous except for Jhalawar, separated by a small section of Kota from Chittorgarh, they form a central core in which there is a high proportion of joint family households, explained to a considerable extent by the high proportions of married young adolescents.

While the proportions of married 10--14 year-olds were recorded in the 1961 Census, it was not noted whether those counted were living with their spouses or not. The meaning of the 1961 Census figures is thus questionable. Were these young adolescents married only in the sense of having had their *shadis*, or had their *muklavas* taken place already and were they living together in the husband's household? It is noteworthy that none of the census ethnographers

Map 8

Rajasthan Districts in First Quintile on Proportions of Males Aged 10--14 Reported as Married (Census of India 1961)

ever addresses this issue or the question of what is meant by a census report of 'married' 10–14 year-old.

Here, it is useful to turn to ethnographic evidence. That marriage took place at early ages in Rajasthan is supported by Rama Mehta's memoir about the Oswals (Vaishya bureaucrats) (Mehta 1982: 141) attached to the Maharana of Udaipur's court. She writes:

> ...it must be remembered that the age of marriage in the Oswal community was between nine and twelve years prior to 1947, and the age at which a woman came to her husband's home was usually about thirteen to fourteen.... Among the Oswals, child marriage was widespread.

> ...purdah becomes a means for minimalizing family disputes, allowing the child-bride to function under the supervision of elders without the possibility of contradicting their commands. This was necessary, since a child-bride had not been tutored to assume responsibility before she entered marriage. For the young bride, the early years of her marriage constituted a period of training and education (Mehta 1982: 146–48).

According to Mehta, the young Oswal brides were ignorant of housekeeping and were trained by their mothers-in-law as they were too young to have been properly trained before marriage. In M-K as well, new brides complained that they did not know how to do the tasks assigned to them by their mothers-in-law. They were often so young that they had to be trained to do household chores by their mothers-in-law or older sisters-in-law. If a girl was the junior daughter-in-law in a joint household in which her own sister was the senior daughter-in-law, the latter might even do the work for her.

Young age for marriage was noted in 13 of the 1961 Census village surveys (nos. 1, 3, 4, 6, 7, 8, 9, 12, 15, 16, 18, 19, and 22). In Kvasara village of Jhalawar district, for example, in which almost half the population was Rajput, another 20 percent Nath and 10 percent Chamar, with nine other small caste communities (Singh and Gupta 1965a: 2), three-fourths of the females aged 10–14 and one-third of the males aged 10–14 were recorded as married. According to the ethnographers, "there is no unmarried female above the age of 14 in the village" (ibid.: 37). In only three villages were there any reports of marriage for girls normally occurring after age 14. Two reports refer to Rajputs (4, 18), and one to Kanjars (2).

That marriage ceremonies may take place at extremely young ages is suggested by the report from Kalijal village in Jodhpur district:

> Among the Jats of the village it is customary to hold the marriages of the girls of the family without consideration of their age at the time of performance of death-feast of some elderly person. The main consideration behind this custom is economy. Even girls in arms who belong to the family are married on the occasion. It is not unusual to see a small girl seated on a brass plate to be married to a boy who may be a little bigger than her. The children are lifted by

the parents who go round the fire to complete the *pheras* [circumambulations of the sacred fire by the bride and groom] (Singh and Pendharker 1967: 14).

In his book on the village of Awan in Kota district, Giri Raj Gupta (1974: 65–66) explains the custom of early age of marriage:

> It is a common practice for girls to marry before reaching puberty. There are several arguments advanced in favour of early marriage. The people believe early marriages tend to protect the chastity of women, ease the transfer of a girl from her father's domain to that of her husband, and make it easier for a girl to adjust to her husband and in-laws. Pre-puberty marriages are also considered to be more sacred and pure than a marriage which takes place later in a girl's life, since the girl has not been contaminated by the pollution associated with menstruation. It is also feared that a girl's approaching sexuality will lead her to relinquish her sacred status as a virgin. It is well known that the Sanskritic scriptures of the Vedic times state that a girl should be married as a virgin and before menarche.
>
> The economic consideration is also very important. A girl married before puberty becomes an economic partner in her conjugal family much earlier. This, in turn, reintegrates the economy of her natal as well as conjugal family.
>
> Traditionally, each incipient family begins with the support of an old family. The young people are responsible for bringing new people into the family, both by marriage and by birth, to replace the old members. Since marriages are expensive events, the family's economy must be preserved by spacing marriages several years apart. The earlier the marriage is organized, the better it is for the family. Parents like to see their responsibilities fulfilled before they retire. Most marriages cost somewhat more than a year's income of the family. In some cases, as among the Rajputs, a marriage may take two or three years of the family's income. Early marriages of the children help the family to space the marriages evenly.
>
> Another advantage of early marriages is that a person benefits immediately from any advantages he has achieved through the marital alliance.

> However, on an average, the boys are usually married between the age of 12 and 16 years, while the girls are married between the age of 9 and 14 years. Analyzing the caste rank and its relationship with age at marriage, it appears that there is little association between the two. One of the major inferences could be that it is not the rank of the caste, but its involvement in agricultural activities which could explain the distribution of age at *sagai* [betrothal] and marriage. For purposes of broader generalization three perceivable trends can be delineated: (1) upper castes marry relatively late, (2) agriculturalists and artisans marry relatively early, and (3) most of the boys and girls among all the castes continue to marry earlier than the minimum ages fixed by the Hindu Marriage Act of 1955, which is 15 for girls and 18 for boys. Obviously, the legislation relating to the age at marriage has had little impact, if any, on the marital practices of the people.

Note Gupta's statement that "a girl married before puberty becomes an economic partner in her conjugal family much earlier". What both Gupta and Mehta suggest is that in some communities and places in Rajasthan, the bride actually does take up residence with her husband's family before the age of 14, and possibly before first menstruation. Needless to say, among illiterate people who do not keep precise records, the exact age of a bride upon joining her husband's household may not be known, but it seems safe to say that brides have, by age 16, joined their mothers-in-law. In the case of such early marriages, the joint family functions to support very young couples not mature enough to manage a household economic enterprise alone. The Rajasthani joint family can thus be understood to be a reversal of the pre-industrial nuclear family in Western Europe, a family founded by an adult male in his mid- or late twenties, trained and ready to support a wife and children, the wife also being in her twenties at marriage (Laslett 1984: 99--101; 1972: 85). Instead of postponing marriage and childbearing as the English pre-industrial family required, the Rajasthani family supports marriage for even physically immature adolescents, and childbearing for sexually mature adolescent wives, by having the family unit joint, composed of at least one adult couple and possible one or more pre-adult couples (couples under age 20).

Prakash Tandon (1961: 124) made this contrast between British and Punjabi assumptions about the age of marriage:

> .... it was in accordance with father's own ideas that uncle preferred to wait for his marriage till he was settled in life. To the old way of thinking this was irrelevant. You married when you came of age and not when you began to earn. Marriage and earning were two separate things. Marriage was a social, familial and religious obligation, while earning was a matter of circumstance.

This Punjabi view is quite in line with the Rajasthani view. The joint familism of the North Indian family can be understood, at least for much of Rajasthan, as more a matter of an adult male and his wife in their thirties or forties taking the lead, with inexperienced married teenagers following their directions, than as a matter of an elderly patriarch in his fifties or sixties ordering about fully adult sons who are men in their twenties to forties.

These findings strongly suggest a kind of joint family composed of a head couple plus a young teenaged couple living together until either the members of the older couple die or the young couple mature and have so many children that they need more living space. The question would then be whether all joint families in Rajasthan, and in India as a whole, are 'protective joint families' of this type.

Of course, the strategy for establishing a couple at a young age may involve a belief that young adolescents are more malleable than older ones, that once a bride has adjusted to her husband's joint family she is less likely to be discontented that she does not have a home of her own (see Kolenda 1987: 104–5).

The Well-Team Joint Family

The high correlation between young adolescent marriage and the two measures of joint family ('married sons' and 'other married relatives') is partly an artifact of the data, since married males aged 10–14 are included in the proportion of married sons in the household sample. Similarly, males and females aged 10–14 who are represented as married are included in the proportion of other married relatives in the sample. What the high correlations between the two measures of joint family and adolescent marriage measure, then, is the correlation between the whole variable (the married sons or other married

Map 9

Seven Districts in Rajasthan in First Quintile on Four Measures: Proportion of Married Sons, Proportion of Married Relatives, Females 10--14 Married and Males 10--14 Married (Census of India 1961)

relatives of all ages) and part of it (the married sons or other married relatives aged 10–14). Thus, the high correlations appear to be a matter of a variable relating to part of itself. Only if the couples which included a spouse aged 10--14 lived separately in their own households separate from the other married relatives would the previous statement be untrue. The ethnographic evidence, however, does not suggest that neolocal residence for such young couples occurs.

One way to find out whether there are other kinds of joint family besides the 'protective joint family' is to remove from the household samples the effects of the presence of married 10--14 year-olds. This was done,[11] and a third measure of family structure was developed, the

Map 10

Seven Rajasthan Districts in First Quintile on Revised Family Structure (Census of India 1961)

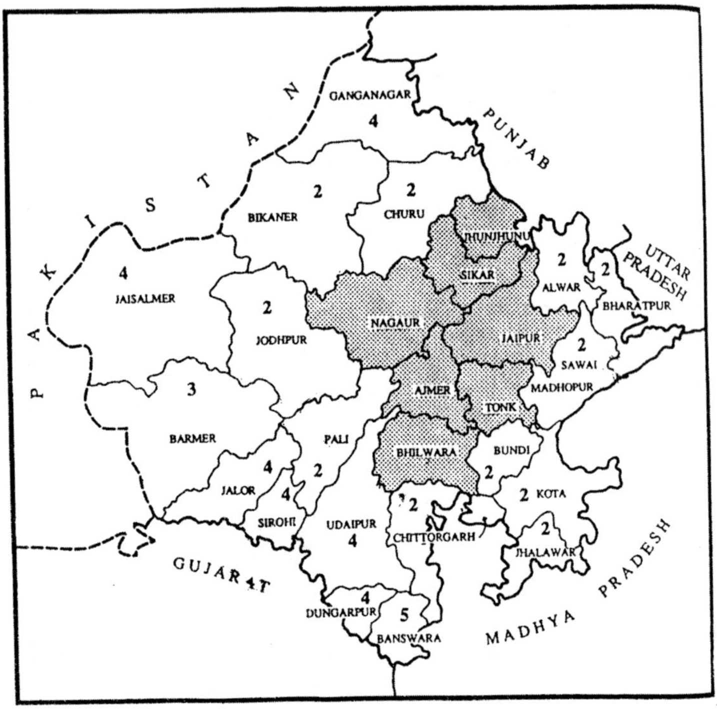

'revised family structure'. How then does Rajasthan appear in comparison with the rest of India when joint family living is measured by revised family structure?

Map 10 shows the seven districts of Rajasthan which fall in the top quintile of all the 326 districts in India on revised family structure. The number, of course, is considerably less than the 15 districts in the first quintile on married sons (see Map 3) or the 11 districts in the first quintile on other married relatives (see Map 4). We may presume that the decline in the ranking of other districts in Quintile 1 on 'married sons' and 'other married relatives' is due to the considerable prevalence in them of 'protective joint families'. Indeed, all these districts fall in the second quintile on the revised family structure

Map 11

Geographical Regions of Rajasthan (based on natural regions)

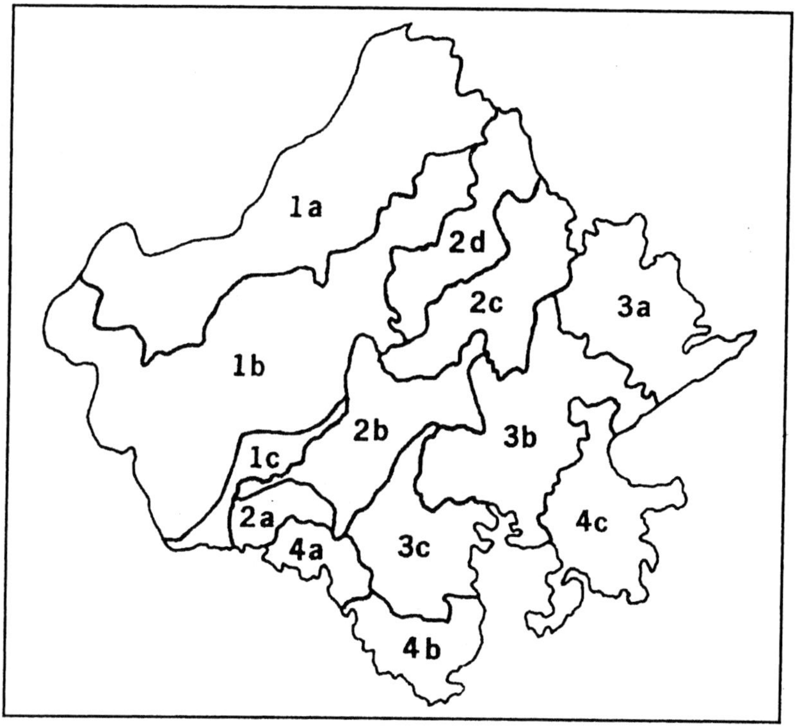

1 **Hot Desert:** *1a* Ganganagar-Jaisalmer region (Raj. Canal area); *1b* Jodhpur region (Dry Desert); *1c* Luni region (Central & Lower Luni Basin). **2 Steppe Desert:** *2a* Jalor region (Jawai Basin); *2b* Ajmer-Pali region (Upper Luni Basin); *2c* Sikar-Deedwana region (Kantli and Didwana-Sambhar Salt Basins); *2d* Churu region (Dry Steppe). **3 Semi-Arid Region:** *3a* Alwar-Bharatpur region (Sota Sahibi and Barh Basins); *3b* Jaipur region (Lower Bansi and Morel Basins of the Chambal Catchment); *3c* Udaipur-Chittorgarh region (Chambal-Mahi Waterparting Zone). **4 Humid Region:** *4a* Sirohi region (Upper Sabarmati-Banas Basins); *4b* Dungarpur region (Upper Mahi Basin); *4c* Kota Region (Chambal Project Area)

Source: A.K. Sen, Cartographic Laboratory, Central Arid Zone Research Institute.

measure, indicating that the frequency of joint families that are not just protecting adolescent brides and grooms is still above average for India as a whole.

How are we to understand the seven districts that are in the first quintile on joint families once the effect of adolescent brides and grooms is factored out? Here I would like to return to the village of

Maharajapur-Kishanpur and the third factor contributing to the occurrence of joint families: the need for the family to function as a work-team and, more specially, a well-team.

To help analyze this factor, I would like to introduce the mapping of Rajasthan into ecological zones by A.K. Sen of the Central Arid Zone Research Institute (CAZRI) in Jodhpur. In the *Agricultural Atlas of Rajasthan* (1972), he divided Rajasthan into four major ecological zones: the hot desert, the steppe desert, the semi-arid region, and the humid region. With Sen's permission, an adaptation of that map is presented here (Map 11). Each of the four major zones is sub-divided into three or four sub-zones, yielding a total of 13 ecological sub-zones. When the seven districts in the first quintile on revised family structure are superimposed on the ecological map, they fall almost entirely into three sub-zones. Two sub-zones (2c and 2d) are in the steppe desert, and one (3b) is in the semi-arid region. Small portions of the seven districts fall into three other sub-zones (1b, 2b and 3a). With the exception of a small portion of Nagaur district, which falls into sub-zone 1b of the hot desert, all seven districts fall into the steppe desert and semi-arid region (see Map 12). What this suggests is that, in Rajasthan, the joint family is a more important adaptation in these two zones than it is in either the hot desert or in the humid region.

Map 10 shows the quintile rankings of all the districts of Rajasthan on revised family structure. In the two sub-zones of southern Rajasthan and Gujarat, all four districts are well below average on revised family structure, falling into either the fourth quintile (Sirohi, Udaipur, and Dungarpur) or the fifth (Banswara). The 4a and 4b sub-zones of the humid region are distinguished from the 4c sub-zone (composed of Jhalawar, Kota and parts of Bundi and Sawai Madhopur districts; see Map 11), by the considerably greater agricultural activity in the latter, called by Misra the 'southeastern agricultural region' (1967: 176–77), due to that region's closeness to the Chambal river waters and its flatter and better soil.

In the hot desert, three of the districts are average to low on revised family structure. Barmer, in the third quintile, is average in an all-India ranking, while Jaisalmer and Ganganagar are well below average.

Map 12

Seven Districts in First Quintile on Revised Family Structure by Geographical Regions in Rajasthan (Census of India 1961)

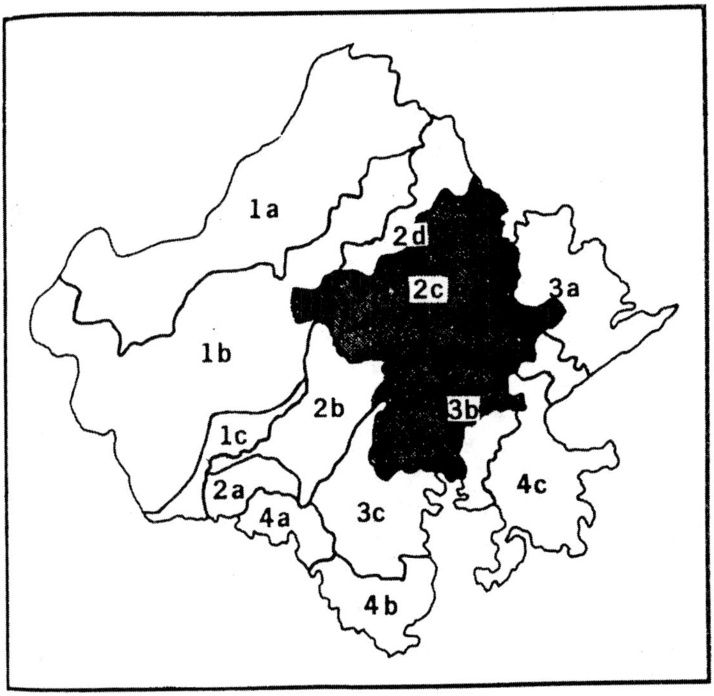

1 Hot Desert: *1a* Ganganagar-Jaisalmer region (Raj. Canal area); *1b* Jodhpur region (Dry Desert); *1c* Luni region (Central & Lower Luni Basin). **2 Steppe Desert:** *2a* Jalor region (Jawai Basin); *2b* Ajmer-Pali region (Upper Luni Basin); *2c* Sikar-Deedwana region (Kantli and Didwana-Sambhar Salt Basins); *2d* Churu region (Dry Steppe). **3 Semi-Arid Region:** *3a* Alwar-Bharatpur region (Sota Sahibi and Barh Basins); *3b* Jaipur region (Lower Bansi and Morel Basins of the Chambal Catchment); *3c* Udaipur-Chittorgarh region (Chambal-Mahi Waterparting Zone). **4 Humid Region:** *4a* Sirohi region (Upper Sabarmati-Banas Basins); *4b* Dungarpur region (Upper Mahi Basin); *4c* Kota Region (Chambal Project Area)

Source: A.K. Sen, Cartographic Laboratory, Central Arid Zone Research Institute.

The strength of the joint family in the steppe desert and the semi-arid region suggests that the joint family is most adapted to areas where there is water for irrigation, but not so little that agriculture is impossible (as in Jaisalmer in the hot desert), or enough so that it is not a serious problem as in the humid region. The joint family as a

Map 13

Quintile 1 and 2 as Compared to Quintiles 4 and 5 on Revised Family Structure by Geographical Regions in Rajasthan (Census of India 1961)

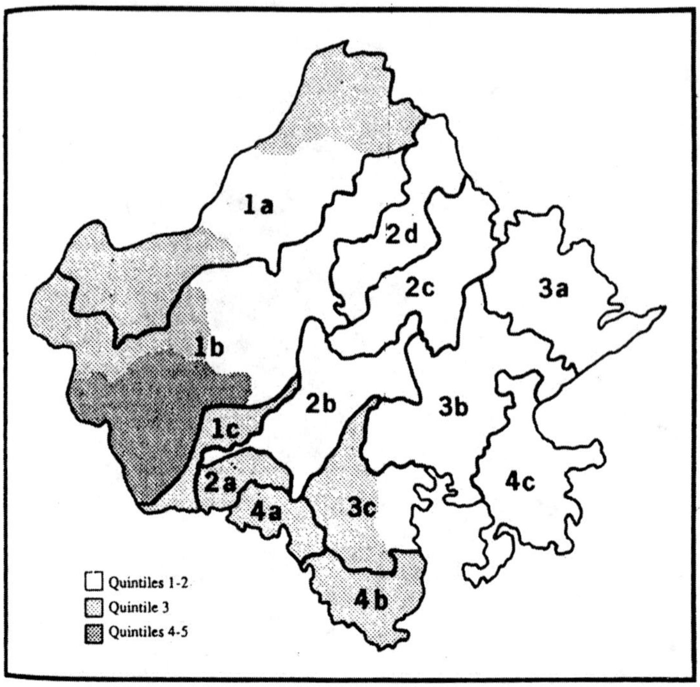

1 Hot Desert: *1a* Ganganagar-Jaisalmer region (Raj. Canal area); *1b* Jodhpur region (Dry Desert); *1c* Luni region (Central & Lower Luni Basin). **2 Steppe Desert:** *2a* Jalor region (Jawai Basin); *2b* Ajmer-Pali region (Upper Luni Basin); *2c* Sikar-Deedwana region (Kantli and Didwana-Sambhar Salt Basins); *2d* Churu region (Dry Steppe). **3 Semi-Arid Region:** *3a* Alwar-Bharatpur region (Sota Sahibi and Barh Basins); *3b* Jaipur region (Lower Bansi and Morel Basins of the Chambal Catchment); *3c* Udaipur-Chittorgarh region (Chambal-Mahi Waterparting Zone). **4 Humid Region:** *4a* Sirohi region (Upper Sabarmati-Banas Basins); *4b* Dungarpur region (Upper Mahi Basin); *4c* Kota Region (Chambal Project Area)

Source: A.K. Sen, Cartographic Laboratory, Central Arid Zone Research Institute.

well-team thus appears to be one effective strategy for coping with the irrigation problems of the steppe desert and semi-arid region.[12]

There are, however, a number of problems with such an analysis, especially when Map 12 is redrawn separating districts in the first and second quintiles on revised family structure from those in the fourth and fifth (see Map 13). It becomes clear that above average proportion of joint families (in the second quintile and above on revised family structure) occur in districts of all four ecological zones – in sub-zones 1a and 1b of the hot desert (Jodhpur and Bikaner) as well as in sub-zone 4c of the humid region (Kota, Jhalawar, and Bundi).

Indeed, Map 13 suggests that Rajasthan is characterized by three revised family structure zones: an 18-district zone with joint families in the first and second quintiles zone of Barmer district, and a fourth and fifth quintiles zone composed of the five districts bordering on Gujarat (Jalor, Sirohi, Udaipur, Dungarpur, and Banswara) and the two Thar desert districts (Jaisalmer and Ganganagar). The problem then becomes: what are the crucial differences between the 18 high joint family districts and the seven low joint family districts?

Some leads emerge when we turn to correlations between different variables. If we take the standard that only correlations over +/-0.608 are suggestive of a substantial relationship between variables, then revised family structure correlates only with adolescent marriage (a correlation of +0.62 and +0.74, respectively, for males and females aged 10--14 who are married). Correlations between +/-0.40 and +/-0.62, which are sometimes accepted as significant by social scientists, are found for proportion of tribals in district's population (+0.46) and for proportion of females in agriculture (+0.511).

The tribal variable suggests the high proportion of Bhils along the Gujarat border, especially in the districts of Dungarpur and Banswara, where over half the population are Bhils. However, as we saw earlier in Table 9.8, the village surveys suggest that Bhils sometimes have low proportions of joint families and sometimes do not. The variable of females in agriculture suggests joint family work-teams or well-teams. However, as shown in Map 14, the districts of Dungarpur and Banswara fall into Quintile 1 on females in agriculture but in the fourth and fifth quintiles on revised family structure, thus actually lowering the correlation between these two variables.

The factor that seems to be common to all seven districts in the fourth and fifth quintiles appears to be a paucity of wells. Let us first consider the districts along the Gujarat border, moving from west to east. The 1961 Census District Gazetteer for Jalor reports that only 9 percent of the land is irrigated (Sehgal 1973a: 61). What geographer V.C. Misra calls the Aravalli region (composed of all of Udaipur, southeast Pali, Sirohi, and western Dungarpur) makes up much of the

Map 14

Rajasthan Districts in First Quintile on Proportion of Females in Agriculture (Census of India 1961)

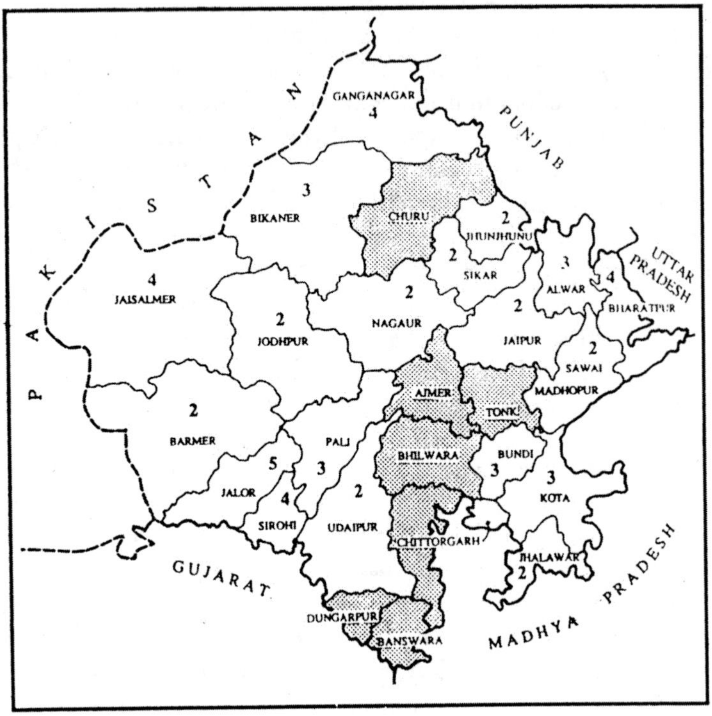

Gujarat border area. "The area being hilly, it is only a small part of the land where irrigation is possible. In Udaipur, nearly two-thirds of the land is barren and is not suitable for agricultural use" (1967: 173).

At the east end of the Aravalli region is Dungarpur, characterized in its District Gazetteer as "stony hills covered with low jungle" (Sehgal 1974: 2), with its cultivated area "confined to valleys and low ground between the hills" (ibid.: 3). Its well irrigation is by the pole-rope system (*dhenkli*) or Persian wheel (ibid.: 79), both methods requiring only one person rather than a team (Michael 1978: 198). Most of Banswara district is composed of hills and forests. Thus, the mountains and hills on the Gujarat border seem to prevent much well-team irrigation.

Map 15

Rajasthan Districts in First Quintile on Child/Woman Fertility (Census of India 1961)

Jaisalmer district likewise, which is almost entirely pastoral in its adaptation to the Thar desert, has "hardly any good wells which can be the sources of irrigation" (Sehgal 1973b: 7) and extremely deep water tables. Ganganagar too, irrigated since 1927 by the Gang Canal, is characterized by "no well irrigation nor tanks and lakes" (Sehgal 1972: 7).

This more refined analysis of well irrigation suggests that the first and second quintiles districts on revised family structure are districts in which, along with the practice of adolescent marriage, well-team irrigation is important, while the fourth and fifth quintiles districts tend to be bereft of wells and hence irrigation methods do not require a team. Some of the Gujarat border districts are high on the variable of young adolescent marriage (all of them are in the first and second quintiles on male adolescent marriage, while on female adolescent marriage, Udaipur and Sirohi are in the second quintile, and Jalor, Dungarpur, and Banswara in the third (see Maps 7 and 8). The Gujarat border districts thus seem to be districts in which more 'protective joint families' occur than well-team joint families.

The census figures I have examined thus suggest that the joint family structure in Rajasthan is associated with an agrarian economic-ecological adaptation which results in adult responsibilities that are incompatible if a single person has to carry them all out. My fieldwork in Maharajapur-Kishanpur likewise suggested that the joint family in Rajasthan is a work-team, associated especially with well-irrigation in semi-arid regions. While the Persian wheel, counterpoise-bucket lift or *dhenkli* are appropriate for water on the surface or close to the surface, and can be operated by a single person (Michael 1978: 198), the rope-and-bucket lift (*charas*) method of irrigation appropriate for deeper water requires the cooperation of at least two people. It is the *charas* method and deeper water that are characteristic of the wells of the steppe desert and semi-arid regions of Rajasthan where Quintile 1 districts on revised family structure are located. The *charas*-teams often consist of brothers, or of a father and son, and may also include a wife or unmarried daughter guiding water into the patches of crop plants. This need for females to help in the fields in a demographic situation characterized by a general shortage of women in Rajasthan may be responded to by an eagerness to 'reserve' wives for sons by the *shadi* ceremony of marriage as early as possible and thus results in early marriage for females and resultant 'protective joint families'.

Fertility, Sex Preference, and the Joint Family in Rajasthan

A final question to be examined is whether the data for Rajasthan show any correlation between the joint family, fertility, and preference for male children. Looking first at fertility, are districts high in proportions of joint families also high in size of family, average number of children per family, and child/woman fertility rates? High correlations between measures of joint family living and these variable would suggest that joint families tend to stimulate fertility more than nuclear families.

Table 9.12 presents the correlation coefficients for the relationships between these measures and proportion of married sons, proportion of other married relatives, and revised family structure. For all three measures, the correlation coefficients are very small, and mostly negative in direction.

Table 9.12

Correlations between Family Size, Number of Children, Child/Woman Fertility and Measures of Joint Families and Early Adolescent Marriage

	Married	*Married*		*Married*	*Married*
	Sons	*Relatives*	*RFS**	*F 10--14*	*M 10--14*
Family size	-0.167	0.014	0.152	-0.377	-0.433
Average number of children	-0.402	-0.245	-0.12	-0.587	-0.556
Child/woman fertility	-0.636	-0.561	-0.49	-0.720	-0.571

* Revised family structure

	Rajasthan			*All India*		
	Mean	*Median*	*Range*	*Mean*	*Median*	*Range*
Family size	5.42	5.48	4.81-6.08	5.26	5.24	2.91-6.59
Average number of children	2.33	2.32	1.91-2.73	2.19	2.18	1.54-3.0
Child/woman fertility	0.795	0.797	0.675-0.949	0.739	0.743	0.0793-0.9942

Thus, no relationship between family structure and these measures appears to be of any importance. The list of means and medians shows something else, however: that the average values on the variables of family size, number of children, and child/woman fertility ratios are higher for Rajasthan than the national averages. On all three values, Rajasthan lies in the second quintile nation-wide. Thus, it seems that Rajasthani families tend to be larger and have more children than the average for the whole of India, and that a woman in her childbearing years has more children under the age of five than the national average.

The correlation coefficients nevertheless indicate that the higher values on these measures in Rajasthan tend not to be in districts with higher proportions of joint families (see Map 15 for districts of Rajasthan with high child/woman fertility rates). This negative relationship is suggested by the fact that the seven districts high in proportion of joint families on revised family structure fall into the second, third and fourth quintiles on child/woman fertility ratios. When a bilinear analysis between measures of joint family and child/woman fertility was run, it was found that about 40 percent of the variance in joint family values overlapped with (negative) variance in child/woman fertility. This value is much lower than the 70 percent and higher (positive) variances for the measures of adolescent marriage. It does, nevertheless, suggest a notable negative relationship between the prevalence of joint families and fertility in women.

The hypothesis that joint families encourage high fertility is thus incorrect. A striking demonstration of this are the figures for Bhilwara district. Bhilwara was the district in Rajasthan with the highest proportion of married sons in the proportion of the household sample (8.98 percent), the third highest proportion of married relatives (24.28 percent), the highest proportion of married females aged 10--14 (63.92 percent), and the highest proportion of married males aged 10--14 (32.48 percent). It was also found to have the third lowest average family size (4.88 persons), the third lowest average number of children (1.91), and the lowest child/woman fertility ratio (0.67451) of all the districts in Rajasthan. Similar results could be shown for Chittorgarh district, which had the smallest average family size (4.81), the second lowest child/woman fertility ratio (0.6965), and the second lowest average number of children (1.93).

The expectation that joint families encourage high fertility may be based on various assumptions -- that a general ideology of 'familism' prevails with joint families, one that encourages wives to reproduce; or that patrilineal joint families partake of a 'patriarchalism' that includes producing sons for the patriline; or that young daughters-in-laws have too little knowledge to avoid childbearing or too little capacity to refuse it. To explain the negative correlation found here between joint families and fertility, however, we may return to the theme of crowding that has come up from time to time in this discussion. When a couple has three or more children, theirs tends to be a nuclear household or supplemented nuclear household, it can be argued, either because they have broken away from the husband's brother's family as they have needed more space, or, by default, because one or both of the husband's parents are dead. One could also argue that a family in Rajasthan has two possible strategies open to it: to get the labor needed in the family economic enterprise by having as many children as possible, or by having the wives-mothers of the family work in the fields. It may be that in the high joint family districts of Rajasthan it is the latter choice that is made.

The second common hypothesis challenged by the data is that Indian joint families are biased in their preference for sons over daughters. If this were the case, joint families would be related statistically to disproportionate numbers of males over females. In fact, the three measures of joint family have an almost zero relationship to sex ratio. The married sons variable has a -0.087 correlation with sex ratio, married relatives -0.072, and revised family structure -0.043. The parallel correlation coefficients between the three measures of joint family and child-sex ratio (the number of males to females in the population under age 5) are also negligible. The married sons variable has a correlation coefficient of -0.097, married relatives of -0.053, and revised family structure of -0.023. This absence of correlation suggests that the joint family culture, if not sexually egalitarian, is not especially male-preferential.

Conclusion

This paper has raised the question: why was there a higher proportion of joint family households in Rajasthan than in other states of India. While this question cannot be said to have been conclusively answered, what this exploration of ethnographic materials and statistical data from the 1961 Census has suggested is that there are interrelated factors contributing to this high proportion of joint families in the population. Chief among these factors are the tradition of early marriage, leading to the need for the joint family to function as protector and guide of young couples, and dependence on the joint family as the work-team. In some parts of Rajasthan, particularly the semi-arid and steppe regions, this work-team is often probably also a well-team. Related to and reinforcing early marriage and the 'protective joint family' are the customs of sibling-set and collateral-set marriages, and multiple weddings on very few auspicious wedding days as a means of curtailing expenses.

Several commonly held hypotheses concerning joint family living have also been tested in the course of this study, and proven erroneous. Among them is the idea that there are clear caste or tribal preferences for joint family living, especially on the part of higher castes, as well as the belief that joint families encourage high fertility and show a marked preference for male children. Finally, data from some of the village surveys suggest that one of the effects of land reforms has been to encourage landholding joint families to fragment themselves into their nuclear components.

Perhaps, the most surprising finding of this study was the high proportions of joint families found among untouchable Chamars, possibly due to their very limited housing. The most important finding, one probably important for understanding the joint family in many parts of India, is the correlation between young adolescent marriage and joint families. This suggests a model family structure quite the reverse of that found in much of pre-industrial Europe (Laslett 1984: 99--101), in which a man was required to be trained in an occupation and able to support a wife and children before he married, and the newly married couple set up its own household from the start. In the Rajasthani model of the family, young people are expected to be married and ready to reproduce when their bodies are mature enough to do so, and the adolescent husband is not expected to be able to support himself and his wife and children on his own, but rather his parents and/or older brothers expect to both support and supervise the young married couple as long as it is either necessary or desired by the couple themselves. A further contrast between the European pre-industrial family and the Rajasthani joint family is that one existed in a demographic context in which many adult men and women remained unmarried all their lives, while the other exists in a context in which virtually all females and almost all males marry.

In one of his essays, Peter Laslett (1977: 15) raises the question of whether there is a polar family type to the Western family:

> ...an 'Eastern' familial category, where all mothers were young when their children were born, and much younger that their husbands with whom they lived in multiple family households having no servants.

A prime candidate for such a polar type 'Eastern' familial category would possibly be the joint family household of Rajasthan.

Acknowledgements

A brief version of this paper was read at the Annual Conference on South Asia at the University of Wisconsin-Madison, 8 November 1986. Fieldwork in Rajasthan was supported by Faculty Research Fellowships of the American Institute of Indian Studies, and by grants from the National Science Foundation and the University of Houston. Statistical analysis of the data was supported by the University of Houston through computer time and two grants-in-aid.

This study would not have possible without the work of Lorriane Haddon, who calculated measures of over 60 variables for 326 districts and territories of India from the statistics in the 1961 Census, and Indira Sapru, who served as research assistant on the project in Rajasthan. Others who contributed to the statistical research and analysis were Albert Ballinger, Diane Ballinger, Nancy Bernard, Pam Brown, David Cohen, Gary Dworkin, Christopher Kolenda, Carolyn Lewis, Kevin Olive, Leslie Pinter, Moniker Reuter-Echols, and Rebecca Story. I am also grateful to Joseph E. Schwartzberg for having called my attention in 1965 to the C-I tables of the 1961 Census of India.

Help in obtaining the scores of census volumes used in the study was given by a number of individuals at several libraries: Gene Jackson, Helen Tatman and Michael Biggs at the University of Houston Library, T. Tsuchiyama and Merry Burlingham at the University of Texas Library, Richard Martin at the University of Virginia Asia Library, and anonymous but helpful librarians at the Louisiana State University Asia Library and the Library of the University of Texas at Arlington.

Thanks are hereby extended to Thomas Rosin and others who made significant suggestions for improving earlier versions of this paper. Ved Vatuk helped me with a calendrical reference. William Skinner's unpublished papers on Chinese demography which he kindly made accessible to me gave me courage to apply ethnographic evidence for Rajasthan.

Notes

1. While these tables are consistently labeled as 'C-I', the title for the C-I table varies among different states.
2. Not all the districts and territories of India as it was in 1961 are included in the study. Excluded are Daman, Diu, Goa, the Yenem portion of Pondicherry, and the divisions of the Northeast Frontier Agency for which data were not available to us. The three divisions of Nagaland are merged and treated as one unit, as are the Laccadive, Amindivi, and Minicoy Islands. The protectorate of Sikkim is included. Note that in 1961, the state of Haryana did not yet exist, nor did a number of subsequently designated districts (Rupar, Punjab; Jind, Haryana; Bulsar, Gujarat; or Rajura, Maharashtra), and that some districts now in Himachal Pradesh were in the Punjab (Simla, Lahaul and Spiti, Kangra, and Kullu). Finally, since these data are only for rural populations, entirely urban districts (Bombay, Madras, Calcutta, and Bangalore) have been omitted.
3. Regional differences in family structure in various European countries both in the present and the past are beginning to be recognized by social historians (Laslett 1977: 16--27; Wall 1983; 52--60).
4. One of the founding fathers of modern cultural anthropology, Lewis Henry Morgan, did conceive of sibling-set joint families. According to Morgan, the second in a series of five successive forms of marriage throughout human evolution was the Punuluan. He described it as follows:

   > It was founded upon the intermarriage of several sisters, own and collateral, with each other's husbands not being necessarily kinsmen of each other. Also, on the intermarriage of several brothers, own and collateral, 'with each others' wives, in a group; these wives not being necessarily of kin to each other, *although often the case in both instances* (Morgan 1964: 325--26, emphasis added).

   My thanks to the anthropologist Edward Norbeck who mentioned this old reference to me.
5. Space does not permit a discussion here of the subject of brideprice or dowry in Rajasthan. Careful examination of the 24 census village surveys treated later as well as other ethnographic evidence indicates that brideprice is much more prevalent in Rajasthan than is dowry. Neither seems to influence in any obvious way the timing of weddings.

6. Czap (1983: 122) noted that large complex households – joint family households, in the Indian term – were also reported for Latvia and Hungary in the 18th and 19th centuries.
7. At the beginning of each village survey report, the titles of all 36 done in Rajasthan are listed. Unfortunately, despite all the efforts of inter-library loan librarians, I was unable to acquire 12 of these.
8. We are dealing here only with Hindu Rajputs; Gagron also had a large population of Muslim Rajputs (see Table 9.4).
9. The issue of the unbalanced sex ratios in India as a whole and in the districts of Rajasthan more specifically is one I do not have the space to discuss. The reader may wish to refer to Miller (1981) on this topic. That measures of joint family do not correlate highly with district sex ratio or child sex ratios in Rajasthan is shown in the last section of this paper.
10. Statisticians hold that correlations from +/-0.60 to 1.00 are worth interpreting. Sometimes this criterion is relaxed to allow for interpretation of correlations as low as +/-0.40.
11. The effects of the married among the 10--14 age group upon the indices of joint family was removed by finding in Table C-II, age and marital status for each district, the number of males aged 10--14 who were reported as married, dividing the number by 5 to correspond to the 20 percent household sample, and subtracting this dividend from the number of 'other married relatives'. The same was done for the figures on females aged 10–14 who were married. The resulting remainder was then divided by the total population of the 20 percent household sample and that proportion was the measure of revised family structure.
12. It is not claimed here that the joint family is the only organization on which Rajasthan agriculturists base a work-team. R. Thomas Rosin (1978: 469) describes a standard work-team for Undhyala village, Nagaur, as:

    > The organization of labor crucial to the irrigation of a second crop was provided by a four-man team, each member of which was an equal partner, usually from separate families which could contribute kinsmen and affines as needed to augment the labor force at the well (see also ibid.: 475, 487 for other details of this work-team).

    Rosin promises to report on a survey of irrigation work-teams in Rajasthan that he made in 1982--83 in the near future.

References

Twenty-four Rajasthan village surveys have been compared and drawn upon in this paper. They are indicated here with an asterisk (*) and can be found in Census of India 1961, Volume XIV, Part VI-A.

* Agrawal, G.D. and G.R. Gupta (1964), Malar, Palodi Tehsil, Jodhpur District.

* Agrawal, G.D. and G.R. Gupta (1965), Nangal Sooswatan, Amber Tehsil, Jaipur District.

* — (1969), Aghapur, Bharatpur Tehsil, Bharatpur District.

* Agrawal, G.D. and L.R. Pendharker (1965), Abhaneri, Baswa Tehsil, Jaipur District.

* Bhargava, R.C. and G.R. Gupta (1965a), Mudh, Kolayat Tehsil, Bikaner District.

* — (1965b), Mukam, Nokha Tehsil, Bikaner District.

* — (1965c), Rangmahal, Suratgarh Tehsil, Ganganagar District.

* — (1966), Bhadwasi, Nagaur Tehsil, Nagaur District.

* Bhargava, R.C. and L.R. Pendharker (1968), Bagor, Mandal Tehsil, Bhilwara.

Buhler, George (trans.) (1886), *The Laws of Manu*, Oxford: Clarendon Press.

Chauhan, Brij Raj (1967), *A Rajasthan Village*, New Delhi: Vir Publishing House.

Czap, Peter, Jr. (1983), 'A Large Family: The Peasant's Greatest Wealth': Serf Households in Mishind, Russia, 1814–1858. *In* Richard Wall, Jean Robin and Peter Laslett (eds.), *Family Forms in Historic Europe*, New York: Cambridge University Press, pp. 105--51.

Dandekar, Hemalata C. (1986), Men to Bombay, Woman at Home: Urban Influence on Sugao Village, Deccan Maharashtra, India, 1942--1982. Michigan Papers on South and Southeast Asia. Center for South and Southeast Asian Studies, The University of Michigan.

* Gulati, B.R. and G.R. Gupta (1966), Goriya, Bali Tehsil, Pali District.

* Gulati, B.R. and L.R. Pendharkar (1965a), Sanwara, Shahbad Tehsil, Kota District.

*— (1965b), Panarwa, Phalasia Tehsil, Udaipur District.

*— (1965c), Bhangarh, Rajgarh Tehsil, Alwar District.

* Gupta, B.R. and L.R. Pendharker (1969), Gagron, Kanwas Tehsil, Kota District.

Gupta, Giri Raj (1974), *Marriage, Relation and Society: Patterns of Change in an Indian Village,* Delhi: Vikas.

Hajnal, J. (1983), Two Kinds of Pre-Industrial Household Formation Systems. *In* Richard Wall, Jean Robin and Peter Laslett (eds.), *Family Forms in Historic Europe*, New York: Cambridge University Press, pp. 65--104.

Johnson, Erwin (1964), The Stem Family and Its Extension in Present Day Japan, *American Anthropologist* 66: 839--51.

Kane, P.V. (1941), *History of Dharmasastra.* Vol. 2, Part 1, Poona: Bhandarkar Oriental Research Institute.

---- (1958), *History of Dharmasastra.* Vol. 5, Part 1, Poona: Bhandarkar Oriental Research Institute.

Kolenda, Pauline (1967), Regional Differences in Indian Family Structure. *In* Robert Crane (ed.), *Regions and Regionalism in South Asian Studies.* Durham, North Carolina: Duke University Program in Comparative Studies on Southern Asia Monograph Series. Monograph No. 5, pp. 147--225 (also in Kolenda 1987).

---- (1968), Region, Caste, and Family Structure: A Comparative Study of the Indian 'Joint' Family. *In* Milton Singer and Bernard Cohn (eds.), *Structure and Change in Indian Society.* Chicago: Aldine Publishing Company, pp. 339--96 (also in Kolenda 1987).

--- (1969), Minas of Maharajapur-Kishanpur. Unpublished manuscript.

---- (1978), Sibling-Set Marriage, Collateral-Set Marriage, and Deflected Alliance among Annana Jats of Jaipur District, Rajasthan. *In* Sylvia Vatuk (ed.), *American Studies in the Anthropology of India*, Delhi: Manohar, pp. 242--77 (also in Kolenda 1987).

--- (1987), *Regional Differences in Family Structure in India*, Jaipur: Rawat.

Kolenda, Pauline and Lorraine Haddon (1987), Marked Regional Differences in Family Structure in India. *In* Pauline Kolenda, *Regional Differences in Family Structure in India*, Jaipur: Rawat, pp. 214--88.

Laslett, Peter (1972), Introduction: The History of the Family. *In* Peter Laslett and Richard Wall (eds.), *Household and the Family in Past Time*, London: Cambridge University Press, pp. 2--89.

---- (1977), Characteristics of the Western Family Considered over Time. *In* Peter Laslett, *Family Life and Illicit Love in Earlier Generations*, Cambridge: Cambridge University Press, pp. 12--49.

---- (1984), *The World We Have Lost Further Explored*, New York: Charles Scribner's Sons.

Lushington, C.S. (1833), On the Marriage Rites and Usages of the Jats of Bharatpur, *Journal of the Asiatic Society* 18: 273–97.

Mehta, Rama (1982), Purdah among the Oswals of Mewar. *In* Hanna Papanek and Gail Minault (eds.), *Separate Worlds Studies of Purdah in South Asia*, Columbia, Missouri: South Asia Books, pp.139–63.

Michael, A.M. (1978), *Irrigation Theory and Practice*, New Delhi: Vikas.

Miller, Barbara Diane (1981), *The Endangered Sex*, Ithaca, New York: Cornell University Press.

Misra, V.C. (1967), *Geography of Rajasthan*, New Delhi: National Book Trust of India.

Morgan, Lewis H. (1964), *Ancient Society*, Cambridge: Belknap Press of Harvard University Press.

Nakane, Chie (1967), *Kinship and Economic Organization in Rural Japan*, New York: Humanities Press.

Pasternak, Burton, Carol R. Ember, and Melvin Ember (1976), On the Conditions Favoring Extended Family Households, *Journal of Anthropological Research* 32: 109–23.

Rosin, R. Thomas (1978), Peasant Adaptation as Process in Land Reform: A Case Study. *In* Sylvia Vatuk (ed.), *American Studies in Anthropology of India*, Delhi: Manohar, pp. 460–95.

--- (1987), Set Marriage and the Continuity of the Joint Family in Rajasthan. Paper read at Rajasthan Studies Conference, Jaipur, December 1987.

Sehgal, K. (1972), *Ganganagar*. Rajasthan District Gazetteers, Jaipur: Central Government Press.

--- (1973a), *Jalor*. Rajasthan District Gazetteers, Jaipur: Central Government Press.

--- (1973b), *Jaisalmer*. Rajasthan District Gazetteers, Jaipur: Central Government Press.

--- (1974), *Dungarpur*. Rajasthan District Gazetteers, Jaipur: Central Government Press.

Sen, A.K. (1972), *Agricultural Atlas of Rajasthan*, Jodhpur: Central Arid Zone Research Institute.

* Sharma, B.L. and G.R. Gupta (1967a), Ramnagar Kanjar Colony, Bundi Tehsil, Bundi District.

* --- (1967b), Kailashpuri, Girwa Tehsil, Udaipur District.

* Sharma, B.L. and L.R. Pendharker (1969), Hasanpur, Tijara Tehsil, Alwar District.

* Singh, Shamsher and G.R. Gupta (1964), Khajoora, Kushalgarh Tehsil, Banswara District.

* — (1965a), Kyasara, Dag Tehsil, Jhalawar District.

* — (1965b), Peepal Khoont, Ghatol Tehsil, Banswara District.

* — (1966a), Bujawa, Jodhpur Tehsil, Jodhpur District.

* — (1966b), Janvi, Sanchore Tehsil, Jalor District.

* — (1967), Bujawa, Udaipurwati Tehsil, Jhunjhunu District.

* Singh, Samsher and L.R. Pendharker (1967), Kalijal, Jodhpur Tehsil, Jodhpur District.

Tandon, Prakash (1961), *Punjabi Century, 1857--1947*, Berkeley: University of California Press, 1968 (1st ed. 1961).

Wall, Richard (1983), Introduction. *In* Richard Wall, Jean Robin, and Peter Laslett (eds.), *Family Forms in Historic Europe*, New York: Cambridge University Press, pp. 1–63.

Part IV

Comparison between Regions of India

10

Woman as Tribute, Woman as Flower

Images of "Woman" in Weddings in North and South India

"Generalized exchange," writes Lévi-Strauss (1969 [1949]: 269) in *Elementary Structures of Kinship*, "extends over a vast area of southern Asia." Here, I compare weddings from two regions of that area to give content to the empty category of woman as object of exchange creating marriage alliances. Gayle Rubin (1975: 159), in her "somewhat idiosyncratic and exegetical reading to Lévi-Strauss and Freud," deplores Lévi-Strauss' obtuseness:

> For instance, Lévi-Strauss sees women as being like words, which are misused when they are not "communicated" and exchanged. On the last page of a very long book, he observes that this creates something of a contradiction in women, since women are at the same time "speaker" and "spoken" (1975: 201).

According to Rubin (1975:201), Lévi-Strauss' only comment on this contradiction is this:

> "But woman could never become just a sign and nothing more, since even in a man's world she is still a person, ...woman is never purely what is spoken about... each woman preserves a particular value arising from her talent, before and after marriage, for taking her part in a duet. In contrast to words, which have wholly become signs, woman has remained at once a sign and a value. *This explains why the relations between the sexes have preserved that effective richness, ardour and mystery which doubtless originally permeated the entire universe of human communications*" (Lévi-Strauss 1969: 496) (emphasis added by Rubin).

Rubin (1975: 201) continues: "This is an extraordinary statement. Why is he not at this point, denouncing what kinship systems do to women, instead of presenting one of the greatest rip-offs of all time as the root of romance?"

Rubin says that because women are persons equal to men in their capacities to communicate, as Lévi-Strauss admits, it is unfair for kin groups allying with others to *use* women as items of exchange, for in such alliance formation women suffer enormously. Lévi-Strauss' (1969: 233) stated purpose in *Elementary Structures in Kinship is* "to find the origin and regulatory function of kinship in exchange in all its forms," to show how gift exchange between groups binds them together, and that the "supreme gift" is woman (1969: 65). He tells us that "men exchange women, and not *vice versa*" (1969: 115). He takes a "paternal perspective" (1969: 132): "we have regarded the woman married by a member of the group as acquired, and the sister provided in exchange as lost" (1969: 132); "the woman is never anything more than the symbol of her lineage" (1969: 116).

Throughout Lévi-Strauss' extensive survey of Eurasian, Australian, and other marriage systems in which different local lineages provide spouses for one another, it is notable that there is only an occasional glance at the "supreme gift," woman per se. The Kachin of Burma rejoice if a daughter is born because of the future brideprice -- "buffaloes, gongs, brandy, clothes" (Gilhodes quoted in Lévi-Strauss 1969: 257); they try to protect their daughters from the very marital kin to whom they are given. Granet (quoted in Lévi-Strauss 1969: 307) wrote of the "feeling of banishment" among Chinese woman. Lévi-Strauss (1969: 306) notes the "hard fate of exile" for women in "patrilineal and patrilocal regimes". Not much is said in *Elementary Structures of Kinship* about weddings, the formal transfer of women: "marriage is regarded everywhere as a particularly favorable occasion for the initiation or development of a cycle of exchanges" (1969: 63).

As does Lévi-Strauss, I treat weddings as occasions on which a woman is given by one kin group to another. My task is both structuralist and interpretive. I read weddings as texts (Geertz 1973: 448–53; 1980; Ricoeur 1981) to seek clues that together create a cultural image of woman that helps to fill the empty category, woman, offered by Lévi-Strauss. Since I have carried out ethnographic fieldwork in both North and South India, I stick closely to cases I know. Notes on the Rajput wedding in the North Indian village of Khalapur were made in spring 1955. I am fortunate that other anthropologists on the Khalapur project also attended weddings and conducted interviews about them; their data supplement my own and indicate that the high-caste Rajput wedding described is procedurally almost exactly the same as the weddings among the high-caste Brahmans and the low-caste untouchable Chamars and Chuhras. My notes on the Nattati Nadar wedding were made during spring 1967. I have also attended higher-caste Brahman and Vellala weddings in southern Tamilnadu; they are much like the Nadar wedding.

This paper is divided into four sections: (1) the social organization and modified generalized exchange systems of the two communities – the Rajput in a North Indian village and the Nattati Nadars in a South Indian one; (2) similarities in the two weddings, followed by brief subsections on the weddings as rites of passage and as Vedic; (3) the differences in the two weddings, followed by a detailing of the clues that reveal the summary image of woman in each culture; and (4) a conclusion with comments on such a reading for the emerging field of comparative symbology. Limitations of space preclude the presentation of an exhaustive description of the two ceremonial complexes; nor do I undertake a painstaking listing or description of all the symbols involved. What I try to learn is whether one can grasp a culture's conception of woman by studying one cultural performance (see Singer 1972:71) -- its wedding. From a feminist perspective, at least, the young woman who is impelled into an arranged marriage with an individual chosen by her elders is, in Rubin's terms, being "ripped-off"; I show that there may be profound differences in the kind and degree of symbolic and concrete depredation.

The Social Organization and Deflected Alliance System of the Rajputs

Generalized exchange does not simply involve one lineage giving a woman to another lineage. The givers have a justified faith that they will eventually be compensated, not by the receivers to whom they give a bride but by some third lineage (Lévi-Strauss 1969: 265). Such one-directional giving of women between lineages tends to develop into a *system of anisogamy* ("marriage between spouses of different status without any implication as to which of them, to the man or the woman, is higher or lower"; Lévi-Strauss 1969: 240). Either the bride-givers are superior, as among the Kachin (Lévi-Strauss 1969: 241; Leach 1961), or they are inferior, as among North Indian Hindus.

"All systems of generalized exchange derive from harmonic systems" (Lévi-Strauss 1969: 289). A *harmonic system* is one in which the rule of residence and the rule of descent match. Patrilineal-patrilocal and matrilineal-matrilocal kinship systems are harmonic; patrilineal-matrilocal and matrilineal-patrilocal are disharmonic. Most Indian marriage systems involve patrilineal-patrilocal regimes, although there are famous examples of matrilineal-matrilocal ones, such as the Khasi of Assam.[1] The seven features of the generalized exchange model of the giving of women are listed in Table 10.1.

Table 10.1

Generalized Exchange of Women in Rajput North Indian and Nattati Nadar South Indian Weddings

	Lévi-Strauss's generalized exchange model	*Rajput North Indian wedding*	*Nattati Nadar South Indian wedding*
1.	Harmonic regime: patrilineal-patrilocal	yes	yes
2.	Arrangement of marriage by elders of kin group	yes	yes
3.	One-directional giving	yes	no
4.	Ranking of lineage giving	no	no
5.	Asymmetric relations between bride-givers and bride-receivers	yes	yes
6.	Cross-cousin marriage	no	yes
7.	Repetition of alliances over generations	possibly between pairs of villages or minor lineages	two-generation alliance when cross-cousin marriage

In India, marriages of youths are arranged by their elders and society is organized in exogamous groups within the bounds of endogamous ones, or castes. An individual must not marry within his or her local unilineage or within various unilineal clans – one's own and often those of various close relatives -- but must marry within the caste connubium, called *jati*.[2]

The main deviations from the features of generalized exchange which Dumont (1957a, 1970) found in his studies of non-Brahman communities in Madurai, Ramnad, and Tinnevelly districts in South India are: (1) the lack of hierarchy or asymmetry in relations between intermarrying families (marriage tends to be isogamous, to take place between two families of equal rank) (1970: 116); and (2) a preference for patrilateral cross-cousin marriage (1957a: 20). Cross-cousin marriage results in repeated marriage between pairs of minor lineages; hence, Dumont calls the South Indian system an *alliance system*. He later sought evidence of repeated alliance in North India, the Indo-Gangetic plains area, where among Hindus various rules preclude the marriage of cousins (Dumont 1966, 1975). Earlier work by Karve (1953: 124) portrayed the region as one where marriages between pairs of families, lineages, or villages were not repeated. Dumont (1966: 105--6) was, therefore, especially pleased to find that in Gorakhpur district, where he did fieldwork, certain communities, including the Sarjupari Brahmans, did repeat marriages between local descent groups, indicating a kind of alliance system even in North India -- a "hypergamous milieu" (Dumont 1970: 116--18).

Are the marriage systems of the Rajputs of Khalapur and the Nattati Nadars of Kanyakumari examples of generalized exchange? I answer this question as I describe the social organization of each caste community as it relates to marriage. The Rajputs of Khalapur are similar in their system of alliance to the Sarjupari Brahmans, and the Nattati Nadars are similar to the non-Brahman caste communities Dumont studied in districts to the north of Kanyakumari.

Khalapur is a large, multicaste village of 5,000 people. The Rajputs are the dominant landowning group, comprising 44 percent of the population. All 500 to 600 male Rajputs are considered descendants of a conqueror who took the village 300 years ago and who founded the local clan, a fragment of the Pundir *gotra* (exogamous patriclan) (Hitchcock 1956). Almost 30 other castes make up the other 56 percent of the population. Many of these work for the Rajputs, either as artisans or as household or agrestic servants.

The Khalapur Pundir Rajputs are related to Pundir Rajputs of nearby villages, so they cannot marry in those villages. They have affinal ties with Rajputs of other *gotra*s in over 200 different villages within a radius of 48 km (Mahar 1965). This should not be envisioned as a continuous area of Rajput dominance; other dominant castes are intermixed with Rajputs, such as Jats, Gujars, and Ahirs. British colonials dubbed the Rajputs one of the "martial races" of northern India (MacMunn 1933; Yeats-Brown 1945). They warred continuously over territory and feuded with traditional enemies (Tod 1829: 32). Hitchcock (1959: 11), who studied the Rajput men of Khalapur, characterizes them as adhering to a martial tradition with a "stress upon the blood relationship between themselves and the kings and heroes of the past".

In Khalapur, the ambience of Moghul times persists, though the British had displaced the Moghuls completely by the mid-nineteenth century. Rajput men's clubhouses are built with Moghul arches and columns, and elders among them still speak resentfully of their subordination to the Moghul emperors. It was Rajput generals and troops on whom the latter largely relied, and Rajput brides were given to form political alliances, and also for political subordination, into the harems of Moghul overlords (Kolenda 1980).

An aspect of the Rajputs' martial tradition was the expectation that a Rajput widow should commit *sati* (the Britishism being suttee) -- burn herself on her husband's funeral pyre or commit suicide in some other way on learning of her husband's death – to indicate her complete devotion to him as her god (Thompson 1928: 15). Although the practice of *sati* was widespread throughout India, especially among higher castes and royalty, "suttee reached its most magnificent and least squalid form among the Rajputs" (Thompson 1928: 57). Both the Moghuls and the British tried to outlaw this form of suicide (Thompson 1928: 57; Stein 1978). Although there are no recent instances of *sati* in Khalapur, there are a number of *sati* votive stones memorializing such heroines of the past.

As for the hypergamous relationships characteristic of generalized exchange systems and reported for other parts of northern India (Dumont 1966, 1975; Vatuk 1969, 1975; Khare 1975; Turner 1975; Madan 1975), the Rajputs of Khalapur deny that *gotra*s or villages are ranked (Hitchcock 1956: 57). But they take wives only from the districts to the south of theirs and give daughters only to the districts to the west and northwest (Mahar 1966: 177–78). The rules for visiting and gift giving are asymmetrical as well, with subordination and the heavier burden of costs on the bride-givers rather than on the bride-receivers. In effect, theirs is a system of directional hypergamy.

The features of the Rajput marriage system as they meet the criteria for a generalized exchange system are listed in Table 10.1: one-directional giving between unequal partners but not cross-cousin marriage. Enduring ties may well exist between a pair of villages rather than between minor lineages (Dumont 1957b: 183–96). The Khalapur Rajput marriage system must be considered one of modified generalized exchange.

In arranging marriages, Rajputs practice village and *gotra* (patriclan) exogamy; they also avoid the geographical subsection *thamba* (a unit including the caste chapter in a cluster of 10 or 12 villages) of the mother's *gotra*. For example, if a child's father's *gotra* is Chauhan and the mother's *gotra* is Pundir, the child cannot marry a Chauhan of any kind but can marry a Pundir who is not from the child's mother's *thamba* (Hitchcock 1965: 60–62). Such rules preclude cousin marriage.

Despite these rules of exogamy, the Rajputs of Khalapur do tend to marry into villages with which they had prior affinal ties. In a study of marriage networks, J.M. Mahar (1966: 146–47, 290, 293–94) found that almost one-half of Rajput marriages were arranged with spouses living in villages that already had marital ties with Khalapur. Of the 602 Khalapur Rajput marriages that had taken place with spouses from 208 villages, 107 had been single marriages in 107 villages. Thus, 495 marriages had taken place in 101 villages. Whether there are "perpetual" alliances across generations between people in particular sets of villages cannot be determined from Mahar's data. In a sample of Khalapur Rajput daughters who were married into villages where there were other married Khalapur daughters (82 percent of the total), Mahar found that 25 percent (66 of 267) were members of sets of two, three, or four sisters -- all married into the same village; about one-third of these (6 percent of the total number of women) were pairs of sisters married to pairs of brothers.[3]

The Rajput rules of *gotra* exogamy prevent a man from marrying his MBD (because he cannot marry into the *gotra-thamba* of his mother) or his FZD (because she cannot marry into her mother's *gotra-thamba*, to which the man belongs). The rules of exogamy do not prevent him from marrying his BWZ or his FBWBD or his FBSWZ. The Rajput system is one of *deflected alliance* (Kolenda 1978). In such a system, one cannot marry a cross-cousin but a man can "repeat" his brother's or his male parallel cousin's marriage by marrying that man's WZ, or he can marry a male parallel cousin's female cross-cousin.

While a system of generalized exchange requires the existence of a minimum of three lineages, each of which gives women in one direction, a system of deflected alliance requires more units. The Rajput system, with its prohibition on two unilineages (*gotras*), requires a minimum of four lineages, each giving women in one direction. Many other North Indian caste communities prohibit more than two *gotras*, not only the candidate's own and her/his mother's but those of either or both the MM and the FM. Dumont (1966:112) has demonstrated that with a four-*gotra* prohibition, the marriage system requires a minimum of nine unilineal units giving women in one direction. As such systems actually operate, of course, far more exogamous unilineages are in the exchange network than the minimum number required.

The Social Organization and Delayed Exchange System of the Nattati Nadars

At the time of European missionary contact in the early nineteenth century, the Nadars were considered to be low Shudras, almost but not quite untouchable. Their traditional work was making sugar and toddy from the juice of the palmyra palm. Through educational institutions established first by Christians and later by local Hindu rulers and the Nadars themselves, many became educated and entered the professions and trades beginning in the 1800s (Hardgrave 1969). Today, they have a wide range of occupations. The Nattati Nadars, however, claim to be a caste of Nadars who were traditionally landlords, some of whom had rather large amounts of land. Like the Rajputs, many of the Nadars have untouchable field labourers working for them; others work in their own fields and/or may work for other landowners, either for other Nadars or for Vellalas or Brahmans. They are considered too low to be served by Brahman priests; rather, they have priests who are Saiva Vellala (a high-ranking caste of Shudra cultivators) or an elder Nadar performs all priestly duties.

The Nattati Nadars among whom I did fieldwork live in sixteen hamlets in two different revenue villages in southernmost Tamilnadu. The Nadar caste chapters in these hamlets together form an almost closed circulating connubium. Features of the South Indian marriage system of the Nattati Nadars of Kanyakumari district are summarized in Table 10.1. The Nattati Nadars' marriage system does not meet one of the requirements of generalized exchange: they lack one-directional giving. The Nattati Nadars claim to be organized into 64 *inti*s (exogamous patriclans), but there are substantial numbers of representatives of only 38 of these in the Kanyakumari *jati*. These are not ordered into bride-givers and bride-receivers, as a pair of *inti*s may give and take brides from one another. Like most South Indian Hindus, the Nattati Nadars prefer cross-cousin marriage. Lévi-Strauss (1969: 406) suggests that South Indian men prefer to marry matrilateral cross-cousins. Nattati Nadar ritual suggests a preference for patrilateral cross-cousins but, in fact, some FZDs and some MBDs, as well as other cross-relatives, are married frequently.[4] In one of the hamlets, as many as 60 percent of marriage are with a cross-relative and about one-third with a first cross-cousin. A brother-sister pair sometimes exchanges marriage with another brother-sister pair, but usually the delayed return of a bride takes place in the next generation. The Kanyakumari Nattati Nadar marriage system can be considered one of delayed exchange. The Nattati Nadars themselves do not phrase the arrangement of marriage as such; they consider it as preference for marriages within the *kutumpam* (family, kindred).

The Nattati Nadars' patrilineal organization is weaker than that of the Rajputs. In one of the hamlets of Kanyakumari, with a population of 208 Nattati Nadars, men belong to seven different *inti*s, compared to the single residential patriclan of the Rajputs in the Khalapur village. Unlike the Rajputs, among whom minimal and minor patrilineages share neighborhoods and joint residences, an entire set of Nattati Nadar brothers seldom reside together. Two or three may be in one village of the caste connubium and one or two in another. There is much movement of residence within the connubium. Since women can also own land, both husband and wife may have land in more than one place and a couple may move so as to be close to the property of one or the other. There is an overall adherence to patrilocal residence, qualified by much intravillage marriage and some uxorilocal residence. It is hard to trace perpetual alliances between local minor patrilines as found by Dumont (1957a: 23; 1957b: 183–96) in areas of Tamilnadu farther to the north, because minor patrilines of permanent locations and long duration do not exist. Gift giving is asymmetrical in that the couple is given more by the bride's people than by those of the groom; and there is a feeling of subordination on the part of the bride's people to the groom's people.

Segregation of the sexes is sharper among the Rajputs than among the Nattati Nadars. Nattati Nadar women remain in a backroom during their monthly menstrual periods, neither cooking nor touching others, and adolescent unmarried girls are carefully chaperoned. Otherwise, woman move about freely with faces uncovered. Rajput women are in *purdah*: they must cover their faces before older men in their marital home; their movement outside the house is limited and must always be in a group; and they spend their lives in women's houses, compounds of rooms built around an open courtyard where the wives and children of patrilineally related men reside. A sizable patrilineage has its own men's clubhouse where the men spend their leisure time and sleep at night. Men also spend much time together in cattlesheds and in the fields. Nattati Nadars live mostly in nuclear family households, possibly supplemented by a grandparent. Although men may congregate around the coffee shops in club-type groups in the hamlet, nearby town, and in the fields, there is undoubtedly more contact between husband and wife among the Nadars than among the Rajputs. A Rajput husband comes to the women's quarters to eat -- though he may well be served by his mother rather than by his wife -- and to have sexual relations with his wife in her room, which she shares with her daughters and small sons. Nattati Nadar husband and wife share a house and often a sleeping room on a full-time basis. Rajputs idealize the sexually segregated lineal and fraternal joint family and live in joint households, compounds, and neighborhoods. The Nattati Nadars give some lip service to the joint family ideal. A newly married couple may briefly reside with the groom's parents, but otherwise they live in nuclear or supplemented nuclear households.

The Rajputs are the dominant caste emulated by others in Khalapur. Other high- and low-ranking castes follow the same sequence of weddings rites in imitation of the Rajputs, who style themselves as traditional warriors. The Nadar wedding sequence is the same as for other non-Brahman Hindu castes in the Kanyakumari area -- the Vellalas, Acaris, and Thevars. They seem to share a regional culture that is not dominated by any one caste community.

Similarities in the Two Weddings

In India, among Hindus the major rites of weddings take three days, while preliminary and successive rites may spread over years. Some of these minor rites are small domestic affairs; the three-day sequence, however, is often attended by scores, even hundreds, of guests and is sponsored by the kindred of both bride and groom. The Indian preoccupation with weddings is manifested not only in the wedding as the major cultural performance of every family, aided by its kindred and often saved for and prepared for from the moment of a child's birth, but in the wedding as the plot of many Hindu religious dramas (Binford, Camerini, and Elder 1975). Weddings are the most vital entertainment in ordinary Hindu lives. As such, they may be treated as a dramaturgical repository of cultural texts.

The marriage is arranged by the elders of the boy and girl to be wed. A party from one group meets a party from the other group to see the possible spouse; if the latter is to their liking, a marriage proposal is made by one group to the other. There should be a satisfactory agreement as to the size of dowry to be given with the bride. Later, the child who has been seen is ritually reserved by the other group and the engagement is confirmed by a gift to the child who is to be reserved. At a subsequent ceremony at the bride-to-be's home, the auspicious dates and hours for the various important rites are determined astrologically. The MBs of each child to be wed are invited to their sister's home for a gift-presentation ceremony just before the wedding. It is especially important that the mother's eldest brother attend, for either he or a priest ties a turmeric string-bracelet on the right wrist of the niece or nephew to ward off evil influences; after the wedding the bracelets are ritually removed.

The wedding almost always takes place at the home of the bride. The bridegroom comes to the bride's house in a procession with his father and other agnates, his MBs and their sons, his FZHs, and his ZHs; his M, FBWs, and FZs are not in the procession. Accompanied by a loudly playing band, the procession enters the bride's neighborhood and one of her male relatives leads the men to the place where they are to stay. There, the host pastes a mark of greeting and blessing on the groom's forehead and presents gifts to him. Then, the groom and his party bathe and are feasted. During the feast, they sit on lengths of clean cloth provided by the family's washerman, and they eat from clay dishes provided by the family's potter.

The following day the groom and his party come to the bride's house for the wedding. Once more there is a ceremonial greeting which includes forehead marking of the groom by a relative of the bride, who also feeds him a sweet and presents gifts to him. A male relative washes the groom's feet. At either the welcoming ceremony when they first arrive or at this ceremony on the wedding day, the groom's party presents the bride's party with gifts for the bride, including articles of clothing and adornment for her to wear during the wedding. The groom is taken to the wedding pavilion and seated facing east, across from the bride's priest. Others of his party sit along the sides of a purified rectangle of ground on which various ritual paraphernalia (grain, grass, and coconuts) have been placed, including the makings of a fire – pieces of wood, camphor, a container of clarified butter – which the priest lights at the proper moment.

The bride is led to the pavilion and seated next to the groom. The priest pours milk, water, and other mixtures over the groom's palms, and the groom is fed sweet food. The bride's father joins the couple's hands, which are tied together with a scarf. The couple rises and circles the fire a number of times. Either during these rounds or as she initially enters the pavilion, the bride steps on a stone symbolizing her steadfastness in marriage. The priest chants *mantras* all during these rites. At certain high points, women's musical voices celebrate the transitions, as does a nearby band or drummer. At the end of the rounds, the couple stands while a tray containing a flaming lamp is circled in front of them to ward off evil influences. The couple then leaves for another room. At that time, or the following day, they play various simple games to foretell their future relationship. The groom also meets alone with women of the bride's family, who welcome him into her family.

Before the bride and groom depart for his home, gifts of money are presented by the bride's people to the members of the groom's party. Then gifts for the bride from her relatives and friends are presented to her male relatives and carefully listed by one of them so that her family may later reciprocate such gifts at marriages in their families. Large amounts of foodstuffs have been prepared for the bride to take with her to the groom's relatives. Her trousseau of household goods, clothing and gifts for the groom's people follow behind her.

When the bride arrives at her husband's home, she is greeted by women of his household. A feast is served to the newly married couple as well as to other guests. After the bride has spent some time at her husband's house, she returns to her parental home. She stays there for some time before taking up more or less permanent residence in her husband's house. Subsequent departures from her parental home to her husband's home are celebrated with farewell ceremonies and gift giving. During the first year or so that she resides at her husband's home, her relatives are obliged to present gifts to her at the autumn festival of lights (Deepawali) and at other festivals.

The above description fits both a North Indian wedding and a South Indian wedding. As I compared the two sets of field notes, I myself was surprised at how similar in outline the two weddings are. There are, of course, some important differences between the weddings of the two regions, as I show later.

The Weddings as Rites of Passage

Arnold van Gennep and, more recently, Victor Turner are prominent students of rites of passage. van Gennep (1960 [1909]: 117) saw the wedding as especially important for that individual who changes residence upon marriage. "In the last analysis a marriage is the incorporation of a stranger into a group" (van Gennep 1960: 141). Indeed, the arrival of the bridegroom and his party to take the bride away to the groom's home, amid the assembled kindreds and neighbors, is what the Indian wedding is about.

Victor Turner's writings on liminality take as their source of inspiration the adolescent initiation rite among the Ndembu of Zambia. He sees such rites of passage as "antistructural", outside the usual social structure with actors leveled to mutual equality, person facing person so that full communication can take place (Turner 1969: 94--165; 1974: 231--70; 1979: 11--59). The Ndembu initiates are stripped to their clothing and may even be stark naked (Turner 1969: 106; 1974: 252; 1979: 19). The Indian bride and groom, by contrast, are vastly overdressed. The Hindu wedding is, if anything, "hyperstructural", presenting a sharpened, highlighted social structure in which each actor carries out highly stereotypic acts dictated by a rigid scenario, playing roles within kinship, intracaste, and intercaste structures. The individuality of the bride and groom is smothered under costumes appropriate for the parts they play. Like the Ndembu initiates, the Indian bride and groom tend to be anonymous (Turner 1979: 19), but they are also meek, submissive, and scared (Turner 1967: 101; 1969: 99, 102–3).

The Weddings as Vedic

The Rajput and the Nattati Nadar weddings are similar in that they are versions of a set of Sanskritic rites. M.P.V. Kane (1941), in his *History of Dharmasastra*, reviews prescriptions regulating marriage in scores of Sanskritic religious law books, written by Brahmans and dating from 4000 B.C. to A.D. 1790 (1974: 427–639). While admitting that there is much variation between regions and even between villages in their wedding customs (1974: 527), Kane (1941: 531, 534) lists a core of rites mentioned by *all* the works of Hindu domestic law: the groom's taking the bride's hand; the offering of oblations to a fire (*homa*); the couple walking around the fire; the couple taking seven steps together (*saptapadi*); the bride stepping on seven small heaps of rice placed to the north of the fire subsequent to going round the fire with the groom; and the couple viewing the Pole Star together. Both Rajputs and Nattati Nadars perform the first four of these six acts; the Rajputs perform all six.

In addition to this small core of common rites, Kane lists 33 others, all of which are prescribed in some of the scores of Hindu law books. Both Rajputs and Nattati Nadars follow 14 of these additional rites: (1) examining the suitability of the bride or groom; (2) settling the marriage; (3) erecting a *pandal*; (4) honoring the bridegroom and his party on their arrival at the bride's village; (5) bridegroom's going to the bride's house; (6) reception of the bridegroom at the bride's house; (7) anointing the bride and groom; (8) coming into the *pandal* of the bride and bridegroom from the inner part of the house; (9) taking hold of the bride's hand; (10) making the bride tread on a millstone; (11) the tying of an amulet string on the bride's hand; (12) entering the bridegroom's house; (13) sacrifice on entering the bridegroom's house; and (14) presenting of the mother of the bridegroom with several gifts (Kane 1941: 531–38).

One might argue that what makes this sequence Vedic is the circling of the fire in the *pandal*, with the groom taking the bride's hand, the couple then taking seven steps, and the bride stepping on a stone. Beyond that we have only the amulet strings and anointings. The seeking of a bride or groom, settling the marriage, and greeting the groom and his party would all take place in many marriages that could not be considered Vedic.

Why do both the Rajput and the Nattati Nadar weddings share these elements of the Vedic model, especially the rounds of the fire? It would be tempting to say that the unity of Hindu culture over the subcontinent is again being documented; that over the millennia, Brahmanical culture from North India diffused so that Vedic weddings are practiced universally. However, the diffusion of features of the Vedic wedding to the Kanyakumari Nattati Nadars may be very recent. Dumont (1957a: 29) has noted that among non-Brahman castes in the districts to the north of Kanyakumari, weddings do not include "sacramental acts like uniting hands or circumambulating the fire". Thus, those Shudra caste communities lack this central element of the Vedic wedding. Kausalya Hart (1982: personal communication) assures me that in the Madurai area of Tamilnadu to the north, circling of the fire is a regular part of non-Brahman wedding ceremonies. It may well be that non-Brahman marriage customs have been Vedicized only in recent decades.

The Rajput wedding is officiated by a Brahman priest, who has a Sanskrit wedding guide to follow. Circling the fire is the high point of the wedding. There is no Brahman priest at the Nattati Nadar weddings; in some, there are Saiva Vellala priests and in others an elder officiates. At one Nattati Nadar wedding, the bride's father (who was also the groom's MB) led the couple in rounds while the *mantras* were sung by college students, who were pupils of the bridegroom, from books they held in front of them. Circling the fire took place after the high point of the wedding, the tying of a golden pendant (the *mangaliyam* or *tali*) around the bride's neck.

Education gives young men access to Vedic ritual. "Going round the fire" is probably to be accounted for more by printed guides and the frequent scenes of Vedic weddings in Indian cinemas than by the services of Brahmans, especially when it is non-Brahman castes whose weddings are under consideration – people whom the Brahmans of Tamilnadu have mostly refused to serve or to teach. The occurrence of the rounds after the *mangaliyam*-tying suggests that it has been added on to that essential South Indian wedding rite. Jamila Feldman (1982: personal communication) tells me that it is becoming fashionable in sophisticated North Indian Hindu circles to include the *tali*-tying; perhaps it is added on to North Indian wedding rounds as a secondary rite.

Differences in the Two Weddings: Relatives' Claims on the Bride and Dowry

There is only one set of wedding ceremonies among the Nadars, not two as among the Rajputs, or so it would seem. Among the Nadars, it is on the night after the wedding rounds that the couple first has marital relations; among the Rajput, it is not until the bride goes to her husband the second time after the second set of wedding ceremonies (*chala*), usually two years or so after the *shadi* (the first set of wedding ceremonies). However, the Nadars, like many other South Indians, have an earlier ceremony parallel to the *shadi* that gives us a clue to the meaning of woman inscribed in the wedding. The ceremony is called "the blossoming and purifying bath" ceremony (*puppu punita nitatal*;[5] the word *puppu* means both blossoming and menstruation).

In North India, a girl's first menstruation is not ceremonialized. Just before the *shadi* in North India, the bride's mother goes to her brothers' houses to invite each of them to her daughter's forthcoming wedding and also to bring a *bhat* – the gift of a man to his sister just before her daughter's wedding. In South India, when a girl first menstruates, she is secluded for fifteen days. Her mother visits each of her brothers to invite them not to her daughter's wedding but to her daughter's "blossoming" – a ceremony on the sixteenth day when each brother should present the newly nubile girl with a *sari* to wear after her purifying baths. Each brother also has the right at that time to claim the girl as a *urimaippen* (the proper girl), or bride for one of his sons who is older than she is. At the wedding, the MB is equally important; he may well lead the couple in the wedding rounds, especially if his ZD is marrying his son. If she does not marry his son, he should be there to receive a gift of clothing from his sister to indicate his approval of the match that has been made for her daughter. There may also be a ritual in which the couple asks his permission and blessing to marry, and he thereby gives up his right to the bride as a wife for one of his sons.

In North India, the MB brings the *bhat* for his ZD's marriage as another installment in the eternal gift giving between the two families of husband and wife, with the greater burden being on the bride's family. The MB has no right to his ZD in North India, but there is a privileged proposal of marriage in the Rajput wedding. At a ceremony on the day before the wedding rounds, during which a bundle of thatch is hung over the doorway (the *mandha* ceremony), the groom may make a demand, which may be for the bride's sister as a bride for his brother. This is a request that should not be refused and is, of course, consistent with the Rajput marriage system of deflected alliance.

The groom's side thus seeking a bride is contrary to the usual pattern of mate seeking among the Hindus of the Khalapur area. There, the bride's elders seek a suitable groom, and it is the groom who is the center of the engagement ceremony (the *rokna*), which the bride does not attend. By contrast, among the Nattati Nadars of South India, it is the groom's elders who seek a suitable bride, and it is the bride who is the center of the engagement ceremony (the *niccaya tambulam*), which the groom does not attend.

This generalization should be qualified by the point that in both communities it is difficult for either a poor man or a widower to obtain a wife; in both areas, such men must *seek* brides. In North India, among the Rajputs and those caste communities imitating Rajputs, there are groomprice marriages and brideprice marriages. In the first, the bride's people give the groom or the groom's father a substantial amount of money and/or costly gifts, such as a wristwatch, a bicycle, or a gold ring. Giving of "dowry" in the sense of groomprice has been reported as common among the higher castes of northern India, including the Rajputs. However, groomprice (specifically, a monetary payment made to an educated groom or to his father) seems to be a rather recent introduction to the Rajputs of Khalapur, while brideprice is reported to have been fairly common in earlier decades. Poorer Rajputs and widowers may still have to give brideprice.

In Kanyakumari, I found no instance of brideprice. A well-off widower may provide all the expenses of his second wedding, which may take place at his family's home rather than the bride's. The usual Nattati Nadar custom is the giving of *sidanam* (land, a house, or money) as gifts to a daughter upon marriage; *sidanam* is owned by the bride, not the groom.

In seeking a mate in both these communities of North and South India, the one sought represents the side which will control considerable wealth – in North India, the groom (or his father) will control the groomprice, so the bride's elders seek the groom; in South India, the bride (or, indirectly, her father and/or brother) will control the *sidanam*, so the groom's elders seek the bride. The sequence of wedding rites allow for gift giving by both sides: in a groomprice marriage, the bride's people give more costly gifts and larger sums of money; in a brideprice wedding, the opposite is the case.

Differences in the Two Weddings: The Image of Woman

One of the girl's FBWs commented angrily to me: "They take a girl and throw her anywhere. She has no say." The comment refers to the marriage being arranged by the elders with little if any consultation with the bride-to-be. When I asked about this, the woman admitted that only an educated daughter might voice any resentment. At the time, girls in Khalapur attended at most three or four grades of school and were hardly "educated". The bitterness of the Rajput women of the bride's patrilineal joint family is voiced from the very first of the massage-baths that the Rajput bride must be given to being the *shadi* sequence of rites.

The preliminary to the bans, the very first ritual gesture, gives away the whole show. Before the *chachi*, who is the mistress of ceremonies, can spread turmeric, flour, and mustard oil (the paste for the massages) on the limbs of the bride, she must spread some of it on the flanks of a local shrine, one devoted to the *sati* worship by the Rajput family. About 30 women of the bride's joint household and of the neighborhood make the offering to the *sati* votive stone.

The bride's father explained that the *sati* was the example of the perfectly devoted Rajput wife, one who committed suicide when her husband died. That she first should be massaged like a bride makes her value clear – especially if it is also realized that a widow, though she lives in her dead husband's family's household, is considered inauspicious and must not attend weddings lest she bring bad luck to the union. The *sati* is a widow to be praised; the widow who lives on is ceremonially dishonored.

Let us look at the other *dramatis personae.* The barber administers the seven baths to the groom, the barber's wife does so for the bride – true in both the Rajput wedding and the Nadar blossoming. Among the Rajputs, the seven women who are the FBWs (*chachis*) and the FBSWs and the Brahman's wife, surround the bride. It is usually one of the *chachis* who is the mistress of ceremonies, who runs the series of ritual massage-baths. Among the Nadars, at the blossoming ceremony, the bathing is performed by the bride's MZs, MBWs, FZs, and FZDs, the *muraikarigal* (proper relatives), who are largely the bride's mother's relatives. Thus, we see a radical difference in the wedding parties of the two brides. The Rajput bride is ushered through her wedding preparations by the women of her father's joint family; the Nadar bride is ushered through by the *muraikarigal*, largely her mother's female kin.

The main ceremony at the Nadar blossoming is a bathing, when the *muraikarigals* pour water over the girl and when her MB is obligated to present her with a *sari.* The purpose of the bathing is to cleanse her after her menstrual pollution. As one non-Brahman informant explained: "This is *atma sutti* [purification of the soul] and *sariya sutti* [purification of the body]. During her seclusion, she was '*titu totate*' [do not touch the polluted]." What is being celebrated is the girl's fertility, ascendant now that her first menstrual period is over. She is a virgin (a *pupottu*, which also means a flower bud).

In the case of the Rajput bride, the baths are to heat her, since turmeric makes one "hot" as for sexual relations. Although the bride does not have sexual relations with her husband during the *shadi*, symbolic sexual relations occur in two ceremonies which take place right after the smearing of the *sati* monument, before the bride herself is massaged and bathed. In the first ceremony, two of the *chachis* pound rice and then rock salt in a brass pan with 1.2 m-long rods. They put both the rice and the salt in new round pots which are then heaped up, one on top of the other near, the doorway. Thus, salt and rice -- semen and egg -- are locked in pure new pottery wombs. The second ceremony follows when these women rub leguminous pulses (*dal*) in a tray with sesame oil. The *bhabhi* (FBSW) explained the meaning of these rites: "These end the girl's virginity." The bathing thus signifies purification in the case of the Nadar blossoming and symbolic sexual intercourse to end virginity and become pregnant in the case of the *shadi* preliminary rituals of the Rajputs. The same seven or five women do the massages and baths for the girl as did the massaging of the *sati*, the pounding of the rice and rock salt, and the rubbing of the *dal* with oil. My notes read:

> February 10, 1955. We asked what the bans meant. M's wife said they indicated that the girl was losing her virginity. Until she had these turmeric baths, she was a virgin. The sister-in-law who does the bans fasts from morning till night on the first day of the bans and eats only after she has performed them... *Dhubru* [sacred grass], milk and oil touched to the girl's feet, keens, forehead, all mean her losing her virginity, they said.

The Nadars blossoming is similar to the Rajput *shadi* in that there is a wedding during the blossoming, although it is a mock wedding. In one non-Brahman blossoming ceremony which I witnessed, the groom in the mock wedding was played by the girl's *patti* (her MM). In the "wedding" the two exchanged garlands. It is appropriate that the *patti* play this role since ideally it would be her grandchildren who would marry, her DD and her SS. Like the Rajput bride at the *shadi*, the Nadar initiate at the blossoming ceremony is presented with gifts by her various relatives, mostly metal cooking and kitchen vessels and metal containers for cosmetics and oils. The Rajput bride's trousseau of quilts and brass vessels and other useful household items are on display during the *shadi*. At both "first weddings" the Nadar blossoming and the Rajput *shadi*, the bride receives gifts with which to begin married life.

At both "first weddings" the girl also is transferred to affinal kin. Sexual relations are promised but do not take place. At the blossoming, the girl is already in the keeping of her affines, the *muraikarigals* and the *maman* (MB), who may ask for her as a bride for one of his sons. She is surrounded by her future affines, most of whom she has known her entire life, many being neighbors or her mother's patrikin among whom she is likely to marry. At the *shadi*, the girl is ambivalently, even bitterly, relinquished to a strange groom who takes her home to his sister and his female patrikin.

The groom's wedding party is comprised of his male agnates, his MBs, and his MBSs. But, the party does not include the groom's mother or his FBWs. The groom's party is of the same composition in both the Rajput wedding and the Nadar wedding except for a very important personage in the Nadar wedding -- the groom's sister.

Among the Nadars, a married sister of the groom is one of his party. She helps the bride change into the *sari* which the groom has presented for her to wear. She brings the Nadar bride to the *pandal* for the wedding rounds and helps to tie the *tali* -- the golden pendant denoting the marital state for women. My notes read:

> Three of four young men sang *mantras* from a book. The band stopped playing. From a tray containing pink tissue paper packages, the groom took the *tali* and put it around the bride's neck, his sister helping him. I think she tied it. The groom also took a gold chain from the same tray, and his sister unfastened it, and together they put it around the bride's neck. The difficulty in putting both around her neck was that she was wearing one or more garlands of flowers, and it was hard to get the red string of the *tali* or the gold chain over or under the garlands. People threw flower petals on the couple during the *tali*-tying, the women yodeling (*kuluvai*).

Even before the wedding, the groom's sister has duties. She is required to give the engaged girl a new *sari* to wear at the engagement ceremony (*nichayya tambulam*). A groom's older sisters have the *mangaliyam* made for him; they pay the goldsmith for melting the gold and molding the *mangaliyam*. In return, each sister is given a *sari* by her parents.

There is no *mangaliyam* in the North Indian wedding; and, of course, the groom's sister does not come to the Rajput wedding. The contrast is clear. Among the Nattati Nadars, the groom's sister helps marry off her brother's wife; among the Rajputs, the brothers' wives marry off their husbands' sister by massaging her, by grinding rice, and by rubbing *dal*, rites which end her virginity.

When the groom is greeted by the bride's brother among the Nadars, one or another of these cross-cousins, one of the *muraikarigal*, may be present. The *muraikarigal* includes the groom's sister who ties the *tali* and may include his other sisters. When he is taken off to be fed for the first time in the bride's house, he is among his own female relatives if he is a Nadar; but if a Rajput, he is among a bevy of strange women. The Rajput groom is served by his new wife's sisters and female cousins (*salis*) and by her brothers' and male cousins' wives (*salhejs*). While a Nadar groom is treated respectfully and affectionately by the *muraikarigals* of the bride, who include his own sisters, the Rajput groom is teased unmercifully by the strange *salis* and *salhejs*. My notes from the Rajput wedding read:

> Chaoli said to him, "Oh, you killed your mother before she could see you married." To this, the boy smiled and wiped a tear from his eye. The girls asked him how many sisters he had. "Oh, we will bring them here and marry them to our boys." "How many are there? We want to see if the boys will go around." A favorite phrase was "lover of one's own mother" [*man ke yar*] and son of a lewd woman [*luchi ke*]. A little song that Chaoli sang was, "We will bring all your sisters here in marriage" [*Behen ko laen ge be*].

The joking here turns on Rajput hypergamy. Since the Rajputs of Khalapur are giving a girl to the groom's patrilineage, they could not, of course, also take girls as wives from the same patrilineage. In the joking there is a fantasy of the situation being reversed. The intense insult of suggestions of both incest and adultery on the part of the groom's mother is more easily tossed off, perhaps because the lady in question is back in the groom's home village and will never come to visit in Khalapur (the custom of *purdah* prohibiting visits to strange villages, even that of one's daughter-in-law's parents).

When the Rajput bride leaves to go with her husband and his all-male party, she goes heavily shrouded in head coverings, in a bullock cart, hardly seeing the way. Weeping, she tears herself away from M, Zs, BWs, and FBWs, and perhaps from her FM. This is the first of a long series of ritual weepings that mark her departures and returns. Every time she meets her brother when he comes to visit her or to get her at her husband's village, she weeps as she embraces him. When she returns from her husband's village, she weeps ritually on her mother's shoulder, chanting the misery of her separation and recalling their mutual sorrows.

After a wedding visit to her husband's home, the bride returns to her parental home to wait until she is fully mature. Then, there is a ceremony when her husband comes again with a party of men to take her for the consummation of their marriage. Her worth is known when soon after the *chala*, the second wedding ceremony, she produces a son. Then, she is finally accepted into her husband's joint family and neighborhood. If she produces a daughter, at least she has proven her fecundity; the next time it may be a son. We may say that the Rajput bride is given as tribute to another family.

After the wedding, the *kalyanam* (the Nadar girl) does not depart from her mother with wails and tears, either ritual or real ones, for the Nadar bride goes away only shortly before her mother is to follow. The mother goes that evening to her daughter's new house to inspect it (*maruvitu kannal*), accompanied by her Zs, HBWs, Bs, and BWs, a largely female procession. She brings vegetables and rice for the groom's relatives to prepare a feast for her and her party. The groom's people serve the meal, and the bride's mother presents the bride with a gift for the groom. Then, on the third, fifth, and seventh days after the wedding, the couple must go together to the bride's parents' house to be feasted. During their first month of marriage, they may spend all their time being entertained by the bride's relatives. They must be called by the bride's parents for the first Deepawali (Hindu festival of lights) after marriage, and they must have gifts sent to them on the first Pongal (South Indian ceremony of plenty) and on the first day of the Tamil month of Adi (July-August). When the bride is finally pregnant, her mother comes to take her to deliver the baby at her parental home.

The South Indian Nattati Nadar family gives their daughter reluctantly to the groom and his kin. If they can afford it, the parents give their daughter a paddy field, so that she will never want for rice, and a house or house plot as part of her *sidanam* (gift to daughter, dowry). These are deeded in her name, not the groom's. The family may even make it beneficial to the groom to live close to them; or, when they are old, they may go to live near their daughter or even with her and her children, something that would be strictly forbidden among Rajputs.

The Rajput bride's father or brother does not stay at his married daughter's or married sister's house for any length of time, but they may come to visit her briefly and to fetch her home. A brother should bring his married sister gifts at Deepawali, Holi (the spring saturnalia), and Tij (the summer swing festival). It is against the rules for any man of the bride's family to accept hospitality at the bride's marital home; if he accepts a meal, he must pay for it. It also is shameful for a man to live in his wife's house, no less at his married daughter's house. A Rajput mother can never visit her daughter in her marital home. Among the Nadars, a woman may travel by herself, going as much as 22 km to Aral village, a popular place for marrying daughters of the hamlet; and a married woman may travel by bus to visit her mother.

A Nadar bride need not wait for her brother or father to fetch her home.

The contrasting basic attitudes of these two communities is reflected in the following statements: "Of course, we would not marry among ourselves!" (a Rajput speaking); "Of course, if we can, we marry within the family [*kutumpam*]" (a Nadar speaking). Among the Rajputs, the bride is not only carefully integrated into her husband's family, but the couple together is integrated into her family as well as into his, as the feasting early in the marriage intends. In North India, the relations between the two families linked by a marriage are continued through the one-way procession of gifts from the bride's family to the groom's. Among the Nadars, the couple is integrated personally into both families; among the Rajputs, the bride is integrated as a person into her husband's family, but the two families strengthen their link only by gifts brought by the bride from her family to her husband's family, or the gifts brought by her brother on the above mentioned three important festival days.

That the couple is a unit from the start among the Nadars is indicated by the house construction often undertaken before a marriage, when a room is added for the anticipated new family. Almost invariably the new room has a kitchen of its own. Among the Rajputs, by contrast, the new couple live jointly with the groom's parents, and often with his brothers' families, and it may be the groom's mother who continues to cook for him. In the Nadar wedding, at the first feeding of the groom in the bride's house, the bride herself does the cooking. Among the Rajputs, the bride may not cook for her husband until after his mother dies. As the Rajputs say when referring to the joint family, "At night two, in the day, one hundred."

Summary of Differences Between the Two Weddings

Let me now summarize the differences between the Nadar wedding and the Rajput wedding in a set of oppositions.[6]

In both of the preliminary rituals, affinal female relatives prepare the bride-to-be. In North India, among the Rajputs, the female affines represent the bride's own extended family, women who symbolically end her virginity so that long before actual sexual relations begin her virginity is lost -- there is no turning back. She is committed and severed, alienated from her extended family by the women who have married into that family. They symbolically "spoil" her to give her away. In South India, among the Nattati Nadars, the female affines represent the kin among whom the girl will probably marry and they purify her, so that as a blossoming "flower" she is ready to be impregnated. In the North Indian rite, the maiden loses her virginity in a tray of rice, ground out by the inmarried women of her own joint family. Thereafter, she is no longer virginal; she has become the

Nadar (South India)	*Rajput (North India)*
1. Delayed exchange marriage system.	1. Deflected alliance marriage system.
2. Nuclear or supplemented nuclear family households.	2. Linear or fraternal joint compounds or neighborhoods.
3. Strict seclusion of women during menstruation; chaperonage of unmarried women.	3. Less strict seclusion of women during menstruation; strict seclusion of married women in the husband's home.
4. First menstruation celebrated.	4. First menstruation not celebrated.
5. MB may claim ZD as a bride for his son.	5. Groom may ask for bride's sister as a bride for his brother.
6. MB brings *sari* at "blossoming" of his ZD.	6. MB brings gifts to Z for her daughter, at the bride's *shadi*.
7. Groom's elders seek bride.	7. Bride's elders seek groom.
8. *Sidanam* (property owned by bride).	8. Groomprice.
9. Preliminary rite purifies the bride.	9. Preliminary rites "spoil" the bride.
10. Preliminary rite by female kin among whom she is likely to marry.	10. Preliminary rites by inmarried women of bride's natal extended patrilineal family.
11. Preliminary bath of "cooling" water.	11. Preliminary baths of "heating" turmeric.
12. Groom greeted by bride's brother.	12. Groom greeted by bride's elder.
13. Attitude in first set of ceremonies: nurturing bride's fertility.	13. Attitude in first set of ceremonies: dedication to her husband like that of a woman who is willing to commit *sati*.
14. Bride's kindred likely to overlap with groom's.	14. Bride's kindred unlikely to overlap with groom's.
15. Brother's wife welcomed by husband's sisters.	15. Husband's sister sent off by brothers' wives.
16. Married with *mangaliyam*.	16. Married with rounds about fire.
17. Mother follows bride after her departure to inspect the bride's home.	17. Bride torn weeping from mother and other women of her natal family who may never visit her at her marital home.
18. Synthesis of two families, that of bride and groom.	18. Permanent subordination of bride's family to groom's.
19. Bride delivers first child at her mother's home.	19. Bride delivers children at her husband's joint family.

devotee of her husband, and she goes, along with gifts and family fortune, as hostage to another fortress, inexorably bound to a husband long before the physical binding itself takes place. In the south, her fertility is celebrated with ritual bathing and adornment, with gifts and congratulations. She is shifted from sister to brother within the family she has always known.

The Rajput of the north and the Nattati Nadars of the south represent two Indian patrilineal, patrilocal groups. In one, the woman is tribute to a group to whom her patrikin and family must always be inferior; in the other, the woman is a flower whose fertility must be fostered, preferably by the closest male relative who is permitted to marry her, her proper bridegroom, her *urumaimappilai*. The strict patrilineality of the north contrasts with the reluctant patrilineality of the south, and both are writ large in the wedding ceremonies themselves. Among the Rajputs, a girl is torn from the bosom of her joint family as a tribute to strangers; among the Nadars, the girl is purified upon her blossoming by her *muraikarigals*, and from among these women, who are close kin, a husband will be found for her. She reluctantly is loaned out to him until she is fertilized, as a flower should be. Then, she returns to the sheltering tree of her mother's house to bear her fruit.

While these clues add up to an image of woman in each wedding, they also suggest an experience for the bride, one that is considerably less arduous for the South Indian bride than for the North Indian bride. In South Indian culture, female fertility and close-knit connubia are valued, while the North Indian culture values hierarchical prestige relations and women are used in the construction of asymmetrical networks. While both communities are patrilineal and patrilocal, with women given by one kin group to another in modified systems of generalized exchange, there are profound differences in the degree of despoilment of the women involved.

Wedding and Comparative Symbology

In this paper I extract summary images[7] of women from various clues. Ricoeur (1981: 175) writes: "A clue serves as a guide for a specific construction, in that it contains at once a permission and a prohibition; it excludes unsuitable constructions and it allows those which give more meaning to the same words." In the South Indian wedding, an important clue is the word for the first menstruation rite for a girl, *puppu*, which means both menstruation and blossoming. The flowers in the girl's hair, the flowers offered in *puja* to the gods, are significant clues that contribute to my reading. The word *puja* may be derived from the word for flower, *pu* (Southworth 1980: personal communication). The woman who is given is a kind of flower. In the North Indian wedding cycle of the Rajputs, their martial tradition -- the all-male party traveling a long distance, their weighted bamboo staves in hand, the bridegroom riding on horseback, the giving of groomprice, the going of the bride along with the all-male party to a strange village, the hypergamic relationship of subordination of the bride's kindred to the groom's, the persistent ambience of Moghul times when Rajput women were offered unilaterally to Moghul rulers -- all seem to make a picture of the bride as tribute.

Other weddings in India suggest other images of woman. Nicholas and Inden (1977: 52, 54) write of the Bengali conception of husband and wife as "the seed and the earth". Fruzzetti and Ostor (1976: 120--124) also speak of the wife as a vessel, of which the husband is the bearer, and of the wife as the *ardhangini*, the half-body of the husband. Bride and groom also may be god and goddess (Allison 1981). Sehgal (1969: 7--8), in a little book that lays out the wedding rites with the Sanskrit verses, says of the bride's father: "From the moment [of the engagement] he looks upon groom and bride as Lord Narayana and Goddess Lakshmi." In the Rajput wedding, the total commitment expected of the bride to her husband, an ideal suggested in the worship of the *sati* votive stone, calls up an image of woman as worshipper of her husband.

The wedding may locate a culture's imagery of woman. Weddings usually are codified, consensually validated, and widely similar within a cultural group. Since they occur almost universally, comparisons of weddings may lead us to comparisons of symbolizations of woman, even as comparisons of pilgrimages may lead us to comparisons of great world religions (Turner and Turner 1978).

Acknowledgments

Fieldwork in Khalapur (1954–56) was supported by the Cornell India Program. Fieldwork in Kanyakumari has been supported by Faculty Research Fellowships from the American Institute of Indian Studies and a grant from the National Science Foundation. In Khalapur, John T. Hitchcock and Shyam Narain Singh attended one of the same Rajput weddings I did and collected other data on Rajputs weddings; Hari S. Saxena provided excellent data on weddings with Brahman informants, as did J.M. Mahar and Raj Jaiswal on untouchable Chamar (traditionally leather workers, now mostly agrestic servants) weddings. Usha Bhagat and I covered the weddings of untouchable Chuhras (scavengers, sweepers). In Kanyakumari, Mary Fainsod (Katzenstein) and Wilda Campbell conducted interviews about and observed weddings among Acaris (goldsmiths) and Thevars (traditional guardsmen and mercenary soldiers, now cultivators) and Nadars. I owe thanks to the funding agencies and to my research associates, as well as to Prema Nathaniel and Saroja Chelliah who worked with me on Nattati Nadar and Vellala weddings in Kanyakumari.

An earlier version of this paper was read at the South Asia Symposium on "System of Communication and Interaction in South Asia," at the University of Pennsylvania, 14 February 1980. I owe thanks to Arjun Appadurai, Carol Breckenridge, and Ward Goodenough, as well as to others in attendance, for their searching questions and helpful commentary; and to Peter Claus, Jamila Feldman, Mattison Mines, David Mandelbaum, and several readers for the *American Ethnologist* who subsequently made helpful suggestions.

Notes

1. Lévi-Strauss (1969: 132) grants that the generalized exchange system might be quite different in matrilineal-matrilocal regimes than in patrilineal-patrilocal ones, but he does not discuss those differences. Louis Dumont (1957a) had demonstrated that there are disharmonic regimes to be found as well in southern Tamilnadu. There have, of course, been myriad criticisms of *Elementary Structures of Kinship*; of

relevance here are the developments from Lévi-Strauss' ideas made by Dumont, whose work, in turn, has stimulated others writing on marriage systems in South Asia.

2. In using either a Tamil or Hindi word, I italicize it throughout.
3. The overall estimate of about 6 percent sibling-set marriages (marriages of a set of sisters to a set of brothers) among the Khalapur Rajputs is low compared to the 29 percent rate found among the Annana Jats of Jaipur. The 82 percent rate of women married into villages in which other women from Khalapur are also married is, however, higher than the comparable figure among the Annana Jats (74 percent) (Kolenda 1978: 253).
4. Neither the Nattati Nadars nor the Rajputs encourage cross-generational marriages, though an occasional one sometimes occurs. Marriages between a mother's younger brother and an elder sister's daughter do occur in other areas of South India. In five of six non-Brahman castes studied by Dumont (1957a: 20) in districts to the north of Kanyakumari, patrilateral cross-cousin marriage was also preferred.
5. Since the analytical sections of this paper were written, two rich studies (Winslow 1980: McGilvray 1982) have appeared that compare various ethnic groups in Sri Lanka in their girls' puberty or first-menstruation rites. The rites in Sri Lanka are very similar to those among the Nattati Nadars and other non-Brahmans of the Kanyakumari area. See Gough (1955) for other puberty rites in South India.
6. Comparisons between women of North India and women of South India have been made by various anthropologists (Kolenda 1967: 172–81, 200, 211, 216; Wadley 1980: 161–67; Miller 1981, 1982).
7. Are the summary images of "woman as tribute" and "woman as flower" "root paradigms" (Turner 1974: 64) of the two weddings? Turner (1974: 67) sought a "root paradigm" or a plot in actual historical events revolving around a hero, but a ritual complex is hardly the same phenomenon. Instead, it is a series of small dramas, the actors always playing the same parts, and finding the paradigm of such action should not be problematic. Both the "root paradigm" and the "summary image" are cultural constructs, one taken by the analyst to be in the head of the hero, such as a Becket or a Hildalgo (Turner 1974: 60–155), the other a picture painted by a ritual complex.

References

Allison, Charlene (1981), *Transforming Two into One: The Process of Uniting a Tamil Bride and Groom*. Paper read at the Society for South India Studies meeting, 7 November 1981, Berkeley.

Binford, Myra Raym, Michael Camerini, and Joseph Elder (1975), *Wedding of the Goddess*. Contemporary South Asia Film Series. South Asian Area Center, University of Wisconsin, Madison.

Dumont, Louis (1957a), *Hierarchy and Marriage Alliance*, Royal Anthropological Institute, Occasional Paper No. 12, London.

— (1957b), *Une Sous-Caste de l'Inde du Sud*, Paris: Mouton.

— (1966), Marriage in India. The Present State of the Question. III: North India in Relation to South India, *Contributions to Indian Sociology* 9:90–114.

— (1970), *Homo Hierarchicus*. Mark Sainsbury, transl., Chicago: University of Chicago.

— (1975), Terminology and Prestations Revisited, *Contributions to Indian Sociology* (NS) 9:197–216.

Fruzzetti, Lina, and Akos Ostor (1976), Seed and Earth: A Cultural Analysis of Kinship in a Bengali Town, *Contributions to Indian Sociology* (NS) 10:97–132.

Geertz, Clifford (1973), Deep Play: Notes on the Balinese Cockfight. *In The Interpretation of Cultures*, New York: Basic Books, pp. 412–53.

— (1980), Blurred Genres: The Refiguration of Social Thought, *The American Scholar* 49 (spring): 165–79.

Gough, E. Kathleen (1955), Female Initiation Rites on the Malabar Coast, *Journal of the Royal Anthropological Institute* 85:45–80.

Hardgrave, Robert L., Jr. (1969), *The Nadars of Tamilnadu*, Berkeley: University of California Press.

Hitchcock, John T. (1956), *The Rajputs of Khalapur: A Study of Kinship, Social Stratification and Politics*, Ph.D. dissertation, Department of Anthropology, Cornell University.

— (1959), The Idea of the Martial Rajput. *In Traditional India: Structure and Change*. M. Singer, ed. Philadelphia: The American Folklore Society, pp. 10–17.

Kane, M.P.V. (1941), *History of Dharmasastra* (Ancient and Medieval Religious and Civil Law), Vol. 2, Poona: Bhandarkar Oriental Research Institute.

Karve, Irawati (1953), *Kinship Organization in India*, Poona: Deccan College Postgraduate and Research Institute.

Khare, R.S. (1975), Embedded Affinity and Consanguineal Ethos: Two Properties of the Northern Kinship System, *Contributions to Indian Sociology* (NS) 9: 245–62.

Kolenda, Pauline (1967), Regional Differences in Indian Family Structure. *In Regions and Regionalism in South Asian Studies*. Robert Crane, ed. Duke University Program in Comparative Studies, pp. 147--225. Monograph No. 5. Durham, NC.

---- (1978), Sibling-set marriage, Collateral-set marriage, and Deflected Alliance among Annana Jats of Jaipur District Rajasthan. *In American Studies in Indian Anthropology*, Sylvia Vatuk, ed. New Delhi: Manohar, pp. 242--77.

---- (1980), Hindu Caste in a Regal Tradition: The Native View, *Rice University Studies* 66(1): 125--36.

Leach, Edmund (1961), Asymmetric Marriage Rules, Status Difference and Direct Reciprocity: Comments on an Alleged Fallacy, *Southwestern Journal of Anthropology* 17: 343--50.

Lévi-Strauss, Claude, 1969 [1949], *Elementary Structures of Kinship*, London: Eyre and Spottiswoode.

MacMunn, George Fletcher (1933), *The Martial Races of India*, London: S. Low, Marston.

Madan, T.N. (1975), Structural Implications of Marriage in North India: Wife-Givers and Wife-Takers among the Pandits of Kashmir, *Contributions to Indian Sociology* (NS) 9:217–44.

Mahar, James Michael (1965), *Affinal Networks and Caste Boundaries*. Paper read at the 64th Annual Meeting of the American Anthropological Association, Denver.

---- (1966), *Marriage Networks in the Northern Gangetic Plain*, Ph.D. dissertation, Department of Anthropology, Cornell University.

McGilvray, D.B. (1982), Sexual Power and Fertility in Sri Lanka: Batticaloa Tamils and Moors. *In Ethnography of Fertility and Birth*. Carol P. MacCormack, ed. London: Academic Press, pp. 25--73.

Miller, Barbara (1981), *The Endangered Sex: Neglect of Female Children in Rural North India*, Ithaca: Cornell University Press.

---- (1982), Female Labor Participation and Female Seclusion in Rural India: A Regional View, *Economic Development and Cultural Change* 30: 777--94.

Nicholas, Ralph, and Ronald B. Inden (1977), *Kinship in Bengali Culture*, Chicago: University of Chicago Press.

Ricoeur, Paul (1981), *Hermeneutics and the Human Sciences*. J.B. Thompson, transl. and ed. Cambridge: Cambridge University Press.

Rubin, Gayle (1975), The Traffic in Women: Notes on the "Political Economy" of Sex. *In Towards an Anthropology of Women*, R. Reiter, ed. New York: Monthly Review, pp. 157–210.

Sehgal, S.R. (1969), *Hindu Marriage and its Immortal Traditions*, New Delhi: Navyug.

Singer, Milton (1972), *When a Great Tradition Modernizes*, New York: Praeger.

Stein, Dorothy (1978), Women to Burn: Suttee as a Normatice Institution, *Signs* 4:253–273.

Thompson, Edward (1928), *Suttee: A Historical and Philosophical Enquiry into the Hindu Rite of Widow-Burning*, London: George Allen and Unwin.

Tod, James (1829–32), *The Annals and Antiquities of Rajasthan*, 2 vols., London: Smith, Elder.

Turner, Edith, and Victor Turner (1978), *Image and Pilgrimage*, New York: Columbia University Press.

Turner, James (1975), A Formal Semantic Analysis of Hindu Kinship Terminology, *Contributions to Indian Sociology* (NS) 9:263–92.

Turner, Victor (1967), *Forest of Symbols*, Ithaca: Cornell University Press.

— (1969), *The Ritual Process*, Chicago: Aldine.

— (1974), *Dramas, Fields, and Metaphors*, Ithaca: Cornell University Press.

— (1979), *Process, Performance and Pilgrimage*, Ranchi Anthropology Series 1, New Delhi: Concept Publishing.

van Gennep, Arnold, 1960 [1909], *Rites de Passage*, Chicago: University of Chicago Press.

Vatuk, Sylvia (1969), A Structural Analysis of the Hindu Kinship Terminology, *Contributions to Indian Sociology* (NS) 3:263–92.

— (1975), Gifts and Affines in North India, *Contributions to Indian Sociology* (NS) 9:155–96.

Wadley, Susan (1980), The Paradoxical Powers of Tamil Women. *In The Powers of Tamil Women*. Syracuse: Maxwell School of Citizenship and Public Affairs, Syracuse University, pp.153–79.

Winslow, Deborah (1980), Rituals of First Menstruation in Sri Lanka, *Man* (NS) 15:603–25.

Yeats-Brown, Francis C.C. (1945), *Martial India*, London: Eyre and Spottiswoode.

11

Sibling Relations and Marriage Practices

A Comparison of North, Central, and South India

To write about sibling relationships without including other familial relationships, for instance those between parents and children, between grandparents and grandchildren, between in-laws – in other words, outside the entire kinship system – is to commit an anthropological sin: taking relationships out of context. Inevitably, other kinship relationships will be mentioned in this chapter. The main justification for looking at sibling relationships under a spotlight is their previous neglect by anthropologists. Much more has been written about the relationship between mother-in-law and daughter-in-law, father and son, and husband and wife in the Indian joint family. The most neglected sibling relationship in the literature on Indian kinship is that of sisters. The least neglected is probably that of brothers, especially the difficulties between brothers when they divide jointly inherited land. In-between is the brother-sister relationship.

Over the past 49 years, I have done ethnographic fieldwork in three different parts of rural India – in the north, in the village of Khalapur, situated in western Uttar Pradesh; in central India, in villages near the city of Jaipur, Rajasthan; and in the south, in Kanyakumari district, Tamilnadu.[1] My consistent concern has been with caste and family among Hindus. In this chapter, I present briefly the cultural expectations for the brother-sister, brother-brother, and sister-sister relationships as they are alike and, especially, as they differ in the three regions. These culturally prescribed sibling relationships are those of adolescents and adults (rather than children), viewed in the context of similar and different kinship and marriage systems. As Weisner (1982: 324) has stated: "Most accounts of the cross-cultural

Plate 21

A pair of Jat sisters married to husbands who are brothers. The two couples form the core of a joint-family household in the Rajasthan village (Photo December 1978, by Pauline Kolenda).

diversity in the expression of sibling ties are closely linked to theories of descent and residence patterns around the world."

What is highlighted by a comparison between sibling relationships in three different regions of India is the relativity of these relationships to the marriage system followed. Each of the three regions has a different marriage system. In north India, marriage alliances are dispersed with a preference for maximizing ties, so that seldom do two sisters marry into the same village or family.[2] The strong brother-sister relationship fits well with the need for concern for the welfare of a married sister, living among strangers. Sisters seldom see each other after marriage, since they are usually married into different villages. Brothers, after marriage, either continue to live with their parents in a joint household, or live near each other, often working together in a joint farming or artisan enterprise.

In central India, the marriage of related women to men of the same village and family is common, so that women have women relatives in their place of marriage. This makes the bonds between sisters unusually strong, especially when a pair or triad of sisters are married to a pair or triad of brothers. Joint families are prevalent in Rajasthan, and married brothers often continue to live together, or else, as in north India, are neighbors and work together and share a family pool of resources. The brother-sister relationship is not as idealized or as strong as in north India.

In south India, it is children of brother and sister who should marry. This means that there is a special closeness between the brother and sister whose children do marry, although there may be enmity between a sister and brother whose children were of the right age, but who did not marry. For the bride in a cross-cousin marriage, her mother-in-law may be her father's sister, or else her father-in-law may be her mother's brother; she does not move into a house of strangers at marriage. A brother may look after the land and gardens given as *stridanam* to a sister when she married; these may return to him later on when her daughter marries his son. Brothers may own land together jointly with their father, and may then divide it after their father's death. This can cause difficulties between brothers, as it can in north and central India. The relationship between sisters is not culturally emphasized, but sisters can maintain their relationships with each other, since travel for women is much freer for women in south India than in central or north India, where *purdah* limits a woman's freedom of movement.[3]

To begin, here are three kinship stories that characterize the three regions to be described and compared.

The Two Television Sets: A Story from North India

During the spring of 1984, my research assistants and I lived in Khalapur with a large joint family, one of the wealthiest and most educated of the village, owning about 120 acres of good sugarcane and wheat land. It was composed of 16 core members: the uneducated elderly parents (the mother in her 60s and the father in his 70s), their three educated married sons (one in his 40s, two in their 30s), and the sons' wives and children. Each son had exactly two sons and one daughter, one of whom was married, so there were eight unmarried children, ranging in age from six months to 15 years. Living with the family permanently, at least until her marriage, was a daughter's daughter, aged 16. By rule of patrilocal residence, this granddaughter was not residing in the "right" village; the "right" village was her father's village, at a considerable distance in a different district. She had lived with her maternal grandparents since the age of four, we were told. Possibly, her parents and grandparents agreed that the latter could better afford the expenses of her education. Living with

Figure 11.1

A Rajput Joint Family of Khalapur

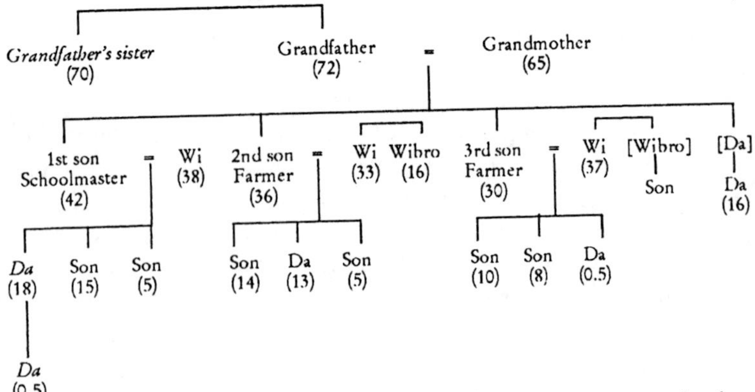

Italics, visitor; [ ], absent; ( ), age of individual above, in years; Da, daughter; Bro, brother; Wi, wife.

the family while they attended the local high school were the second son's wife's brother and the third son's wife's brother's son.[4] While we were there, the grandfather's elderly married sister and the eldest son's married daughter, with her 6-month-old daughter, each visited for a number of weeks (see Figure 11.1).

The eldest of the three sons was the most educated, having both a BA and an MA degree; he was a teacher of social science in the local high school. The two younger brothers both had completed high school; both worked on the land, aided by a hired servant. They were very aware of the latest agricultural methods, true examples of rational farmers. The second son, who was the main manager of the family farm, once listed for me the dozens of different new wheat and sugarcane seeds he had tried over the years, each recommended by the local government agricultural officer. The family had a tractor, but also maintained cooperative relations with other farmers to work together on sowing and other tasks.

The division of labor was one in which the two younger brothers did all the work in the fields, while the eldest brother contributed his teacher's salary to the family income; he also was expected to negotiate with government distributors to get good seed and fertilizer or to obtain the products in a market in a nearby town. The three brothers were in agreement that all the children should be educated through high school, even the girls. Because they could foresee the small portions of land (at most, 20 acres) each of their six sons would eventually inherit, they had purposely limited the sizes of their families. Despite the rationality of the three sons, the integration of their joint family was fragile.

The second brother complained to me about what enormously hard work farming is. He hinted that the older schoolmaster-brother should be making more effort to get them good seed and fertilizer. He did not complain about his good-natured younger brother.

The schoolmaster-eldest brother, indeed, may have neglected his agrarian duties, since he yearned to be free; he wanted to build a house in town where he could live a more sophisticated life, socializing with the educated elite, serving his guests tea out of bone china cups, as they sat on chairs around a polished table. It was he who had rented rooms to us; the cash we paid in rent was probably meant to help toward the cost of that town house.

What undoubtedly contributed to the two farmer-brothers' overwork, even though they had a full-time male field servant, was the fact that all eight boys (six sons plus the second son's wife's brother and the third son's wife's brother's son) attended school. Three of them (aged 5, 5, and 8) were too small to do heavy field work. The schoolmaster's eldest son was the oldest of the sons, but the schoolmaster would not allow him to do anything but study, since he wanted him both to pass his final year of high school and to get admitted into college. That left four boys big enough to help, a son of each of the two farmer-brothers, plus the two relatives of the farmer-brothers' wives, who lived with them while going to school. On school holidays, the farmer-brothers rounded up these four boys to help in the fields, while the daughter's daughter, also off from school, and the visiting elderly aunt carried huge baskets of bread and pots of curry out to the fields to feed the team of workers.

In a large joint family such as this one, siblings are not just full brothers and sisters but also cousins, for in north Indian Hindi kinship terminology, cousins are also called "brother" and "sister". Thus, 11 of the 12 children in this household could address each other as "brother" or "sister". One of the three boys attending high school was a mother's brother to these children, since he was an in-marrying wife's brother.

In general, the "brothers" and "sisters" seemed to get along. Only between the two little boys, both aged 5, parallel cousins to each other (their fathers were brothers), did there appear to be any bad feelings. These little fellows, constant companions, sometimes broke into arguments. Additionally, the head couple's daughter's daughter, the 16-year-old high school student who lived with her grandparents but whose home village was in another district, complained to us that the household chores she was required to do -- we noticed that she was always up very early in the morning sweeping the courtyard -- limited the time she had to study. Whether the other two boys (the second son's wife's brother and the third son's wife's brother's son), who were in high school, resented the schoolmaster's eldest son's freedom from chores, we do not know.

While the schoolmaster dreamed of living in town, it was his children who were causing the greatest expense to the joint family. His eldest child, a daughter, had been married a year before, at the age of 17, to an engineer. She lived with her husband in the city. This girl did not quite finish high school, since her wedding took place during the examination period of her 12th and final year. It was a joke around the house that she could not take her last year's exams and graduate because she got married instead. It was rumored that the joint family gave a lakh (100,000) of rupees (then roughly equivalent to $10,000) in cash to the groom's father as part of the wedding arrangement. Gifts such as a television set and a scooter had also been given. The wedding had been attended by scores of guests, all of whom the bride's family fed luxuriously. This first daughter's wedding had strained the joint family's resources.

None of the other children of the three brothers was yet of marriageable age. The eldest was the schoolmaster's 15-year-old son. When he married probably depended upon whether he went to college. If he did, he would marry at a later age, but the joint family would have his college expenses to meet. It would probably be at least four years before either of the younger brother's children would be old enough to marry, but the brothers were already putting money into an interest-yielding bank account toward the second son's eldest daughter's wedding. She was 13 and in the 7th grade.

The strain between the brothers was symbolized by the two television sets in the large joint family women's quarters. The schoolmaster was unusual in having a private room on the roof of the women's quarters (originally built when the high school first opened in 1948 as a temporary residence for the principal and his family). Except for the two small boys of five who still slept with their mothers, all nine of the other men and boys slept in the cattleyard, where the grandfather had built a fine men's clubhouse.

The schoolmaster kept his books and fine clothes in his room, where he also had a television set. He watched it alone unless he specifically invited others to see some special program. Even his wife and children were excluded from viewing the schoolmaster's television set. After his elder brother bought a set, the second brother bought one that was kept in his wife's room in the inner courtyard, where only women, girls, and unmarried boys were to be seen during the day.[5] That television was watched by the women and children.

It was the second brother who most resented his eldest brother – his teaching job to which he wore white shirts and fancy suits, his room on top of the women's quarters, and the high cost of his daughter's wedding, expenses the whole family had had to bear. The second brother could see looming ahead the costs of this brother's son's college education. While the schoolmaster-brother dreamed of a westernized city life, his next brother dreamed of getting his portion of the family land and living separately.

Not long before we knew them, this second brother had lost his temper (probably due to excessive drinking on Holi, the Hindu spring festival) and had marked off the outer courtyard of the women's quarters into fourths, saying that his father and the three brothers should each take an equal share of the women's quarters. His dramatic gesture and his anger frightened the women, who all got along harmoniously.

The second brother probably did not relish years of hard work ahead, the benefits of which his eldest brother would enjoy, as the eldest brother's family ate from the family harvests, made possible by the two farming brothers, while the joint family's savings were likely to go into the college education and marriage of the schoolmaster's eldest son. So far the brothers had not separated. Perhaps they will not do so as long as their elderly parents live. When the third and youngest brother told his father that he, too, might buy a television, the old man snorted, "Why don't you open a shop?" (meaning a television shop). The youngest son had not yet bought one when we left in mid-1984.[6]

The Untrained Daughter-in-Law: A Story from Central India

The Jat women were agog with the event one morning in the winter of 1966. It seemed that Kasturi, a handsome girl of about 13, had walked 14 miles home from her husband's village all alone, something an adolescent girl would ordinarily never do.

Her husband's brother and uncle had come to Maharajapur to take her back to her marital village some days before, and it had been very reluctantly that her father had allowed her to go with them. These men from her father-in-law's village had come twice and been refused. Kasturi had been married in her *shadi*, the first wedding ceremony, two years before, and the family was saving to celebrate the second wedding ceremony, the *muklava*, which usually takes place after the bride has reached menarche. But her husband's male relatives had come early, before the *muklava* had even been scheduled, asking that she be sent to help her mother-in-law right away. Let them skip the *muklava*, they had suggested, she was needed now.

There was, of course, the possibility that if her father refused a third time that the husband's people might stop coming, and when it was time for the *muklava*, they might refuse to come to it. Then what would they do? What man would offer a bride-price for a girl who was half-married already? So Kasturi's father had allowed her to go.

One reason Kasturi was needed was because her sister, who was married to Kasturi's husband's elder brother, the mother of four children, was coming back to visit her parents and natal family in Maharajapur. She brought her new baby and her toddler with her. While Kalavati, Kasturi's sister, was to be visiting at home, her mother-in-law would be left without sufficient help in cooking for her large joint family. Because her elder sister was coming home, Kasturi had to go to the village and house in which both sisters had husbands who were brothers. In this part of Rajasthan, it is common for sets of sisters to marry sets of brothers.

All the women felt sorry for Kasturi, who complained that she had never been so badly treated. Her mother-in-law had expected her to churn the milk, to cut the fodder, to do many chores that she did not know how to do, chores that her mother had never required of her. Her older sister, Kalavati, sighed, "If only I had been there, I could have helped her and shown her what to do!" Now, the women felt that when Kasturi was sent back, she would not be allowed to visit home again for several years. That would be her punishment.

The Substitute Bride: A Story from South India

Again a scandal, with all the village of Arole marveling, shaking their heads, and laughing. That day in the summer of 1980, a big wedding was to take place among the Nadars, a lower-caste community of cultivators. Both bride and groom came from Arole itself, but they were not related. She was not a *murai penn*, a proper girl or proper bride, for her groom, because she was not his cross-cousin. Like most communities in Kanyakumari, 'proper' mates were the children of brother and sister.

The groom had a high school education and a job at the mill, and his father, a cultivator, did not want his son to marry any of his sister's daughters. They were uneducated. Nor did his wife's brothers have a suitable daughter. So he arranged a marriage for his son with an educated girl, one with eight years of education. The day of the wedding had come, a feast was ready, and the guests had arrived.

Then suddenly, the bride refused to go through with it. She refused to marry this groom. Her relatives could not prevail upon her. Educated girls have minds of their own. But all was ready! What to do?

A south Indian solution was found. The father caught the next bus into town, and he went to his married sister's house and asked for his sister's daughter in marriage. The sister and the girl herself readily agreed. The girl was decked in her best sari, and the wedding proceeded.

Universals in Indian Marriage and Siblingship

Before presentations of each of the regions, some background features universal to marriage and siblingship in India are listed. The term *universal* is used here in the sense of "that which is applicable to a large number of instances" rather than "the whole world at all times" (Fabian 1983: 3). Deviation from these Indian "universals" are more likely to occur among urban, educated, and middle- and upper-class people than among rural people.

First of all, weddings are a focus of Indian culture, ideally celebrated lavishly for days, even, in the past, for weeks, with many guests attending. Parents begin saving for a child's, especially a daughter's, wedding almost from the day of birth.[7] Indians are notorious for bankrupting their families or going deeply into debt in order to transact and celebrate weddings. Many of the cultural expectations with respect to attitudes and rights between siblings are written into various wedding rituals. For example, all over India, it is essential for a bride's or a groom's mother's brothers to attend the wedding, and it demeans the mother and child if the brothers fail to attend without an acceptable excuse.

Second, marriages are arranged by the bride and groom's elders; and third, they must be arranged between a couple from the same endogamous group (*jati*) or caste. Nowadays it is usually expected that a bride should be a few years younger than the groom and that he should be the taller and the better educated of the two. Besides trying to find a match of the right age, height, and education, the elders must be concerned about various rules of exogamy; a bride or groom cannot marry into his or her own patrisib, and there may be other stipulations as to who cannot be wed, even within the same *jati*. Elders seek a boy or girl from a "good family," with a reputation for honor and for enjoying a reasonable standard of living. They often stipulate that they seek a boy or girl from a large family and/or a sizeable lineage, so that their child, once married, will not find himself or herself without aid from marital relatives. As for the wedding itself, there are considerations of gift-exchange and dowry or bride-price, the dates for the events, the numbers of guests, and so on, which must be discussed and agreed upon.[8]

The elders must beware of deception and humiliation when seeking a mate for a girl or boy. It is particularly tempting to deceive bride-seekers or groom-seekers when a girl or boy has some handicap such as deafness, blindness, or lameness, and usually those who wish to pass off such a child as normal seek a mate residing in a distant place. An honest, well-off father is likely to offer a good dowry or bride-price to help compensate for such defects. Some successful men have gotten their start through such dowries and from continuing financial support from a grateful father-in-law. There is a certain shame to a family if it is known that the father, father's brother, or grandfather has made more than a few proposals to potential brides' or bridegrooms' elders and been refused. Then gossip begins that there must be something wrong with the girl or boy on whose behalf the elder has acted.

In rural areas where it is common for bride and groom to be young teenagers who will not be receiving much education, neither bride nor groom sees the other or knows much about the other when they wed. As the age of marriage and number of years of education have gone up over the past 60 years, potential grooms and brides are increasingly requesting the opportunity to see the proposed partners before the engagement is fixed. Such viewing of the other, which may even include a brief conversation between the couple, is invariably in the presence of relatives from both sides. In communities where cross-cousins marry, a pair is likely to have known each other as children, but girls usually are kept away from boys their age and older once they reach puberty.

Self-selection of a mate through meeting members of the opposite sex at college, at work, through friends or relatives, or even more casually – eventuating in what is called a "love marriage" – is universally frowned upon; there is the implication that before wedding the bride and groom must have known each other too well.[9] Since a fair proportion of love marriages are also intercaste or interreligious marriages, they threaten the third universal feature of Indian marriage, that one must marry within one's own endogamous group, *jati*, and religion. Universally, intercaste and interreligious couples are socially ostracized by their families and *jatis*.

Fourth, one's behavior and success in social life, work, and studies reflect not just on oneself but on the good name of one's family and *jati*, especially the local *jati* chapter members, those who live together in the same village and neighborhood. Villagers are always talking about children who have given their families or *jatis* a good (or bad) name. Universally, the sure way for a girl to give her family a bad name is to indulge in a premarital flirtation or sexual relationship, or worse, to be thought to be promiscuous, or worst of all, to become pregnant. While an unmarried pregnant daughter should be ostracized, even killed, by some local norms, in fact she is more likely to be quickly married off to an elderly widower or bachelor who would otherwise have a great deal of trouble finding a young wife. A bad name is given to his family or *jati* by a boy who is known to be a thief, a gambler, or one who prefers to wander about and play rather than work.

Fifth, spinsterhood is almost unknown in India.[10] High-caste Hindu women are only allowed to marry once; such a prohibition holds among some lower castes as well, but generally middle- and lower-caste widows under age 40 are mated again, often to their dead husband's brother.[11] Men of all communities can marry repeatedly and, except among Christians, may have more than one wife at the same time.

Sixth, the purpose of marriage is to produce children; while a childless marriage occasionally endures, childlessness is the main cause for separation of a married couple. A husband may take his barren wife back to her parents or to her married brother's house and leave her there, never to return for her. This is a kind of *de facto* divorce, the most common kind to be found in rural India, where there are still few legal divorces.[12] Such a man usually takes another wife; in rural areas, bigamy for a man is not forbidden. Unless aged, a widower who can possibly afford it will almost always take another wife. In making village censuses, I have found such men with frequency, some of whom have had three or more wives and may thereby have had many children.

Rural Indian couples usually expect to have several children. There is no Indian cultural ideal for a two- or one-child family. Among the most enlightened rural people these days, people who appreciate the importance of family limitation, the ideal is two sons and one daughter.

Seventh, typically then, an Indian grows up in a family with two or more other siblings. Families with four, five, or six children are quite common. Table 11.1, which presents the sizes of sibling-sets among a 5 percent random sample of minimal patrilineages (*khandans*) in Khalapur, western Uttar Pradesh, illustrates this point.

Table 11.1

Sizes of Sibling-Sets in a 5 percent Sample of Minimal Patrilineages (Khandans), Khalapur, Western Uttar Pradesh (1985)

*Number of surviving children** *(n = 661)*	*Number of married women (n = 200)*	*Percentage of married women*
0	23	11.5
1	31	15.5
2	24	12.0
3	32	16.0
4	31	15.5
5	22	11.0
6	19	9.5
7	11	5.5
8	4	2.0
9	1	0.5
10	2	1.0

*308 girls and 353 boys; median = 3 children per married woman; mean = 3.31 children per married woman; mean = 3.73 children per existing sibling-set (excluding women with no children).

In 1985, 45 percent of married women in the sample had four or more living children. Most of the 23 women who had no children were recently married and would probably have children in the future, and, of course, many of the other women were still in their

Table 11.2

200 Sibling-Sets Displayed by 35 Combinations of Sons and Daughters Belonging to 200 Married Women Found in a 5 Percent Sample of Inimal Patrilineages in Khalapur, Western Uttar Pradesh (1985)

Number of sons	*Number of daughters*	*Number of occurrences*	*Rank of combination (top 1/2)*
0	0	23	1
0	1	15	4.5
0	2	5	16
0	3	1	
0	4	1	
1	0	16	3
1	1	11	6
1	2	10	7
1	3	5	16
1	4	4	18
1	6	1	
2	0	8	12
2	1	18	2
2	2	15	4.5
2	3	8	12.5
2	4	4	18
2	5	1	
3	0	3	
3	1	8	12
3	2	6	16
3	3	7	13.5
3	4	3	
3	5	1	
3	6	1	
4	0	2	
4	1	4	
4	2	7	13.5
4	3	4	18
4	4	1	
5	0	1	
5	1	1	
5	2	2	
5	3	2	
5	5	1	
7	3	1	

childbearing years and would have more children, so these statistics suggest that in Khalapur, children grow up in sibling-sets of three or more. Indeed, these figures indicate that at least one-fourth of the children are in sibling-sets of six or more.

Table 11.2 lists the 35 different combinations of sons and daughters that these 200 married had.

While the most common combination was no sons and no daughters (23 occurrences), again because of the childlessness of the newly married, the second most common combination was the present cultural ideal of two sons and one daughter (18 occurrences). That there is some preference for sons is indicated in the total: out of the 661 children, 353 (53%) were sons and 308 (47%) were daughters.[13]

An *eighth* universal relates to the frequency of fairly large sibling-sets. It is quite common for older children to help care for their younger brothers and sisters. Everywhere in India, children of ages 5–10 can be seen carrying baby brothers and sisters. Strong affection for an older sister may stem from her surrogate-mother role, but boys usually help out with the child care, as well, and the responsibility that older children are taught to take for their younger siblings seems to preclude displays of overt jealousy toward them. Beals and Eason (in Charles D. Nuckolls, ed. *Siblings in South Asia*, New York: Sulfad Press, 1993, Ch. 4) emphasize how sibling rivalry is less present in South Asia than in North America. Minturn noticed its absence among the children of the Rajputs of Khalapur (Minturn and Hitchcock, 1966). By sibling rivalry, Minturn meant showing "hostility or resentment to a new baby" (Minturn and Hitchcock, 1966: 137). Older Rajput brothers and sisters do "shout at or even slap an erring child" (Minturn and Hitchcock 1966:119), although "bullying...is strongly discouraged" (Minturn and Hitchcock 1966: 136).

Ninth, all over rural India, there is the expectation that an older brother should marry before his younger brothers, and an older sister before her younger sisters. There are various implications of this rule. If the elder daughter was given in marriage with a huge dowry, the community and she herself are both likely to expect that the younger daughter will be given with an equal dowry. There can sometimes be a long delay as the family tries to accumulate enough savings before the arrangement of the younger sibling's marriage. Often, the parents simply cannot afford to spend as much on the second or subsequent children's weddings as upon the first. Parents may feel they must get a large dowry when their sons marry in order to pay large dowries when their daughters marry, or if bride-price is given, the reverse holds. If a family has spent a great deal on the education of a son, they may expect a large dowry to defray their debts or make up for that expense. The reverse – high bride-price for educated brides – has not yet developed, but if such a girl's father is wealthy, he may choose a son-in-law who will accede to his father-in-law's wishes with respect to job and residence.

In some sibling-sets, the younger sister is considered to be more beautiful than her older sister, or a younger brother may be considered healthier, better looking, better educated, or having better prospects than his elder brother. In such cases, the younger sibling may receive proposals before the elder is married. There are folk stories about how the beautiful daughter was allowed to be glimpsed by the groom's elders out seeking a bride, while the less beautiful daughter was actually given at the wedding. Parents almost always insist that the older be married off before the younger. As we shall see, in some parts of Rajasthan, the parents avoid these problems by marrying off two or more sons, or two or more daughters, at once.

There is an interdependence of fate among the siblings with respect to marriage. Birth order is a factor as it relates not only to the resources the parents have at the time a child is marriageable but also to the "desirability" of his or her older sibling's marriage contributing to a sibling's status when marrying. If an older brother or sister has indulged in either a "love marriage" or intercaste or interreligious marriage, this will affect a family's reputation within its caste community and almost certainly hurt the chances of marriage for the younger siblings. Once a family has allowed one such "undesirable" marriage, it may find itself having to accept others by default, because more conformist families within their endogamous group, *jati*, will refuse to give a bride or groom to the family with the deviant son or daughter. People are likely to think, "If one daughter is 'bad', then the other daughter may be bad, too." A "good" marriage, on the other hand, is likely to enhance the chances of the younger siblings to attract offers from the elders of other desirable mates, or to have the offers made on their behalf accepted. Weisner (1982: 323) has identified this phenomenon as "the norm throughout most of the cultures of the world: brothers and sisters are decisive participants in each other's fate concerning sexual access, marriage, or property."

Since the sororate is quite widely practiced, the younger sister, indeed, may repeat her sister's marriage to the very same man. With the levirate, a man may accept his older brother's widow.

Part of an elder's plan for a sibling-set may include a decision to let one son (practically never a daughter, unless she is crippled) remain unmarried. When there are three brothers, two may be married, and the third, well past a marriageable age, may have his food cooked for him by the wife of one of his brothers and may adopt one of his brother's sons as his heir. If one of his brothers dies prematurely and his community practices the levirate, he may, of course, receive his brother's widow as a wife.

The younger the rank of a sibling in a sibling-set, the more likely it will be that his or her marriage will be arranged not by the grandfather, father, or father's brother, but, because of the deaths or incapacity of the elder family members, by the eldest brother. The younger sibling in such a position may feel quite nervous because of the brother's lack of experience in such tricky matters as arranging marriages, and the younger sibling may also be doubtful about how seriously the elder brother will perform his duty. In villages, however, marriages are rarely arranged by a single elder without his taking the advice of others.

Tenth, another universal feature of larger sibling-sets in Indian families is that the father or grandfather often establishes a plan for a division of labor among male siblings, or a division of labor emerges among them. A common division of labor is: one or two brothers farm the land while the other brother, who has been educated longer, holds a job as a teacher or clerk. The better-educated brother is usually expected to contribute cash from his earnings for the weddings and other expenses of his nephews and nieces, or for other joint-family expenses, while he, in turn, gets grain, vegetables, milk, and *ghi* (clarified butter) from the family farm. Prevalent in north India more than in south India, the educated brother leaves his wife and children in the village to be looked after by his brothers while he works outside.[14]

Education is still very rare for daughters in rural families. But education for both boys and girls tends to delay marriage. Those few girls who go beyond four or five years of schooling are not married before or at puberty, as is typical for less-educated girls, but a few years later when they finish 8th, 10th, or 12th grade. These girls thus have a longer time to establish close relations with parents and siblings than girls who marry earlier. This is especially important for the relationships between sisters, who usually see little of each other after marriage unless they are married into the same household or village, as occurs among the Jaipur villagers discussed below. Sisters may attend school and study together and become girlfriends. An older daughter, still unmarried because she is attending middle school or high school, tends to take on more responsibility in the house. She may do much of the cooking and may be even more of a surrogate mother to her siblings than if she had married when she came of age.[15]

The *last* universal has to do with the terms "brother" and "sister", which refer not just to full brothers and sisters but to parallel cousins, the children of mother's sisters and father's brothers. In north Indian kinship terminology, these terms are used for all cousins (including mother's brother's and father's sister's children -- that is, cross-cousins – as well as second and more distant cousins, both parallel and cross-), as well as for the other offspring of one's parents. To distinguish between a full brother and a cousin, the English term "cousin-brother" is often used; similarly, the term "cousin-sister" is used. Since married brothers may live in the same household or, more likely, be neighbors, children may associate as much with their cousin-brothers and cousin-sisters as with their full brothers and sisters. In address, just the term "brother" or "sister" is used without the closeness of the relationship indicated. The pattern in Rajasthan in central India is similar.

In south India, one's parallel cousins, the children of father's brothers and mother's sisters, are called by terms for brother and sister, but not one's cross-cousins, the children of father's sisters or mother's brothers. While parallel cousins are brothers and sisters, cross-cousins are ideal as husbands and wives. It is customary all over India to extend kinship terms, especially those for brother and sister, to unrelated people within one's village and *jati*.

As detailed in this section, weddings are a cultural focus in India, indicated by their high expense in resources, kinship obligation, time, and interest. The arrangement of marriages by elders of the bride and groom is essential to the preservation of the Indian caste system, and the arrangement of marriages between very young brides and grooms is probably essential to the preservation of the Indian joint family: a young person allowed to choose a mate may not choose someone within his or her *jati*, and older brides and grooms are more likely to want to have some say in the choice of a mate and less likely to adjust docilely in a joint family household. There are fewer joint families where there are older ages of marriage (Kolenda and Haddon, 1987; Kolenda, 1989). The requirement that the bride be virginal ensures the authority of elders who must protect the virgins in their families; the illiterate young woman has no honorable alternative to a marriage arranged by elders, and it is these very elders who may threaten to outcaste a wayward girl. Love between a man and woman is not considered a proper or good basis for marriage in India, and a healthy, normal young woman remaining unmarried is not an acceptable possibility either in most caste-communities.

Just as rigorous is the expectation that the married woman should produce children; there are few childless couples; a woman's failure to produce children is generally considered an acceptable reason for a man to take another wife, either keeping or separating from his first wife.

Rare also is a family with an "only child"; Indians usually grow up in families with one, two, or more siblings. There seems to be relatively little sibling rivalry in the Indian family, perhaps because of the strong emphasis on duty and obligation as opposed to individual freedom and individual gratification. Siblings enjoy or suffer an interdependence of fate, as the action of one, including actions relevant to marriage, affect the reputation of the entire family. One aspect of this interdependence is the rule that an older child should marry before a younger one.

Siblingship is wide in India. One's brothers and sisters include one's parallel cousins, and in north India, all one's cousins; cousins of second and further degree in distance are still "brothers" and "sisters". Indeed, the children of parents' friends often are called "brother" and "sister". Since the incest taboo between brother and sister is strongly adhered to, this "siblingizing" of others rules out a whole series of potential mates whom a boy or girl might meet and be attracted to – another prop to the arrangement of marriage by the elders.

The inevitability of marriage for women, the arrangement of marriage by elders within a caste, the elaborate celebration of the weddings of virginal brides, the high valuation on children and family, and the prevalence of large sibling-sets in India are universals found in all three of the regions presented in this chapter and, indeed, in most part of India.

Regional Comparisons in Sibling Relationships

For all three regions presented, it is rural Hindu villagers who are compared. The styles of life of the three differ. Khalapur, in north India, is dominated by Rajputs, a martial caste who engage in patrilineal feuding and rivalries. They fancy themselves warriors and were cattle rustlers until the end of the nineteenth century. In the 1950s, they had agrestic servants who were untouchable Chamars, and they had, and still had in the 1980s, servants from other castes such as carpenters, barbers, washermen, sweepers, and potters. They also have private household Brahman priests. They are quite ready to defend themselves and their dependents and did so during the turbulent centuries before the twentieth century.

Representing central India, in Rajasthan, the Maharajapur-Kishanpur Jat and Mina peasants were, until land reform in 1958, agrarian tenants. The Jats and Minas of Maharajapur were tenants of the Maharaja of Jaipur. Those of Kishanpur were tenants either of the *mahant* (supervisor) of the Kishan temple there or of one of the two *jagirdars* (vassals of the Maharaja) who had property there. The Minas also traditionally had been highway robbers and housebreakers, and, in the 1960s, they were still considered to be thieves, even though they had become tenant farmers in the late 1920s. The Jats allowed themselves to be "protected" by the Minas, giving them bags of grain after each harvest in payment for their "protection". If robberies occurred, the police came from the nearby town to arrest the Mina men; it was assumed that any theft must have been done by a Mina. They assumed that one of them was guilty, and they would keep all of them locked up until the name of the robber of the current incident was forthcoming.

Representing south India, in Tamilnadu, the Vellala and Nadar cultivators of Kanyakumari had similarly employed mercenaries (the Thevars or Maravars) to protect them. And like the Jats, the Vellalas and Nadars paid Thevars bags of grain for protecting them. Neither the Jats and Minas nor the Vellalas and Nadars were preoccupied with patrilineal feuds, as were the Rajputs of Khalapur. This was probably because the groups of central and south India did not consider themselves to be primarily warriors and because they had little land and only small local patrilineal groups, as compared to the large holdings and patrilineages of the Rajputs in the very large village of Khalapur.

North India: Khalapur, Western Uttar Pradesh

Let us look first at the western Uttar Pradesh village. Khalapur is mostly Hindu; only about 10 percent of its huge population (in 1984, about 9,700) is Muslim. Like many other Hindus in north India, the 20-odd caste-communities there practice village exogamy, as well as *jati* endogamy (marriage within the network of village chapters of a particular caste), patrilocality (the rule that after marriage a couple lives in the husband's village), and patrilineality (recognition of patrilines to which new sons must be continually added). In Khalapur, as in other villages in Uttar Pradesh (Gould 1960, 1961; Marriott 1959; Rowe 1960) and Delhi State (Lewis 1958), there is a tendency to maximize marriage ties by arranging marriages for daughters in different villages, and by not giving more than one daughter in each generation to a particular village. As Karve and other observers of north Indian Hindu life have noted, because of these ways of maximizing marriage ties, the bride almost always enters her husband's household as a stranger; she cannot expect to find there a father's sister, a sister, or a cousin-sister (Karve 1965: 125) (see note 2). Therefore, she not only does not know her husband but also does not know any of his kinswomen.

Since brides, until recently, have been quite young, typically under the age of 16, this exile for a girl at such an early age was, and often still is, traumatic, often sung about in women's songs. The transition for a young bride is eased by the custom in Khalapur and elsewhere of having the first and most important wedding ceremonies when the girl has not yet reached puberty, while the second set of ceremonies takes place a year or more later, after the girl has reached puberty. While the girl may go with her groom and his all-male party to her husband's village after the first set of ceremonies, she stays only with his womenfolk in the women's part of the house, and she may not see her husband at all. She returns home to her parental home after only a few days and remains with them until the second set of ceremonies a year or more later. The physical marriage usually is not consummated until after the second set of ceremonies when the girl has come of age. The first ceremonies establish the relationship between the two sets of kin and makes the marriage binding. The second ceremonies commence the actual cohabitation for the couple themselves.

Of course, a bride's adjustment to all the women of her husband's household is her greatest challenge; typically she sees her husband only briefly at night during her first years of marriage. However, in these early years, her life is made easier by her long visits to her parental home. In the years of marriage just after the *chala* (second ceremonies), the girl, often pregnant or with her first child, is in her parental home and village as much of the year as she is with her mother-in-law in her father-in-law's village (*sasural*). As years go by and she has more children and becomes more mature herself, and as her parents die off and her brother's wife becomes head of her once parental home, a woman returns to her home village less frequently and may only return for her brother's children's weddings. It is quite common for married sisters to return to help during their brother's children's weddings.

It is often held in north India that the affection between a brother and sister is great. The role of the brother as a sister's protector begins early, and at the time of a wedding, a new bride may be accompanied to her husband's house by none of her relatives except her small brother, old enough to be able to function on his own (between the ages of 6 and 12), but not old enough to be a sexual threat to the women of the groom's house. The role of the brother in north India is as the one who should check on the welfare of his sister. This is particularly true at three festival times of the year: (1) Bhaiya Dooj, right after the festival of lights (Diwali) in October or November, (2) Rakshabandhan, in August, when a sister ties a bracelet on her brother's wrist, and he gives her a gift, and (3) Tij, also in August, when swings are strung from trees for women's enjoyment. On these three holidays, an adult brother should go with gifts to his married sister's marital village to see how she is faring. Often, he will escort her home at this time for a visit in her home village. His concern and gift-giving is not limited to his sister, but extends to her children. He, along with his father, should present jewelry to his sister's newborn child, and when each of her children marry, he must present special gifts in a special ceremony.

The culturally expected affection between a married sister and her brother is functional for the sister who is off among strangers. Women have often told me that they loved their brothers more than their husbands. It used to be quite common in Khalapur for women to have on their forearms above the wrist a tattoo showing a stick-figure boy and girl holding hands. If one asked, "Is that you and your husband?" the answer would be, "No, me and my brother. If I have that on my arm, I will have the same brother in my next life."

Facilitating this cultural expectation of love between brother and sister is the customary prohibition upon a daughter's inheriting a share in the joint-family land. Although daughters have a recent legal right to a share in inherited family land, Sharma's (1980: 39) statement, "A good sister does not claim the land which her brother might inherit," holds true still for rural north India. Sharma (1980: 57) suggests that maintaining a positive relationship with her brother in much more important and potentially beneficial to a married woman than would be land in her natal village that she would be dependent upon her brother, or some other male, to till for her. While landownership for women is common in Kanyakumari, as described below, it is rare in most parts of India.

In north India, a woman's brother is also, from her husband's point of view, a *sala* (wife's brother). The term *sala* has the connotation of "pimp" in English, and it is a curse word in Uttar Pradesh and Punjab. The brother who is supposed to be a woman's protector, in giving her into marriage, is causing her to be injured by the sexual activities that a marriage entails. This attitude towards the man giving a woman to a bridegroom is part of a wider honor-and-shame ideology, in which the honor of a family and of the men in that family are entwined with the virtue of its women. While honor requires that a sister be kept virginal and protected from predatory men, the brother who gives his sister in marriage has not only ceased to protect her but has delivered her up to be spoiled and harmed. The term *sala* connotes all of that (see Hershman 1981; Kolenda 1990).

In these parts of north India, far more than in south India, as will be seen below, a wedding is the establishment of an alliance between two distinctly different minimal patrilineages (*khandans*) always located in two different villages. There is an inequality between these two sets of men, with the bride's men being inferior to the groom's.

There is a ritual joking relationship between the inferior *sala* and the superior groom. During the wedding, there is much enactment, in both the ritual of etiquette and the ritual of joking, of the inequality between the two male wedding parties – the groom's men, who are guests, and the bride's men, who are the hosts (Kolenda 1990). Usually, by the end of the first set of wedding ceremonies, the *shadi*, the groom and the *sala* have become friendly, but the etiquette of subordination forbids the *sala* from taking hospitality or from tarrying when he goes to his married sister's marital home to take her back to her natal home. If he accepts so much as a glass of water, he should pay for it. He should go and fetch her and bring her back. He may stay longer for a wedding, funeral, or birth ceremony, but at such, he is a guest, and it is only during such formal occasions that he may stay overnight in his married sister's marital village. In Khalapur, a sister has cause for joy if her older brother marries, since the dowry given by the bride's people to the groom's at a brother's wedding may become the dowry given for this sister's wedding. Wedding gifts similarly may circulate from in-marrying wife to out-marrying sister.

However, one of the eternal triangles in north Indian kinship is that between a man, his wife, and his sister. The latter's jealousy is ritualized in a ceremony after the *shadi* when the groom and his party arrive home with the new bride, and the groom is greeted by his mother and the other women. His sister bars their way, and she does not let them enter the women's quarters until the bridegroom-brother gives his sister some jewelry or other valuable.[16]

Once a brother is married, and especially after their parents are dead, his married sister's visits to her natal village are partly by grace of his wife. Since a visiting married sister should be treated as a guest and not be asked to do arduous work while visiting, her presence increases the brother's wife's work. Additionally, it is customary for the married sister to take gifts, including food, back to her husband's house when she returns. Responsibility for the preparation of the food falls on the brother's wife. And money spent on gifts for married sisters take away from what might be spent on the brother's wife or upon his children. In other words, the loving relationship between brother and sister may be made ambivalent by the brother's wife's less-than-welcoming ways toward her husband's married sister. This is perhaps the process by which a woman's place of refuge, her parental home, becomes less and less available to her. By adapting herself to the ways of her mother-in-law and her husband's brothers' wives, and by bearing children, the married sister may feel less and less the need for such a refuge.

For the brother, there may be the problem of being fair not just to both wife and sister but to all his sisters. And once his daughters marry, he has gift-giving responsibilities to them that need to be coordinated with gift-giving responsibilities to his sisters (see Nuckolls, in his, ed., *Siblings in South Asia*, New York: Sulfad Press, 1993, Ch. 8). The brother's obligations increase again when he becomes mother's brother to his sister's children, an affectionate, present-giving uncle (*mama*). When Khalapur children run away from home, it is likely to be the mother's brother's village that is their destination.

In north India, the effect of the rules of village exogamy and patrilocality is that men of the same patrilineage continue to live together, and, indeed, a common Hindi term used for the local *jati*-chapter who live together is *biradari*, brotherhood. The relationship between brothers is one of authority between the eldest and the younger in anticipation of the joint family these men may later belong to, the continuation of the family they enjoyed together before any brother was married. The kinship terminology does not reflect this authority difference, there being a single term *bhai* for both older and younger brothers; *bhai* is also used for all male cousins of varying degree and for friends and even casual acquaintances of one's own generation, for all men except for one's wife's brothers or one's brother's wife's brothers (the *salas*) (Dumont 1966: 99; Vatuk 1969: 175). Since there is sharp segregation between the sexes in Khalapur, women being secluded in women's quarters, men having their own clubhouses, a man lives very largely in a world of brothers, fathers, grandfathers, uncles, sons, and nephews, the men of his minimal patrilineage. Sometimes adjectives supplement the term *bhai*, and "big brother" and "little brother" are used, and sometimes the eldest brother is called *bhai sahib* to indicate special respect for him.

In the middle- and lower-ranking castes in Khalapur, and in north India more generally, widows are allowed to take a second mate (Singh 1947). The preferred mate may be the dead husband's younger brother. So, a brother may inherit his dead brother's wife. In higher castes, like the Brahmans and Rajputs who proscribe remarriage for a widow, brothers may look after a dead brother's wife and children. And when a brother is away in the military and working far away, his brothers look after his wife and children.

The partitioning of the joint family in north India usually seems to involve bad feeling between the two or more families dividing a residence and/or land. After parents are dead, it is rare in Khalapur for married brothers to continue to share a single kitchen. Typically, the blame for the breakup of the two or more brothers' joint household is allotted to their wives. Villagers often observe that sisters-in-law cannot get along. Early in their relationship, they vie for the favor of their mother-in-law; later, they are likely to quarrel over children. The fact that it is increasingly difficult to manage cooking for a household, as there are more and more members, is overlooked in the public justification of the partition of the joint household. After the breakup, the brothers may continue to be somewhat soured on each other, but the sons of the two brothers are likely to be hostile. Cousin-brothers seem to bear grudges long after the division, even after their fathers' deaths.

This persisting hostility can be played out in the practice of the levirate among the untouchable Chuhra sweepers of Khalapur (Kolenda 1987b). Among them, the underlying assumption seems to be that a woman has come in marriage to the men of a family, to a father and his sons, although she is sexual partner only to one of them, her husband. If her husband dies, she should then mate with her husband's brother. She is not considered to be compromised in any way if she does so. However, the dead husband may not be survived by a brother, or his brother or brothers may already be married. Frequently, it is suggested that a widow "sit with" her husband's cousin-brother (his father's brother's son) – "sit with" because only the first marriage is a true marriage. Once a woman has mated outside the father-sons unit into which she married, her new husband has the right to sell her. And this is not an empty threat; several of the Chuhris of Khalapur were bought wives. A woman who was sold not only had no say in a transaction planned primarily to profit the seller, but she was totally cut off from all her relatives, although eventually she might be able to reestablish relations.[17] Therefore, only one of the 12 Chuhra widows who had this choice (out of the 24 Chuhra widows whose marital careers I traced) (Kolenda 1982: 212–19) chose this option. A Chuhra widow's fears with respect to her husband's patrilateral parallel-cousin were well-taken, given the often intense hostility between cousin-brothers (Kolenda 1987b).

Among Hindus of north India, once sisters are married, they see each other when both visit their home at the same time, as when both are working at their brother's child's wedding, cooking for guests and helping in other ways. Married sisters are not allowed to visit each other in their marriage-villages, although this is not the case everywhere in the north (see Sharma 1980). They cannot even attend the weddings of each other's children or attend each other's funeral. They can only meet on their natal, parental home ground where they were girls together.

The great importance of siblingship in north India is also indicated by the taking of fictive brothers and sisters in the ceremonialized ties of *dharam-bhais* and *dharam-bahans*, brothers or sisters by duty and affection. Usually these are women friends of different castes who exchange gifts and food in a little ceremony and pledge to continue their friendship indefinitely, marking it by a periodic exchange of gifts. The assumption that the relationship is for life suggests a similar attitude about the relationship between blood-related sisters or brothers.

Central India: Jats and Minas of Jaipur District, Rajasthan

In some parts of Rajasthan, and certainly among the Jats and Minas (important Rajasthani cultivating castes) living in Jaipur and Nagaur (Rosin 1978, 1987) districts, many marriages (almost two-thirds in the Jat-Mina villages of Maharajapur-Kishanpur) are in sibling-sets or collateral-sets (Kolenda 1978: 253; 1987a: 189--90). That is, sets of two or three brothers or cousin-brothers marry sets of two or three sisters or cousin-sisters – often in a wedding of two, three, or more couples at once. As in north India, there are two ceremonies, traditionally one before and one after the eldest bride has reached puberty. When sisters are married at the same time, the younger bride may be very young indeed, under the age of 10, since in Rajasthan brides are often under the age of 14 (Kolenda 1989: 87--91). The younger bride will usually not begin to reside with her husband and with her mother-in-law and elder sister (who is also her husband's brother's wife, her sister-in-law) until she has herself come of age, often several years after the *muklava*. In the story from central India, Kasturi, in being sent to her mother-in-law before the *muklava*, was an exception to the general rule.

Although the Jats, Minas, and other caste-communities in Rajasthan are patrilineal, patrilocal, and practice village exogamy, in this area a bride does not enter a household or community of strange women. Not only is there often a sister in the same household or nearby, but a father's married sister or cousin-sisters, or other women from her home village, may also have married into the same household, patrilineage, hamlet, or village. Therefore, a bride usually is not among total strangers. In the Jaipur village of Maharajapur-Kishanpur, almost three-quarters of daughters were married into villages in which there were other women married in from Maharajapur-Kishanpur (Kolenda 1978: 253: 1987a: 190).

Rajasthan is a premier place in India for joint-family living, and sibling- and collateral-set marriage seems to facilitate joint families by double-bonding them (Kolenda 1978, 1989). Not only are the component adult men brothers in relationship, but their wives are sisters to each other. The older sister who is also the sister-in-law may become the protector and guide to her younger sister/sister-in-law. Since girls may join their mother-in law at age 13 or 14, they may be quite untrained in household chores. The older sister may do the chores for her little sister and gradually train her in them.

Joint families among the villagers of Jaipur district endure beyond the death of the brothers' parents, and when breakup between the married brothers who have resided together takes place, there is not the bitterness that attends such breakup in Khalapur to the north. The brothers are more ready to see and say that breakup is necessary because, for instance, the elder brother now has too many children for the space they all share. And they do not blame their wives for the breakup. Since these peasants were until the late 1950s tenants of Jaipur royalty, clergy, or nobility, they could not build a new house without the landlord's permission, and there was no division of landownership to quarrel over. In Rajasthan, land is not the issue anyway, since there is plenty of land. What is needed is water, and until land reform, the wells were built by the landlords or with materials supplied by the landlord.

Joint families endure in this region because the irrigation system – driving bullocks down a ramp as they pull a leather pouch of water from the well – requires two men on the well. These men are usually father and son, or brothers (Kolenda 1978: 249; 1987a: 185) The irrigation system also requires a woman or older boy or two in the fields to guide the water into the patches of growing plants. Thus, while children are small, one wife stays at home and looks after the children while the other wife works in the fields guiding water, or else one tends the children and cooks while the other forages for fire wood and other forms of fuel.

A number of writers have observed that ecocultural factors influence the activity settings of siblings (Weisner 1989: 16) and of parents and children. Such factors include demographic ones, subsistence patterns, and the division of labor. The Rajasthani well team, based on the fraternal joint family, is an example of the interplay between the ecological adaptation made by these arid-zone farmers and their family structure.

The peasants themselves do not explain the purpose of sibling-set marriage as a way to bind the joint family so that it is an especially effective productive unit; they see it as a means of reducing costs of entertainment. If two wives have a single set of parents and siblings between them, there are half as many relatives to entertain at a wedding, birth or death feast. Whatever theoretical or practical explanations are offered, the Rajasthan family structure seems to promote family bonding. A sister can be expected to feel more affection for children who are not only her husband's nephews and nieces but also her own. If her sister/sister-in-law dies, she is more willing to nurse her dead sister's baby. That sisters/sisters-in-law do find their association agreeable is indicated by the number of instances in Maharajapur-Kishanpur of pairs of sisters who continue to live together as widows of brothers at a time when they no longer need to do so since each could presumably be supported by a married son.

This system of joint-family households seems to work far better than the system in Khalapur, in which sisters-in-laws are strangers to one another and hence rivals. The hierarchy among the women is clear when the younger sister-in-law is already used to being younger sister. The levirate here also seems to work well, women being more willing to join their dead husband's brother when he is married to her sister. The kind of child-rearing pattern found so widely in India, in which an older sister has been the caretaker of her younger brothers and sisters, may well mean that the younger sister/sister-in-law sees her older sister/sister-in-law as a caring mother-figure.

A survey of ethnographies from Rajasthan clearly indicates that middle- and lower-ranking castes and tribals generally give bride-price rather than dowry, or else little in the way of gifts is exchanged at marriage (Kolenda 1989). A Rajasthani married woman's brother, thus, is not obliged to bring his married sister gifts and to visit her in her marital village three times a year – at the Hindu holidays of Bhaiya Dooj, Tij, and Holi -- as in Khalapur. The obligation of a brother to look after married sisters and, later, his daughters is not so strong in this area, where a man or his elders must pay a bride-price to get a bride. While in Maharajapur-Kishanpur, the giving of bride-price was not publicized, instances of it were known to us. The few young men who had completed 8th or 10th grade were in demand as bridegrooms and hence probably would not be required to give bride-price by hopeful fathers of brides, but, as yet, the giving of dowry among the Jats and Minas of Maharajapur-Kishanpur has not begun.

The contrast between north India (with the strong obligation on the part of a man toward his married sisters and the giving of dowry and then gifts throughout her marriage) and Rajasthan (with its weaker brother-sister bonds and bride-price) indicates the necessity of the culturally prescribed brotherly feeling to get the tasks of dowry giving and gift-giving done. A brother in north India protects his married sisters in a solidly material way. In contrast, in the Jaipur region of Rajasthan, a new bride may receive the reassurance she needs in her husband's village from the other women from her home village, so her brother's periodic visits to check on his married sister are less necessary. The bond between brother and sister is not so strong as in north India, but the bond between sisters who are also brothers' wives or who reside in the same marital hamlet or village may be very strong.

So, in the Jaipur region of Rajasthan, brothers are brothers all their lives because they reside in the same household, hamlet, or village, and so are sisters if they live in the same place of marriage.

South India: Vellalas, Nadars, Thevars and Acaris of Kanyakumari District, Tamilnadu

In south India, the preferred marriage is between the children of brother and sister, which anthropologists call cross-cousin marriage. This means that for a couple in a cross-cousin marriage, a mother's brother is a father-in-law as well as an uncle, and a father's sister is a mother-in-law as well as an aunt. Presumably, the advantage for a bride in south India is that upon marriage, she does not enter a household of strangers, since either her mother-in-law is her father's sister or her father-in-law is her mother's brother. In either case, there should be affection already existing between them.

In the hamlets studied in Kanyakumari district, Tamilnadu, live Vellalas, Thevars, Nadars, and Acaris. While the latter community's traditional occupations of carpenter and goldsmith are still followed, the first three are now almost entirely cultivators, although the Thevars were mercenary soldiers until the mid-nineteenth century. Even in the 1960s, as mentioned above, they served as guards for Vellalas and other cultivators. Among these caste-communities, perhaps one-third or more of marriages take place within the hamlet; unlike north and central Indian Hindus, there is no rule of village or hamlet exogamy. While all these caste-communities trace descent patrilineally and recognize patrilineal descent groups, the men of a single patriline do not necessarily continue to stay together in adulthood. Ready movement of a couple and their children from one hamlet to another is common, couples with children going wherever the means of livelihood seems most promising. Since women can own property, it is sometimes advantageous for a couple to live near her land, especially if the husband owns little or no land.

One of the difficulties of this system of cross-cousin marriage is the matching of the marital pair from among the possible cousins who could marry. I think of one young man who showed me the photographs of seven possible cross-cousins he could marry, since he could marry a daughter of either one of his mother's brothers or of one of his father's sisters. Since he actually married only one of these, his parents were left with somewhat strained relations with all their older brothers and sisters whose daughters were not chosen.

Another difficulty is the increasing preference for arranging a marriage with an outsider when one has a son or daughter who is well educated and likely to have a prestigeful and/or lucrative occupation. So, a man with a son who is an engineer may not want that son to marry his sister's or wife's brother's daughter who has never gone to school. In such situations, a man may end up with angry sisters, his wife with angry brothers.

In Kanyakumari, it is not unusual for more than one sibling of one family to marry more than one sibling in another. As in Jaipur district, a pair of brothers may marry a pair of sisters. Unlike the places sampled above in north and central India, however, there is no prohibition on exchange marriage in Kanyakumari, so a brother and sister may marry a sister and brother. This is another way for blood and marital ties to reinforce each other. Since intravillage marriage is allowed and since women are not kept in the kind of strict *purdah* of northern and central India, a mother can go and visit her married daughter in south India, whereas in northern and central India, she may not -- marriage is not likely to be so traumatic.

There is a saying in the Kanyakumari area about divers for pearls, that a diver prefers to dive with his sister's husband or his wife's brother, rather than with his brother. The sentiment here is that brothers have no reason to want the other to survive, since one's death would give the other a larger share of their jointly inherited landed property. But a man does not want his sister's husband to die, lest he have to care for her, nor does he want his wife's brother to die, since the wife's brother is the source of support to his sister and, hence, to her husband, as well.

This picture of affection between brothers-in-law must be modified by the fact that in Kanyakumari, non-Brahman caste women may own land, garden, houseplot, and houses. At marriage, a wealthy father tries to give his daughter a banana garden, a coconut garden, a paddy field, and a house. This is called *stridanam*, women's property. It is not dowry (called in Hindi *dahej*) in the north Indian sense, because it is hers, not transferred to her husband's elders, as in northern India. A Kanyakumari husband, however, may not rest content with his wife's economic resources, land, or garden often tilled by her brother or father, and may pressure her to sign the property over to him or to sell the property for some purpose of the husband's. So women are often caught between the demands of a husband, who wants to use her property for his ends, and her brothers and father, who want her to retain it. A woman who manages to retain property may give it to her daughter when her daughter marries her brother's son – a way in which property given by a brother returns to him.

Actually, there is a great difference in the brother-in-law relationship between south India and north India. In south India, the bride's brother is not seen as the one who is giving the bride in marriage, and sexual activity for a woman is not thought of as injury.

Her destiny lies in the kinship rule that children of brother and sister should marry. A girl's proper bridegrooms (*murai mappillais*) are well known to her and to her relatives from her childhood. Her mother's brother has a right to ask for her as a bride for his son when she is feted in her coming-of-age ceremony. She should marry her mother's brother's son, this ritual says. If the mother's brother does not ask for her – possibly he doesn't have a son of the right age, or possibly all his sons are already married – he should, nevertheless, attend her puberty rite. When the girl does marry, she and her husband must honor her mother's brother by getting his blessing before the wedding ritual. In south India, the kindred "give" the girl in marriage; in north India, her brother gives her in marriage, and in doing so makes himself the most cursed of men, a *sala* (Differences in the conception of sexuality in north and south India are noted in Kolenda 1984, and a discussion of the *sala* appears in Kolenda 1990).

There is a contrast between the role of the sister at her brother's wedding in north and south India. Whereas the groom's sisters resist their brother's return with the bride in north India, in the south, it is the groom's eldest sister who actually ties the *tali*, the wedding pendant, around the bride's neck, and it is the groom's older sisters who should pay the costs of making their brother's bride's *tali*. While in north India the sister must be bribed with a gift to let her brother and his bride come in, in south India the sister actually performs the symbolic act that makes the bride her brother's wife.

The patrilineage is a much less unified social unit in south India than in north India. In Kanyakumari, there is not the patrilineal feuding that there is in Khalapur. North India is a "hypergamous milieu" (Dumont, 1966: 94, 110): a married woman's brother is inferior to her husband and his patrilineal brothers, and in his married sister's village he should be only a brief guest. In south India, brothers-in-law – a man and his wife's brother or a man and his sister's husband – are much more likely to live near each other, and there are no barriers to asking a brother-in-law to help with a chore. In central India, as represented by the Jaipur villages described above, although brothers-in-law always live in different villages, their relationship is not unequal, and a brother-in-law may be called on for help, as when a family is digging or repairing a well, and more hands than usual are needed.

As for sisters, there is a good deal of sororal polygyny and practice of the sororate among the middle and lower castes of Kanyakumari.

Woman marry at later ages in Kanyakumari than in north and central India, usually not until 17 or 18, and have their own separate households almost immediately upon marriage. Married sisters may well live in the same hamlet due to intrahamlet marriage, but with freer movement for women married sisters can visit each other by taking a bus from one hamlet to another.

Comparisons and Conclusions

The emphases in sibling relationships as I have been impressed with them center round marriage. So, in north India, the brother is above all the trustee of his married sister; he should keep in touch with her to see that she is being treated well; he should, if he can, bring her gifts and bring her home for visits. In central India, the double-bonding of the joint family through sets of brothers marrying sets of sisters is especially noteworthy. While in south India, the marriage or non-marriage of the children of brother and sister may result in lifelong closeness between the families of a brother and a sister, or in lifelong enmity. Table 11.3 summarizes these comparisons.

Table 11.3

Summary of Similarities and Differences between Three Different Regions of India[a] with Respect to Sibling Relationships

	North	*Central*	*South*
Parents arrange marriages	+	+	+
Jati endogamy	+	+	+
Patrilineality	+	+	+
Patrilocality	+	+	P or M[b]
Wife visits home frequently	—	+	+
Maximize marriage ties	+	—	—
Bride knows other women	—	+	+
Bride knows husband before marriage	—	—	If cous: +
Two wedding ceremonies	+	+	—
Wedding traumatic for bride	+	—	—
Joint household	+	+	—
Characteristic form of marriage	With stranger	Brother set with sister set	With cross-cousin
Dowry/bride-price/stridanam	Dowry	Bride-price	Stridanam

[a]Represented by Khalapur village, western Uttar Pradesh, Maharajapur-Kishanpur Villages, Jaipur District, Rajasthan, and Kanyakumari district Hindu villages.
[b]P, patrilocal; M, matrilocal.

To comment on Indian sibling relations in comparison to those reported for siblings studied in the United States, there are some similarities and differences. The American psychologist Victor Circirelli (1982: 276) states that some studies have found, "the relationship between brothers was the poorest when they were at different occupational levels." The occupational difference between the north Indian high school teacher and his farmer-brothers seems to illustrate this generalization.

An issue of sibling rivalry in American families is commonly school achievement. Ross and Milgram (1982: 236) comment on the extreme pressure on the child in a family who is "to become the first who has ever obtained a college degree." As more children in India go to school, more such rivalry is likely to emerge. In the north Indian joint family, such pressure was already being exerted on the schoolmaster's eldest son.

While arguments between siblings are likely to arise in the United States at the time of the settling of their parents' estate, will, or property, such strain is highly institutionalized in the Indian joint family owning land together. It is the wise Indian father or eldest brother who tries to get the division of family land agreed upon by the various joint owners long in advance of its eldest member's death.

Cicirelli (1982: 281), in summarizing findings from American studies of siblings, cites a study by Troll (1971) which concludes that "sisters play a major role in preserving family relationships and providing emotional support to their siblings" during their entire lifespan. The possibility of sisters holding families together in India varies with the kinship system. As has been mentioned, virtually all Hindu women marry, so we must ask the question: Do married sisters hold families together? What we mean by family and what we mean by holding together will also vary regionally. So, in the Jaipur area of Rajasthan where frequently sets of Jat and Mina sisters marry sets of brothers, sisters tend to hold together the fraternal joint family in which both women are married to the brothers. But, in both this area and in western Uttar Pradesh where Khalapur is located, women are invariably married into villages other than their natal villages, a requirement of village exogamy, so sisters are not in a position to hold together their sibling-set composed of their brothers and sisters. The brothers should be in the natal village, and some of the sisters will be in other villages. All members of a sibling-set are likely to be together after marriage only when all gather for a parent's funeral or for a marriage of a brother's child in the home village.

Among the Kanyakumari caste-communities, in south India, where there is a preference for cross-cousin marriage, the brother and sister whose children wed are likely to feel especially strongly bound together, but the frequent rivalry and jealousy connected with marriage arrangements also tend to undermine affection among adult siblings. Certainly, the way in which adult married sisters solidify sibling relations differs greatly in India from such processes in the United States.

Cicirelli (1982: 268) has suggested, again primarily with American families in mind, that "the relationship between siblings is highly egalitarian, with the siblings of approximately equal power in the relationship. Each sibling feels free to say or do as he or she pleases in the relationship." Relationships among siblings in India are not supposed to be equal. In south Indian languages, one cannot speak of just a sister or just a brother, but must speak of older sister and younger sister, older brother and younger brother. An older brother has authority over younger brothers and sisters. After adulthood, brothers are superior to sisters. These, at least, are norms that are general to India. Seldom does a person feel as much respect, however, for an older sibling as for a parent or grandparent.

These materials from India illustrate Thomas Weisner's point that in India, Africa, Polynesia, and other parts of the world obligations bind siblings throughout their lives (1982: 322).

Studies in the United States and elsewhere indicate that over 80 percent of American adults have living siblings and almost all maintain contact with siblings (Cicirelli 1982: 269, 271–72). A perusal of the results of American studies suggests that the sibling relationships among Americans are more voluntary and of less economic importance than those we have looked at in India, where brothers own land together and may farm together (illustrated by Khalapur, western Uttar Pradesh and Maharajapur-Kishanpur, Rajasthan), where married sisters may be part of a combined agricultural enterprise (Rajasthan, central India), where a brother gives his daughter land as part of her dowry when she marries his sister's son, and where this land, in turn, becomes his daughter's daughter's dowry when that girl marries his son's son (her mother's brother's son) so that the land returns to the original patriline (Kanyakumari district, south India). Land given out as dowry in one generation may return in the following generation, if the right combination of cross-cousin marriages occur.

Ritual obligations are similarly more institutionalized in rural India: a brother must bring gifts to his sister after her marriage and when any of her children marry, a sister must tie the marriage pendant for her brother's wife in the south Indian wedding, and so on. Again American customs are more voluntary: a brother may be a groomsman and a sister may be a bridesmaid in an American wedding, adult siblings may or may not exchange Christmas gifts and so on. This difference of obligatory siblingship versus voluntary siblingship is a general contrast between a culture structured largely on kinship relationships and one that is less structured on kinship relations.

Notes

1. Fieldwork in Khalapur was done October 1954 to June 1956 and February to June 1984; fieldwork in the Jaipur villages was done September 1966--January 1967, May 1967, June-July 1969, and for a week or two in 1974 and 1978; fieldwork in the Kanyakumari hamlets was done in February-April 1967, July-August 1969, January-March 1974, May-August 1978, and May-August 1980. After the writing of this essay, I visited both Khalapur and Kanyakumari a number of times in the 1980's and 1990's. My fieldwork has been supported by the following institutions: Cornell University, Ford Foundation, American Institute of Indian Studies, National Science Foundation, Smithsonian Institution, and University of Houston. I owe thanks to them, as well as to many research assistants, most importantly Usha Bhagat Dave, Indira Sapru, Prema Nathaniel, Prabha Roy Joshua, Saroja Chelliah Srinivasan, Mary Fainsod Katzenstein, and Wilda Campbell.
2. In a study of marriage among 14 different caste-communities in the village of Khalapur, J.M. Mahar found that about two-thirds of women had the experience of marrying into a village in which she found no previously known kinswoman (Mahar 1966: 156).

3. The term *purdah* comes from the Hindi word *parda*, or curtain. It refers most noticeably to the requirement that women veil themselves, particularly their heads and faces, in the presence of strange men and in the presence of older men related through the husband; it is required also that they keep silent in such circumstances.

In Khalapur, *purdah* involves strict segregation of the sexes among all caste-communities, both high and low, and both Hindu and Muslim (about 10 percent of the population in the village of Khalapur is Muslim). A married couple is separated, with the wife living in a women's quarters and the husband in a men's clubhouse or cattleyard. A woman is required to leave her natal village upon marriage and live in her husband's village, in a compound of rooms built around a courtyard, with no windows looking outside and only a single doorway (locked at night), with her husband's mother, his brothers' wives, his sisters, and possibly more distant female relatives of the husband. The men, who share a men's clubhouse or cattleshed, always at some distance from the women's quarters, are father and sons, sometimes a father's brother or brothers and sons, and possibly more distant male relatives. Males over the age of six enter the women's quarters mainly for two purposes – to eat and to have sexual relations. A mother, sister, or daughter is more likely to bring a man his food than is his wife. Sexual relations are carried out surreptitiously, when a man slips into his wife's room in the middle of the night. Husband and wife never share a bed for the whole night; a woman often sleeps with her small children A companionable relationship between husband and wife is not a cultural ideal in north India and the architectural arrangements do not encourage companionship between them.

In the Jaipur villages, the women of all castes also cover their heads and faces from strangers and older male relatives of the husband, but there are not separate women's quarters and men's quarters. Two brothers, their wives, and their children are likely to share a household, with the men sleeping at night in an alcove at the locked entrance to the courtyard, and married women and their small children sleeping in rooms around the inside of the courtyard. Thus, the house is built like a small fortress, with the men as guards. Separation between the sexes is maintained in the fields where both men and women work, women working together or with children, the men at a distance but keeping an eye on the women. Whenever my research assistant and I would go up to a cluster of women working in the fields of the Jaipur villages and start to talk to them, their menfolk would immediately come over and take over the conversation, expecting the women to remain silent.

In the south Indian hamlets of Kanyakumari, there is no requirement that women veil themselves. Households are usually nuclear in composition, husband, wife, and children inhabiting a small, clearly separate house. While the women and children are expected to remain quiet while the husband talks to strangers, there is much more conversation between the sexes and across the generations within the Kanyakumari household than in north or central India.

An excellent treatment of *purdah* in South Asia is Papanek and Minault (1982).

4. Only large villages in India have high schools, so children from villages without high schools may reside with relatives who live in villages that do have them. This was the case with these two students.
5. Adult men were excluded during the day from the inner courtyard, where each of the three wives had her own cooking area and spent most of her time. Around three sides of the inner courtyard were the women's private rooms for sleeping and storage of food supplies, clothing, and other belongings. The fourth side was the entranceway from the outer courtyard, a much larger open area where the old mother of the three married sons often sat with elderly women friends sunning herself in winter, where clothes were dried, and where men sat on cots to take their food brought to them by one of the children. Individual husbands slipped into their wives' rooms through the inner courtyard at night, something that was never openly spoken about.
6. Carstairs (1957), Wiser (1978), Sharma (1980), and Bennett (1983) have written about rivalrous relations among brothers. Carstairs suggests that the rivalry is related to the perception on the part of one or all sons that their father prefers one son, usually the eldest, over the others, or else to the quarrels over partitioning the jointly owned land. Wiser portrays a rivalry between two brothers over decades.
7. The term "dowry", as used in India, refers both to personal and household goods that a bride takes with her to her new home, what might be covered by the term "trousseau", as well as valuables and money handed over to the groom's father or elder to be spent as he sees fit. The dowry in the second sense was given in premodern times by royal communities and some high castes, and it is given increasingly nowadays when the bridegroom is educated and is

considered to have good future prospects. Equal exchange of gifts and/or the giving of bride-price was and is usual among middle and lower Hindu castes (see Sharma 1980: 137–43; Kolenda 1967, 1989). Nuckolls states that in the Andhra communities (numbering over 50,000 people) where he worked, "there was only one wedding in four years." He continues:

> Most people seemed to think they were too expensive. Marriages were commemorated simply and unceremoniously by a payment of fifteen rupees to the headman. More important seemed to be the earlier rituals which commemorated the alliance when the marriage partners were still children. In the first ritual, a sister and brother confirm the future marriages of their children when the sister takes her brother's newly born daughter and bathes her with turmeric water on her lap.... In the second ritual, the brother takes the umbilical cord of his sister's newly born son and puts it in his house, under the pot where his family keeps its "cold rice gruel" (the staple food of this area). These rituals confirm that the cross-cousin marriage of the siblings' two children will take place. Villagers easily dismissed the importance of formal weddings, but agreed that early promissory rituals were absolutely indispensable (Nuckolls, personal communication, June 15, 1989).

The two Andhra customs that Nuckolls describes can be seen as parallel to the two marriage rites in north India and central India, one before puberty and one after; the infant rites by the aunt and uncle seem to be roughly equivalent to the first wedding rite in north and central India, the payment to the headman the rough equivalent to the second rite. One could argue just as well that the first Andhra rite is equivalent to the engagement ceremony in north India. The lack of ritualization of cross-cousin marriages in Sri Lanka was noted by Yalman (1967). In Kanyakumari, in south India, the puberty rite for the girl after her first menstruation seems to replace the first rite, the wedding itself is the second rite (see Kolenda 1984). In the village in Karimnagar district, Andhra Pradesh, studied by Philip and Carol Bousley, there were infant and child weddings, roughly equivalent to the north and central Indian *shadi*, with cohabitation not taking place until after the girl had reached puberty (Bousley 1969).

There are places and communities in South Asia in which weddings are not celebrated or only minimally celebrated. Yalman (1967) suggested for Sri Lanka that wealthy families tried to make advantageous marriages with non-relatives and to celebrate these lavishly, while marriages between cross-cousins, especially among the poor, were not ritualized at all. I have attended lavish weddings between cross-cousins in Kanyakumari, and even poor families extended themselves to celebrate weddings, whether between cross-cousins or between an unrelated bride and groom.

8. Sharma (1980) gives an excellent account of the arrangement of marriages in rural Punjab and Himachal Pradesh, where negotiations tend to be in the hands of the older women.
9. Sharma, talking about villages in the northern Punjab and eastern Himachal Pradesh, puts it this way:

> The most honorable form of marriage is that where there is no element of prior sexual attraction between the partners. There should also be the appearance of maximum trust between the two families, and hence the minimum need actually to subject the boy or girl to any kind of "looking over" (although this almost always does take place in practice, however discreetly disguised as a casual social visit) (Sharma 1980: 40).

10. Spinsterhood is common in a few communities such as the Parsis, some Christian groups, and the Nambudiri Brahmans (of Kerala) among whom, until the twentieth century, only eldest sons could marry, so many Nambudiri women were left without husbands.
11. The term "mated again" is purposely used in this passage, because even middle- and lower-caste people generally accept the Hindu idea that a woman should only be married once to a single husband. Dumont (1970) has referred to the remarriages among middle- or lower-caste people as secondary marriages. The people themselves have special terms for these secondary marriages, distinctly different from the term used for the first and only true marriage (see Kolenda 1982).
12. Sharma (1980: 155–66, 176) presents nine cases of divorce in northwest India initiated by women. She makes the point that where bride-price is given for women, men are unlikely to desert or evict their wives, since it is costly for them to try to get another, but where there is dowry they may allow wives to leave (Sharma 1980: 163–64).
13. B.D. Miller (1981) has explored various explanations for the disproportionate sex ratio in India. In Kolenda and Haddon (1987) the correlation between the prevalence of joint families and a preference for sons is noted, based on statistical data in the Census of India for 1961. Ajit Kumar Sinha (1974) explains son-preference as due to a Hindu requirement for salvation. He writes: "It is believed by the Hindus that a man may attain salvation or *moksha* only when a son is born to him." He adds that a wife is seen as an instrument for the procreation of a son.

14. In her description of a Maharashtrian Brahman landed family over 60 years, Irawati Karve (1963) found it common for several brothers to do no work: "The idleness of certain males in the joint family might be owing to the deliberate policy of the head who, owing to this, gets a sort of moral right to divide the property in an unequal way" (Karve 1963: 260–61).
15. Various researchers have given attention to siblings as child caretakers. See, for example, Weisner (1982) and Watson-Gegeo and Gegeo (1989).
16. Hershman (1981: 218) reports that in Punjab a sister does not allow her brother to circumambulate the wedding fire until he has paid her an amount of money.
17. Sale of a woman must be distinguished from bride-price. With bride-price, a sum of money is given by the groom's people to the bride's, but a ceremonial wedding and feasting, along with other gift-giving, takes place. The bride-price is just one of several prestations exchanged. With sale of a woman, there is no celebration, and the woman is suspected of having behaved immorally. In some cases, she has become pregnant outside of wedlock, but in other cases, a male relative has found it to his advantage to sell the woman.

References

Bennett, L. (1983), *Dangerous Wives and Sacred Sisters*, New York: Columbia University Press.

Bousley, P. (1969), *A Study in Caste Ranking*, Master's Thesis in Sociology and Anthropology, University of Houston.

Carstairs, G.M. (1957), *The Twice-Born*, London: Hogarth Press.

Cicirelli, V.G. (1982), Sibling Influence throughout the Lifespan, *In* M.E. Lamb and B. Sutton-Smith (Eds.), *Sibling Relationships: Their Nature and Significance across the Lifespan* (pp. 267--84), Hillsdale, NJ: Erlbaum.

Dumont, L. (1966), 'Marriage in India: The Present State of the Question. Part Three: North India in Relation to South India,' *Contributions to Indian Sociology* 7: 99–102.

Fabian, J. (1983), *Time and the Other*, New York: Columbia University Press.

Gould, H. (1960), 'The Micro-demography of Marriages in a North Indian Area,' *Southwestern Journal of Anthropology* 16: 476–91.

— (1961), 'Further Note on Village Exogamy in North India,' *Southwestern Journal of Anthropology* 17: 297–300.

Hershman, P. (1981), *Punjabi Kinship and Marriage*, Delhi: Hindustan Publishing.

Karve, I. (1965), *Kinship Organization in India*, Bombay: Asia.

— (1963), A Family through Six Generations, *In* L.K. Bala Ratnam (Ed.), *Anthropology on the March* (pp. 241–62), Madras: The Book Center.

Kolenda, P. (1967), Regional Differences in Indian Family Structure, *In* R. Crane (Ed.), *Regions and Regionalism in South Asian Studies* (pp. 147–225), Monograph 5. Durham, NC: Duke University Program in Comparative Studies of Southern Asia.

— (1978), Sibling-set Marriage, Collateral-set Marriage and Deflected Alliance among Annana Jats of Jaipur District, Rajasthan. *In* S. Vatuk (Ed.), *American Studies in Indian Anthropology* (pp. 242–77), New Delhi: American Institute of Indian Studies.

— (1982), Widowhood among 'Untouchable' Chuhras. *In* A. Ostor, L. Fruzzetti and S. Barnett (Eds.), *Concepts of Person: Kinship, Caste, and Marriage in India* (pp. 172–220), Cambridge: Harvard University Press.

— (1984), 'Woman as Tribute, Woman as Flower: Images of 'Woman' in North and South India,' *American Ethnologist* II: 98–117.

— (1987a), *Regional Differences in Family Structure in India*, Jaipur: Rawat.

— (1987b), Living the Levirate: The Mating of an Untouchable Chuhra Widow. *In* P. Hockings (Ed.), *Dimensions of Social Life: Essays in Honor of David G. Mandelbaum* (pp. 45–67), Berlin: Mouton de Gruyter.

— (1989), The Joint-Family Household in Rural Rajasthan: Ecological, Cultural and Demographic Conditions for Its Occurrence. *In* J.N. Gray and D.J. Mearns (Eds.), *Society from the Inside Out: Anthropological Perspectives on the South Asian Household* (pp. 55–106), New Delhi: Sage.

— (1990), 'Untouchable' Chuhras through their Humor: 'Equalizing' Marital Kin through Teasing, Pretence and Farce. *In* O. Lynch (Ed.), *Divine Passions* (pp. 116–53), Berkeley: University of California Press.

Kolenda, P. and Haddon, L. (1987), Marked Regional Differences in Family Structure in India. *In* P. Kolenda, *Regional Differences in Family Structure in India* (pp. 214–88), Jaipur: Rawat.

Lewis, O. (1958), *Village Life in Northern India*, Urbana: University of Illinois Press.

Mahar, J.M. (1966), *Marriage Networks in the Northern Gangetic Plain*, Ph.D. Dissertation in Anthropology, Cornell University.

Marriott, M. (1959), Social Structure and Change in a U.P. Village. *In* M.N. Srinivas (Ed.), *India's Villages* (pp. 96--109), Calcutta: Development Department of West Bengal.

Miller, B.D. (1981), *The Endangered Sex*, Ithaca: Cornell University Press.

Minturn, L. and Hitchcock, J.T. (1966), *The Rajputs of Khalapur*, New York: John Wiley.

Papanek, H. and Minault, G. (Eds.) (1982), *Separate Worlds: Studies of Purdah in South Asia*, Columbia, MO: South Asia Books.

Rosin, T. (1978), Peasant Adaptation as Process in Land Reform: A Case Study. *In* S. Vatuk (Ed.), *American Studies in the Anthropology of India* (pp. 460–95), Delhi: American Institute of Indian Studies.

Rosin, T. (1987), *Set Marriage and the Continuity of the Joint Family in Rajasthan*, Paper presented at Rajasthan Studies Conference, Jaipur.

Ross, H.G. and Milgram, J.I. (1982), Important Variables in Adult Sibling Relationships. *In* M.E. Lamb and B. Sutton-Smith (Eds.), *Sibling Relationships: Their Nature and Significance across the Lifespan* (pp. 225--249), Hillsdale, NJ: Erlbaum.

Rowe, W.L. (1960), 'The Marriage Network and Structural Change in a North Indian Community,' *Southwestern Journal of Anthropology* 16: 299--311.

Sharma, U. (1980), *Women, Work, and Property in North-West India*, London: Tavistock Publications.

Troll, L.E. (1971), 'The Family of Later Life: A Decade Review,' *Journal of Marriage and the Family* 33: 263--90.

van der Veer, K.W. (1971), *I Give Thee My Daughter: A Study of Marriage and Hierarchy Among the Anavil Brahmans of South Gujarat*, Assen: van Gorcum.

Vatuk, S. (1969), 'A Structural Analysis of Hindi Kinship Terminology,' *Contributions to Indian Sociology* (n.s.) 3: 94–115.

Watson-Gegeo, K. and Gegeo, D.W. (1989), The Role of Sibling Interaction in Child Socialization. *In* P.G. Zukow (Ed.), *Sibling Interactions across Cultures* (pp. 54–76), New York: Springer-Verlag.

Weisner, T. (1982), Sibling Interdependence and Child Caretaking: A Cross-Cultural View. In M.E. Lamb and B. Sutton-Smith (Eds.),

Sibling Relationships: Their Nature and Significance across the Lifespan (pp. 305–27). Hillsdale, NJ: Erlbaum.

---- (1989). Comparing Sibling Relationships Across Cultures. *In* P.G. Zuckow (Ed.), Sibling Interaction across Cultures: Theoretical and Methodological Issues (pp. 11–25), New York: Springer-Verlag.

Wiser C.V. (1978), *Four Families of Karimpur*. Foreign and Comparative Studies/South Asian Series S. Syracuse, N.Y.: Maxwell School of Citizenship and Public Affairs, Syracuse University.

Yalman, N. (1967), *Under the Bo Tree*, Berkeley: University of California Press.

Part V

Caste in India

12

Caste in India Since Independence

In the first part of this paper, I shall deal with issues related to the established definition of caste – the rural local systems of interdependence between castes, endogamy, fission of castes, caste as related to occupation, and purity and population. In the second part, I shall be concerned with the emergence of segmentary opposition of blocs of castes within the political arena, and the unification of caste with similar rank, identity, and economic interests.

I

Issues Related to the Established Definition of Caste

A caste is a large-scale kinship group into which a member is born and within which he or she must marry. Caste as a system operates in the rural areas of India. It is a set of interdependent specialist caste groups centering around those caste groups that control land, produce food and cash crops. These large-scale kinship-specialist groups are ranked locally along a dimension of purity-impurity, with the priests who serve the gods being the most pure while specialists who do manual "dirty work" are impure. The groups with high or purer standings avoid physical or commensal contact with those of low or impure standings, on penalty of becoming impure themselves, because there is contagion from impure to pure.

While this purity-impurity concept is often considered to be "religious" (Dumont 1970), the ranking of castes is sometimes associated with the Hindu religious concepts of *samsara* (reincarnation) and *karma* (quality of actions), the idea being that actions during one's past lives determine present life conditions including one's caste. Thus, the highest ranking castes, the Brahmans (learned in religious teachings and the purest priests for household and temple worship), the Kshatriyas (the ruling or dominant castes, often considered to be equivalent to the ancient Vedic king), and the Vaishyas (the tradesmen and merchants) may believe that their high caste status is due to good action in past lives. At the same time, the servant and artisan castes – considered to be equivalent, if their work is "clean", to the ancient Vedic Shudras, and, if their work is "dirty", to the untouchables – may cringe from admitting that their lowly lot in life is due to inferior action in past lives.

The plight of the lowest ranked caste groups, the so-called untouchables, became a political issue during the movement for independence for India during the 1930s and 1940s. Under the Communal Award of 1932, the British granted to these lower castes, referred to as "depressed classes", separate electorates for choosing representatives to central and provincial legislative bodies. Mahatma Gandhi, the spiritual as well as political leader of the independence movement, protested against the award as an attempt by the British to divide the Indian population. Negotiations with the spokesman for the untouchable community, Dr. Bhimrao Ramji Ambedkar, resulted in the Poona Pact, assuring untouchables "an early removal of all social disabilities" (Aggarwal and Ashraf 1976:28). Thereafter, Gandhi made the abolition of untouchability and the amelioration of some of the conditions under which these disadvantaged Indians lived prominent parts of his program.

After independence, Ambedkar headed the assembly formulating the Constitution of India (1950). It abolishes untouchability and prohibits discrimination in "access to shops, public restaurants, hotels and places of entertainment", or in the "use of wells, tanks, bathing *ghats*, roads, and places of public resort", or in admission to educational institutions. Article 23 forbids forced labor, commonly part of the dominant caste rule or feudal regime. Article 25 allows for free entrance to Hindu religious institutions. In addition to these protections in the Constitution, in 1955, the parliament passed the Untouchability (Offences) Act. About one-seventh of the seats in state legislatures and in parliament are reserved for untouchable representatives; however, incumbents are not selected by an exclusively untouchable electorate, though only candidates from untouchable castes may stand as candidates from such constituencies.

If we ask whether the traditional caste system is breaking down in India and whether those who suffered most severely under it are now better off than they were when independence was achieved, we imply ten questions. These are:

1. Is the system of interdependent occupational groups, the local rural caste system, declining?
2. Are traditional occupations associated with castes dying out?
3. Are low castes upwardly mobile?
4. Is caste endogamy, the rule that members of a caste must marry within the caste, broken? Or are intercaste marriages occurring with frequency?
5. Are the boundaries of castes being maintained by members' changing memberships?
6. Are the avoidances between high "pure" castes and lower "impure" castes lessening? Is there less belief in the Hindu pollution concept?
7. Is caste segmentation as strongly endorsed by Hinduism as it might have been before independence?
8. Are the lower castes, dependent upon higher caste superiors, better treated than before independence? Is exploitation of low castes by high castes continuing, decreasing, or increasing?
9. What is the relationship between caste and politics?
10. Is there evidence that a class system is emerging in India?

The first seven questions will be addressed in the first section of the paper, the last three in the second. One caveat which must be made is that almost all generalizations advanced in this paper are undoubtedly overgeneralizations. On many of these questions, we have, at best, spotty information, and far from all-India, both rural and urban, coverage. What is presented here is a sketch of the condition of caste in India; some parts of that sketch are based on rather few hints and clues.

Background Thinking

Before taking up each of these questions in turn, let me briefly trace transformations in the way caste has been thought about over the first thirty-five years of independent India. World War II was a watershed in Indian studies. There were a few notable anthropologists and sociologists who did research in India both before and after World

War II. These include G.S. Ghurye, D.N. Majumdar, Nirmal Kumar Bose, David Mandelbaum, and S.C. Dube. Except for Ghurye, even these anthropologists did most of their work after World War II. The new breed of anthropologists who descended on rural India after World War II were wedded to the concept of face-to-face interaction with their subjects over a lengthy period of time. They were social anthropologists doing micro-sociology. Two early volumes of these village studies were *Village India*, edited by McKim Marriott (1955), and *India's Villages*, edited by M.N. Srinivas (1955).

During the 1950s and early 1960s there were two favorite concepts among social anthropologists: the dominant caste, an adaptation from African studies (Evans-Pritchard's concept of "dominant clan") and the *jajmani* system, taken from a book written by a missionary, William Wiser, published in Lucknow in 1936. The two ideas fit together nicely. A village was dominated by a dominant caste, which controlled land, usually had high caste ranking, and sizeable numbers. Above all, its members controlled land. Other castes served this dominant caste and each other. The potter made pots for the dominant caste and other caste people; the shoemaker made shoes, the launderer washed clothes, and so on. Virtually, all Indianist social anthropologists in the 1960s wrote a piece on the *jajmani* system (Gould 1958; Beidelman 1959; Rowe 1968; Elder 1970; Kolenda 1963). At that time, E.R. Leach could write an essay (1960) emphasizing the essence of the caste system as interdependence and cooperation; granted it was *hierarchical* interdependence and cooperation, but it was, nevertheless, interdependence and cooperation. Above all, the caste system was *not* a competitive system, Leach held, and if it were to become competitive, it would no longer be a caste system.

From independence until the mid-1960s social anthropologists were concerned with the village; theirs was an inward-looking view in which the village was treated as a single system. The caste system of India should be understood as a local system operating only at the local level. There were, however, some demurrers. Oscar Lewis (1955) spoke of "rural cosmopolitanism", involving the marriage links between the caste chapters of different villages. Morris Opler (1958) wrote a paper on the "extensions" of the village. Louis Dumont could suggest that marriage alliances integrated castes and this implied regional social integration within a caste. But, the weight of the work done focused upon the village as a system. There was concern in the 1950s and 1960s about hierarchy -- were castes ranked? If so, how?

With how much consensus? And with how much diversity in opinion? (see Marriott 1960, 1968; Mahar 1958; Marriott, Freed, and Nicholas 1967). Generally speaking, rather high consistency was found in the ranking of the local castes within a village on the basis of ritual transactions involving food, water, and touch.

Within anthropology in the 1970s there was something of a debate between two leading theorists of caste – Gerald Berreman (1981) and Louis Dumont (1970). The key difference between them was that Berreman was concerned about how people at the bottom of the caste system feel. His verdict: deprived – deprived in every way. Dumont, on the other hand, did not dwell on the feelings of those deprived ones, but saw that the system included everyone; each, according to his or her contribution, was rewarded. And, the Hindu ideology held that the Brahman priest deserved more reward than did the day laborer in the field. Dumont saw the beauty of the caste system in its inclusiveness. Whereas in the West an ethnic group might be excluded, in the Hindu system it was ranked. In the local caste system there was an essential community consciousness; everyone was included. Wiser (1958) saw it as a kind of *noblesse oblige*. The *Dharmasastras* or the *Bhagavad Gita* might phrase it as one's *dharma*, one's religiously-given duty to care for others even though their lowly conditions could be believed to be the result of their past actions in previous lives (*karma*). While Dumont and Wiser might suggest that the local system provided security for all castes' members, needless to say that Berreman, Beidelman (1959) and other anthropologists saw the system as exploitative, particularly of the low castes and untouchables.

We have noted that the caste system is primarily a rural social-economic-political system – one with many speciality castes centered around the landholding castes, often called dominant castes. This is a system quite suited to a subsistence economy producing relatively little surplus, or producing only sufficient surplus to support a modestly organized government. There are six important changes that have taken place since independence and had a substantial impact on the rural local caste systems of India: (i) the establishment of universal adult franchise; (ii) the legal outlawing of untouchability and the enactment of legislation protecting ex-untouchables, sometimes referred to as a policy of compensatory discrimination; (iii) the great increase in the productivity of grains, especially wheat; (iv) the explosion in educational facilities and the multiplication in the numbers of people attending schools and colleges; (v) the increase in white-collar jobs – such as, teachers, government officials, people in business, stenographers – an expansion of the modern sector of Indian society; and (vi) the tremendous expansion of the infrastructure of Indian society – buses, roads, railways, airways, electrification, hydraulic power, and so on.

However, whatever security the caste system offers is a casualty of the Indian version of rural modernization (such as, cash cropping and scientific-technological agriculture). The caste system, in the sense of the *jajmani* system, so dwelled upon by anthropologists of the 1960s, is probably now increasingly broken. The *noblesse oblige* of the old dominant caste, which needed lower caste people to serve it and support it and which had no use for the surplus food produced on their lands but to have it consumed by numerous dependents, has been replaced very frequently by a profit motive. Or, as some villagers put it, by "greed". Twice-born man has become economic man. Dumont (1970) has seen the root motive of capitalism in Mandeville's argument that individual greed leads to the prosperity of all. The question is: Does capitalistic self-interest lead to the welfare of all when the balance between numbers of people and resources available is so disproportionate? What happens to the dependents who do not have the land or wherewithal to participate in the new cash crop cultivation?

The Declining *Jajmani* System

Social anthropologists have called the cooperative system of exchange of goods and services among members of different castes in a locality the *jajmani* system, since the individual served is commonly called a *jajman*. The term comes out of a religious context meaning one who pays to have a ritual performed. Since the client served is given a name from the religious context, it is sometimes said that these services should not be seen as economic transactions so much as ritual ones, and it has been suggested that the function of the *jajmani* system is not so much the exchange of specialities as the process whereby the priests have been kept from having to defile themselves by doing impure work; the lower castes "absorb" impurity for them (Hocart 1950; Gould 1958).

There is a good deal of evidence from rural village studies indicating that the *jajmani* system is in decline as a result of the introduction of manufactured goods, which purchasers prefer to the hand-made local craft goods -- mill-made cloth and shoes, manufactured brass vessels instead of pottery ones, and so on. Population increase has also meant that landholdings have fragmented; many are so small that landholders cannot afford the traditional panoply of servant and artisan dependents. And cash cropping has meant that producers prefer to sell their produce, rather than share it with their dependents. Either unemployment or population pressure or both have led to some specialists leaving the rural areas. Their lot partly depends on whether their particular skill is in demand. In rural areas, carpenters probably continue to be well-employed, while water-carriers have largely been displayed by courtyard pumps, or else people can no longer afford to employ them. Where irrigation or other improvements have fostered a more prosperous agriculture in some places, employment of some *jajmani* specialists may actually have increased.

Artisans have had varied fates. Some -- goldsmiths, launderers, sweepers -- have moved in considerable numbers to the city or provincial towns, where their services are more likely to be in a demand. Some anthropologists report that villages are becoming depopulated as their contingents of artisan and servant castes leave for towns (Karve and Ranadive 1965: 12; Mencher 1972: 51). It is the very group *not* included in the *jajmani* system -- the agrestic servants -- however, that are becoming the rural proletariat, as tractors and other labor-saving machines displace manual laborers. Oddly enough, except for Jan Breman's study in southern Gujarat (1974), Edward Harper's study of the Malnad of Karnataka (1961), and a collation of references made to systems of agrarian relations by Beidelman (1959), we know relatively little about agrestic servants in the "traditional" caste system. They also were involved in more or less permanent dependency relations with the landed castes. This is a matter begging for further study.

'Modern' Occupations for Villagers

While some villagers journey to urban areas, others are turning to new occupations while remaining in their villages. They may work in sugar mills or other kinds of factories. They may be absorbed in the building of the infrastructure -- working on railways, road construction, and in the telephone and power companies. With the increase in bus transportation, some have started tea shops, grain mills, and auto repair shops at bus stands (Elder 1970; Miller 1976; Kolenda 1978: 53).

There are some success stories of middle-caste cultivators who have taken up modern urban occupations and done well. An instructive and illustrative example is provided by Raymond Owens and Ashis Nandy who have described the Mahisyas (a Bengali cultivating caste), members of which have co-opted engineering machine businesses in Howrah, near Calcutta. Owens found that Mahisya *jati* members hired each other as apprentices, workers, and partners. As a cultivating caste, Owens suggests, Mahisyas more readily entered a business requiring manual labor (Owens 1973; Owens and Nandy 1977). The authors conclude their study by describing the transformation in Mahisya community life that has come about through their economic success:

> The entire social, political and cultural structure of the community has been radically changed from that which existed in the first two decades of the twentieth century. At that time all aspects of community life were dominated by Brahmins. One might say that Brahmin status was summated at the top of society. From the inception of semi-representative government in 1885 until 1915 the local Ward Commissioner and the head of the local Brahmin caste panchayat were one and the same person. Brahmins owned most of the land in the community, which had been the case since the seventeenth century. The Brahmin caste panchayat regulated all social and religious activities. Even religious celebrations (*pujas*) paid for by members of other caste groups had to be held in the name of a Brahmin, and at feasts carried out in conjunction with such *puja*s people were fed in order of the status of their castes. Brahmins were fed first on an elevated platform; then the other twice-born castes were served on a slightly less elevated platform; next the rest of the fourteen or so castes from which a Brahmin would take water were fed in the courtyard; and finally, outside the gates, those few castes from which a Brahmin would not take water, which included the Mahisyas, were fed. By the time of our research, the Mahisyas had

become the area's dominant economic group, owning most of the land in the community and 71 percent of all the engineering factories. All local candidates for Ward Commissioner were Mahisyas in 1967, and a Mahisya factory owner was elected that year to parliament. Through their new economic power Mahisyas also dominated most of the community's voluntary associations, which had multiplied many times over during the economic rise of the Mahisyas. Feasting by caste rank could no longer be observed in the community; and at *pujas* sponsored by voluntary groups if any favouritism was shown in presenting *prasad* (food blessed by the deity) it was to offer it first to club officers or the largest financial contributors to the *puja*, who were mostly Mahisyas. When we asked respondents to rank castes in the community, Mahisyas were found to have moved from a position at the bottom of society to a rank of fourth or fifth from the top, a position congruous with that of the Bengali merchant castes (Owens and Nandy 1977: 196--97).

Another study of a low caste, which traced the rise of many of its members out of their low condition, is Hardgrave's study of the Nadars of Tamilnadu, whose traditional caste work was climbing the palmyra palm tree to tap its sap in order to make sugar and toddy. Unlike the Mahisyas, the Nadar's social ascent involved the acquisition of education, which they first obtained through attending schools run by European (usually English) missionaries (Hardgrave 1969).

New Dominant Castes

The rural economy began to change in the mid-1950s with the beginnings of the Community Development Programme, which later spread throughout India. There then began, in 1965, an increase in the production of food grains (especially wheat, and to a lesser extent, rice) as a result of the introduction of high-yielding seeds, chemical fertilizers, and the pumping of water through electricity – the green revolution. What has happened since the green revolution began is an accelerated transformation of the rural social structure. The hero in India is no longer the Brahman or the Kshatriya, but rather the kulak or the yeoman -- sometimes could the 'bullock capitalist' (Rudolph and Rudolph 1980) -- the surplus food-producing farmer.

Before, when there was not such a large urban population, almost all food was consumed within the village, and the dominant high-caste landholders disdained manual labor and tended to depend upon low-caste tenants, bondsmen, and day laborers to do the actual production of crops in the fields. The situation is different now. Many of the old dominant castes have become urban or modern in their occupations (Bhatt 1978: 305). Jats have tended to displace Rajputs in Rajasthan; non-Brahmans have displaced Brahmans in Tamilnadu (Béteille 1962; Sivertsen 1963; Gough 1960; Mencher 1972). There has been a rise to dominance of the middle and lower cultivating castes (Bhatt 1978: 306). More will be said about the political implication of these new powers later in this paper.

Intercaste Marriage

Are the boundaries of castes being maintained? Are all marriages endogamous within caste connubia? In a nation that is largely rural in residence, with almost 70 percent illiteracy, most marriages are arranged by elders who almost invariably arrange them between individuals of the same caste connubium, the bride and groom having little to say about the mate chosen. Educated males seem increasingly to have a choice in selecting their brides, and educated brides seem to have at least "veto" power with respect to a bridegroom, but higher education for men, and especially for women, is still rare.

Occasionally, marriages are arranged between persons of contiguously-ranked connubia within the same caste complex. So, for example, Tamil Brahmans of the "Iyer" surname are divided into several traditionally endogamous groups, or *jatis*. Nowadays, however, some marriages are taking place between brides and grooms of different Iyer *jatis* -- thus a Vadama may marry a Vatima. Furthermore, people of the same caste from widely distant places are now more likely to marry than has been true in the past. So, an educated bride of the Nattati Nadar caste, whose connubium is located in the Kanyakumari area of southern Tamilnadu, may marry an educated groom from a different Nattati Nadar connubium to the north, around the town of Usalampatti, in central Tamilnadu.

As Andre Béteille (1965: 63) has said, "the relevant question in examining intermarriage is the amount of structural distance spanned in each particular instance." There is probably still rather little intercaste marriage between members of castes or connubia that are structurally distant from one another in terms of local or regional caste ranking, despite the encouragements of some reformist organizations like the Tamilnadu political party, the All-India Anna Dravidian Progressive Federation (All-India Anna Dravida Munnetra Kazhagam, AIADMK). There appears to be some widening of connubia, however, especially because of the shortage of educated bridegrooms. Enough of such marriages, of course, might result in a fusion of adjacent castes, though I am unaware of any documented case of the fusion of two connubia by intermarriage as yet.[1]

Ritual Pollution

The custom of avoidance of lower caste persons' pollution by high caste persons seems to be inapplicable in modern occupational contexts -- factories, business firms, universities and colleges, and government offices. In urban areas generally, where many transactions are impersonal, there is seemingly no concern about the caste identities of the transactors. Milton Singer (1972) has spoken of the "ritual neutrality" of this modern sector of the economy. Both he and Shils (1960) have talked about the compartmentalization in the lives of modern men who follow the rules of purity in the home, but ignore them outside the home. Modern western Brahmans usually continue to be vegetarians but they have greatly relaxed other pollution restrictions.

While such extra-domestic "ritual neutrality" would seem to mark progress in the dissipation of Hindu pollution practices, Joshi (1980: 221) points out that untouchables themselves see these private rules of commensality as an index of profound prejudice against untouchables.

In his study of a Harijan elite in the state of Bihar, Sachchidananda (1976: 42) found that these highly educated Harijans, who were legislators, social workers, and public servants (almost all worked for the government), were still discriminated against, more so in rural areas than in cities. Such discrimination took place particularly with respect to eating with guests of other castes at ceremonies. He further points out, however, that none of these highly educated Harijans had been tortured, suggesting "that climbing up the socio-economic ladder through the acquisition of achieved traits is evoking less resistance even from those who are the champions of the status quo" (ibid: 45).

That discrimination in workplaces in the modern sector does occur is attested to by the infrequent case in which an untouchable has the courage and wherewithal to complain. A recent one is that taken by a transport dispatcher at Delhi's Palam Airport, who protested against being addressed by a pilot "as a *chuda* (sweeper) – a reflection on a Jatav's cobbler caste". He is reported to have said in Hindi, "Which s.....gave you sweepers employment? I can have you sacked in no time." It took the transport dispatcher five years and Rs 3,00,000 (over $4,000) in legal fees and other expenses before a judge fined the pilot Rs 250 (about $30) and one month's imprisonment (*India Today*, 1982: 61).

Marc Galanter, a scholar of Indian law, has found that very few cases have ever been brought under the Untouchability (Offences) Act, and of those, few have been decided in favor of the untouchables. Of the 476 taken by the *Harijan Sevak Sangh* (The Service Society for the Children of God – the Untouchables) between 1961 and 1966, only 90 cases (19 percent) resulted in convictions; and the median fine in such cases was Rs 10 (a little over $1). Galanter concluded: "It is, simply, very hard to win one of these cases" (1972: 278). He believed that legislation protecting untouchables could be improved and that other kinds of initiatives could be taken by the government to seek out "patterns of discrimination". However, he noted, "there is no interest in the intellectual community in the mechanics of programs for attacking untouchability, no debate about alternatives, no assessment of prospects" (ibid: 276).

Caste and Hinduism

With respect to the relationship between caste and religion, let us consider two touchstones. The first is a statement made by M.N. Srinivas (1962: 76) when he raised a question which he refused to answer: " 'What will happen to Hinduism when caste disappears?' It raises such far-reaching issues that I cannot hope to deal with it satisfactorily here." The other is a statement made by Louis Dumont, who said that the caste system would go only if there was a turning against the Brahmans. There is a certain inconsistency in the causal relationships of the predictive propositions made by these two scholars: one, that if caste goes, religion will go; the other, that if religion, at least the apical position of the priest, goes, the caste system will go. The two are similar in their emphasis upon the close relationship between the caste system and the Hindu religion.

Actually, many centers of Hindu religious learning have been in decline since independence. Some writers (Embree 1974; Bharati 1974) see a new, modern kind of Hinduism as being characteristic of western-educated urban men, one based on the teachings of the nineteenth century reformers like Vivekananda and Ramakrishna, who did not emphasize the importance of caste as related to Hinduism, but rather emphasized mystic union and social service as the best modes of religiosity. Ainslie Embree suggests that vocal public opinion does not support the caste-Hinduism connection when he reports:

> A rather bizarre illustration of the ambiguities of secularism was provided in 1969 when the Sankaracharya of Puri, one of the most prestigious figures of Hindu orthodoxy, began making public speeches in which he stated that ritual pollution and the idea of untouchability were scripturally sanctioned. Not surprinsingly, he was able to quote chapter and verse. The fierce public outcry that followed indicated how sensitive a nerve he had touched. The leaders of the Jana Sangh were content to say that they disagreed with the Acharya's interpretation of the *Shastras*, but many spokesmen for the modernising groups, true to the neo-Hindu approach, began earnest exercises in textual criticism to show that the scriptures, far from sanctioning untouchability, preached equality and brotherhood (Embree 1974: 116).

Yet, while secular standards serve as measures for public policy, Hinduism thrives. India is on the move – on buses, trains, airplanes, jets – and one of the most popular destinations is an important Hindu temple or religious center. The motorized pilgrimage is packing the roads of Tamilnadu. The impurity of these temples (open in the 1930s since the Gandhian and Ambedkar advocacy of temple-entry to low castes and untouchables, and open, now, even to non-Hindu foreigners), does not seem to be troubling these pilgrims. Hinduism without purity-impurity and even without Brahmans and possibly without caste seems to be a real possibility. This statement must be qualified, however, by the fixity of the revulsion that seems to be felt by vast numbers of Hindus toward their untouchable fellow citizens.

II
New Kinds of Caste Organizations

Caste and Political Party Fissioning

Both the strength and the weakness of caste organization in India have been its tendency to fragmentation. J.H. Hutton (1961: 50) spoke of the "fissiparous tendencies of castes". These tendencies seem to characterize political parties in India – witness the evolution of the DK to the DMK to the AIADMK. One can trace similar fissions in the Congress, the communists, the Lok Dal, and so on. Weiner (1982: 342) points out that there are now "three Congress parties, two Communist parties, two Janata parties, two Lok Dals, two Dravida parties, two Muslim Leagues, and countless small state parties". The same tendency to fission in the farmers' organizations may greatly deplete their strength, and, of course, their threat to the rural proletariat. This characteristic of the Indian caste system -- to solve differences by separation rather than by compromise – seems to be reflected in the new social structures brought about with a democratic electoral system – the political parties.

Caste Blocs

As stated in the foregoing, there is no evidence, despite occasional intercaste marriages, that fusion of contiguously ranked connubia is taking place, although caste blocs have emerged as political combinations directed toward winning elections and achieving other benefits. One of the prime examples of such a bloc (in this instance a bloc of non-Brahman, non-untouchable castes), is the DMK party of the southern state of Tamilnadu. By 1952, the DMK had become a political power in south India; the DMK candidates won most of the Tamil local elections in 1967, and since then the party or its fission party, the AIADMK, has usually held the chief ministership and the plurality of seats in the Tamilnadu state legislature. Through the medium of cinema especially, their Tamil chauvinism and their anti-Brahmanism were powerfully conveyed. Discrimination against

Brahmans applying for seats in universities and schools and for employment became well established, and south Indian Brahmans in greater numbers than ever poured into the cities – Madras, Bombay, Delhi, and Calcutta. By the mid-1960s there was only one other important political party that seemed to have a strong caste basis: the Republican Party representing mostly the untouchable Mahars of Maharashtra (Zelliot 1970; Lynch 1969).

More recently, the combination of democracy and modern agriculture has brought about a farmers' movement. Regional organizations are already well established – the Shramik Sanghatana led by Sharad Joshi in Maharashtra, the Ramizhaga Vivasayigal Sangam led by C. Narayanaswamy Naidu in Tamilnadu, and the Lok Dal in the northern plains. And, many demonstrations in several parts of the countryside have taken place – such as the Malprabha agitation in Karnataka in 1980 – expressing demands for higher prices for cereals and oilseeds, a higher subsidy on diesel fuel, and complaining about the high price of electrical power. The unification of the various regional farmers' organizations into an all-India movement might seem to be the next logical step, but given the Indian penchant for fissioning of social units, unification is unlikely to be brought about.

Does the rise of the farmers' movement signal the development of a competitively integrated caste system? Both the Tamil and the Maharashtrian movements see the urban food consumers as their enemy. To quote C. Narayanaswamy Naidu of the Tamil agriculturalists:

> When we were said to have attained freedom in 1947, there was an acute shortage of food grains in our country. Five year plans were made. We continued to import food grains from Thailand, America, etc. One day they declared that we should attain self-sufficiently in food grains and to this end all our farmers should intensify their cultivation. They implored us to "grow more food".
>
> They laid the trap for farmers: loans at 4.5 percent, fertilisers, hybrid variety seeds, insecticides, farm implements, etc. The farmers were lured into the trap. All in the name of making the country prosperous. But what happened? It might have worked well in the case of a few. There has been an unequal exchange between countryside and towns. We didn't get fair prices for our produce.

Middlemen, traders, manufacturers profited from the green revolutions.

The reverse stock of 20 million tons of food grains in 1980 was the blood and sweat of farmers, Naidu argued (Rajadurai 1980: 2170).

Sharad Joshi of the Maharashtrian organizations poses Bharat, or the countryside, against India, the city. The poverty of the countryside, he agrees with Naidu, is a result of low prices for food produced by the farmers. The opposition between the countryside and city is a form of rivalry not predicted by sociologists. And, so far, these movements have taken the tack of trying to convince agriculturalists at all levels that their interests are all the same – although both Joshi's and Naidu's organizations have been suspected of representing the interests of the larger landowners (those with 10--15 acres). Neither organization includes the landless low castesmen. And, the question is: After complaining about the exploitation of the city food middlemen, will these organizations complain about the economic drag of non-productive supernumeraries? Will they turn on the landless low castes in an organized way?

In his Gandhi Memorial Lecture (1977), M.N. Srinivas saw dual cultures as having emerged in independent India. One is a modern urban middle class culture, the other the culture of the rural poor. Srinivas saw the better-off landowners as "eager to become part of the urban middle class". "Educated members of the dominant castes prefer to socialize with their urban peers and ignore, as far as possible, their links with their rural relatives." He further says, "the overall hierarchy that then emerges includes the urban middle class and the rural poor with the richer section of the dominant landowning castes occupying a crucial position between the two" (ibid: 3).

Srinivas' suggestion that the dominant landowning castes have the crucial position seems true, but these farmers' movements suggest that larger numbers are still oriented toward rural life, at least to the rural agricultural economy. It may well be that the old entrenched dominants like the Rajputs and Brahmans are urban-oriented, while the new ascendant dominants like the Jats and Vellalas are rural-oriented. The present political party situation seems to reflect this kind of caste bloc picture: the wealthiest of the landed and the landless supporting and being supported by the Congress (I), the farmers supporting one or another or a few different opposition parties.

Violence Against Untouchables

There is ample evidence to suggest that economic tensions in India are being vented in violence. Communal incidents have begun to occur after thirty years of peaceful coexistence between Hindus, Muslims, Christians, Sikhs, and Jains. In the late 1970s, Hindu-Muslim riots re-emerged. In the spring of 1982 Christian-Hindu riots occurred in the district of Kanyakumari in Tamilnadu, one of the most literate districts in India. In October 1982, in Delhi, Sikhs sought to attack the convening national parliament itself. Magazines and newspapers have been regularly reporting "bride-burnings" as a bridegroom's family, trying to extort dowry money from a bride's family, drives a bride to suicide, or, through a contrived accident, kills her. Atrocities against members of the scheduled castes (SCs) are a part of this pattern of blood-letting, as stories of atrocities against rural untouchable agricultural laborers appeared in the late 1970s.

Actually, highly educated Harijans do not function as leaders of their deprived castefellows. While Sachchidananda (1976) says that there is a great gulf between these educated people and the other members of their caste, and quotes some who claim that there has been no untouchable leader of Ambedkar's stature produced since independence, he also reports stories narrated by his survey respondents about serious threats to their lives when they have tried to help their weak castefellows in villages (ibid: 134). Sachchidananda speaks of "years of exploitation and failure of the present government machinery to fully protect the Harijans from the onslaughts of the upper castes struggling hard to cling to their diminishing power which keeps the Harijans in a state of inertia" (ibid: 135).

Harijans continue to be the most disadvantaged group within the Indian population: 90 percent are in the rural areas; 95 percent are involved in agriculture as compared to 67 percent of the total population (ibid: 162). Very few live in cities; yet only about 28 percent own or rent land, the others being largely landless laborers. Very few have been able to obtain land under land reform programs. Since independence, the untouchables probably have lost ground economically in the countryside (Joshi 1980: 203–5). The patterns of systematic deprivation of a social group that has been the presumed beneficiary of a policy of protective discrimination reflects the severe difficulty of inducing upward mobility at the lowest rungs of the Indian social hierarchy as it may portend a center of future social and political conflict.

Caste and Class

Modernization creates differentiation within a caste. The process has been identified in varied locales. Andre Béteille describes it as follows:

> Each caste tends to become increasingly heterogeneous in terms of occupation, income, education and rural-urban residence. The process of horizontal extension is accompanied by vertical differentiation. Internal differentiation has proceeded much further among some castes than among others. Those most open to westernisation are most differentiated – the Brahmins, Kayasthas, Nairs. Peasant castes remain more homogeneous and less changed (1977: 63–64).

A single caste extending over a region usually includes within it segments that still operate within the traditional caste systems, and others that are modernized. Hardgrave's study of the Nadars of Tamilnadu examines such diverse structures within the same caste. Not only do segments within a *jati* differ in degree of modernization, but the segments, families, and lineages within a *jati* may have members in both traditional caste relations and in modern occupations (Kolenda 1978: 149).

A number of social scientists have suggested that new identities may gradually outweigh caste identity: school ties, professional ties, possibly region, neighborhood, and cultural ties (Kolenda 1970: 20--23; Barnett 1977). Differences in income, occupation and style of life are contained within the same caste, and except among some urban elite, the caste social unit is too strong to allow a solidification of social classes across caste boundaries, though the inducements for action in the political sphere may be stronger than the constraints of ritual purity and social autonomy.

Conclusion

This analysis and review is intended to portray in broad outline what might be happening to caste in India. Whenever we as scholars talk about this topic, we grossly overgeneralize – we take a village study from here, a political demonstration from there, or take a handful of each and suggest that that is what is happening all over India. Obviously, that is far from satisfactory; but until we have more complete and better coverage by social scientists, that will be about as good as we can do. Available evidence suggests the following propositions:

1. The inclusive local system that provided for everyone in the village, at least minimally, seems to be broken.
2. To a considerable extent artisans and some servants are still supported and needed; but many have had to seek new kinds of employment.
3. Landless agrestic servants are increasingly supernumerary and suffer increasing deprivation. The fundamental question is: Are they also viewed as expendable? Can they be absorbed in either the rural or urban economy elsewhere?
4. Castes as connubia, as large endogamous kinship groups, are very much intact. There is little intercaste marriage. There is some very slight trend toward fusion of connubia within a caste complex.
5. Pollution seems to be increasingly "the custom of my grandmother" except for a deep-set feeling against the untouchable.
6. There are important indications that blocs of higher and lower castes are forming within the political arena.

References

Aggarwal, Partap C. and Mohammed Siddiq Ashraf (1976), *Equality Through Privilege*, New Delhi: Shri Ram Centre for Industrial Relations and Human Resources.

Barnett, Steve (1977), 'Identity Choice and Caste Ideology in Contemporary South India,' in K. David (ed.), *The New Wind: Changing Identities in South Asia*, The Hague: Mouton.

Beidelman, T.O. (1959), *A Comparative Analysis of the Jajmani System*. Monography of the Association for Asian Studies VII. Locust Valley, New York: J.J. Augustin.

Béteille, Andre (1962), *Caste, Class and Power*, Berkeley: University of California Press.

--- (1965), 'Caste and Social Status,' Seminar 70. Reprinted in Romesh Thapar (ed.), *Tribe, Caste and Religion in India*, Delhi: Macmillan.

--- (1977), 'Caste and Social Status,' in Romesh Thapar (ed.), *Tribe, Caste and Religion in India*, Delhi: Macmillan.

Berreman, Gerald D. (1981), *Caste and Other Inequities*, Delhi: Manohar.

Bharati, Agehananda (1974), 'The Language of Modern Hinduism: Cognitive Models and Ethnoscientific Analysis,' in Robert J. Miller (ed.), *Religious Ferment in Asia*, Lawrence, Kansas: University Press of Kansas.

Bhatt, Anil (1978), 'Dominant Caste and Political Process,' in M.N. Srinivas, S. Seshaiah, and V.S. Parthasarathy (eds.), *Dimensions of Social Change in India*, New Delhi: Indian Council of Social Science Research.

Bhattacharyya, Jnanabrata (1979), 'Inequality and Radical Land Reform: Some Notes from West Bengal,' *Asian Survey*, 19:718–27.

Brass, Paul R. (1981), 'Congress, the Lok Dal, and the Middle-Peasant Castes: An Analysis of the 1977 and 1980 Parliamentary Elections in Uttar Pradesh,' *Pacific Affairs*, 54:5–41.

Breman, Jan (1974), *Patronage and Exploitation*, Berkeley: University of California Press.

Dumont, Louis (1970), *Homo Hierarchicus*, Chicago: University of Chicago Press.

Dushkin, Lelah (1972), 'Scheduled Caste Politics,' in J. Michael Mahar (ed.), *The Untouchables of Contemporary India*, Tucson: University of Arizona Press.

Elder, Joseph W. (1970), 'Rajpur: Change in the Jajmani System of an Uttar Pradesh Village,' in K. Ishwaran (ed.), *Change and Continuity in India's Villages*, New York: Columbia University Press.

Embree, Ainslie T. (1974), 'The Social Role of Religion in Contemporary India,' in Robert J. Miller (ed.), *Religious Ferment in Asia*. Lawrence, Kansas: University Press of Kansas.

Galanter, Marc (1972), 'The Abolition of Disabilities – Untouchability and the Law,' in J. Michael Mahar (ed.), *The Untouchables in Contemporary India*, Tucson: University of Arizona Press.

Gough, E. Kathleen (1960); 'Caste in a Tanjore Village,' in E.R. Leach (ed.), *Aspect of Caste in South India, Ceylon, and North-West Pakistan*, Cambridge: Cambridge University Press.

Gould, Harold A. (1958), 'The Hindu Jajmani System: A Case of Economic Particularism,' *Southwestern Journal of Anthropology*, 14:428–37.

Hardgrave, Robert L., Jr. (1965), *The Dravidian Movement*, Bombay: Popular Prakashan.

— (1969), *The Nadars of Tamilnad*, Berkeley and Los Angeles: University of California Press.

Harper, E.B. (1961), 'Moneylending in the Village Economy of Malnad,' *Economic and Political Weekly*, 13:169–77.

Hocart, A.M. (1950), *Caste*, London: Methuen.

Hutton, J.H. (1961), *Caste in India* (fourth edition), Oxford: Oxford University Press.

India Today, 1982, 'Caste Abuse,' 15 September: 61.

Isaacs, Harold R. (1965), *India's Ex-Untouchables*, Bombay: Asia Publishing House.

Joshi, Barbara R. (1980), 'Ex-Untouchables: Problems, Progress, and Policies in Indian Social Change,' *Pacific Affairs*, 53:193–222.

— (1982), 'Whose Law, Whose Order: "Untouchables," Social Violence, and the State in India,' *Asian Survey*, 22:676–87.

Kannan, C.T. (1963), *Intercaste and Intercommunity Marriages in India*, Bombay: Allied.

Karve, Irawati and J.S. Ranadive (1965), *The Social Dynamics of a Growing Town and Its Surrounding Area*, Poona: Deccan College Research Institute.

Kolenda, Pauline (1963), 'Toward a Model of the Hindu Jajmani System,' *Human Organisation*, 22:11–31.

---- (1978), *Caste in Contemporary India: Beyond Organic Solidarity*, Menlo Park, CA: Benjamin/Cummings.

Kothari, Rajni (1970), *Caste in Indian Politics*, New Delhi: Orient Longman.

Leach, E.R. (1960), 'Introduction: What Should We Mean by Caste?' in E.R. Leach (ed.), *Aspects of Caste in South India, Ceylon, and North-West Pakistan*, Cambridge: Cambridge University Press.

Lewis, Oscar (1955), 'Peasant Culture in India and Mexico: A Comparative Analysis,' in McKim Marriott (ed.), *Village India*, Chicago: University of Chicago Press.

Lynch, Owen (1969), *The Politics of Untouchability*, New York: Columbia University Press.

Mahar, Pauline (1958), 'Multiple Scaling Technique for Caste Ranking,' *Man in India*, 39:127–47.

Marriott, McKim (1955), *Village India*, Chicago: University of Chicago Press.

---- (1960), *Caste Ranking and Community Structure in Five Regions of India and Pakistan*, Poona: Deccan College Monograph.

---- (1968), 'Caste Ranking and Food Transactions: A Matrix Analysis,' in Milton Singer and Bernard S. Cohn (eds.), *Structure and Change in Indian Society*, Chicago: Aldine.

Marriott, McKim, Stanley A. Freed, and Ralph Nicholas (1967), *Hindu Caste Ranking*, The Lewis Henry Morgan Lecture, University of Rochester, Rochester, New York.

Marriott, McKim and Ronald B. Inden (1973), 'Caste System,' *Encyclopaedia Britannica*, 3:982–91.

---- (1977), 'Toward an Ethnosociology of South Asian Caste Systems,' in K. David (ed.), *The New Wind: Changing Identities in South Asia*, The Hague: Mouton.

Mayer, Adrian C. (1958), 'The Dominant Caste in a Region of Central India,' *South-Western Journal of Anthropology*, 14:407–27.

Mencher, Joan P. (1968), 'Structure of Politics in the Villages of Southern Asia,' in Milton Singer and Bernard S. Cohn (eds.), *Structure and Change in Indian Society*, Chicago: Aldine.

---- (1972), 'Continuity and Change in an Ex-Untouchable Community of South India,' in J. Michael Mahar (ed.), *The Untouchables in Contemporary India*, Tucson: University of Arizona Press.

Miller, D.B. (1976), *From Hierarchy to Stratification: Changing Patterns of Social Inequality in a North Indian Village*, New York: Oxford University Press.

Opler, Morris E. (1958), 'The Extension of an Indian Village,' *Journal of Asian Studies*, 16:5–10.

Omvedt, Gail (1981a), 'Maharashtra Rasta Roko, Kulaks and the Left,' *Economic and Political Weekly*, 28 November: 1937–40.

---- (1981b), 'Capitalist Agriculture and Rural Classes in India,' *Economic and Political Weekly*, 26 December.

Orenstein, Henry (1965), *Gaon: Conflict and Cohesion in an Indian Village*, Princeton: Princeton University Press.

Owens, Raymond L. (1973), 'Peasant Entrepreneurs in a North Indian Industrial City,' in Milton Singer (ed.), *Entrepreneurship and Modernization of Occupational Cultures in South Asia*, Duke University, Program in Comparative Studies on Southern Asia, Monograph No. 12, pp. 133--66.

Owens, Raymond L., and Ashis Nandy (1977), *The New Vaisyas*. New Delhi: Allied Publishers.

Patwardhan, Sunanda (1972), *Change Among India's Harijans*, New Delhi: Orient Longman.

Rajadurai, S.V. (1980), 'Tamilnadu Green Power on the March,' *Economic and Political Weekly*, 15 (no. 52, December 27, 1980), p. 2170.

Rowe, William L. (1968), 'Changing Rural Class Structure and the Jajmani System,' *Human Organisation*, 22:41–44.

Roy Burman, B.K. (1977), 'The Problem of Untouchables,' in Romesh Thapar (ed.), *Tribe, Caste and Religion in India*, Delhi: Macmillan.

Rudolph, Susanne Hoeber and Lloyd I. Rudolph (1967), *The Modernity of Tradition*, Chicago: University of Chicago Press.

---- (1980), 'The Centrist Future of Indian Politics,' *Asian Survey*, 20: 575--94.

Sachchidananda (1976), *The Harijan Elite*, Faridabad, Haryana: Thomson Press.

Shils, Edward (1960), *The Indian Intellectual between Tradition and Modernity: The Indian Situation*, The Hague: Mouton.

Singer, Milton (1972), *When a Great Tradition Modernizes*, New York: Praeger.

Silvertsen, Dagfinn (1963), *When Caste Barriers Fall*, London: Allen and Unwin.

Srinivas, M.N. (1962), *Caste in Modern India*, London: Asia Publishing House.

— (1977), *The Dual Cultures of Independent India.* Gandhi Memorial Lecture 1977, Bangalore: Raman Research Institute.

Weiner, Myron (1982), 'Congress Restored: Continuities and Discontinuities in Indian Politics,' *Asian Survey*, 22:339–55.

Wiser, William (1958), *The Hindu Jajmani System*, Lucknow: Lucknow Publishing House.

Zelliot, Eleanor (1970), 'Learning the Uses of Political Means: The Mahars of Maharashtra,' in Rajni Kothari (ed.), *Caste in Indian Politics*, Delhi: Orient Longman.

Part VI

Inequality

13

How Should We Think About Inequality?

Or No Tears for Losers

What are the positive benefits of equality? The writers to be considered here suggest that equality gives access to political and economic power, the right to compete in the marketplace, and to compete for a good education and better occupations. Alexis de Toqueville, the nineteenth century French observer, saw other implications of equality in his comparison of American democracy with French aristocracy – independent thought, individual search for truth, readiness to form personal opinions, willingness to try new occupations and pursuits, self-reliance, devotion to hard work, activism, skepticism concerning authority, rejection of a clerical hierarchy or of a mediator within the religious realm, disbelief in magic, humane concerns for others of all stations, insatiable curiosity, and eagerness to travel (Toqueville 1980, Vol. 2: 3–7, 15, 37, 72, 138, 165, 288).

Lest only such ample goods be seen to result from equality, we may also note Toqueville's observation of the chronic restlessness of the seemingly happy egalitarians he found in America; consider also his remark that "in the ages of equality all men are independent of each other, isolated and weak" (Toqueville 1980, Vol. 2: 15).

It is probably a taken-for-granted truth for most Americans that equality is a good thing and that inequality is bad. That inequality causes illness is an assumption of this symposium.* Thus, we are unlikely to take up Toqueville's point that equality may leave people "isolated and weak", but we are rather likely to assume that equality leads to good experiences including good health. What, then, should we mean by inequality in America?

---

* A preliminary version of this paper was presented in a workshop on social inequality and illness, organized by Arthur J. Rubel and Susan Abbott, held at the University of California-Los Angeles, December 1–2, 1981.

To get some idea of what ordinary Americans think about inequality I asked one – a freshman at the University of California-Berkeley. "What is meant by equality here in America?" I queried.

"In what context do you mean?" he questioned in turn. "In politics? Like in mathematics, it's two equals two."

"What would equality mean there?" I continued.

"Of the same value. Two is 'of the same value' as something else."

The conversation went on:

I: "Hmm. 'Of the same value.' I'll note that down. And what about in other contexts?"

He: "Well in economics, it's equal chance to get ahead. Not that everyone has an equal chance. Some people have a head start, but there should be room in society so that one can advance oneself. So it's not: once a peasant, always a peasant. A person should be able to change his class. Here in America you can go from being a peasant to being an aristocrat, because in the United States social class is a matter of having money, so a peasant can make a lot of money and become an aristocrat. Then what job you have is important. Like *you* are a member of the UMC – the upper-middle class, the great upper-middle class – because your occupation is college professor."

I: "Well, what about inequality here in America?"

He: "Well...racism is a perfect example of inequality in American society."[1]

If we switch from ordinary language to not-so-ordinary language, we may see how anthropologists are currently using the concepts of equality and inequality. I'll draw on some of their thinking in the sub-field of the anthropology of women and the social anthropology of the Indian caste system. I will also draw on the observations of some other social thinkers including John Rawls, author of *A Theory of Justice*, and sociologists Lillian Rubin and William Ryan. This may yield an inventory of definitions and lead us to new issues.

Inequality and Women: Equality as Identity and Unranked Differences; Inequality as Ranked Differences, Victimization and Differential Power

One of the first books on women by women anthropologists during the recent women's movement is Rosaddo and Lamphere's *Women,*

Culture and Society (1974), a collection of articles, by now widely read. Thinking of the two social segments of men and women, Lamphere defines equality as identity. Equality between males and females would entail identical social roles for both. Since nowhere, Lamphere says, are the gender roles identical, and furthermore, since everywhere the roles of women are considered to be interior to men's, women are universally oppressed.

In three books (Dahlberg 1981; Sanday 1981; Leacock 1981), the universal subordination of women has been called into question. Some argue that roles of men and women are very close to identical in some cultures; so the Geertzes refer to the Balinese as 'unisex' (Greetz 1973: 417 and Greetz and Greetz 1975, cited by Sanday 1981), and Estioko-Griffin and Griffin (in Dahlberg 1981): describe the hunting-horticultural Agta of the Philippines, a cultural group among whom women carry on all the same subsistence activities as do men. There are some other cultures which are good candidates for cultures in which the roles of men and women are close to identical; among modern industrial societies, Sweden probably comes closest (Kolenda 1982: 47–48).

Other anthropologists discuss cultures where the roles of men and women are not identical but the two sexes are, nevertheless, equal. Both Peggy Sanday and Eleanor Leacock have labelled one common pattern of sex roles as separate but equal. Before automatically rejecting that notion because of our association of "separate but equal" with school desegregation efforts, we might pause and see what is being said. A number of studies of women in other cultures suggest that women's roles are different from men's but are not considered by the people themselves to be inferior to men's; this is true among the !Kung of the Kalahari desert of southwestern Africa (Draper 1975; Lee 1981), the Mbuti of Ituri forest in Central Africa (Turnbull, cited in Dahlberg 1981), among the Iroquois (Brown, cited by Sanday and Leacock 1970), the Montagnais-Naskapi (Leacock 1981) and other native American cultural groups (Sanday 1981; Kolenda 1982: 47–48), as well as other. Equality may thus be equivalent to *unranked* differences. We may refer to this kind of equality as complementary equality. In some cultures this may be antagonistic complementary equality (Sanday 1981: 75, 89, 108–110, 169, 181).

What about inequality? Peggy Sanday (1981) is trying to arrive at a theory of, as the title of her book suggests: *Female Power and Male*

Dominance. Her measure of male dominance is composed of two features: first, exclusion of women from political and economic power, and second, male aggressiveness toward women, including beating and institutionalized rape. She calls a society "equal" if it has neither exclusion of women from political and economic power, nor male aggression toward women; unequal if a society has both, while the plus-minus society is one in which there is access to political and economic power for women, but also male aggressiveness. She characterizes these latter societies as ones having a "myth of male dominance."[2] Sanday, in fact, found only a minority of her Human Relations Area File sample of societies to be characterized as unequal – only 28 percent (35 of the 124) – while 32 percent (39 societies) were equal, and 40 percent (50) had myths of male dominance (Sanday 1981: 174).

We thus have inequality as ranked differences (Lamphere), and now as being powerless (with no access to political or economic power) and victimized (being objects of physical assault) (Sanday). The opposite, equality, may be understood as unranked differences (Leacock, Sanday), as well as identity in social roles (Lamphere). For anthropologists of women, equality may be equivalent to identical gender roles. A key question then becomes: under what conditions are differing gender roles evaluated as unequal? Cultural values must be brought to bear to understand inequality between the sexes; there is nothing inherent in the content of the gender roles themselves. Sanday theorizes that male dominance arises only under certain conditions in the non-western societies she studied – above all under *stress* as in regions of chronic food shortage, or in famine, or migration into dangerous territories, or under siege from overwhelming enemies. Under such conditions, ideologies often develop or old ideologies are elaborated, which explain bad luck as due to the nature of woman. This is a kind of scapegoat theory.

Inequality and Caste: The Problem of Unequal Social Conditions and Unequal Benefits; Justice as Fair Inequality

Gerald D. Berreman (1979) in *Caste and Other Inequities* emphasizes the suffering that systems of institutionalized inequality entail for those at the bottom. He sees the low castes suffering in the caste systems of India, the United States, Japan, and that of the Rwanda in Africa. Critical of the views of Louis Dumont (Berreman 1979: 155–63) who wrote on the Indian caste system in *Homo Hierarchicus* (1970), he finds Dumont ignoring the pain of those in the lower reaches of the caste system and accepting the ideology formulated by the learned Brahmans, which serves to justify their own purity and high rank and the impurity and inferiority of others. It is true that although Dumont occasionally notes the suffering of untouchables[3], his emphasis is upon a system of interdependent specialist castes that provides a living for all within it. For Dumont, indeed, the opposite of equality in the Indian context is not inequality, but hierarchy; for him, the caste system of India is not institutionalized inequality so much as it is institutionalized hierarchy. He emphasizes the point that "hierarchy" was originally used in the religious context and that the hierarchy of the caste system in India is essentially religious. The religious element in the Hindu caste system is especially ritual purity-impurity – an idiom through which the different ranks within the caste hierarchy are expressed. Hierarchy reflects an ideology which is implemented in a social system of interdependent segments. He claims that although castes differ in degrees of purity-impurity (and hence differ in rank in the caste hierarchy), all are rewarded commensurate with the contribution each makes to the whole community, as these are evaluated according to shared cultural values (Dumont 1970: 105). Since it is the Brahman priests who communicate, on behalf of the whole community, with gods, spirits and the high-caste dead, they make the most important contribution, and are of the highest rank and purity. Berreman and Dumont disagree about the lot of the untouchables. Berreman sees them as deprived; Dumont probably sees them as minimally, but presumably adequately, cared for. Implicit in Dumont's position is an answer to Berreman's indictment that the lowest castes are seriously deprived; his answer: this unequal system ideally ensures the welfare of all its participants; granted the rewards are unequal. Given Dumont's assumption that hierarchy is inevitable in human society, the caste system of India is not such a bad social system. So we have two different meanings of inequality – Berreman's: inequality means deprivation and suffering for the inferior; Dumont's: inequality is hierarchy which includes all.

The Harvard philosopher, John Rawls (1971), offers us a model for a just society. A just society is one in which people are equal – they have equal access to occupations and positions in society – and they receive equal shares of resources. The only grounds on which one individual or occupation would be given more than the standard share would be if its contribution to society improved the lot of the individual or occupation which was worst-off in the society. Rawls' scheme seems to go beyond both those of Berreman and Dumont. In Dumont's, contributions are rewarded differentially depending upon the social value of the contribution made, but there is no attempt to give equal shares, nor is there any special concern for the worst-off. In Berreman's there is compassion for the suffering of the lowest strata of society, but no suggestion of the proper procedures to correct the situation. Rawls' theory of a just society takes into account the likelihood that some members of society may make valuable contributions to the general welfare (parallel of Dumont's insight about the reason for the unequal rewards to various castes in the Indian caste system), but he makes as a crucial criterion of reward for any such unusual contribution the requirement that it benefit the worst-off (a stricture that would presumably satisfy Berreman).

In Rawls' ideal society, the standard by which contributions would be assessed would be on the basis of whether an added reward for some contributors would hurt the lot of the worst-off. It is one of the few philosophies around that has a built-in concern that no one should be a loser.

The Problem of Structured Inequality

In a later major work, *From Mandeville to Marx*, Dumont writes about *homo aequalis*, the archetypal MAN of Western Culture, the opposite of *homo hierarchicus*, the Man of caste India. Following Toqueville, Dumont transforms equality into individualism, and individualism is very much an ideology that developed in Western Europe with the concepts of economics and economic systems. Dumont claims that before Quesnay, Adam Smith, Locke, and Mandeville, there was no distinction in western thought between economics and politics.[4] Economics and individualism are related because western individualism operates in the free competitive marketplace. The individual competitors in that free market are assumed to be, at least initially, equal contenders.

The Mandeville in the title of Dumont's book refers to Thomas Mandeville's *Fable of the Bees*, first published in 1714, a popular work in the eighteenth century. When the bees were affectionate, altruistic and unselfish, the fable tells, their hive produced little but "sloth, poverty and boredom in a much reduced population" (Dumont 1978: 64); but when each was striving to fulfill his material needs, motivated by pride and a love of luxury, the hive prospered (Dumont 1978: 63–78). Dumont concludes about Mandeville, "in his philosophy of individualism...is...the idea that passions are so arranged that 'their apparent discords harmonize to the public good'; ...it is when a competitor does not will it that he works for the public good" (Dumont 1978: 69–70). So Mandeville's fable suggests that egoistical competition between equal participants results in the welfare of the whole society.[5]

There is a common thread in the ideologies of both Dumont's Brahmanical interpretation of the caste system and Mandeville's *Fable of the Bees* (1924). Just as the castes interact so as to ensure the welfare of all, so in the marketplace, where each contender is motivated by his own self-interest, the process of free competition has as its outcome a prosperous society. The comparison of caste and the bees implies that social ideology must be concerned with the general welfare; in that sense any ideology is altruistic. One cannot expect an ideology to be accepted and shared, unless people see it as good for themselves. These is a difference, however, in the outcome from these two ideological systems: in the caste system all participants are cared for (according to Dumont's ideal model, not according to Berreman's empirical one), while in the Mandeville bee society, the whole society prospered, but presumably not necessarily all of the bees. In all likelihood, some of the losers in the general rivalry did not do so well.

Berreman believes a thoroughly egalitarian society is possible in the future. In such a society, there would be no castes or classes and hence no deprived low castes. He is, however, curiously silent about the basis of economic interdependence in such a future egalitarian society. How would various specialists serve each other?

Does Rawls perhaps help us here? In such an egalitarian society of the future a principle of justice such as Rawls' might apply. There are many questions that would have to be raised about the implementation of such a principle – who would be the judge of whether a contribution benefited the most disadvantaged? If even the most disadvantaged agreed that a contribution benefited them, how much additional reward beyond the standard compensation all equal citizens receive would the contributor be awarded? How could one ensure that unusual benefits would be so allotted and that they were not to be expropriated by force or appropriated by stealth?

Rawls himself admits that he is writing about a hypothetical ideal situation of contract. He admits that his scheme cannot cover the social situation of inequality into which all are born in modern society (Rawls 1971: 7). He writes:

> In justice as fairness the original position of equality corresponds to the state of nature in the traditional theory of the social contract. This original position is not, of course, thought of as an actual historical state of affairs, much less as a primitive condition of culture. It is understood as a purely hypothetical situation characterized so as to lead to a certain conception of justice. Among the essential features of this situation is that no one knows his place in society, his class position or social status, nor does any one know his fortune in the distribution of natural assets and abilities, his intelligence, strength, and the like (Rawls 1971: 12).

Rawls' hypothetical conditions are so far from any modern society that the usefulness of his theory for changing social structure is limited. His ideal of reward being contingent on a member of society's contributing something of value even to the least well-off member of society may continue to be a worthy ideal for a future society, however.

What Berreman seems to be concerned with is the discrepancy between the egalitarian ideology (which he clearly accepts) and reality – a reality which includes American racism and Indian casteism. Berreman says nothing about the competition entailed in the egalitarian western system, nor does he say what the deprived in caste systems ought to be given – presumably, at least equal chance to compete for position, including occupation and property. Certainly, that is a common reaction of Americans or Europeans to Indian caste, that people should have a chance to find their own level in life, and should not be assigned an occupation and a way of life by heredity, an assignment they cannot alter. In Dumont's caste hierarchy, there are no losers, because all are included and cared for; in Berreman's the untouchables are not losers because they have never had the opportunity to play the occupational game. In the individualistic competition of the West (which Berreman might prefer to Indian caste), the ideologies of which Dumont traces, there are losers, but neither Dumont nor Berreman focus on their condition. A competitive economic system may make for a prosperous society even as Mandeville taught with his fable, but at the cost of losers in the competitive processes.

The Preoccupation with Political and Economic Power

All the writers I have drawn upon – Berreman, Dumont, Sanday, Rosaldo and Lamphere – have a common concern with political and economic power. Dumont suggests that although the idea of hierarchy (his form of inequality) is included in religious ideology, yet there exists high status in India for those with not just religious status, but for those with secular (political and economic) power, even though the religious ideas would not logically lead to high status for those with *artha*, wealth and power. The inconsistency is one of the central problems in *Homo Hierarchicus* (Kolenda 1978). In *From Mandeville to Marx,* Dumont is again concerned with an inconsistency. Individualism is an ideology for people striving for profit, economic success, while it ignores the problem of order and power. For Berreman, power is a given, but its expression in a caste structure often involves severe deprivation for some segments of the population; he also emphasizes that the deprived, such as the lowest castes in a caste system, do not like it; he disagrees with social theorists (Cox 1948; Berreman 1979: 3) who claim that the low castes accept their position in a caste system as just. Sanday defines female power as political and economic power, at least in part, and Rosaldo and Lamphere are concerned with power for women. This consistent preoccupation with economic and/or political power reflects a covert issue in our own Euro-American culture: the actual inequalities in the distribution of political and economic power in an ideologically egalitarian system.

Fredrik Barth (1964) holds that interaction produces results which become social structure, and that seems to be the case with economic competition. The results of the competitions of the past become the structure of the present. After all, in *From Mandeville to Marx,*

Dumont only got as far as Marx, who died over a hundred years ago. Meanwhile, since the times of Marx, the economic organization of the West has taken shape, one characterized and dominated by large complex organizations, hierarchical in command. The local caste system in India is simplicity itself compared to the hierarchical organizations *we* have. Those who have won in the earlier competitions and can transmit their gains and winning positions to their heirs can limit the game only to certain players. The biggest inequality of access is access to the proper rites of passage, certified by ritual paraphernalia – diplomas, certificates, degrees. As John Ogbu has put it, "educational credentials (have) crystallized as the society's main institutionalized strategy for job placement and remuneration" (Ogbu 1981: 278). In both capitalistic and socialistic societies there has been considerable concern with giving all children schooling so that all could start life on an equal footing, but it is accepted in both types of societies that some students will do better in their studies than others. Even as in Mandeville's Beehive, presumably some bees will be outdone by others.

Then beyond access there is the problem of being considered a legitimate player. Only certain kinds of players will be taken seriously. Even once in the general game, only a few will gain entry to the biggest games going on. Then, there are countless other inequities – in the distribution of information, contact with the "right people", benefits of encouragement, luck, and so on.

The Losers

None of our thinkers – Berreman Dumont, Lamphere and Rosaldo, Leacock, Sanday – gives much attention to the losers. Presumably, in fact, the only way the deprived in our society, at least, get sympathy is by being conceived of as not having been allowed to play in the first place. Calvinism is far from dead. Max Weber (1918) was not so wrong, perhaps, in his suggestion that western culture is pervaded with the Calvinistic concept that worldly success is a sign of spiritual salvation in a religious realm. One's success in wealth, occupation and prestige are measures of one's true worth. Losers are the damned, by the Calvinistic principle of predestination.

The competition in American life is an occupation game, as American sociologists (e.g., Duncan and Blau 1967) have pointed out, and increasingly, an individual American's occupation depends upon the amount of education he or she is able to acquire. It appears that by the 1970s and 1980s, only those who have managed to acquire high numbers of years of education are in the competition in our free labor market. William Ryan observes:

> Most of us, like most horses, spend our lives in ordinary, everyday work. The stereotypes who fit the metaphor -- the biology majors, for example, who cheat and spite each other in order to get a place in medical school, the new MBAs who sprint off their marks into the maze of the executive suite -- these are familiar to most people only at second hand. The working lives of most people are nothing like a race. If one walked down the aisles of a factory, the length of an assembly line, the sections of a department store, the rows of desks in an insurance company, how in the world would one go about distinguishing the fast winners from the slow losers? The answer is that that is not an issue. It is simply assumed that they are all losers. In the legendary race of life, most of us are not even participants (Ryan 1981: 28).

Ryan points out that one-fourth of the American population owns nothing, many of them owing more than they have, so that their "wealth" is actually negative. He continues:

> The persons in the next quarter own about 5 percent of all personal assets. In other words, half of us own 5 percent, the other half own 95 percent. But it gets worse as you go up the scale. Those in the top 6 percent own half of all the wealth. Those in the top 1 percent own one-fourth of all the wealth. Those in the top one-half of 1 percent own one-fifth of the wealth. That's one-half of 1 percent -- about one million persons, or roughly 300,000 families (Ryan 1981: 14).

> ...it has been calculated that for a young man born into a family in which the father does unskilled low-wage manual work, the odds against his rising merely to the point of his becoming a non-manual white-collar worker are at least three of four to one; the odds against his rising to the highest level and joining the wealthy upper class are almost incalculable.

For the son of a middle-level white-collar worker, the odds against his rising to a higher-level professional or managerial occupation are two or three to one. On the other hand, the odds are better than fifty to one that the son of a father with such a high-level occupation will not descend the ladder to a position as an unskilled or semi-skilled manual worker (Ryan 1981: 17).

Lillian Rubin, in her book on fifty working-class families in the San Francisco Bay area (1976), speaks of the restless discontent which working-class women feel, that is often "too frightening to talk about" and for which the woman usually blames herself. Rubin comments:

> Such turning inward with self-blame is common among the women and men I met – a product, in part, of the individualist ethic in the American society which fixes responsibility for any failure to achieve the American dream in individual inadequacy. That same ethic – emphasizing as it does the isolated individual or, at most, the family unit – breeds a kind of isolation in American life that is common in all classes but most profoundly experienced in the working class, partly, at least, because they have fewer outside resources (Rubin 1976: [illegible]9).

> ...those who have bought into the system, who believe in the ethic of hard work, who believe in the American myth that everyone can pull themselves up by their bootstraps if only they have the will and the brains. What, then, are such people to say to themselves when they don't succeed? They *know* they have the will. There's little left but to accept that they don't have the brain – a devastating self-image from which all people must seek periodic relief and surcease...Most of the time, (they) tend to deal with this injury to personal dignity by containing their anger and pain. But in their effort to bind their wounds – to restore dignity and affirm self – they redefine success so that it is more compatible with their modest accomplishments, and they accumulate possession as the visible symbol of their achievements and status. Often, however, it's not enough; it doesn't work. Some find the respite they need in angry explosions, some in deep withdrawals. Again and again, the men and women I met, recall parents, especially fathers, who were taciturn and unresponsive (Rubin 1976: 36).

What Ryan suggests is that half the American population is not even engaged in the competition for success and that the overwhelming majority own very little, and, at least by the criterion of property ownership, are losers. Rubin suggests that failure in the American success game leads to psychological disturbance. If we put Ryan and Rubin together, a proposition emerges: Most people are either not involved in or find themselves losers in the American occupational competition. Losers are likely to be psychologically disturbed by the incongruity between their position and their rightful expectations given the work ethic and success vision that is so typically American.

Victimization

There is the issue of victimization raised by both Berreman and Sanday and obliquely by Ryan and Rubin. This introduces the idea that the winners do not just exclude some players or handicap others, but that they exploit and assault the losers and the non-players. The losers or non-competitors as victims or targets for displaced aggression should be included in our concern with equality-inequality. Such ideas suggest that the suffering of losers is not just the result of having accepted an untrue ideology but also the result of being targets for the hostility of the more powerful and presumably more successful. The implications for mental and physical illnesses of victimization of losers bear investigation.

Conclusion

In this paper, I have tried to take some leads from some recent writings on equality and inequality within anthropology and to some extent within sociology and philosophy. Some of these writings point us toward inequality as hierarchy, deprivation, powerlessness, victimization, ranked differences in social roles, and exclusion from access to paths to advancement and to political and economic power. If we accept Dumont's idea that the ideology of the West is individualism as our form of egalitarianism, then there is a serious lacuna in that ideology, aside from its general inaccuracy as a description of the structure of our society. There is little concern for losers. Rawls' theory of justice makes that omission clear, but his theory fails to treat the issue of inequalities perpetuated through the transmission of power, advantage, and position over generations, the problem of the fair allocation of rewards, and the likelihood or expropriation of resources through force and threat, and the temptation to victimize the weak.

Notes

1. I owe thanks to Christopher Kolenda for answers to this question and for permitting their use here.
2. Sanday did not include a minus-plus type, a society without access to political and economic power for women, but also no male aggressiveness, a type under which I would say recent American society would fit. We, of course, have some aggression toward women – beating and rape – but we do not approve of it; it is considered to be reprehensible behavior – not so, among the South American jungle horticulturalists, the Yanomamo (Chagnon 1977), among whom a woman is said to believe her husband's love is to be counted in the number of scars on her scalp. American women also have some economic and political power, although rarely do they have any at the highest levels where crucial decisions are made.
3. Actually there are passages in *Homo Hierarchicus* which indicate Dumont's awareness of cruel treatment of untouchables. In one (Dumont 1970: 82), he speaks of a South Indian Paraya who showed him welts on his back from being beaten. "...in...Tinnevelly, I saw marks of blows on the back of an untouchable, blows which he had received for having crossed the village of a martial caste (the Maravar) wearing sandals."
4. Dumont (1970: 165) claims that the distinction between economics and politics does not occur in Indian thought -- the concept of *artha*, something which a king should strive for, includes both power and wealth.
5. What Dumont is concerned with in *From Mandeville to Marx* is the failure of western ideology to include a realistic treatment of the problems of order. Since Dumont assumes that hierarchy is inevitable and that the function of hierarchy is to make possible social

order, then if an ideology does not treat of hierarchy, the hierarchy that will, nevertheless, inevitably exist will be essentially unregulated – there won't be agreed-upon rules for hierarchy. In the West, we, in fact, are ruled by such extra-ideological hierarchy, and because it is outside our ideological awareness, it is likely to be criminal or barbarian rule. (Dumont's prime example is Nazi rule in Germany.) Hierarchical relations outside an egalitarian ideology are thus non-ideological and in Dumont's term, "shame-faced".

6. Like Gunnar Myrdal (1944), Dumont sees the western ideology as egalitarian, yet we have racism, of which both European social thinkers believe Americans are ashamed.

   Racism itself would appear to be an ideology. Dumont, however, precludes the possibility of seeing a society as composed of several ideologies, some of them possibly contending. In his first endnote in *Homo Hierarchicus,* he explicitly limits himself to concern with a 'global ideology', so an entire society's ideology, refusing to consider the multiplicity of ideologies that might exist in a society (Dumont 1970: 263).

References

Barth, F. (1964), *Models of Social Organization*, Occasional Papers No. 23, Royal Anthropological Institute, London.

Berreman, G.D. (1979), *Caste and Other Inequities*, Manohar, Delhi.

Brown, J.K. (1970), Economic Organization and the Position of Women Among the Iroquois, *Ethnohistory*, 17: 151–67.

Chagnon, N. (1977), *The Yanomamo: The Fierce People*, Holt, Rinehart and Winston, New York.

Cox, O.C. (1948), *Caste, Class and Race*, Doubleday, New York.

Dahlberg, F. (1981), *Woman the Gatherer*, New Haven, Yale University Press.

Draper, P. (1975), '!Kung Women: Contrasts in Sexual Egalitarianism in Foraging and Sedentary Contexts', in R. Reiter (ed.), *Toward an Anthropology of Women*, Monthly Review Press, New York, pp. 77–109.

Dumont, L. (1970), *Homo Hierarchicus*, University of Chicago Press, Chicago.

— (1978), *From Mandeville to Marx*, University of Chicago Press, Chicago.

Duncan, O.D. and P.M. Blau (1967), *The American Occupational Structure*, Wiley, New York.

Estioko-Griffin, A., and P.B. Griffin (1981), Woman the Hunter: The Agta of the Philippines, in F. Dahlberg (ed.), *Women the Gatherer*, Yale University Press, New Haven.

Geertz, C. (1973a), Deep Play: Notes on the Balinese Cockfight, in *Interpretation of Cultures*, Basic Books, New York, pp. 412–53.

Geertz, H. and C. (1975), *Kinship in Bali*, University of Chicago, Chicago.

Kolenda, P. (1978), Seven Kinds of Hierarchy in *Homo Hierarchicus*, *Journal of Asian Studies*, 35: 581–596.

— (1982), Equality Lost: Male Dominance Rejected and Explained, *Reviews in Anthropology*, 9: 47–62.

Leacock, E.B. (1981), *Myths of Male Dominance*, Monthly Review Press, New York.

Lee, R. (1981), Politics, Sexual and Non-sexual, in an Egalitarian Society, in G.D. Berreman (ed.), *Social Inequality: Comparative and Developing Approaches*, Academic Press, San Francisco, pp. 83–102.

Mandeville, B. (1924), *Fable of the Bee; or, Private Vices, Publick Benefits*, F.B. Kaye (ed.), Oxford University Press, Oxford (originally published in 1714).

Myrdal, G. (1944), *The American Dilemma: The Negro Problem and Modern Democracy*, Harper, New York.

Ogbu, J.U. (1981), Education Clientage, and Social Mobility: Caste and Social Change in the United States and Nigeria, in G.D. Berreman (ed.), *Social Inequality: Comparative and Developing Approaches*, Academic Press, San Francisco, pp. 277–306.

Rawls, J. (1971), *A Theory of Justice*, Belknap Press of Harvard University Press, Cambridge.

Rosaldo, M.Z. and L. Lamphere (eds.) (1974), *Women, Culture and Society*, Stanford University Press, Stanford.

Rubin, L.B. (1976), *Worlds of Pain: Life in the Working-Class Family*, Basic Books, New York.

Ryan, W. (1982), *Equality*, Vintage Books, New York.

Sanday, P.R. (1981), *Female Power and Male Dominance*, University of Pennsylvania Press, Philadelphia.

Slater, P. (1970), *The Pursuit of Loneliness: American Culture at the Breaking Point*, Beacon Press, Boston.

Toqueville, Count A. de (1980), *Democracy in America*, Alfred A. Knopf, New York (originally published in 1834 (Part I) and 1840 (Part II).

Turnbull, C. (1981), Mbuti Womanhood, in F. Dahlberg (ed.), *Women the Gatherer*, Yale University Press, New Haven, pp. 205–19.

Weber, M. (1918), *The Protestant Ethic and the Spirit of Capitalism*, Talcott Parsons (trans.), Scribner's, New York (originally published in German in 1904--5).

14

Demonizing Dalits

Scouring the Sources on the Sikh Pogrom

My review of Vijay Prashad's *Untouchable Freedom: A Social History of a Dalit Community* (New Delhi: Oxford University Press, 2000) was published in the *Journal of Social History (USA)* in 2002. The review is reprinted below, preliminary to the body of this paper.

> *Untouchable Freedom* purports to be the social history of the Chuhra sweepers of Delhi from 1860 to 1960. In many ways an excellent book, I found it very enlightening. However, I also found two problems. Let me explain the first.
>
> In the mid-1950s I did ethnographic fieldwork in a *basti* (colony) of 'untouchable' (nowadays, Dalit) Chuhras in Khalapur village in Saharanpur district, Uttar Pradesh, India. All one hundred or so were lineally or affinally related to each other. Most of the adults had worked outside in various cities, mostly on sanitation crews of municipalities, railways or the military, or as cleaners in private homes and offices. Some had done other kinds of work -- one oldster had once worked in coal mines; another, a handsome young man, had been a ticket-taker at the Race Course Cinema in Delhi. Most of the work experiences the Chuhras told me about had taken place before 1947, before the British rulers had left. Indeed, they were generally of the opinion that urban sanitation jobs were more plentiful under the British than after. My unpublished data indicate that the older Chuhra men and women had all worked in several different cities. Out-migrating men often left their families in the village to clean cattleyards and latrines for higher caste patrons *(jiijmans)*, and when the men came back to the village, they did

sweeping work, and/or share-cropping, construction work, raised animals for owners on a half-and-half basis, cut harvest wheat, worked on sugar-making teams, raised and sold pigs, etc.

All this I relay to the reader to explain why I am unconvinced by Vijay Prashad's assessment in chapters one to three that the Delhi Municipal Corporation (DMC) had a stranglehold on the sweepers it employed. I do not dispute the fact (taken from archival records) that, as told in chapter 1, the DMC in 1884 made the sweepers of Delhi their direct employees, rather than letting them continue as servants of individual households. The DMC did this because all the sweepers of a *mohalla* (section of town) so readily went on strike if one of the householders abused one of them. Under the DMC, the sweepers were not allowed to strike nor take private clients; they also were badly paid. Nor do I doubt Prashad's account in chapter 2 that beginning in 1912, because the British land law for the Punjab left artisans and menial castes landless, Chuhras began migrating to Delhi where they joined the municipal sanitation crews, so that by 1921, 82.5% of DMC sweepers were Chuhras. Nor can I question Prashad's account in chapter 3 that the colonial sections of Delhi had better water supply, drainage and sewage than the native sections. What I doubt is Prashad's statement that the Chuhras always migrated from villages *with their families* because local landlords would not allow *only part of a family* to serve them or to stay in the village (p.43); clearly that had not been the case in Khalapur, just across the river from the Punjab from where, Prashad says, the Delhi Chuhra sweepers came. The Khalapur data make me doubt the implication that DMC sweepers were all permanent residents of Delhi, or that they could not get other kinds of work than sanitation work.

Prashad says that because the Delhi British went to the summer capital, Simla, that only 25% of the usual DMC crews were employed during the hot season (p.17). Does he mean that the other 75% remained unemployed for those months because they could not return to their villages and could not get other kinds of work? Are there DMC records on the length of employment of their Chuhra employees? Were there not temporary sanitation workers as well as permanent ones?

What I especially doubt is Prashad's crediting the DMC and thus presumably the British with making the Chuhras into sanitation workers (sweepers). He cites H.U. Weitbrecht's 1887 article in *Indian Notes and Queries* that said the Chuhras in the Punjab were agricultural laborers, not sweepers (p.25). This claim is belied by the 1881 Census of the Punjab wherein Ibbetson begins his account of the Chuhras, with "The Chuhra or Bhangi of Hindustan is the sweeper and scavenger *par excellence* of the Panjab... " (Ibbetson 1883 [1916: 293]). And this is long before 1912 when the Chuhras began to migrate to Delhi to work for the DMC.[1]

Turning to chapters 4 through 6 – these chapters focus more broadly on the Chuhras of the Delhi region and on Dalits generally, rather than on the DMC Chuhras alone. Chapter 4, the longest and strongest in the book, concerns the Hindu *versus* Muslim political struggle between 1909 and 1947 in anticipation of a post-British democracy, as this related to Chuhras, now increasingly called Balmikis. On one side were B.R. Ambedkar (the Dalit statesman), the Communists, and the Dalits' own Adi movement (claiming that the Dalits were the original pre-Aryan inhabitants of India), all contending that the Dalits were not Hindus. On the other side were the Arya Samaj, the Hindu Mahasabha and other militant Hindus who claimed that Dalits were Hindus. The Dalits were betrayed partly by some of their own leaders, who gave into Hindu militants' blandishments, but especially by the British who insisted on counting Dalits in their censuses as Hindus. They also ignored Dalit demand for a separate country, Achutistan, upon partition of India.

Chapter 5 concerns Gandhi's attempt to persuade India that sweeping was the highest profession, and his failure to see that the Harijans ("children of God"), as he called untouchables, needed emancipation, not just a better image. Chapter 6 concerns municipal sweepers after Independence in 1947 when they were allowed to voice their demands even less than before, culminating in the 1957 police firing on striking DMC sweepers.

Now for my second problem with this book: in the Introduction, Prashad cites claims that the Congress-organized gangs that massacred at least 2,500 Sikhs in Delhi after Prime Minister Indira Gandhi was shot by her two Sikh bodyguards in October, 1984, were composed largely of Churha-Balmikis. I wonder how solid the evidence is for that accusation.

ENDNOTE

1. Ibbetson, Denzil 1916 Panjab Castes: Being a Reprint of the Chapter on "The Races Castes and Tribes of the People" in the Report on the Census of the Panjab, published in 1883 by the late Sir Denzil Ibbetson, K.C.S.I. Lahore: Government Printing, Punjab.

In this paper, I consider the accusation made by Vijay Prashad in the introduction to his book, *Untouchable Freedom* that Bhangis "many of them working as sweepers in the corporation comprised the bulk of the local miscreants who attacked the Sikhs" (Prashad 2002: ix, quoting from the December 1984 report made by the People's Union for Democratic Rights, entitled *Who are the Guilty?*) And that "several young men of the Balmiki community seemed to lead the way in the conflagration" (Prashad 2000: x). What is referred to are the attacks upon Sikhs involving conflagrations of homes, businesses and religious centers in several parts of Delhi after the assassination of Prime Minister Indira Gandhi by her two Sikh bodyguards on October 31, 1984. More than 2,700 Sikhs were killed during the attacks that lasted from October 31 to November 4, 1984.

Since I consider these to be serious accusations against Bhangis and Balmikis, it seems important to check them.

Let me first clarify proper names. The sub-title of *Untouchable Freedom* is *A Social History of a Dalit Community.* Bhangis are a Dalit or ex-untouchable or Scheduled Caste whose traditional caste work was and is to clean latrines, toilets, cattleyards, and to sweep those places, as well as streets and lanes. In cities, Bhangis commonly work on municipal garbage collecting crews. They are to be found in the Punjab, Haryana, Uttar Pradesh, Delhi and probably elsewhere in northern India. In many places, the name "Bhangi" alternates with the name "Chuhra" as their proper name. Denzil Ibbetson, the Director of the 1881 Census of the Punjab wrote that the name Chuhra was derived from the group's previous tribal status; presumably, there was a Chuhra tribe. Balmikis are Bhangis/Chuhras who believe in Balmiki or Valmiki who is credited with having written one version of the famous Hindu epic, the *Ramayana.* The

B/Valmikis believe in B/Valmiki as an ancestor and/or a deity. In many Bhangi/Chuhra neighborhoods or colonies, there are shrines or temples dedicated to B/Valmiki.

As for my interest in pursuing the accusations in Prashad's book, cited above, it can be explained by my strong affection for one colony of Chuhras. Let me explain. I did ethnographic fieldwork in a village in western Uttar Pradesh between 1954 and 1956 when I got to know extremely well a small colony of about 100 Chuhras/Bhangis/Balmikis. I did fieldwork in Khalapur in Saharanpur district again for four or five months in 1984 and stayed there for shorter times in 1985, 1986, 1997, and 1998. I suppose it is my affection for the West Colony sweepers of Khalapur that makes me concerned when the "good name" of the Bhangis and Balmikis was denigrated in Prashad's introduction. That has prompted me to check the references Prashad listed in support of that denigration.

I

Introduction to the Book, *Untouchable Freedom*

Vijay Prashad's *Untouchable Freedom* is about the sanitation workers employed by the Delhi Municipal Corporation (DMC) from 1863 to 1957. In the latter part of the nineteenth century the so-called Mehtar sweepers of the DMC were from a number of caste-communities, namely, "Khatiks, Sansis, Chamars, Chuhras, Reghars, Lodhas among others" (Prashad 2002: 21), but by the 1920s almost all were Chuhras from the Punjab (*ibid.*:44–45). By the 1930s, most of these Chuhras considered themselves to be Valmikis; that is, they had been convinced by Arya Samaj preachers that they were the disciples of Valmiki, the author of one version of the Hindu epic, the *Ramayana* (*ibid.*:90)

Prashad is surely mistaken when he says:

> The bulk of the Balmiki community today labours as sweepers hired by the municipalities of Delhi where they work under the close supervision of Hindu overseers and Jamadars (*ibid* : xv)

because he overlooks the many who live and work in other cities and in villages of Punjab, Haryana and western Uttar Pradesh. He himself cites interviews he had with Balmikis living in other cities such as Jalandhar (*ibid:* 166). This slip aside, it is the Bhangis-Chuhras-

Valmikis who work for the DMC who are the Dalit community he is concerned with.

The first chapter in Prashad's book is about the Delhi Municipal Corporation's decision in 1892 (*ibid.*: 10) to employ the sanitation workers directly rather than having them employed by individual households. In that way, the sweepers would not be allowed to go on strike as they had been able to do quite effectively when they worked for separate households. Carefully supervised by overseers, they were henceforth held to strict schedules, fined for any insubordination, forced to pay bribes to get and keep their jobs, and paid badly. So they lost control over their own work arrangements.

In chapter 2, the reason for the Churhas' migrating from the Punjab beginning about 1912 is explained – as a result of the Punjab land legislation under the British that took land away from untouchables and artisans (*ibid:* 36). Chapter 3 details the better sewage and sanitation services in the British part of Delhi as compared to the native parts.

While the first three chapters in *Untouchable Freedom* concern the sanitary conditions and the sanitary workers of Delhi from the 1860s to the 1930s, chapters 4 and 5 concern the struggle from 1909 to 1947 between various social, religious and political organizations to convince the Balmikis/Chuhras to count themselves as Hindus or to convince them that they were *not* Hindus. What was at issue, of course, was the proportion of the population of British India that was Hindu as compared to the proportion that was Muslim, seen as so very important to politicians and other activists, as they anticipated the democratic state that would be established after the British rulers departed. The more Hindu voters there were, the more likely leaders elected would be Hindu. Organizations like the Arya Samaj, the Hindu Mahasabha, and the Harijan Sevak Sangh preached that untouchables were Hindus, while the Mahar leader Ambedkar, and various Adi movements claiming that the untouchables were the original pre-Aryan inhabitants of the South Asia peninsular, and various Balmiki organizations, as well as traditional Chuhra religious practices, argued that Chuhras and other untouchables were *not* Hindu. The latter non-Hinduists were defeated when census officials decided that Chuhras represented an occupational category (of scavenger) rather than a tribal name and counted Chuhras as Hindus in the Census (*ibid.*: 86), as well as Ambedkar's compromise on reserved electorates, and the rift between the two large untouchable caste-communities in the Punjab, Uttar Pradesh, and Delhi, the Chamars and the Chuhras (*ibid.*: 89–90). Prashad concludes that the Chuhras conceded to the Hindu militants in their acceptance of Valmiki as their guru and with this, their consequent identity as Hindu. Despite their concession to the militant Hindus, most were supporters of the Congress party, that stood for a "secular" non-religious post-independence state. Prashad does not discuss the RSS and other Hindu nationalists that advocated a Hindu state (*Hindutva*) in these chapters even though the RSS was in existence during the period covered.

Chapter 6 in *Untouchable Freedom* concerns the Balmikis in the post-Independence years of 1946–57. It reiterates the facts of the horrendous living conditions of the DMC sanitation workers by describing Mahatma Gandhi's six-month sojourn in 1946 in a colony of untouchable sweepers in Delhi. Special tents and buildings were erected for Gandhi near the sweepers' Valmiki shrine, 50 meters from the homes of the sweepers. Gandhi found that he could not live in the house of a sweeper family. He "declared that the actual homes of the dalits appeared worse than the worst prison cell he had experienced in India and South Africa" (*ibid.:* 137–38), nor could he bring himself to take food from them. The Gandhian episode illustrates the contradiction between the Congress party's advocacy of equality while at the same time ensuring the perpetuation of what Prashad calls "bourgeois-landlord power" with its subordination of the lower castes. He writes:

> The Balmikis found themselves as clients of political patrons particularly after the patrons organized the disorganization of the Balmiki political organs. Social service agencies withdrew in favour of temple organizations, militant unions lost their dynamism and accepted the leadership of the Congress' class collaborationist union, Indian Trade Union Congress (INTUC), which the more radical among them named Brahmanism (*ibid.*:144).

Chapter 6 culminates in the strike by DMC sanitation workers in 1957 when, unarmed and using Gandhian tactics of non-violence, the strikers were fired upon by the Delhi police. The strike was followed by legislation passed in Parliament forbidding those who provide public utilities to strike. Garbage collection, sweeping, cleaning of latrines – in other words, the work of the DMC sanitation workers – was such a public utility.

The message of chapters 1 through 6 of *Untouchable Freedom* is that after more than forty years, the Balmiki/Chuhra sanitation workers of the DMC were serfs in debt-bondage, living in appalling conditions, with no obvious champion to lead them toward freedom. Indeed, they mistakenly "followed" their oppressors.

The story Prashad has told in chapters 1 through 6 is sympathetic toward the Balmiki/Chuhra/Bhangis. He regrets the turns in the story when some of these Dalits asserted their independence, but were then defeated. So I have been puzzled as to why Prashad put in an introduction accusing Bhangis and Valmikis of being killers and burners in the pogrom against the Sikhs in Delhi in November 1984.

II
Reading the Sources on the Sikh Pogrom

It is generally agreed, as Prashad states in the first paragraph of his introduction with the reference to Bhangis as "the bulk of the local miscreants who attacked the Sikhs", that the attacks on the Sikhs in Delhi in the early days of November 1984 were organized and supervised by Leaders of the Congress (I) political party (*ibid.*: ix), a party headed by Prime Minister Indira Gandhi's son, Rajiv, who immediately succeeded his mother as Prime Minister. On the following page, Prashad states: "Among the dalits of Delhi, several young men of the Balmiki community seemed to lead the way in the conflagration" (*ibid.*: x). The Bhangi "local miscreants" and Balmiki "conflagration leaders" are accused of composing the mobs who actually perpetrated the attacks, looting, murders and burnings during the Sikh pogrom.

In the first part of this paper, I have explained that at least some Bhangis are Chuhras, and some Chuhras are B/Valmikis. They are to be found in villages and cities in Uttar Pradesh, the Punjab, Haryana and Delhi. As sweepers, latrine cleaners, garbage collectors, they are considered among the lowest of "untouchables" or, by the more current label, the lowest of "Dalits".

In his lengthy entry on Bhangis in *The Tribes and Castes of the Northwestern Provinces and Oudh*, published in 1896, the British ethnographer, William Crooke, cited "five main sub-castes" as classified by the 1891 Census of India. These were Balmiki, Dhanuk, Hela, Lal Begi and Patharphor (Crooke 1896: Volume I, p. 270). Already in the late nineteenth century, there was a sub-caste of Bhangis called Balmikis, although the Balmik referred to was a character in stories about the Bhangi culture hero, Lal Beg.

In the same entry on Bhangis, Crooke said:

> There are various titles used to designate the tribe. Thus, they are known in the Western districts of the province and in the Punjab as Chuhra, Chura, or Chuhara, which is by some derived from their business of collecting or sweeping up scraps (*chura-jharna*)...(Crooke 1896, Volume I, p. 260).

So, Chuhras were, and, indeed, are often called Bhangis. Although, as indicated, not all Bhangis are Chuhras.

Note that the reference to the Bhangi miscreants cited above said that many of them worked for "the Corporation". The Corporation means the Delhi Municipal Corporation (DMC); so we may presume that many of the miscreant Bhangis were Chuhras, because Prashad has stated that most of the sanitation workers for the DMC were Chuhras. So it is likely that the young Balmiki men said to have been "leading the conflagrations" of Sikh properties would have been Chuhras, who are also called Valmikis or Balmikis; there is, of course, not a perfect coincidence between the two. That is, perhaps not all Chuhras are Balmikis, and perhaps not all Balmikis are Chuhras, but a considerable overlap is likely.

The quotation: "the Bhangis – many of them working as sweepers in the corporation – comprised the bulk of the local miscreants who attacked the Sikhs" is referenced in footnote 2 of Prashad's introduction as from PUDR, *Who are the Guilty? Report of a Joint Inquiry into the Causes and Impact of the Riots in Delhi from 31 October to 10 November* (New Delhi: PUDR, 2nd edition, December 1984, p. 3).

A quotation from a Sikh woman survivor of the massacre who said the killing had been done by "the *kanjars* and the *bhangis*" is referenced in footnote 3 as coming from Uma Chakravarti and Nandita Haksar, *The Delhi Riots: Three Days in the Life of a Nation* (New Delhi: Lancer, 1987: 43).

On page x, Prashad references in footnote 4 the following sentence:

> The screen between the acts of violence and the political structures that work at the behest of certain dominant classes enables the latter to disown responsibility for making violence as a means to realize their agenda (as in the 'excesses' of the period of the National Emergency)

to an article he wrote himself, Vijay Prashad, "Emergency *Assessments*", *Social Scientist,* Nos. 280–1 (September-October 1996, p. 52).

The sentence about "young men of the Balmiki community seemed to lead the way in the conflagration" seemed to be referenced in footnote 5 that said:

Pradip K. Datta, *et al.*, 'Understanding Communal Violence: Nizamuddin Riots', *Economic and Political Weekly*, 19 November 1990; Uma Chakravarty, *et al.*, 'Khurja Riots, 1990–91: Understanding the Conjuncture', *Economic and Political Weekly,* 2 May 1992; and my own research during the 1992–94 period.

So it would appear that my task was to read five sources. I could, of course, not read Prashad's own research notes, referred to in footnote 5, just quoted, but through the collections of the University of California-Berkeley library, I was able to obtain all five published sources Vijay Prashad cited in his introduction to *Untouchable Freedom.*

What became clear was that only two of the five sources had anything to do with the Sikh pogrom of 1984. Prashad's own published article focused on the Emergency period of the mid-1970s. The articles by Datta, *et al.* and by Chakravarty, *et al.* concerned later Hindu attacks on Muslims that took place one, in a part of south Delhi, Nizamuddin, in 1990, and the other, in the town of Khurja, south of Delhi, in 1990 and 1991. That left the PUDR pamphlet, *Who are the Guilty?* and the quotation from an interview with one Sikh woman survivor in a very long book on the Delhi riots. The latter, a single observer's report, is hardly sufficient to support any generalization about the role of Bhangis in the Sikh pogrom. So we are left with the PUDR pamphlet. And what I have to say is about that source. In a third part of the paper, I will comment on the roles of the Balmikis in the Nizamuddin and Khurja attacks on Muslims.

PUDR stands for the People's Union for Democratic Rights. That organization, along with the PUCL, the People's Union for Civil Liberties, sent a team of investigators to the trans-Jamuna and West Delhi areas where Sikhs had been attacked. They interviewed people between November 1st and November 10th, 1984. The first edition of *Who are the Guilty?* was published soon after the team's investigations, in November 1984. The second edition, used by both Vijay Prashad and myself, was published in December 1984. According to its authors, the report is

> based on case studies carried out in the trans-Jamuna and West Delhi areas. It is by no means exhaustive and covers only partially the killings, arson and brutalities committed in other parts of Delhi (PUDR 1984: 1).

To be fair to Vijay Prashad, let me quote the passage in his book in which the 'Bhangi miscreants' are mentioned. It follows:

> In the aftermath of the pogrom against the Sikhs in Delhi (1984) in which 2,500 people perished in a few days, reports filled the capital of the assailants and their motives. It was clear from the very first that this was no disorganized 'riot' and the organized violence visited upon Sikhs was engineered by the Congress(I) to avenge the assassination of Indira Gandhi. Of the assailants, we only heard rumours, that they came from the outskirts of the city, from those 'urban villages' inhabited by Jats and Gujjars as well as *dalits* (untouchables) resettled there during the National Emergency (1975--7). The People's Union of Democratic Rights (PUDR) published a pamphlet, just after the carnage, which reported 'the Bhangis -- many of them working as sweepers in the corporation – comprised the bulk of the local miscreants who attacked the Sikhs'. For many middle-class residents of the city, this news simply reaffirmed their stubborn conviction that the 'low castes', being prone to violence and devoid of any promise or potential beyond that required strict control (Prashad 2000: ix).

The PUDR report explains the sequence of moves made by the Congress(I) organizers of the pogrom. The first phase involved the spreading of anti-Sikh rumors such as reports that Sikhs were celebrating, rather than mourning, the death of Indira Gandhi; that a train-load of dead Hindus had arrived in the Old Delhi station from the Punjab, presumably killed by Punjabi Sikhs, and that Sikhs had poisoned the Delhi water supply. The authors of the pamphlet say:

> ...we came across evidence of policemen in vans touring certain localities and announcing through loudspeakers the arrival of the train and the poisoning of the water (PUDR 1984: 2).

In the second phase, on the night of October 31–November 1, "groups of armed young people" in various vehicles came into "places like Munirka, Saket, South Extension, Lajpat Nagar, Bhogal, Jangpura and Ashram in the south and southeast, the Connaught Circus shopping area in the centre and later the trans-Jamuna colonies and resettlement colonies in other areas in the north" with cans of petrol. "......they went round the localities and systematically set fire to Sikh houses, shops and gurudwaras." These arsonists were directed by "well known Congress (I) leaders and workers. Local Congress(I) people identified Sikh houses and shops"(PUDR 1984: 2).

The first reference in the pamphlet to Bhangis appears in the following passage:

> In some areas, like Trilokpuri, Mangolpuri and the trans-Jamuna colonies, the arsonists consisted of Gujjar or Jat farmers from neighboring villages and were accompanied by local residents, some of whom again were Congress(I) activists. In these areas, we were told, Congress(I) followers of the Bhangi caste (belonging to the Scheduled Caste community) took part in looting (PUDR 1984: 2).

In the above passage, Bhangis are presented as looters, not leaders in conflagration or assassination, and it is local Bhangis who were Congress(I) followers who were said to have been the looters.

In the succeeding paragraph, sentences are in the passive voice and/or agent-less, so that young Sikh males "were dragged out, beaten up and then burnt alive", "we came across reports of gang-rape of women", "in some areas of Mangolpuri...even children were not spared" (PUDR 1984: 2). The phrasing leaves it unclear who did the dragging out, gang-raping and murdering of children.

Next comes Part II "Socio-Economic Composition of the Assailants". Again mention is made of "Jats and Gujjars from neighboring villages. A large number of Scheduled Castes people were also a part of the mob" (PUDR 1984: 3).

Three of the affected communities had been established in the course of an "urban resettlement drive initiated by the Congress(I)." Inhabitants of these three resettlements had been active Congress(I) supporters and had been counted on to populate the Congress(I) rallies in the city of Delhi. The paragraph continues:

> In other words, there exists in such areas an established organizational network, through which masses are mobilised for demonstration of Congress(I) ostensible popular support (PUDR 1984: 3).

The inhabitants of the resettlements were Jats, Gujjars and Scheduled Caste people. Elsewhere, Jats and Gujjars from "urban villages" were dominant in the "riots, murders and looting" in "West and South Delhi". Furthermore,

> much of the police force which is stationed in this area and around is drawn from these communities. For this reason, on various occasions there had been a noticeable complicity in these areas between the criminals and the police (*ibid.*).

Then comes the paragraph about the bulk of the local miscreants who attacked the Sikhs being Bhangis. The paragraph reads as follows:

> As for the Scheduled Caste communities who were displaced due to the acquisition of land for urban expansion those from the Valmiki community utilised the benefits of the reservation policy and came into the city where they found jobs in the policies [*sic*], UPSC, etc. The Bhangis went into the Corporation, while the third major group, the Dhanaks, considered the lowest caste, were engaged in a variety of odd jobs. Among the Scheduled Caste communities living in the resettlement colonies, the Valmikis were predominantly supporters of Jagjivan Ram, while the Bhangis are solid supporters of Congress-I. Information gathered by us from the trouble spots in these areas suggest that the Bhangis – many of them working as sweepers in the Corporation – comprised the bulk of the local miscreants who attacked the Sikhs (PUDR 1984: 3).

There are a number of problems with this last quoted paragraph. Bhangis are distinguished from Valmikis, and it is the former who are said to work for the Corporation and were the "miscreants", while

Vijay Prashad said in his book that the vast majority of the Corporation sweepers were Chuhras. Are the Chuhras equivalent to Bhangis? Aren't most Valmikis Chuhras? The authors of the pamphlet seem to write as though Bhangis and Valmikis are two different caste groups.

Whatever may be the case so far as the separate or single identity of Chuhras, Bhangis and Valmikis in the pamphlet, the localities wherein the bulk of local miscreants who attacked the Sikhs were said to have been Bhangis were the three resettlement colonies. I conclude that the Bhangi attackers on Sikhs were local people residing in the resettlement colonies. It seems clear that Vijay Prashad misleads the reader when he quotes the passage about "the bulk of the local miscreants" without any specification of locality, so that the reader understands (or has been led to misunderstand) that everywhere in Delhi the attackers upon the Sikhs were Bhangis.

Although Prashad did mention the urban villagers, the Jats and Gujjars, he seems to impose almost all the guilt of the attacks on Sikhs upon Bhangis. He insufficiently treats the activities of Congress leaders and the police in the attacks on the Delhi Sikhs.

Long passages in the PUDR pamphlet are concerned with the failure of the police, the highest officials, administrators and the army to act to quell the massacre. In many places, the police participated in the attacks on the Sikhs, and officials ignored pleas to take action. The army, called in very tardily, lacked guides to the affected areas and orders for the actions they were to take.

> In the Kingsway Camp, residents claimed that seventy percent of the loot was to be found in the police lines, suggesting that the police took a leading role in the plundering (PUDR 1984: 5).

> Army officers complained that they were not provided with scouts by the police to lead them to the trouble spots... the deployment of troops followed a strange pattern. They were deployed by the civil authorities in stages, and in almost every case they were deployed after houses in the trouble spots had been burnt to cinders and the massacre was over (PUDR 1984: 9).

There follows a section on the roles of Congress(I) members, with the names of many prominent Congress(I) Members of Parliament and councillors given, cited as organizers of the violence and/or participants in it; a section on the media and opposition parties, neither of which took positive actions, and a section on the public. With respect to the public, the authors of the pamphlet note:

> The long record of uninterrupted depredations by the Sikh extremists in Punjab had possibly created a desire for retaliation that blinded even those who are regarded as responsible people among the Hindus (*ibid.*: 25). The only signs of courage and initiative in an otherwise ominous landscape were demonstrated by those Hindu and Muslim neighbours who helped Sikh families in the affected areas (*ibid.*: 15).

Then follow case studies from Sultanpuri, Mangol Puri, and Trilokpuri, the three resettlement colonies. The population of Sultanpuri is described in the report as follows:

> The resettlement colony of Sultanpuri has a mixed population of Hindus and Sikhs employed in various occupations. Many of the Hindus belong to the lower castes and are employed in various bodies as safai karamcharis. Among the Sikhs are Sikligars (who specialize in preparing metal gratings for building construction), charpoy weavers from Alwar, scooter rickshaw owners, TV mechanics, electricians, and shop keepers. Some also work as scooter rickshaw drivers, rickshaw pullers, vendors and labourers. It is significant that the members of the two communities lived in perfect harmony prior to the riots (PUDR 1984: 17).

The Sikhs of Sultanpuri were attacked late on November 1st. Eyewitnesses attested that the mob was composed of local people and "outsiders believed to be Jats of neighbouring villages (Mundka is one such village)" (*ibid.*). The mob was led by *pradhans* (probably local leaders) "linked to the local Congress MP." The police disarmed the Sikhs and killed some. Local kerosene suppliers provided fuel for burning houses and pyres (*ibid.*)

Without going into the gory details of the Sultanpuri massacre, we may note the one reference to "sweepers" (presumably the reference to *safai karamcharis* in the paragraph above on the inhabitants of Sultanpuri means people like Bhangis, Valmikis, and Chuhras). Referring to camp II that some of the Sikh survivors were taken to we are told:

> The same sweepers who only a few days ago looted their houses and killed their husbands and sons have managed to sneak into the camps for the ostensible purpose of doing the sanitation work (PUDR 1984: 19).

Both the terms "sweepers" and "safai karamcharis" are imprecise, out I presume Bhangis, Valmikis and/or Chuhras are meant.

The cast of characters in the atrocities in Mangolpuri and Trilokpuri is similar to that in Sultanpuri. The police not only failed to protect Sikhs, but threw them to the mobs. "...the assailants were from the nearby Jat villages and were accompanied by local Scheduled Caste people" (PUDR 1984: 19–20). Nearby were well-known Congress(I) workers and the local Congress (I) MP.

How does a scrutiny of the PUDR pamphlet modify Vijay Prashad's portrayal of the Bhangis as the "bulk of the local miscreants who attacked the Sikhs" and "the young men of the Balmiki community leading the way in the conflagration"? As noted above, the quotation concerning Bhangis as "the bulk of the local miscreants" referred only to three resettlement colonies, and the Bhangi "miscreants" were both local residents and supporters of the Congress(I) political party. *No passage in the PUDR pamphlet suggests that the young men of the Balmiki community led the way in committing arson. Rather leadership is repeatedly attributed to Congress (I) officials.* The police cooperated with these officials either by staying at a distance, or by ignoring what went on near them, or by participating in the attacks.

Exactly how the burning of Sikh property was done is not made clear in the pamphlet. It tells us that armed young men came in from outside in vehicles with cans of petrol. Who the leaders were who brought about the conflagrations is not stated. But the burners were outsiders, not locals, the pamphlet says. And all Bhangis referred to were local people.

I do not claim that no Bhangi or Valmiki attacked Sikhs or burned their property; the accusations made by survivors like the single Sikh woman survivor quoted in Chakravarti and Haksar's *The Delhi Riots* and the observations of those in camp II who believed the sweepers now serving the camp were the same who had attacked their homes and killed their men must be given their due; but that Vijay Prashad has exaggerated their participation by suggesting that they were the majority (the "bulk") of the attackers all over Delhi (when the PUDR investigators only went to two parts of Delhi and found the bulk of miscreants to be Bhangis in three resettlements only) and that they took leadership roles. The PUDR pamphlet gives no evidence that either Bhangis or Valmikis were leaders. Leaders rather were Congress(I) elected officials; their roles as leaders is very well documented. Members of other caste communities were involved; specifically Jats and Gujjars and policemen were very much involved.

III
Valmikis in Nizamuddin and Khurja

Before closing, let me comment on the article about the Hindu attacks on Muslims in the Nizamuddin section of Delhi and in the town of Khurja.

The paragraph in *Untouchable Freedom* that leads up to the footnote citing the Nizamuddin and Khurja articles reads as follows:

> Among the dalits of Delhi, several young men of the Balmiki community seemed to lead the way in the conflagration. If the Balmikis offered fealty to the Congress in the early 1980s, by the end of the decade most indications showed that a set of them had begun to work closely with the Hindutva movement, first in anti-Muslim actions in Delhi and Khurja (among other places) and subsequently as part of the caravan to Ayodhya to participate in the 6 December 1992 destruction of Mir Baqi's mosque (Prashad 2000: x).

Already I have said that the articles on the Nizamuddin and Khurja attacks contained no mention and no information about the Sikh pogroms. Prompted by the paragraph just cited, we may ask: Do either of the articles show that the Balmikis worked with the Hindutva movement in Delhi? Do either of the articles show that the Valmikis worked with the Hindutva movement in Khurja? Does either article state that Balmikis participated in the caravan to Ayodhya and the destruction of the mosque in Ayodhya?

The Nizamuddin article discusses the invasion by "Hindus from other parts of the city, ably supported by the police," (Datta 1990: 2487) of a *jhuggi* (a settlement of temporary flimsy dwellings) established by some Muslim refugees from Bangladesh, near the old established Delhi Muslim neighborhood of Nizamuddin. Two Muslims were shot by the police and about fifty others were injured (*ibid.*). Without going into the complexities of the situation, I can answer the questions about the Valmikis briefly and easily. The only mention of Valmikis in the entire lengthy article is the following sentence:

> Recently its [Sufi shrine in Nizamuddin] vulnerabilities were exposed by communal tension, when an enclave of scheduled castes living at its periphery insisted on erecting a conspicuous Valmiki Mandir next to the historic Kali Masjid (erected during Feroz Shah Tuglaq's time) (Datta 1990: 2488).

Whatever communal tension there had been between the Muslims of either the old Nizamuddin neighborhood or of the Bangladeshi *jhuggi* and the "enclave of scheduled castes" with respect to the Valmiki shrine is not described. There is no mention of Valmikis being involved in the attack on the Bangladeshis; there is no mention of their interest in the Hindutva movement; there is no mention of participation in the Ayodhya mosque episode in the Nizamuddin article by Pradip K. Datta *et al.*

The paper on the Khurja riots (December 15, 1990) is a very lengthy report by six social scientists who interviewed a variety of local citizens in March and April of 1991 about the riots. Its main point is that the Bharatiya Janata Party (BJP) with its anti-Muslim policy and message fomented the Khurja riots in order to win in the elections of June 1991. At the beginning of the article, we are told how riots were triggered by simulations of riot:

> The December 15, 1990 riot in Khurja, a small town in western U.P., was preceded by a prolonged simulation of rioting. Fireworks and bombs were exploded every night for more than two weeks all over the city in both Hindu and Muslim 'mohallas' while taped cassettes reproducing sounds of fighting, frenzy and panic were played on loud-speakers. Rumours that killings had taken place in Khurja and elsewhere were spread about five days before (Chakravarti *et al.* 1992: 951).

At the same time, the campaign to rebuild the Ram temple at Ayodhya, supported by the BJP and related groups was going on.

Without going into the many details given of the BJP and related groups' efforts to prove to the public that Hindus were really being physically endangered by Muslims, let me say something about the role of the Valmikis.

In the Khurja article, there is some evidence for Prashad's claim that a set of Valmikis had begun to work with the Hindutva movement by the end of the 1980s (or more accurately, the early 1990s when the Khurja riots took place). The authors of the Khurja report note that since there were sizeable numbers of poor Valmikis in Khurja, they were:

> ....courted by all the major political parties include the BJP. The BJP devoted special attention to the mobilisation of Valmikis and were able to make enough inroads with them to be able to use them to spearhead communal aggression (Chakravarti *et al.* 1992: 958).

One of the Khurja riots started with the stabbling of a government employee, supposedly by three Valmikis. The author states:

> Three Valmiki youths were allegedly involved in the assault, including Ballo, the son of Mathrawali. However, the site of Salim's stabbing was an especially volatile area, since it occurred in the trisection of Baramohalla (inhabited by Valmikis), Tarinan Teraha (a Muslim area) and another lane populated by Gaddis (Muslim cowherds).
>
> This somewhat familiar pattern of conflict between lower caste groups and lower strata Muslims, with the segregated and marginalised groups of both communities living in proximity with each other, may have acquired a particular profile from the fact that the SCs, along with Muslims, are a numerically dominant group in town. Khurja is a reserved constituency for the Lok Sabha seat......
>
> The three assaulters of Salim were released by the police after Mathrawali and some BJP leaders are alleged to have threatened widespread rioting. Salim was sent to Delhi by a group of Muslims and Hindus (which included Valmikis) for treatment. But next day *Aaj* published the false report that Salim had died. Rioting started at about 9 am on December 15 at Baramohalla between Valmikis and Muslims but the epicenter quickly shifted to Sarai Sheikh Alam

where upper caste Bania and Brahmin residents surrounded a numerically small Muslim population concentrated in a few houses (Chakravarti *et al.* 1992: 258).

It is not clear from the above narrative concerning the stabbing of Salim what the motives of the accused Valmiki attackers were or were supposed to have been. Since one of the three alleged/arrested Valmikis was the son of an important politician and the three were released from the police through her offices and that of "some BJP leaders", and since threats of riots were used to leverage the release, and actually riots did break out after Salim's death was inaccurately announced, possibly the stabbing was plotted by some BJP member or members. However, as in the instance of the Valmiki shrine in Nizamuddin, an important ingredient in tension or conflict between Muslims and Valmikis was the residential pattern whereby Valmikis and/or other SCs and Muslims live in adjoining colonies. The implication: neighbors often have altercations. Also Salim, in fact, survived his wounds, and both Muslim and Hindu citizens, including some Valmikis, paid for his travel and treatment in Delhi. It was *Aaj*, a particular newspaper, that printed a false report of Salim's death.

The Khurja analysis makes clear that the leadership in the riots was taken by teachers and merchants, supporters of the BJP, and that mobs included people from a number of caste-communities – namely, "malis, ahirs, khatiks, valmikis, jogis and banias" (*ibid.*: 959).

Again as with the Nizamuddin article, there is no evidence of Balmikis making up "the bulk of the local miscreants". In Khurja, some poor Valmikis seemed to have been used as tools by caste BJP politicians. It is hard to say whether they were supporters of the Hindutva movement or not. There is no mention of Balmikis participating in the caravans going to Ayodhya or in the destruction of the mosque in Ayodhya in December 1992. Indeed, both the Nizamuddin and Khurja articles were published before the destruction of the Ayodhya mosque took place.

IV
Conclusion

To conclude my exercise in checking references, I found that Vijay Prashad's portrayal of sweepers (Bhangis, Chuhras, Balmikis) in recent riots to be both misleading and exaggerated. In none of the references he supplies is there mention of young Balmiki men taking the lead in conflagrations. Balmikis were not reported to have been involved at all in the Hindu invasion of the Bangladesi Muslim colony in Nizamuddin. In *Who are the Guilty ?* the report of the PUDR on the Sikh pogrom in Delhi, Bhangis were reported to be "the bulk of the miscreants" in only three resettlement sections of Delhi, and the report makes it clear that leadership was in the hands of Congress (I) officials, that the police were nonfunctional, and that other caste-communities besides Bhangis were involved.

A multiplicity of castes was involved also in the Khurja riots. In Khurja, three Valmikis were accused of a stabbing, a non-killing, reported falsely in the press as a killing. It was the false press report of a killing that triggered an anti-Muslim riot. The BJP may have had some success in hiring Valmikis to attack Muslims.

Since there is such a poverty of evidence for Vijay Prashad's characterization of the Bhangis and Balmikis as dominant participants in either the Sikh pogrom or the invasion of the Bangladeshis' colony in Nizamuddin, or the Khurja riots, we must assume that Prashad has much evidence for predominance in his own interview notes, or else he had some other reason to exaggerate the role of Bhangis and Valmikis in these horrible instances of violence.

It is only in the introduction and epilogue of the book that the role of Bhangis or Balmikis in the Hindutva movement of the 1980s and 1990s is mentioned. It is by equating the struggles of the Arya Samaj, the Hindu Mahasabha and other Hindu militants (including the efforts of Mahatma Gandhi) of the 1909--1947 period to convince untouchables that they should call themselves Hindus with the anti-Muslim Hindutva movement of the 1980s and 1990s that the author of *Untouchable Freedom* can bridge the 1957 end of his history with the Sikh pogrom and the BJP-inspired riots. So historians struggle to make their historical accounts relevant to contemporary events.

In *Untouchable Freedom,* Prashad makes clear that the inadequacies of the DMC sanitation service in the past were readily blamed on the sweepers themselves rather than on the antiquated sewage system, the insufficiency of the water supply, the obsolete technology still used, and the disappearance of agricultural villages that had absorbed the waste as fertilizer. Referring to the poor sanitation of Delhi in the late 1880s, Prashad wrote:

> The rais [elite] simultaneously indicated that the city's problems stemmed from its rapid expansion of scale, from the diversion of the funds to the colonial enclaves and from the structural decay of its infrastructure.
>
> Nevertheless, the sweepers bore the brunt of their recommendations, since the rais found the colonial rulers obdurate on the other issues (Prashad 2000: 6).

It seems to continue to be easier to blame the powerless sweepers when the rulers are obdurate.

References

Chakravarti, Uma and Nandita Haksar (1987), *The Delhi Riots: Three Days in the Life of a Nation*, New Delhi: Lancer.

Chakravarti, Uma, Prem Chowdhury, Pradip Datta, Zoya Hasan, Kumkurn Sangari, Tanika Sarkar (1992), 'Khurja Riots 1990--91: Understanding the Conjuncture', *Economic and Political Weekly*, May 2, 1992: 951--65.

Crooke, William (1896), *The Tribes and Castes of the North-Western Provinces and Oudh*, Calcutta: Government Printing.

Datta, Pradip, Biswamoy Pati, Sumit Sarkar, Tanika Sarkar, Sambuddha Sen (1990), 'Understanding Communal Violence: Nizamuddin Riots', *Economic and Political Weekly*, 10 November 1990: 2487--95.

People's Union for Democratic Rights, People's Union for Civil Liberties (1984), *Who are the Guilty? Report of a Joint Inquiry into the Causes and Impact of the Riots in Delhi from 31 October to 10 November*, New Delhi.

Prashad, Vijay (1996), 'Emergency Assessments', *Social Scientist*, nos. 280--281 (September--October).

Prashad, Vijay (2000), *Untouchable Freedom: A Social History of a Dalit Community*, New Delhi: Oxford University Press.

Index